MICROSOFT SQL Server Black Book

MICROSOFT SQL Server Black Book

Patrick Dalton

CORIOLIS GROUP BOOKS

an International Thomson Publishing company I(T)P®

Albany, NY • Belmont, CA • Bonn • Boston • Cincinnati • Detroit • Johannesburg • London
Madrid • Melbourne • Mexico City • New York • Paris • Singapore • Tokyo • Toronto • Washington

Publisher
Keith Weiskamp

Project Editor
Paula Kmetz

Production Coordinator
April Nielsen

Cover Artist
Gary Smith

Cover Design
Anthony Stock

Layout Design
Nicole Colón

Compositor
Rob Mauhar

Copyeditor
Joanne Slike

Proofreader
Bonnie Trenga

Indexer
Edwin Durbin

CD-ROM Development
Robert Clarfield

Microsoft SQL Server Black Book
Copyright © 1997 by The Coriolis Group, Inc.

All rights reserved. This book may not be duplicated in any way without the express written consent of the publisher, except in the form of brief excerpts or quotations for the purposes of review. The information contained herein is for the personal use of the reader and may not be incorporated in any commercial programs, other books, databases, or any kind of software without written consent of the publisher. Making copies of this book or any portion for any purpose other than your own is a violation of United States copyright laws.

Limits of Liability and Disclaimer of Warranty
The author and publisher of this book have used their best efforts in preparing the book and the programs contained in it. These efforts include the development, research, and testing of the theories and programs to determine their effectiveness. The author and publisher make no warranty of any kind, expressed or implied, with regard to these programs or the documentation contained in this book.

The author and publisher shall not be liable in the event of incidental or consequential damages in connection with, or arising out of, the furnishing, performance, or use of the programs, associated instructions, and/or claims of productivity gains.

Trademarks
Trademarked names appear throughout this book. Rather than list the names and entities that own the trademarks or insert a trademark symbol with each mention of the trademarked name, the publisher states that it is using the names for editorial purposes only and to the benefit of the trademark owner, with no intention of infringing upon that trademark.

Published by The Coriolis Group, Inc.
An International Thomson Publishing Company
14455 N. Hayden Road, Suite 220
Scottsdale, Arizona 85260

602/483-0192
FAX 602/483-0193
http://www.coriolis.com

Printed in the United States of America

ISBN 1-57610-149-5

10 9 8 7 6 5 4 3 2

*This book is dedicated to my children
and to the memory of Jeffery Simms.*

*To Jennifer, Jamie, and Sterling, with love and thanks for being
my life. You can accomplish anything you set your minds to.*

Contents

Introduction xvii

Chapter 1   Preinstallation Considerations 1
   What Is A Device? 3
   What, Then, Is A Database? 5
   What Are Character Sets And Sort Orders? 6
   What Is The Recommended System Configuration? 8
   Where Should The Microsoft SQL Server Be Installed? 10
   What's Stored In The Master Database? 11
   The Master Database 12
   The Pubs Database 13
   The Model Database 13
   Tempdb 13
   The Msdb Database 14
   Be Careful With Memory 15
   What Security Model Will Be Used? 16
   Spring Cleaning 17
   Protocols 18
   Services 19
   What About The SQL Mail Client? 19
   Should I Use The Default Location For My Devices? 19
   What Hardware Should I Install Microsoft SQL Server On? 20
   Finally 22
   Summary 23

Practical Guide To Preinstallation 24
The Preinstallation Checklist 25

Chapter 2 Installing Microsoft SQL Server 33

Installing A Production Data Server 35
SQL Server A (The Base Level) 35
SQL Server B (Middle Of The Road) 37
SQL Server C (The High-End Beast) 39

Before Installing SQL Server 40
Creating Your SQLExec Account 40
One More Account To Go 41
Setting Up A Mail Client 41
One Last Time 42

Summary 43

Practical Guide To Installation 44
SQL Server Installation From Start To Finish 45
Post-Installation Issues 63

Chapter 3 Development Versus Production 67

Setting Up The Development Environment 70
Third-Party Tools 70
Data Modeling 71
Server-Level Parameters 72
User Connections 73
Tempdb in RAM 73
Sort Pages 73
Resource Timeout 74
Read-Ahead Optimization 74
Priority Boost 75
Max Worker Threads 75
Lock Escalation Parameters 75
Fill Factor 76

Application Parameters 78
DBCC PINTABLE 78

Registry-Type Tables 78
List-Type Tables 79
Setup Scripts 79
Sample Server Setup Script 80
Scripting Objects 82
Third-Party Management 83
Transferring Objects 83
Transferring Data 86
BCP 87
INSERT/SELECT 89
DBArtisan 89
Permissions 90
Users And Groups 91
Summary 91

Practical Guide To Transferring Objects 93
Registering Servers 94
Moving Objects From Server To Server 97
Warning Messages 98
Pitfalls 99

Chapter 4   Replication   101
Data Distribution Models 103
Two-Phase Commit 103
Replication Consistency 104
Terminology 104
Publisher 105
Subscriber 105
Distribution Server 105
Transaction Log 105
Synchronization 106
Horizontal Partitions 106
Vertical Partitions 106
Articles 107
Publications 108
Push 109
Pull 109
Server Roles 109
Publisher Server 109
Subscriber Server 110

Distribution Server 110
Scenarios 111
Considerations 111
Central Publisher 113
Central Publisher With Remote Distribution 114
Publishing Subscriber 114
Central Subscriber 115
Multiple Publishers Of A Single Table 118

Events And Processes 120
Log Reader Process 120
Synchronization Process 121
Replication Distribution Process 121
Communication Failures 122

Prerequisites For Replication 122
Memory 123
Working Directory 123
Same Character Set 123
Protocol 123
Trusts 123
Disk Space 123
SQL Executive 124
User Connections 124
Primary Key 124

Summary 125

Practical Guide To Replication 126
Installing The Distribution Database 127
Setting Publication Options 129
Creating Publications And Articles 131
Setting Subscription Options 134
Subscribing To A Publication 135

Chapter 5 Structured Query Language (SQL) 137
ANSI-Compliant SQL 139
Syntax 141
Comments 141
Pubs Database 141
Authors 142
Sales 142

Titleauthor 142

SELECT Statements 143
WHERE Clause 147
ORDER BY Clause 149
GROUP BY Clause 151
Join Conditions 153
Aliases 156
Aggregates And Functions 157
    SUM() 157
    MAX() 157
    MIN() 158
    AVG() 158
    COUNT() 158
    CONVERT() 158
    GETDATE() 159
    DATEDIFF() 159
    DATEPART() 159
    SOUNDEX() 159
    SUBSTRING() 159
    UPPER() 160
    CHARINDEX() 160
    RTRIM() 160
System Functions 160
    ISNULL() 161
    USER_ID() 161
    USER_NAME() 161
    DATALENGTH() 161
    COL_LENGTH() 161
Calculated Values 161
Optimizer Hints 164
Subqueries 165
Union 167
INSERT Statements 168
    Identity Columns 170
    Stored Procedures 170
    Triggers 170
UPDATE Statements 170
DELETE Statements 172
Batches 172

  Cursors 175
  Summary 178

Practical Guide To SQL 179

Schema Changes 180
Backing Up Data 181
Renaming Objects To Be Modified 182
Scripting Objects 183
Converting And Inserting Old Data 184
Cleaning Up The Environment 185
A Word On Constraints 186

Chapter 6 Stored Procedures 187

Consistent Data Manipulation 190
 Enter Stored Procedures 190
 Establishing Standards 190
 Getting Data 191
 Modifying Data 192
Modular Programming 193
Reduced Client Processing 194
Network Traffic 194
Calling A Stored Procedure 195
Query Optimizer 196
Query Plan 196
Parameters 198
Variables 198
 NT Server Registry 200
Maintenance 202
Return Codes 203
Additional Rules 203
Nesting And Recursion 204
System Stored Procedures 205
Custom Stored Procedures 209
External Stored Procedures 212
Remote Stored Procedures 212
Startup Stored Procedures 213
Prior To Production 214
Summary 215

Practical Guide To Stored Procedures 216
Parsing A String 217
Redundant Code 218
Reduced Network Traffic 219
Calling Procedures Within Procedures 221

Chapter 7 Views 223
Syntax For Creating Views 226
Normalized Data 226
Partitioned Data 228
Vertical Partitions 228
Horizontal Partitions 228
Multiple Tables 229
Computed Values 230
Security 230
Updates 230
Underlying Objects 231
Performance 231
Restrictions 232
Summary 233

Practical Guide To Views 234
Determining Column Needs 235
Partitioning And Combining Data 236
Checking Index Coverage 237
Modifications 239

Chapter 8 Triggers 243
Data Integrity 246
Syntax 247
Business Rules 248
Permissions 249
Nesting 250
More On Triggers 250
Virtual Tables 251
Inserted Tables 252
Deleted Tables 252
Virtual Table Usage 252

Global Variables   252
INSERT Triggers   253
UPDATE Triggers   254
DELETE Triggers   254
Limitations   255
Multiple-Row Considerations   256
Performance   257
Summary   258

Practical Guide To Triggers   269

Remove The Foreign Key Constraints   261
Define The Business Rule   264
Identify The Child Records   265
Graphically Represent The Trigger Firing Order   266
Write A Test Script   268
Check The titleAuthor Table   270
Create The Trigger   272
Test The Trigger   274

Chapter 9   Rules, Defaults, Constraints, And User-Defined Data Types   277

Rules   279
   Creating Rules   281
   Binding Rules   281
   Changing Rules   282
   Dropping Rules   282
Defaults   283
   Creating Defaults   283
   Binding Defaults   284
   Changing Defaults   284
   Dropping Defaults   285
Constraints   285
   Primary Key   285
   Unique   286
   Foreign Key   286
   Default   286
   Check   287
User-Defined Data Types   287

Entity Definition 287
Create Table Statement 288
Dependency 290
Summary 290

Practical Guide To Rules, Defaults, Constraints, And User-Defined Data Types 291

Defining The Domains 292
Creating The Scripts 293
Printing Out A UDT Listing 295
Building A Table Structure 296
Maintenance And Troubleshooting 298

Chapter 10 Error Codes 299

Errors In Microsoft SQL Server 301
Method Or Madness 302
Service Packs 302
Research 303
Summary 303

Practical Guide To Error Codes 305

Query/Connection-Based Errors 307
Server Configuration Errors 310
Connectivity Errors 315
Transaction Log Errors 319
Table And Index Errors 320

Chapter 11 Performance Tuning And Optimization 327

What Is Performance? 330
Performance Monitor 332
Windows NT 335
Data Models 335
Application Design 336
Establish A Baseline 337
Keep It Simple 338
SQL Server Trace Flags 339
SQL Trace 339

SQL Probe   340
Summary   342

Practical Guide To Tuning And Optimization   344
Using The Performance Monitor   345
Using SQL Trace   350

Chapter 12   Newsgroups And The Internet   353
Accessing The Internet   356
Browsers   357
Functions   357
Search Engines   360
Knowledge Base   362
Service Packs And Patches   364
TechNet CD-ROM   364
Microsoft SQL Server Books Online   364
Newsgroups   365
Summary   369

Practical Guide To Free Agent Installation   370
Installing The Newsreader   371
Configuring The Source News Server   376
Subscribing To Newsgroups   378
Preferences   381
Newsgroup Etiquette   387

Appendix A   Classes, Training, And Consultants   389

Appendix B   The Pubs Sample Database   395

Glossary   399

Introduction

Welcome to the world of Microsoft SQL Server! Here is finally a client/server database product that can deliver world-class performance at a price that most enterprises can afford not only to purchase, but also to support. SQL Server's ease of use, coupled with the incredible feature set that accompanies it, delivers enterprise-level client/server computing to everyone. *Microsoft SQL Server Black Book* will focus on the tasks involved in harnessing Microsoft SQL Server's capabilities to create a solid production data server. This book focuses on the current release of Microsoft SQL Server while using many techniques that can be applied as far back as version 4.21.

Writing *Microsoft SQL Server Black Book* has been the most challenging task I have undertaken in a long time. I was asked to write it to fill a void in the market, to deliver a book that focuses on creating production servers with hands-on, step-by-step processes for installing, configuring, and troubleshooting Microsoft SQL Server. I have tried to keep the language of the book as plain-English and matter-of-fact as possible, because that is the way I teach. I have supplied you with substantial technical background, while also supplying numerous examples. This book can be used as a tutorial or desktop reference to help you get Microsoft SQL Server to fulfill your organization's needs.

I have been through many classes as a student and as an instructor—about topics ranging from adult learning principles to Microsoft SQL Server Administration. From these classes, I have acquired a great deal of knowledge that can be applied to creating a solid production data server with Microsoft SQL Server. I want to share that with you and help you head off the problems that you may encounter configuring your servers.

I am a business owner, a consultant, a DBA, and a teacher—as most likely are many of you. I have fought and continue to fight the same battles that you do on a daily basis. That is why I think this book can be such a great value to you! Hopefully my experience will help you develop solid database systems in your Microsoft SQL Server environment.

Each chapter is broken into two sections. The first part of each chapter presents explanatory material about the chapter topics. The second page of this first part is a blank Administrator's Notes page, for you to write on and refer back to later. The first part of the chapter ends with a Summary section, which is a bulleted list of the important points of the chapter. The second part of each chapter (the Practical Guide) supplies you with some step-by-step tasks that reinforce the content of the chapter and provide hands-on practice. Chapters 1to3 cover the installation and configuration of Microsoft SQL Server for both development and production environments. Chapter 4 explains the setup and terminology needed to implement replication between SQL servers. Chapters 5 to9 discuss the SQL language and the many objects that can be created for and utilized in client/server applications. Chapters 10, 11, and 12 cover the troubleshooting and tuning skills you will need to support your system over the long haul.

One of the points I emphasize in this book is that you can solve any technical problem you are facing with the tools available to you. What are those tools? How do you research answers to your questions? How do you know if you can trust the sources you consult? How do particular features really work, and will they work for you? I cover all these questions and more in the pages of this book. I hope that you enjoy reading it this as much as I have writing it.

Prerequisites

This book is geared toward readers with a broad range of backgrounds. Many readers may have never worked with Microsoft SQL Server before, so I have tried to write a book that can transform a beginner into a power user. At the same time, I have added plenty of advanced concepts and techniques to each chapter that experienced DBAs can use to get your server running like a thoroughbred.

The book assumes a basic understanding of Windows NT. The exercises and examples will run on any machine that can run the client utilities for Microsoft SQL Server.

Technical Support

If you find any errors or need further help with any topic in this book, you can reach me on the Internet through my email account: pDalton@msn.com. Please do not hesitate to send me feedback—whether positive or negative—concerning this book. If you have technical difficulties with the CD-ROM, please contact Robert Clarfield at The Coriolis Group: techsupport@coriolis.com. If you find a problem with one of the products on the CD-ROM, contact the appropriate vendor through its Web site.

Acknowledgments

I would like to thank a few people that have been key in my personal and professional life. Without each of these people I would not have been able to write this book or to have the drive required to succeed in today's fast-changing technical environment.

First, I would like to thank my wife Diane. She has provided support day in and day out for years now. She puts up with my technical side and still loves me for the great big kid that I can be at times. I would also like to express my gratitude to my sister, Cathy, and her husband, Lee. They have both helped me through some troubled times of my life and have given me unwavering support.

I would like to thank a few other individuals who have played significant roles in my life. In my early military career, I had the good fortune of being under the tutelage of Sergeant First Class Howell. He was a Vietnam veteran with great wisdom and patience and a strong work ethic; he has had a profound influence on me. Later, at Cray Computer Corporation, I came to know Bob Hoeglund, for whom I held and still hold a great deal of respect. He gave me the opportunity to learn as much as I could about every aspect of databases and computers and how they work.

I would also like to thank all the students in my classes. Without your hard questions and late evenings after class, I would not be the DBA that I am.

I would also like to thank Kenny Simms for his valuable assistance in this endeavor. Kenny is a former student. He has contributed hours of research—both on the Internet and in the Knowledge Base—to ensure the quality of the chapters in this book.

I would also like to thank Paula Kmetz, Senior Project Editor at The Coriolis Group. Her understanding and patience is the only reason I have completed this book. She has even put up with my sense of humor and comments throughout the project. Her efforts, and those of others at The Coriolis Group are greatly appreciated.

Finally, I would like to thank my parents. First, my mother, for her support when I was young and for all the sacrifices she made to ensure that I had what I needed for school and all those projects. I would not be the person I am today without the help and confidence my mother gave me. Over the last 15 years or so, my father and I have come to know each other as adults, and I value the friendship we share. He has helped me come to understand what it is like to sacrifice for the good of the ones you love.

Chapter 1

Preinstallation Considerations

The Preinstallation Checklist
- The Windows NT Section
- Determining Memory Requirements For The Server
- Microsoft SQL Server Installation Issues

Administrator's Notes…

Chapter 1

Today's database administrators face many challenges in setting up a data server, regardless of version or manufacturer. An often-difficult task is to get the installation to match the needs of the production environment. I like to look at as many things as possible prior to running Setup to ensure that the production machine is configured to the requirements of the user and the application load placed on the server.

Let's look at some of the basics of Microsoft SQL Server. Understanding these basic components is important to the planning process. This process is valuable for a first-time installation of Microsoft SQL Server. If you are planning your first installation or reinstallation, the following pages might help clear the fog.

What Is A Device?

The terms *device* and *database* are often confused. The basic storage container for Microsoft SQL Server is a *device,* which is an operating system file that resides on the physical disk, or hard drive, of the server. A device is the container that allocates space to Microsoft SQL Server on the server's hard drive. Microsoft SQL Server does not acquire disk space on the server dynamically. You must specify the amount of disk to set aside for it to use. This allocation is accomplished through the device.

The space that you set aside for devices is essentially lost to the rest of the machine. A device cannot be made smaller. You can, however, expand a device to make more room for your databases to grow—provided you have enough free disk space. You can—and will—have multiple devices on your server. Databases can span multiple devices to accommodate their growth.

A device carries with it a file extension of .DAT. This is important to know if you are in a multiple-programmer environment and are using the data server for file services as well as data services. For example, in File Manager or Windows NT Explorer, note the physical file C:\MSSQL\Data\master.dat. You can highlight this file, hit the Delete key, and if it is not currently being used by Microsoft SQL Server, it will be deleted like any other file. If it is in use, Microsoft SQL Server and the operating system will not allow it to be deleted. This prevents an accidental delete.

The only acceptable way to recover the space given to a device is to drop the device and re-create it with a smaller size. When you drop a device, ensure that you go to the file system and delete the physical file. If you do not remove the device file, you will receive an error message when you re-create the device with the same name. Once you remove the file, you use the Enterprise Manager to re-create the device with a smaller size. You can then restore any contents of the old device to the new device, provided all the objects fit in the new space.

Try to avoid creating one big device that takes up the whole hard drive. Doing so will not give you the flexibility you need from the server. You will be very limited in your options down the road and will have to jump through some fairly complicated hoops to change this configuration on a production machine.

From a slightly different perspective, a device can be thought of as a large, empty office. This space is rented or leased by your company. If your business expands beyond the square footage you have set aside, you must acquire more office space to accommodate the growth. This can be achieved by expanding the existing office into adjoining space in the same building or perhaps in another office building altogether.

This growth scenario applies to your devices as well. I will use this and other analogies a lot throughout this book to help you associate Microsoft SQL Server to a real-world example. Many of my students have found they frequently do not remember the exact piece of information they need but can draw on these analogies to figure out what to do.

What, Then, Is A Database?

Databases are also considered containers. They hold the objects that make up your server's purpose in life. Tables, views, indexes, and stored procedures are all objects that reside in your database. You can, and often will, have multiple user-defined databases residing on your server. These databases are where the production information and code reside. Other databases are installed on your server to give it the intelligence it needs to function; I will cover these databases in a few different areas throughout the book. However, our focus will be on setting up a production system, not on the inner workings of Microsoft SQL Server.

One of the most common mistakes new users make is to confuse the device and the database. You place your databases *within* your devices. To understand this, think of a database as a division within your company. For instance, Human Resources deals with very specific kinds of information, so you would logically put all of that type of information in a container for centralized management and access control. Accounting is an area that often requires more security than others, and the information generated from this area would justly be placed in a separate container for security reasons. You would not scatter information for the Human Resources department throughout all the offices; instead, you would put all those functions and resources in one place. The same applies to databases and good database design.

An interesting point for all PC-based database programmers is that Microsoft SQL Server does not store the information or data in the database. Remember, the database is a container. Instead, the server stores your data in a table. The index you create for fast access to data is not stored in the table with the raw data; it is stored as another object within the database. A database is a collection of objects. This concept is not hard to follow, but it is different enough from the organization of other database programs that it is sometimes a stumbling block for the small-system programmer. An MIS department accustomed to dBASE or Microsoft FoxPro databases will struggle with this at first. Since this structure is common to most large database systems today, you should become familiar with it.

In addition, you should focus on the database level when administrating your system's security. Your users will be granted a logon ID for connecting to the server, but this does not allow them to get to the data they need. This is done by adding users and groups to each database individually on a need-to-know basis. This method of security keeps unwanted users from browsing where they should not while allowing others to do their jobs.

Returning to the office analogy, let's compare a database to the Accounting department in your company. This department might have a door you must pass through, and once you pass through that door, you would see all the cubicles and desks where the actual work is done. This door might be locked in the evening or even require a passkey to enter during the day.

The same idea can be applied to a database. The records and files are not strewn around the office; they reside in filing cabinets and in folders or ledgers for ease of access. These organizational tools can be related to Microsoft SQL Server objects. You use tables, stored procedures, and indexes to find what you need when you need it.

The security model that Microsoft SQL Server uses is also similar to the passkey entry requirement. No one gets access without a valid key or password. I will not try to recommend a security method here because of the diverse requirements in the market today. However, I will say that Microsoft SQL Server will accommodate a strict security model very well and still allow for the simple, trusting models required by smaller companies growing into Microsoft SQL Server.

During installation of Microsoft SQL Server, you will not be concerned with these divisions or security, but you should make a few assumptions on the amount of disk space you will need to accommodate these areas and how you will accommodate these needs.

What Are Character Sets And Sort Orders?

Another preinstallation issue is choosing a character set and sort order. A *character set* is the basic text and symbols that are loaded in your system. Regardless of the character set you choose, the first 128 characters are the same. The extended characters, including language-specific characters, reside in the remaining half of the character set. Your decision depends on whether you are doing business overseas or in other languages and need to store text and special characters. In most cases, the default is fine and should provide you with what you need to function.

You should make this determination prior to installation. Changing character sets can be a daunting task with many system ramifications. If your company is concerned about character sets, chances are you are experienced in these issues and this feature should be nothing new to you.

Another interesting issue concerns *sort orders*. Sort orders determine the way the data is organized when stored by Microsoft SQL Server. The default sort order for Microsoft

SQL Server is dictionary order and case-insensitive. This is fine and probably the best default setting. It is not, however, the fastest setting you can use on your system.

Microsoft is not trying to slow you down. Most programmers are not as careful as they could be and do not always exercise consistent case sensitivity when they write code. The default for Microsoft SQL Server should be used if you have legacy systems that might contain this kind of SQL code.

The fastest sort order is binary. The use of this setting has some impact on how you perform certain tasks down the road, so choose it carefully. It will change all of your SQL scripts, stored procedures, and client pass-through code to be case-sensitive. If you type a statement and use a different case than was specified when the table was created, you will get an error message. Say, for instance, you have a table called *MyTable* on your system. To access it, you type "mytable". An "Object Not Found" error is returned.

Binary sort order poses a few issues in developing client software, and great care should be taken when using it. Your ad hoc queries might not return what you expect back from the server, either. A capital "F" does not equal a lowercase "f". Reports are not inherently smart enough to tell the difference, and your code needs to allow for this.

If you store, access, and check for case sensitivity on your entire system, binary is the way to go. I have configured two identical machines installed from scratch with the same data sets stored in different sort orders. My tests have proven that binary is faster for a lot of common operations. If you are putting third-party applications on your server, make sure they run as expected in this sort order. If in doubt, call the vendor or technical support for the product in question.

I often use binary sort orders as an example of a setting that restricts programmers in a way they might find difficult. Because of the case-sensitive nature, programmers must write code with more care than they would otherwise. The end result is faster, but getting there might be more difficult.

Users of the system should also be considered when selecting binary sort orders. If a system allows for ad hoc reports or queries and a user does not know that the data is stored with case sensitivity, he or she might not get the expected results. This can be dangerous when converting legacy systems. Make the decision to use a binary sort order only after carefully weighing the impact on your entire organization.

Under "Performance Comparisons" in the Microsoft SQL Server Books Online, select Topic 5 from the SQL Server 6.0 Setup Guide for more information.

Another consideration in choosing a character set and a sort order is whether you are setting up a distributed server environment. If you are, you must use compatible character sets and sort orders among your servers. If you are going to share, replicate, or distribute data, use a common character set and sort order throughout your enterprise. Do not forget that in business today we must occasionally share data with other companies. If your system interacts with another company's system, again make sure the character sets and sort orders are compatible.

What Is The Recommended System Configuration?

Let me first comment on the Microsoft recommendations for your system and what I have found to be a more realistic configuration for your server. Microsoft's recommendations should be taken with a grain of salt and applied with care to each environment. Likewise, my recommendations—or anyone else's, for that matter—should not be followed blindly. Recommendations are intended to give you an idea of where to start and should not be considered the end solution or setting for your system.

The system requirements for installing Microsoft SQL Server are actually very easy to meet, often leading the administrator into a false sense of security with regard to how well the server will perform. See Table 1.1 for system requirements.

The minimum CPU recommendation of an Intel-based 80486 is, in my opinion, a poor choice for a production machine unless you have very few users and are going to configure the server as a data server only. This type of machine should be considered a candidate for development environments or servers with only the lightest of loads in a production situation. Given the low cost of Pentium-based processors, I

CPU	80486
RAM	Minimum 16MB Minimum 32MB required for replication
Hard Disk	Minimum 60MB Additional 15MB for Microsoft SQL Server Books Online
File System	FAT or NTFS
OS	Windows NT Server 3.51 or higher

Table 1.1 Microsoft system requirements for an Intel-based system.

would recommend no less than a Pentium-class machine in a production environment. Taking into account the upgrade and support paths for these machines, even a Pentium Pro system is well within the reach of just about any enterprise.

I am not suggesting you throw your current machine away or scrap your plans for a cheaper alternative. I know budgets and real-world requirements often do not allow a top-of-the-line machine for your project. The idea is to put your best-performing machine where it will do the most good.

If you are using existing hardware for your data server, take a good inventory of what makes the target machine tick. Know the particulars of the disk access time and memory configuration. Benchmark the machines where possible to get an idea of how well it is performing against others in the same class. You might find a less-expensive alternative to the planned configuration.

RAM is another highly performance-sensitive item that can make or break your server. The minimum recommendation of 16MB is for a bare-bones server that will perform on a limited basis as a data server. The 32MB reference for a replication server is more in line with a minimum memory configuration for a production server. In most production environments, server configurations range on average from 64MB RAM to 128MB RAM, with the occasional 256MB machine. On a high-volume multiuser system, servers with a greater amount of RAM would be much more efficient.

Do not forget the option of moving to a multiple-processor machine. Some existing servers can be upgraded to multiple-processor configurations very reasonably. Many unique situations require individual configuration considerations, but adding RAM to a machine is the best first step in getting better overall performance. The best rule of thumb is to look at the system load and determine if you need more RAM in your system. If your server is starved for RAM, you will know very quickly, and increasing the RAM is relatively inexpensive.

Hard drives are an often-overlooked performance bottleneck on database servers. Consider the performance of your disk controller and disk access times to make sure you have not slowed your fast machine to a crawl with an older disk thrown in a new box. The axiom that you are only as fast as your slowest link really applies here. I have seen administrators spend extraordinary amounts of time troubleshooting performance issues on data servers with older disks or 16-bit network interface cards. Be sure to look at all the pieces. No piece in the chain of client-server communications should be overlooked.

Where Should The Microsoft SQL Server Be Installed?

Keeping in mind that the optimum configuration is not always possible, I will describe what I think is the best place to install a Microsoft SQL Server on your network. In a strictly Microsoft network environment (which we all know is not very practical with the number of legacy systems out there), Microsoft talks of *domain structures*. While this book will not stray into domain configuration issues, there are some fundamental pieces of information that will apply whether you are setting up in a totally Microsoft environment or a NetWare/Microsoft mix. Your data server should be used solely as a server on the network. Try not to place additional services or processes on your data server, because they will add to overhead and slow the performance of the data services.

Primary domain controllers (PDCs) have the useful role of logging people on and off your Microsoft network. They also handle synchronization with backup domain controllers (BDCs) on your network. Any type of domain controller is not the optimal location to install Microsoft SQL Server.

Gateway Services for NetWare is another of the services you should consider moving off your Microsoft SQL Server. This service allows for NetWare files to be shared through Microsoft shares on your server. Although this is often a convenient way to get to your files, putting these files on your database server adds to the overhead of that machine.

You should strive to install your server on as clean a machine as possible—one that will only be used for database services. This means that you should not set up Microsoft SQL Server on a primary or backup domain controller. Keep shared file access off your database server. Having users copy files to and from the server will move the disk heads unnecessarily. Disk I/O is the slowest thing your data server will do. Do everything you can to keep it to a minimum. Also avoid sharing printers, modems, or like services on your Microsoft SQL Server. All of these processes are burst performance-related loads; Murphy's Law will always ensure that one of the biggest file transfers or print jobs will hit your server at the same time a large query is running, causing the whole system to appear to hang.

As you might be noticing, Microsoft appears to be moving toward a distributed server network. All the servers do not have to be on independent machines, but this configuration will help distribute the load across your network, allowing you to put lighter-weight and lower-cost servers in place for mail and file services and put your money where production is, such as on data services. This distribution can be a good thing, but many companies fail to recognize this until they have put all their eggs (applications, services, and files) in one or two baskets (servers). Plan for growth. By definition, databases will grow given even normal use. Over time any system that is being used in production will expand not only in feature and function, but in the amount of data as well.

If possible, place Microsoft SQL Server on a machine by itself. Install it as a server that is part of a domain (provided you are using the Microsoft domain model). Place any other applications on separate machines when possible. If multiple applications are running on the same machine, you are complicating the process unnecessarily. In addition, beware of disk-intensive applications running on your database machine. If an application is writing to disk and Microsoft SQL Server is writing to disk, these processes will compete for disk I/O and slow down both applications.

The cost of adding a low-cost machine with a good-size disk to the network versus the cost in performance by having all these services running on the same box quickly becomes a non-issue.

Prior to installing Microsoft SQL Server, you should create a domain or local user account under which the SQL Executive service will perform its tasks. This account setup is covered in detail in the next chapter, which includes step-by-step installation on a few different machines.

What's Stored In The Master Database?

The server's system catalog and all the environmental information is stored in the master database, which is contained within the master device. The master database is the brains of your server. Great care should be taken when modifying any information contained in the master database. You should get in the habit of backing up your master database whenever you make environmental changes to your server, including changing the sizes of databases or adding users. The following items should trigger a backup of the master database:

- CREATE, ALTER, or DROP statements (SQL)
- DISK statements (SQL)
- Altering a transaction log
- Adding or removing a mirrored device

- Adding or dropping remote servers
- Adding or dropping a login ID
- Any change in server configuration

Check bu_list.doc (the reminder document) on the CD-ROM. Print it out and put it in a clear, visible place to help keep your system in a good recoverable state.

The size of the master device is another important consideration. By default in current versions of Microsoft SQL Server, the master is set to 25MB. This value is totally dependent on the system that it must support. Many things affect the size of the master device. For most production systems, you must alter the size of the master device when adding major components to the server. Most end up in the 30MB range unless they need an abnormally large Tempdb. Upon installation, I usually change this setting to 30MB to avoid having to resize it a few weeks down the road. The additional 5MB of disk space will not hurt the server and provides more flexibility right off the bat. Keep in mind, however, that the size of the master device can be increased after installation.

Having a good understanding of the master device and its components will help you in later configuration and troubleshooting issues. By default Microsoft SQL Server stores the master database, the Pubs database, the model database, Tempdb, and the Msdb database in the master device. Let's touch on each one of these databases for just a moment to ensure a solid understanding of their functions.

The Master Database

System tables and environmental information are stored in the master database. Tables such as Sysdatabases, Syslocks, Sysprocesses, and Sysusages store critical information about your server. Other tables, such as Sysobjects, keep track of the objects that reside in each database on your server; each database has a copy of these tables.

The server will allow you to edit these and other important tables through raw SQL; however, I strongly recommend that you do not modify data in any of the tables in the master through SQL commands. Such modifications should be attempted only when absolutely necessary and only by someone with an intimate understanding of Microsoft SQL Server. Plenty of tools are available in Microsoft SQL Server to protect you from yourself. Use these tools at your disposal to make server changes.

This is not to say that you cannot check these tables for information needed to run your client-server applications effectively. I have often used information in system tables to find certain server-side permission or relation information. You can read data all day long without making direct modifications to these tables. By default all users of a database will have some kind of permission to access the system tables for that database. This is a requirement for the system to run well and cannot be avoided.

To clarify, let's look at this kind of information in a different light. You probably have committed to memory the layout of all the furniture in your house or apartment. If you woke up in the middle of the night and made a trip to the kitchen to get a drink of milk, you would probably make that trip fairly well even without the lights on. The system tables store the information you take for granted, similar to the location and size of the coffee table, the doors, and so on. Incorrectly changing these stored values by hand would in effect move the furniture on you. This would not lend itself to a good environment for getting to your data. It could in some cases crash your server, rendering it useless.

The Pubs Database

In a production environment, Pubs does you no good and should probably be removed. This database is used as a learning tool and for testing the basics of your installation. Once your production machine is up and running, you can remove this database from the master device.

The Model Database

The model database is like a stencil for creating new user-defined databases. This stencil gives you a starting point for your CREATE DATABASE statements. The system tables for user-defined databases are stored in the model. Any stored procedures or users that need to exist in all your user databases should be placed in the model database. By placing them in the model, they will be copied to each successive database that is created. Be careful when placing things in the model. This action will increase the minimum size of your databases and may add unnecessary objects to databases.

Tempdb

I often refer to Tempdb as a pad of Post-it notes: very small scratch paper that you use for a short period of time and then discard when you no longer need the information on each piece of paper.

Many things can affect the space required for Tempdb. This database is part of the master device by default and resides on disk. This "scratch pad" is shared by all the users on the server for worktable space and to resolve join issues in processing your queries. If you have many users on your system, you might need a bigger Tempdb. You might also need a bigger Tempdb if your users have the ability to write their own ad hoc queries or reports, or if a query returns a large number of rows.

So how big is big enough? This is a newsgroup topic in itself. You really have to look hard at what your server is going to handle and make your best guess. Following are some guidelines to optimize performance:

- Keep your queries under control.
- Limit the ad hoc report and free-formed query abilities against your system.
- Use indexed columns for your join conditions and sorting needs whenever possible.
- Watch all ORDER BY statements. This is covered in more detail later.

You can place Tempdb in RAM to get better performance out of your server. This is not always the best move, and I will tell you why in Chapter 11, "Tuning And Optimization." If you are going to place Tempdb in RAM, install it to disk and test the performance. Then move it to RAM and test it again. If your tests show a good margin of improvement, then leave it in RAM. Otherwise, change it back to disk. You'll wish you had later when you start seeing the "Can't Allocate Space in Tempdb" error messages.

After you have installed your server, made setting changes, and established some of the basic configuration options, back up your master database. You might as well get used to it now and make a habit out of performing a backup whenever you change the server configuration. It's better to restore your master from a backup than to reconstruct it from memory and any notes you might have in a folder somewhere.

The Msdb Database

The Msdb database is perhaps the most versatile piece of your server. This is basically your server's to-do list. You can add tasks to this database that will be performed on a scheduled recurring basis. You can also view the history of the defined tasks and their execution results. The Msdb database is the component that allows you to proactively manage your data server. Used primarily by the SQL Executive service, the Msdb is created on two separate devices: one for your data and one for the transaction log. We will cover these pieces later in the book.

Be Careful With Memory

Microsoft SQL Server should not be installed with a memory footprint larger than available memory. This configuration option can be set to more than the system has installed. (Microsoft SQL Server will try to start with that setting, too.) In some situations the server will start and run *very* slowly, and in others it will appear to hang. You can fix this memory setting by starting the server with the -f switch. This starts the server in a basic configuration and then allows you to go in and change the memory setting. This memory setting is configured after installation. You should pick a setting, make the changes on your server, and then monitor the impact of that setting. Never assume that your math is correct or that what you heard someone else has done is right for your situation. Test it first.

To set or configure the memory for your server, do the following:

1. Start the SQL Enterprise Manager.
2. Select the Server menu option.
3. Select the Configure menu option.
4. When the Server Configuration dialog box appears, select the Configure tab.
5. Scroll to the Memory option and modify the memory settings (see Table 1.2).
6. Make the changes based on your hardware configuration.
7. Stop and start the MSSQLServer service to let the changes take effect.

This memory setting is in 2K units and can be a little confusing. You must convert the MB value of the RAM on the machine to the equal number of kilobytes. This is done by multiplying the MB value by 1024. Subtract the amount of memory that Microsoft Windows NT needs (at least 12MB), then divide that number by 2. This result will give the amount of memory in 2K units that you should give Microsoft SQL Server, provided no other services or applications are running on the server.

Whenever possible, allow yourself a small threshold of extra memory. By doing this you will not bring your server to a crawl by turning on a service or adding a process to your server without changing the memory setting for Microsoft SQL Server. This can be as small as 2MB or as large as 20MB depending on your hardware. See Table 1.2 for memory recommendations.

Hardware	SQL Server	2K Setting
16MB	4MB (—)	2048 (—)
24MB	8MB (—)	4096 (—)
32MB	16MB (18)	8192 (9216)
48MB	28MB (34)	14336 (17408)
64MB	40MB (46)	20480 (23552)
128MB	100MB (108)	51200 (55296)
256MB	216MB (226)	110592 (115712)
512MB	464MB (472)	237568 (241664)

Memory settings do not take into account other processes running on the server. My recommendations for memory are in parenthesis.

Table 1.2 Memory recommendations for Microsoft SQL Server.

I do not recommend setting a Microsoft SQL Server up with less than 32MB of RAM in a production environment. My settings reflect a system with only minimal services running to allow for best performance. No other applications should be running on the database server.

What Security Model Will Be Used?

In Microsoft SQL Server, you have three choices when it comes to data security: standard security setting (default), integrated security, and mixed security. The *standard security* setting requires each user to supply a valid login ID and password to attach to the server. This validation is separate from the network login scheme. This setting supports connections by non-Windows NT validated users accessing your data server.

Integrated security allows you to use the network login and password supplied to Microsoft Windows NT as a security mechanism for access to your data server. If users are validated with a login and password by Microsoft Windows NT, they can connect to the server. This provides you with the one login, one password scenario that many companies are looking for. Keep in mind that just because a user can connect to the server does not mean he or she has access to your database.

Mixed security is used when you want your Microsoft Windows NT users to supply only one login and password to be on the network and connect to your server. This method would also allow other network users to connect to the server as long as they can provide a valid database login and password. In the mixed-legacy environments of today's businesses, this is a very popular method of implementing security.

Microsoft SQL Server uses an interesting security model that has two levels of security. First, you must be allowed to connect to the server. Then, for each database you are granted access to, you are granted rights and permissions on a case-by-case basis.

To explain this concept using our office example, say that you have been given a key to get into the office building. This key gives you the right to enter and walk through any hallways and public areas to function and find your way around. Then, for access to certain areas in the building, you need an access card (or permission) to get into each office or room (database) you do business in. If you are not granted access to, say, the Human Resources department, you simply cannot access this area (database). By assigning security on a departmental level, you can give your users freedom to do their jobs while protecting sensitive data from people who should not see it.

This model is very good for a few reasons. In a lower-budget design, you can have both the production databases and training or development databases coexist on the same server. You don't have to worry about adding to an existing system and having users gain rights by association to other databases. Users are restricted by default and granted access by the owner of the database to do what they need. No one except the SA (system administrator) has rights in a database unless they own it.

Spring Cleaning

As mentioned, in a production environment, Pubs does you no good and should probably be removed. Likewise, you should periodically look for things like Pubs within your system. The tables, or copies of tables, store procedures that are left to sit until no one knows any longer what they are or what they do. In over half the systems I have worked on (even in the one I am developing right now), I have made a copy of something and left the original in place, changed my copy until it was just the way I wanted it, and forgotten to remove the original or the test copy I ran to see if the system was faster. Keep your system as clean as possible and you will have less garbage to clean up later. Each object you define in your system takes up resources of some kind.

Protocols

I have read a few good white papers on benchmarks of protocols and which runs what type of operation best. You might have to support multiple protocols on your network. Keep in mind the default Named Pipes is slower than IPX/SPX or TCP/IP. You should try to use one of the latter two for client connections because they connect faster and transfer results better. Use as few protocols as necessary to reduce network traffic. I will not try to cover Windows NT tuning and optimization in this book; several good books are currently available that address this topic thoroughly. Microsoft SQL Server allows for multiple protocols to be supported and used simultaneously. Obviously, the number of protocols you are trying to support will have an impact on performance. Keep the list as small as possible, and you will be just fine. You can change your network support at any time after installation by rerunning Setup and selecting the Change Network Support radio button. See Table 1.3 for a list of the available protocols and the purposes they serve.

You may drop support for Named Pipes altogether. Before doing this, however, make sure you have another protocol installed for client connections to your server. Also ensure that the client configuration utility is installed and returns the expected values on the server. All software that runs on your server runs as a client. Adminis-

Named Pipes	SQL Server default protocol.
Multi-Protocol	Required to use integrated security. Supports encryption.
NWLink IPX/SPX	Allows Novell IPX/SPX clients to connect.
TCP/IP Sockets	Allows TCP/IP clients to connect. Uses port 1433.
Banyan VINES	(Check SQL Books Online or Banyan documentation for configuration issues.)
AppleTalk ADSP	Allows Apple Macintosh-based clients to connect.
DECnet	Allows PATHWORKS connectivity. (Check SQL Books Online or the DEC documentation.)

Microsoft SQL Server always listens on Named Pipes by default.

Table 1.3   Microsoft SQL Server protocols (Net-Libraries).

trators often take this for granted and have the perception that the Enterprise Manager, for example, is really the server. It is just a client and must connect like any other.

 You cannot change Net-Library configurations during upgrades. Any existing configuration is carried over and can then be changed by rerunning Setup.

Services

As mentioned, try not to have a lot of extra services running on your machine. Each of these services takes up processor time and resources. Administrators often forget that these services run all the time and automatically unless they are changed. I will cover the services required for Microsoft SQL Server in later chapters.

What About The SQL Mail Client?

Having your Microsoft SQL Server send you a mail message or report automatically is a great feature. I have found this to be a tremendous benefit in setting up a new system. Microsoft SQL Server will interact with a number of mail clients through MAPI (Mail Application Programming Interface). Good step-by-step setup instructions are given in the Microsoft SQL Server Books Online. Perform a search on Mail, and look up your particular mail system and how to configure it to run with Microsoft SQL Server. Do this early in the process, and it will help keep you informed of just what your server is doing. Keep in mind, however, that too much of a good thing will slow processes down. Making the call to the external stored procedure for mail does take time. Use it with some thought.

Should I Use The Default Location For My Devices?

Whether to use the default location for devices depends on whether you have a disk configuration that will better support a separate area for your data. In most single-disk situations, the default directory is fine. If you are installing on a machine with a multiple-disk subsystem or RAID system installed, then putting the data files on high-performance disks will improve performance and should be done at installation.

What Hardware Should I Install Microsoft SQL Server On?

This question comes up at least once in every class I have taught. I do not like to generalize all servers into one hardware configuration. But usually there are things I like to have on a server and things I do not.

Any server purchase you make today will be outdated by the time you unpack the box. Hardware changes on a daily basis, which is very frustrating. I like to buy servers with a good expansion path. A lot of potential expansion allows me to keep up with changes in the industry better. I buy brand-name servers because I don't like to invest money in machines that have poor technical support and might not be supported next year. I *always* check the hardware compatibility list for Windows NT Server. This is a must. I check each component, from CPU to disk controller, when needed. This ensures that I will not have an operating-system problem with the server I am configuring.

I like to configure my servers with a RAID disk subsystem for my data. When reliable access to the data is critical, I require some sort of RAID configuration for the data to reside on. With the ability of Microsoft Windows NT to implement RAID at the operating-system level, this is easily accomplished with even a limited budget. I try to keep the operating system and program files separate from the data. I usually place these files on a separate disk and controller from the data, and I mirror the disk and controller when budget allows. This provides the maximum amount of protection from hard drive failures while keeping performance at the highest-possible levels (see Figure 1.1). The number of disks in the RAID array can be as small as three and as many as the disk subsystem will support.

Not everyone can afford this type of configuration for their hardware. It is, however, what I recommend for a fault-tolerant data server. If money is an issue, cut the mirrored disk and controller out of the boot drives. The RAID disk subsystem would be the last thing I would give up. Use the built-in, software-driven, RAID option on Microsoft Windows NT servers only as a last resort. I would use that feature and set up my own fault-tolerant disk system for storing my data only if no other option were available.

Given the many ways Microsoft SQL Server can write backups of databases to shared drives on other machines, a tape drive for backups is not required on the data server as well. This can be a nice feature if you run around-the-clock operations and need to keep performance at high levels 24 hours a day. Removing the backup load to

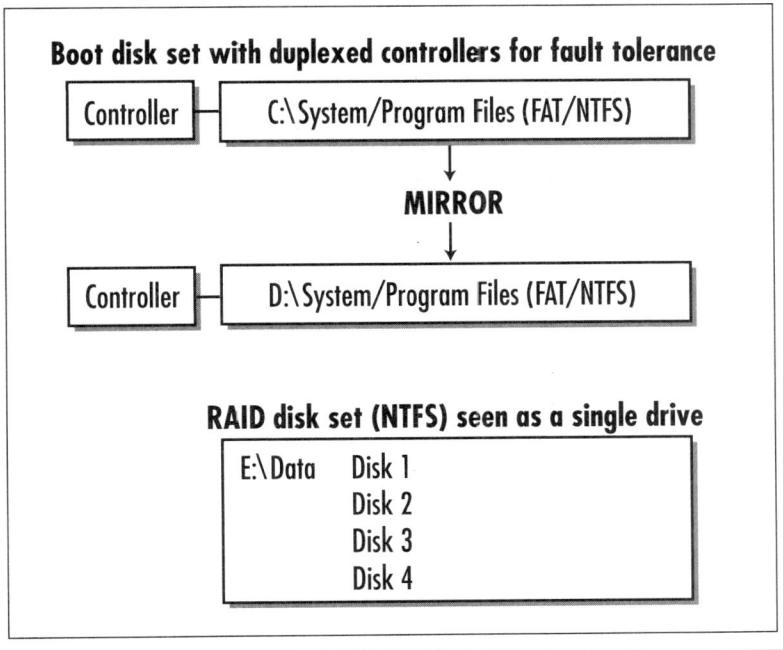

Sample hard drive configuration.
Figure 1.1

another machine is in keeping with the distributed-load concept becoming popular in many enterprises today.

A brief comment on backup strategy: Use the Dump and Load commands to create backups of your databases, then back up the resulting backup device file. Microsoft SQL Server uses the file system to store data, utilizing 2K pages and a starting point and offset algorithm to access data. Your file backup software does not care about 2K pages, and this can cause problems for Microsoft SQL Server. Your backup files can be damaged when you need them to be stable and error-free. For example, a SCSI disk can use bad-sector remapping to fix a problem automatically, and this can confuse Microsoft SQL Server.

I always specify more RAM than I think I will need for the server. I like to have at least 64MB of RAM for a production server. This gives plenty of space for Microsoft SQL Server and a good amount of data cache and procedure cache for performance. You cannot go wrong by adding RAM. Even on a 80486 processor, giving it additional RAM will allow it to run very well.

Invest in a good network interface card—something with as much bus speed and bandwidth as possible. If your data server were a fire engine, you would not want to use a garden hose on it to put fires out.

I usually do not go overboard on the CD-ROM. Since I rarely use it for production purposes, I try to keep this to whatever speed comes with the server. The only time I look at a faster CD is when I plan to mount a database that resides on a CD-ROM for read-only purposes. In this situation, I look at getting the fastest CD-ROM I can afford.

Do not get caught up in expensive monitors or sound cards. This is a place to save your money and buy some more RAM. Keep it simple. Video memory is not an issue on a data server. There is no reason for a sound card in a data server unless you want it to say, "I am slowing down now. Please let your users know. Never mind, they already know." If you follow the recommendations in this book, your server will be just a data server. This is best for your users.

Verify you have network functionality before installing Microsoft SQL Server. One of the hardest things to do is troubleshoot problems when you have no idea what is working and what is not. Assume nothing. I have always used the break-it-down-into-the-simplest-form approach in troubleshooting. If you cannot get out on the network, no one will be able to connect to your server for data.

Consider using a redundant power supply and surge protection for your unit. Keeping the data available should be any DBA's primary focus. Use a UPS that is reliable and test it occasionally. A untested backup strategy is just that: untested. If you think you're under pressure now, wait until the UPS or backup won't restore and the system your boss has invested thousands of dollars in does not work.

Finally

If you are setting up a system for a third-party application, beware of the requirements for that system. Find out ahead of time what special configurations will need to be set to let a particular piece of software run well. You might find that a system configured to run one application well might not allow another to run well at all. If this case arises, contact the vendor to determine how you can adjust your server configuration to best provide for both situations.

The old saying "hindsight is 20/20" is a testament to being prepared. You cannot see all failures or issues ahead of time; we are all human and make mistakes. By preparing yourself for these mistakes, you will know where to look, how to look, and what action to take to solve the problems that arise. The largest compliment I can get as an instructor is to have students call me or email me with a problem, tell me what they think they should do to fix it, and be right on target. This shows they are thinking things through and coming to the right conclusions; they are just lacking the confidence (which will come with time) to take the actions needed to fix the problem. The fact you are reading this book shows you are making an effort to be prepared.

Summary

The information in this chapter might seem like a lot to think about before you install the server software, but it will help you make better decisions about the type of machine you need. Following are the major points:

- Ideally, you should install Microsoft SQL Server on a standalone server that does nothing but serve data to clients. This is not always possible, but it should be the goal to work toward.

- More RAM is better. Use at least 32MB in a production server for best results. Upon installation, set your master database to 30MB to save time later.

- Be careful when choosing a character set and sort order. Faster is not always better.

- Use a RAID disk subsystem for your data when possible, with hardware-level RAID being the choice over software-level RAID on Windows NT.

- Use a separate drive for boot and system information, and mirror that drive with a separate controller for each drive. This disk configuration will give you a very flexible and fault-tolerant system.

- Configure your memory setting and check it to ensure it is correct. Remember that the memory option is in 2K increments.

- Use the Microsoft SQL Server Books Online often. Even though there are some known inconsistencies in them, they are a great resource that is underutilized by many professionals.

- You'll need to increase the size of Tempdb. How much depends on your system and the way it will be used. Be cautious about putting Tempdb in RAM. Test this before doing it; you might not gain as much as you think.

- Back up your master database every time you change the server environment.

Practical Guide To Preinstallation

This section will walk you through gathering some preinstallation information about your system that will help you install your server right the first time.

The Preinstallation Checklist

The preinstallation checklist (preinstall.doc) contained on the CD-ROM accompanying this book can be printed out for your convenience. This document will help you get through the installation process as painlessly as possible. Let's walk through this document step by step and fill it out for an example server. I will choose an Intel-based Pentium 133MHz single-processor machine with two hard drives—one with 1.2GB and the other with 4.3GB. Our machine will have two controllers, one for each hard drive, and 64MB of RAM. It will run as a regular data server in a Microsoft Windows NT TCP/IP network environment.

The preinstallation checklist is a memory-aid document. Each line of the document has a comment or question that should be answered in whole or in part before installing Microsoft SQL Server.

The Windows NT Section

The Windows NT section is intended to remind us of the operating system issues that might come up during the installation and configuration of our server. Check the Hardware Compatibility List (HCL) published by Microsoft for each component used in your server. If your hardware does not exist on the approved list, you should be careful; things might go wrong. However, just because a piece of hardware is not on the list does not mean it will not work. You should check whether NT will install and run properly. Keep in mind that Microsoft will not support hardware configurations that contain any component not on the Hardware Compatibility List. This fact should be enough to make you stay away from nonsupported components when running Windows NT.

Most of the issues in this section will become common sense once you have set up a NT server and configured it for running SQL Server. This is intended to help those of you who might not be as familiar with Microsoft Windows NT as you would like. For more information on installation and configuration of Microsoft Windows NT 4, see *Windows NT 4 Administrator's Black Book*, published by The Coriolis Group. The first area of the preinstallation checklist is displayed in Figure 1.2.

Configuring a TCP/IP network is not covered here. What is covered in this section are the key entries necessary for your server to exist on an IP-based network.

Each machine on an IP network needs a unique address. This address is like a street address for your house. The mail carrier needs to know what address to deliver mail

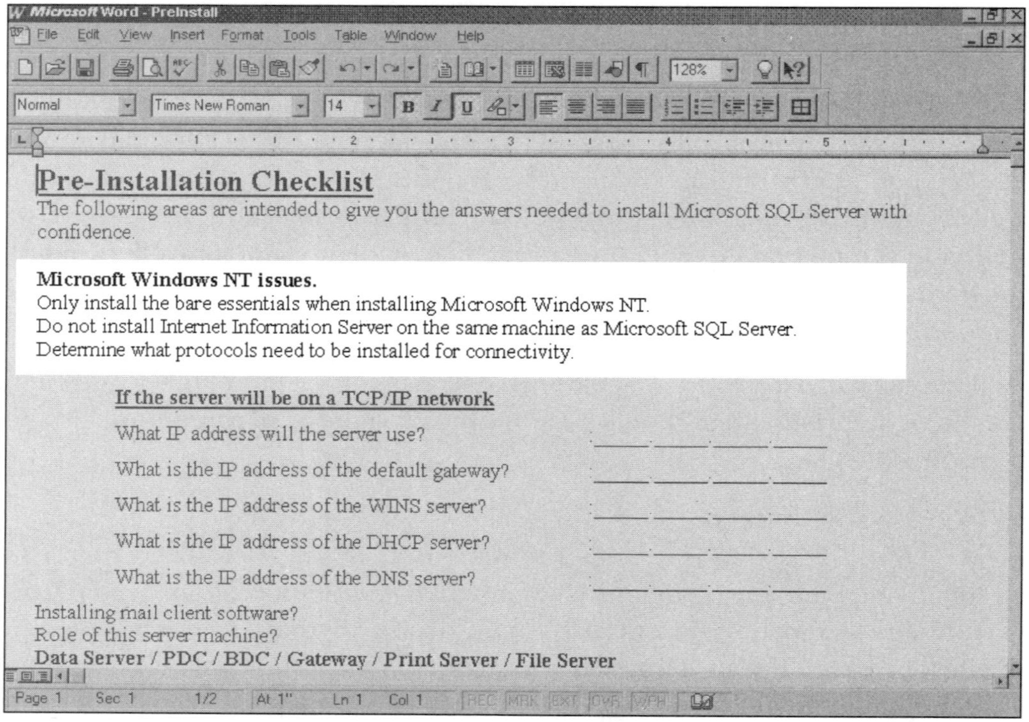

Preinstallation checklist showing Windows NT issues.
Figure 1.2

to—the same applies to your machine. The network must know your address to deliver packets.

Then there is the default gateway entry. This entry is the primary exit point for your network. (To understand this concept, you can compare it to your local post office knowing what other post offices to send packages to.) In a lot of networks, this entry is reserved for the 123.123.123.1 address (the final "1" being the machine, and the rest being address space). Putting the gateway at address 1 makes life easier when you need to remember the address of the gateway. There is no other significance to the "1" in the address.

Next is a WINS Server IP address entry. In a Microsoft network, a WINS server provides Windows Internet Name Services or Resolution of your machine name to an IP address. Internet names are the 123.123.123.4 address that the network knows you to be, and the Window's name is the MY_PC name the users know your machine as.

Next is an address for a DHCP Server. This is not a required entry, but it is a valuable one from a network administration standpoint. The dynamic host configuration protocol server leases addresses dynamically to machines on your network that are DHCP-aware. This eliminates the need for static IP addresses on a network and can be a great benefit in a large enterprise. Last in the list is an entry for the DNS server, or the domain name server. This server allows you to have a central list of names and IP addresses stored in a server environment so that you can query this server for a name or IP address instead of maintaining a separate LMHOSTS file on each machine. Figure 1.3 shows the checklist with these settings filled in.

The final entries in this section stress keeping these topics in your mind as you move through setting up your server. I like to install any mail client and verify the mail works before installing Microsoft SQL Server. I can do this ahead of time because I have configured the SQL Mail Client enough to know each system's setup methods.

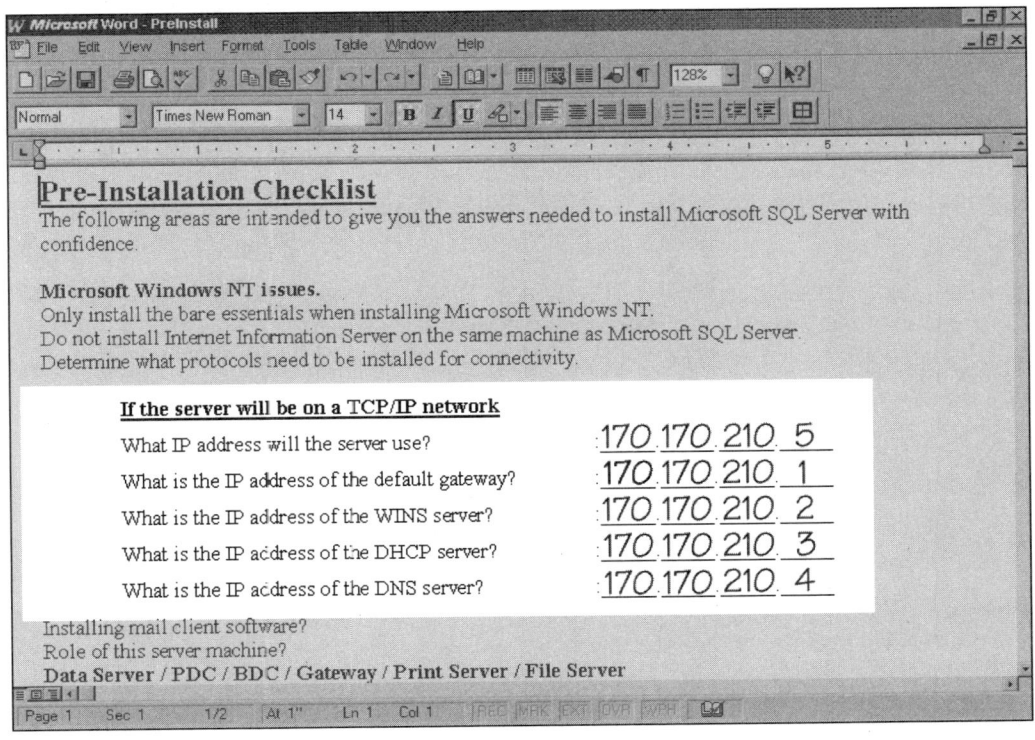

Preinstallation checklist showing TCP/IP address settings.
Figure 1.3

If you are not sure how to configure the mail client, wait until you have installed Books Online, then look up "Setting Up Mail." There are very good step-by-step directions that cover the majority of mail issues.

By setting up mail early when possible, I can make sure mail is working from the client side before adding Microsoft SQL Server to the configuration and having to troubleshoot two problems. Be sure to know the role of your machine. The more tasks it must perform in the background, the harder it will be to troubleshoot performance problems down the road. As mentioned several times in this chapter, I highly recommend having Microsoft SQL Server on a machine by itself whenever possible. Answer the questions shown in Figure 1.4 prior to installing Microsoft SQL Server.

The previous paragraph is very important. Many of the problems people encounter setting up Microsoft SQL Server are related to some subtle configuration issue. By testing your network connectivity prior to installation, you will save time down the

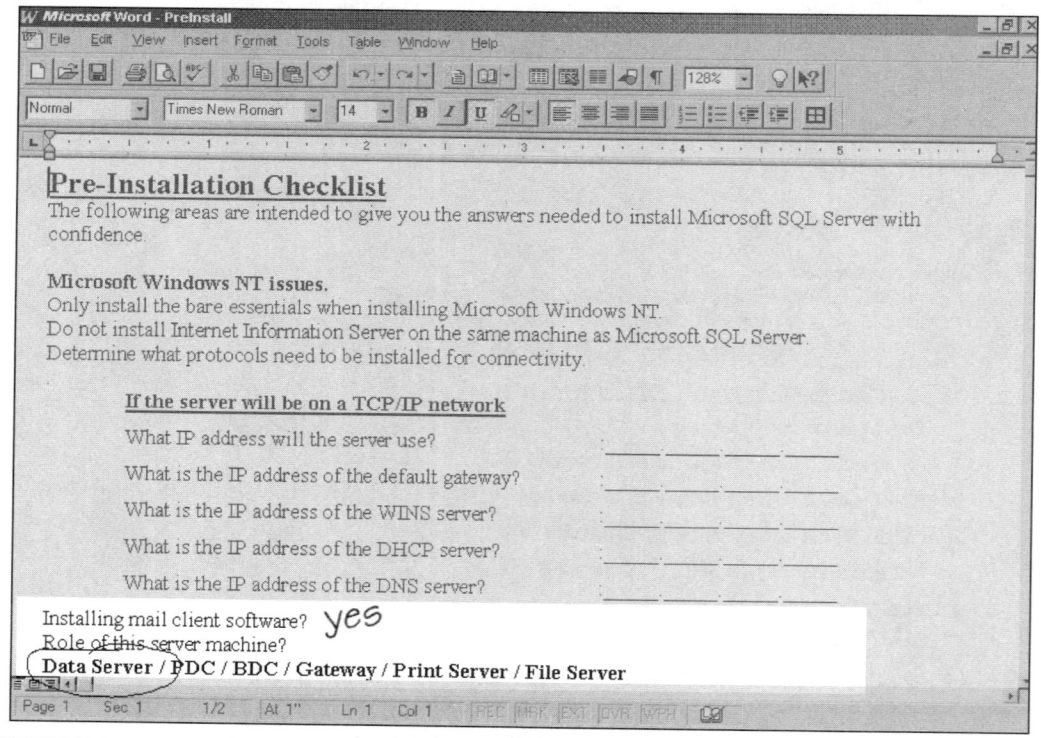

Preinstallation checklist showing server role questions.
Figure 1.4

road. Never assume something works. If you get the "Service Failed To Start" message when you boot a Microsoft Windows NT Server, follow through and find out what went wrong. Many services are dependent on other services running before they can start. Test that NT networking is functional before installing Microsoft SQL Server. This verification will keep you from chasing connectivity problems due to NT configuration.

Determining Memory Requirements For The Server

This section of the worksheet is intended to help you get the memory setting of your Microsoft SQL Server as close to optimum as possible from the beginning. This memory setting is critical to your server's performance, and each server should be looked at separately. No two servers are alike when it comes to this setting.

You should use all the tools available to you when determining the memory usage on your server. The built-in Performance Monitor application and the Task Manager utility are great resources for finding out how much memory is being taken up by Windows NT and any other services running on your server.

Filling in the blanks is pretty straightforward. How much physical RAM is in the server? This is the raw MB value installed on the server.

Next is a small table for listing any applications or services that might be required to run on the server. I realize that we do not live in a perfect world; there will be times when you must run another application on your server in order to support production. List the memory footprint of each of those applications in the table and total them at the bottom.

Notice that only three slots for applications are provided. This is intended to remind you that adding applications is not a good thing and should be limited whenever possible. See Figure 1.5 for memory configuration for this server.

Available memory is totally dependent on the way you have installed NT and what services are running. Check this value with the Performance Monitor and the Task Manager before assuming it is correct. To be safe, never assume less than 12MB of RAM for the operating system.

Now subtract the total from the table list from the installed memory and put that on Line 3. This is what you have to work with for Microsoft SQL Server along with any periodic applications that might be launched on the server. Try to allow a few MB of RAM as a cushion for safety before deciding how much memory to give Microsoft SQL Server.

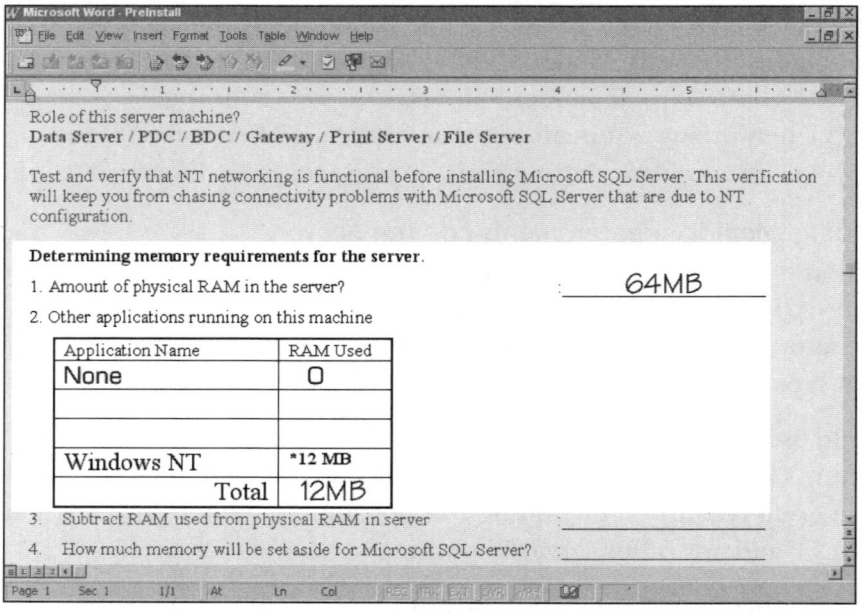

Preinstallation checklist showing memory configuration for example server.
Figure 1.5

Now in Line 5 you convert this amount that you want to set aside for the SQL server. To do this we should multiply the 46MB by 1024 to get the number of kilobytes. The resulting 47104K should be divided by 2 to get the number of 2K units the Microsoft SQL Server uses for the memory setting. Place the 23552 in the blank for Line 5 (see Figure 1.6). This value will be placed in the memory configuration option after you install Microsoft SQL Server.

Microsoft SQL Server Installation Issues

Some of the questions asked by the setup program are similar to the questions in this section of the checklist. Take a minute and look at the list. We will then fill it in based on our test scenario.

Size of the master device, character set, and sort order were covered in detail earlier in this chapter and are listed here as a reminder to verify that the default is really what you want. Fill in the blanks with the appropriate values.

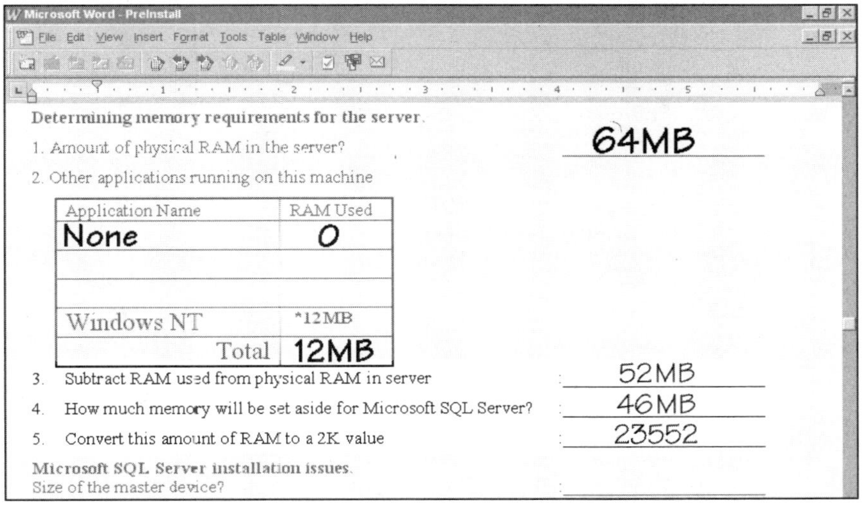

Preinstallation checklist showing calculation of 2K memory setting.
Figure 1.6

In the SQL Executive Account space, you would fill in the user account name that you will define in the User Account Manager for Domains. This account will be covered in detail in the next chapter. The name "SQLExec" is one that is used in the Microsoft curriculum and should be used when possible. If you choose a different name, be sure it is descriptive enough so that you can easily recognize it.

I have chosen to remove the Pubs database from the server. I make every effort to keep the server as clean as possible. This can be done after the installation is complete. You might want to leave the Pubs database around until you have tested your ability to run client queries against the server. Once you have some data out there to run against, feel free to remove the Pubs database.

The location of your data depends on your disk subsystem. In our example system, we have two disks to work with—one for the operating system and application files and the other strictly for data. I would create a data folder on the D: drive and place my data files in that location. See Figure 1.7 for specific notes on installation of SQL Server.

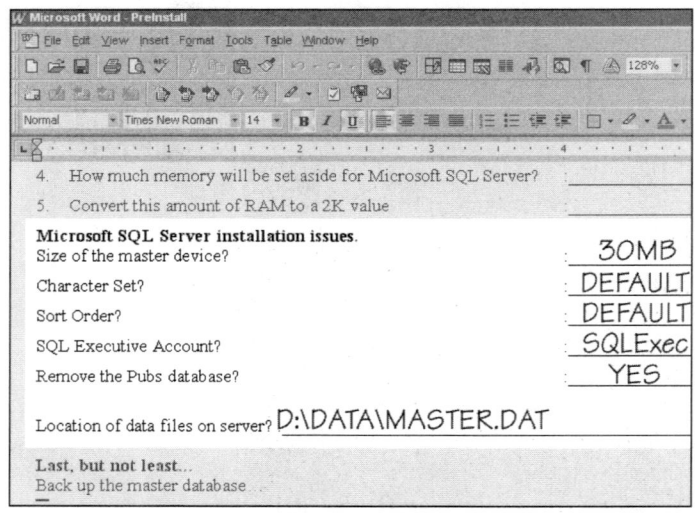

Preinstallation checklist settings.
Figure 1.7

The last thing you should do after installing your server is to perform a complete backup of the server and save that backup as the starting point for your server. The configuration settings and choices you have made up to this point would be saved, and you would not have to remember what you did months before.

A helpful reminder: *Back up the master database!*

Chapter 2

Installing Microsoft SQL Server

SQL Server Installation From Start To Finish

- Creating The SQL Executive Service Account
- Creating The Microsoft SQL Server Service Account
- Granting Service Rights
- Installing Microsoft Exchange Client
- Running Setup
- A Quick Tour Of The SQL Server Program Group

Post-Installation Issues

- Configuring The Server Service
- Changing The Memory Setting To Reflect The Hardware
- Testing SQL Mail

Administrator's Notes...

Chapter 2

Installing A Production Data Server

Because of the incredible number of different server configurations in today's business community, I will use three different machines as examples in this chapter and show how each one can be configured. Choose the configuration that most closely matches your server and follow the information regarding that machine type.

This chapter is intended to be an installation tutorial. If you feel confident installing Microsoft SQL Server, you might want to skip to the Summary section for this chapter, located just before the Practical Guide. By reviewing the Summary, you can see if you need to go back into the chapter to review any installation steps you might be unsure of.

SQL Server A (The Base Level)

This server is a good candidate for a small-enterprise production server or a development server for a small to medium MIS department. Frequently such departments have grown into a need for client-server databases. This type of machine would also handle replication distribution tasks very well for a medium-sized enterprise. (See Chapter 4 for an extensive discussion of replication.)

One other point to consider for this type of server is using it in conjunction with the Distributed Transaction Coordinator (DTC). With Microsoft's increasing focus on the distributed server environment, you should consider smaller servers in your plans. These servers can become valuable in supporting your needs. Also, by separating processes across multiple servers, you can include some legacy systems and save money.

With a little planning, even these smaller servers can be very useful in a production environment. From an audit trail or tracking standpoint to a centralized error-handling and task management scenario, these servers are becoming a part of many enterprises. Learning how to integrate them into your plans will make you look very good in the eyes of any management group trying to resolve growth issues at lower costs.

You may want to look for a network task server application to help manage your network resources and extend the life of your legacy hardware.

Base-level server configurations would typically involve an i486-based server, possibly with 48 to 96MB of RAM. Even a smaller amount of RAM should not pose a real problem for most basic environments. As long as the target system meets the minimum RAM requirements for Microsoft SQL Server, you will be fine. Keep in mind, however, that adding RAM to one of these servers can have a great impact on performance and should be one of the first things you consider. Also included in this group are slower Pentium machines. These lower-speed Pentium servers will surely become commonplace in smaller enterprises.

When specifying a server for your needs, always consider the environment and the clients your machine will be servicing. Most desktops and workstations being purchased today are Pentium 100MHz machines with 32MB RAM. If you have a dozen of these Pentium workstations picking on a poor little 486/66MHz server, your SQL server might not be able to keep up with the requests for data during peak periods.

When choosing a smaller server, you should keep the amount of available RAM in the server as high as possible. Keep the additional tasks of file, print, and gateway services off these types of servers. You may notice a slower connection time with these lighter-weight servers. However, once you *have* connected to one of these servers, you should get acceptable query response times under a light load. This is usually exactly the machine a small office or satellite location needs from a data server.

Example Configuration For Server A

Our example server in this class will be an Intel-based 486/100MHz processor with 48MB RAM. Since this is an entry-level server, we will use a single hard drive with 740MB of free space left after installing Windows NT. This server will run Windows NT Server 4.0 (version 3.51 would do fine as well). The file system for this server will be NTFS and not FAT for file-level security reasons. This server will be running on a TCP/IP network with a PCI network interface card and will run as a standalone server in a Microsoft Windows NT domain. Take special care during installation of the operating system to make the correct installation choices for the network. Accidentally installing NT servers as domain controllers is easy to do and should be avoided.

Avoid putting any additional overhead on this type of server. Starting an application or service can place a burden on the functionality of the operating system or Microsoft SQL Server and bring your data services to a crawl.

We will take advantage of Microsoft SQL Server's ability to write backup files to network drives. This will negate the need for installing any type of tape backup system. Since the system will back up data while users are in the database, you should be aware of when these backups will occur. Scheduling your backups around peak activity is important with a server of this size. By using this backup strategy, you eliminate the need for a tape drive and the disk and/or process overhead of the entire backup routine (with the exception of the actual data dump). Chapter 11, "Tuning And Optimization," discusses backup strategies and how they can affect performance.

SQL Server B (Middle Of The Road)

This server is a good medium-duty server. Usually at this point, many companies begin to consider multiple-processor machines—even if they don't yet actually purchase them. At this stage in a company's growth, purchasing machines that support multiple processors as expansion options is a smart move. Take the time to ensure you can expand your server down the road. By definition, databases will always grow, and there are few things that you can do to prevent a good system from slowing down over time with increased use. Making good purchasing decisions is as important as hiring good people to fill critical positions in your company.

In addition, spending money on as current a processor architecture as possible at this level is a good idea. Take the time to look at what machine will supply the most processing bang for your buck. Check the results of independent tests for different machines. You'll find that many show that Intel-based servers are closing the performance gap with other architectures—and are less expensive and cheaper to support. I have had very good luck going with the established name brands. I also insist on good technical support.

The CD-ROM accompanying this book includes a few excellent white papers from Compaq and other sources. These white papers can be found on Compaq's Web site at www.compaq.com or on any of the appropriate sites listed in the documents themselves. Regardless of the make of your server, these white papers do a very thorough job of helping you configure it to run well in a production environment. (In Chapter 12, you'll find more on using online sources to answer your configuration questions.) There is a wealth of information out there for you to use—some of it is good and some is junk. You should take the time to learn what is and is not valid advice.

Configuring data servers can be a difficult task. Adding one nonconforming task or application can throw your performance into a downward spiral. Always begin by breaking down the problem into simplest-possible form. Then look for the obvious problem. Never assume that something is working fine.

When I am asked to recommend a server, I try to get a good feel for how the server is going to be used in the future. With this middle-of-the-road class of server, you must start to look at fine-tuning your hardware choices for maximum performance. It is common to have multiple drives in these servers; this should be considered, since multiple drives will increase your system's fault tolerance (an important goal of any database administrator). If you cannot afford to purchase all of the components for a fault-tolerant server at one time, you should plan their addition as budgets permit. In many scenarios in this range, it is a good practice to propose during the bid process some sort of plan to upgrade or migrate the server hardware as the use and load of the server matures. Management does not view this approach as overspending but as good business planning. In most of the system consulting I have done over the last few years, I have found that including estimated costs for migrating and improving the server over time actually helps "sell" the idea of purchasing hardware and software to prospective clients. These estimates add value to your recommendations, both short- and long-term, and they give decision makers the realistic information they need to plan and budget IT resources.

A Word On RAID

A middle-of-the-road server should incorporate the ability to add disk space as painlessly as possible. Be leery of using the Microsoft Windows NT Server software implementation of RAID as a solution for your disk subsystem needs. Although this is better than not having a fault-tolerant disk system at all, a hardware-based solution is preferable. Using a hardware-based RAID system relieves your server from the burden of disk I/O while decreasing the amount of CPU processor time spent handling disk activities. Some of the better RAID systems have some very impressive throughput with high capacity and built-in caching. Some even support hot swap disks that, in the event of a failure, allow you to replace the bad drive in your system with an off-the-shelf disk without ever having to power down your server. Not all servers justify this kind of expense, however. Use your best judgment and choose a disk subsystem with great care.

If you must use the software-level implementation of RAID, I suggest starting with a mirrored disk configuration. By choosing the mirror configuration, you will keep performance up as much as possible while maintaining some kind of tolerance. For more information on how to configure Microsoft Windows NT for the software implementation of RAID, see your Windows NT documentation.

Example Configuration For Server B

Let's take a moment and look at an example server configuration in this class. Typically these servers have up to 128MB RAM and are configured with RAID disk subsystems. For our example, we'll use a Pentium Pro 200MHz single-processor server with 128MB RAM. We will again be using a good PCI network card for maximum throughput and two disk drives. The first drive will be for installing the operating system and program files; the second will be for data. Due to costs, we are not going to go with a RAID system. Instead, I will use a 1.2GB hard drive for the C: drive and a 4.3GB hard drive for the D: drive. I will use two separate controllers for the hard drives for maximum throughput of data.

This system will be a great candidate for adding a mirrored disk down the road as funding becomes available for adding fault tolerance. Choose a good disk controller that supports multiple disks or a system that will support the addition of a disk and controller for establishing a mirror—or, in the case of adding the extra controller, for duplexing the data drive.

SQL Server C (The High-End Beast)

Because of the prohibitive cost of a quad-processor or higher monster server, most small- to medium-sized companies do not purchase a high-end server. These machines, of course, do provide some incredible numbers when it comes to throughput and horsepower. Having recently rolled out a major system utilizing a Compaq Proliant 200MHz dual-processor Pentium Pro system at the heart of the data services, I am impressed with the performance of both Microsoft SQL Server and Windows NT on this platform.

Despite their high cost, multiple-processor machines are of great interest to the majority of students in my classes. Given the cost difference between these high-end Pentium machines and the mainframe/RISC machines, as well as the performance of Microsoft SQL Server, the multiple-processor machine is quickly becoming a hot topic. Many companies have purchased expandable machines and are looking for answers on how to take advantage of this architecture. As we explore topics later in this book, I will describe how efficiently these monster machines can run your queries.

Example Configuration For Server C

Although Microsoft SQL Server runs on other hardware (Alpha machines, for example), it must run on the Microsoft Windows NT operating system. I am focusing on Intel platforms because of their cost-to-performance advantages over other hardware platforms. These machines should be running with between 128MB and 256MB of RAM. Our example server in this class will use 256MB RAM. In addition, RAID level 5 subsystems are usually the order of the day for these machines. These servers usually have between 8 and 32GB of hard drive to work with. Redundant power supplies and a replacement drive on the shelf are musts when these systems go online.

These high-end servers are not something that the average programmer should jump into. Great care should be taken to configure these machines to suit their final environment. I recommend having a consultant handle the initial hardware configuration for you if you have even the smallest doubt as to whether you can do it on your own. It's not that difficult, but this kind of system is expensive enough that a mistake can cost you thousands of dollars to fix. Also, I have seen many servers that run at a much lower speed than they should because of one incorrect setting or configuration option. The most common question I get is: "Why is this fast machine running so slowly?"

Before Installing SQL Server

Let's take a few minutes and go over in detail a few installation and configuration issues before SQL is installed. The topics covered in this section can help you solve many of the problems associated with installing Microsoft SQL Server without any training or guidance. I have seen many newsgroup messages that could have been avoided had the reader followed these suggestions.

Creating Your SQLExec Account

Before you install the server software, you should take a moment to create a user account for the SQL Executive account to use once you have installed the server.

This account is created with the User Manager for Domains. The name you choose is not as important as the permissions you give.

I usually choose a name that makes sense to me. "SQLExec" is used in Microsoft's training and course materials, so we'll use that name here. This domain account should be granted the Log On As A Service right so that it can get to the server when it needs to. Do not place any account restrictions on this login. Select a password in accordance with good security practices and make sure that the checkboxes for User Must Change Password and Account Never Expires are set properly. See Figure 2.1 on page 45 (in the Practical Guide section of this chapter) for the proper settings.

One More Account To Go

While I am on the subject of creating user accounts, I usually create a user account for the SQL Server service to use. It's not a requirement for the server to use an account other than the local system, but there are some compelling reasons to do so. Having the server run under the permissions of an account with a password is much more secure. In the event that some unauthorized user gets access to your server, this extra security precaution can save you some headaches. When you create an account for the server, make sure you grant the same permissions as you did for the Executive service account.

This account can also be used for a mail client application. However, you should create the account before attempting to configure the SQL Mail Client or your server. In practically all mail systems, SQL Server must run under the same account as the mail client you install and configure.

Changing the account that SQL server runs under is done through the Control Panel under Services. Select the Services icon and when the window opens up, double-click the MSSQLServer service. In the Services dialog box, click the Startup button. In the bottom of the User Properties dialog box, fill in the domain name, the account name, and the password, then select OK. See Figure 2.2 on page 46 in the Practical Guide for the User Properties dialog box.

Setting Up A Mail Client

If you are going to take advantage of the SQL Mail Client and email notifications on your SQL server, you should take the time to install and test the mail client for the mail system you are running before you install Microsoft SQL Server. Using email in your applications can provide you with a proactive management tool that many systems lack.

Using the **xp_sendmail** external stored procedure in your triggers and user-defined stored procedures can be done very efficiently. Be aware that each mail system is configured slightly differently; you should consult the section on installing the specific mail client in SQL Books Online for any issues associated with your mail system. Microsoft SQL Server will send and receive mail from any MAPI-compliant mail system running on your network. Some additional overhead is involved with sending mail from inside your SQL code, so expect a slight delay in the execution of scripts or triggers that send mail. Since the use of email in your code has little to do with installation, I address this topic later in the book. Mail does, however, play a huge part in setting up a proactive server that will alert you to potential problems before they get out of hand.

Make sure that you create the accounts that mail must run under, and be sure to log in as those accounts when installing the mail client software. With Microsoft Exchange, for example, you need to set up a profile that matches the account that Microsoft SQL Server runs under as a service. Failing to do this will cause configuration problems when attempting to get mail features to work properly. I will walk through setting up a Microsoft Exchange client later in this chapter.

One Last Time

I know that budgets and office politics come into play when deciding what kind of server to buy or what upgrades are required to meet your needs. Take what I have said here with a grain of salt. Few scenarios allow the best-possible design to be implemented. Fight only the battles you feel need to be fought.

Fortunately, Microsoft SQL Server is a very robust application. You can put an awful lot on a SQL server and make it do just about anything you can imagine. It runs well on every machine I have ever installed it on—from a 486/66 with 32MB of RAM to a huge multiple-processor beast. I have not found a bad system yet—only ones that are improperly configured.

Regardless of the server you choose to install Microsoft SQL Server on, you will be tempted to add a service or two to this server. Placing additional services on any of these servers will cause changes in the way you should configure Microsoft SQL Server. Most administrators will be tempted to place some extra files or network tasks on the higher-end machines I have talked about here. Fight that urge!

Summary

- Take time to analyze your server requirements—both current and future needs. Do not forget to consider distributed processing in your plans.

- Check out the Man-O-War Task Server on the CD-ROM accompanying this book. This application can be a valuable tool on your network.

- Place as much RAM in your server as budget allows. The more the better, up to the 128MB range. Insufficient memory limits the number of users and lengthens query response times.

- Install your operating system and verify network connectivity before installing Microsoft SQL Server.

- Create an account for the SQL Executive and the Microsoft SQL Server service to run under. Creating these accounts will allow you to implement better security on your servers and to easily configure email services. These accounts should be granted the Log On As A Service right with a good password assigned for security purposes.

- Install, configure, and test your mail client software prior to installing Microsoft SQL Server. It is very important to ensure that mail can be sent through your client software before assuming that the SQL mail client can send mail. If you cannot send mail from the client, Microsoft SQL Server will not be able to send mail.

Practical Guide To Installation

This section presents step-by-step instructions for the installation and configuration of Microsoft SQL Server and its related services.

SQL Server Installation From Start To Finish

The first step in installing Microsoft SQL Server is to create the accounts needed for the services themselves to run under. To install the product, it is not required that this be done first, but I have found that most easy-to-miss service configuration problems can be avoided by creating the correct user accounts before installing any software. All three of our example servers would use the same account information and would require the same information regardless of hardware.

Creating The SQL Executive Service Account

To create an account for the SQL Executive service, follow these steps:

1. Log on to Windows NT as Administrator.
2. In the Administrative Tools program group, open the User Manager For Domains.
3. Select New User from the User menu.
4. In the User Properties dialog box, input the information in the following steps (see Figure 2.1). Make sure that you provide a secure password for this account.

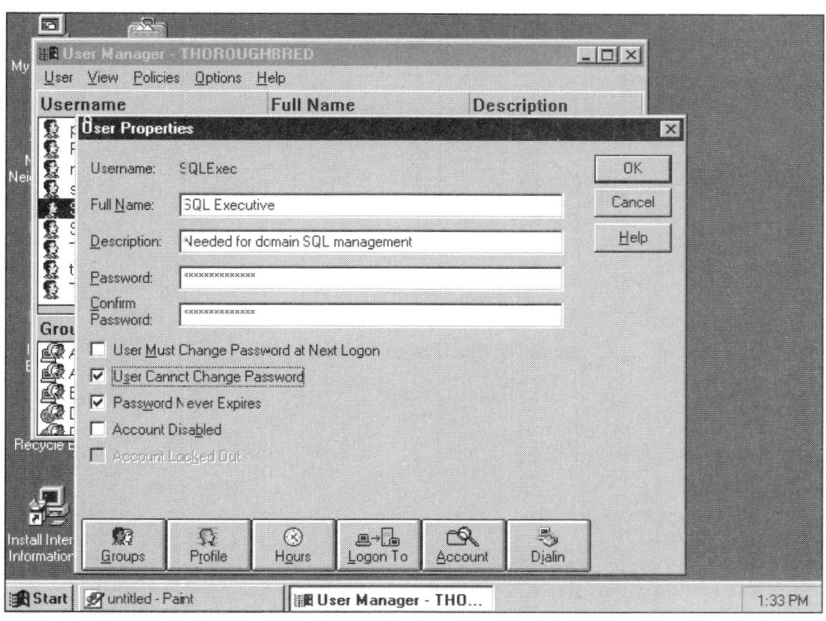

User Properties dialog box showing the SQL Executive account settings.
Figure 2.1

Installation 45

5. Clear the User Must Change Password at Next Logon checkbox.
6. Select the User Cannot Change Password checkbox.
7. Select the Password Never Expires checkbox.
8. Click the Groups button.
9. In the Group Membership dialog box, add this account to the Administrators group.
10. Click OK to close this window. Click Add, then Close to complete the user account.

Creating The Microsoft SQL Server Service Account

Next, create an account for the Microsoft SQL Server service. I usually name my server so that I can identify the different servers in my enterprise. Be creative and come up with a good descriptive name. The user account name you choose should be unique as well. You only need one account for the SQL Executive account for multiple servers, but you should have unique server names for the SQL Server accounts in your domain. For this example, we'll use "MySQLServer".

1. In the User Properties dialog box fill in the information in the following steps (see Figure 2.2). Table 2.1 supplies the settings the example servers will use.

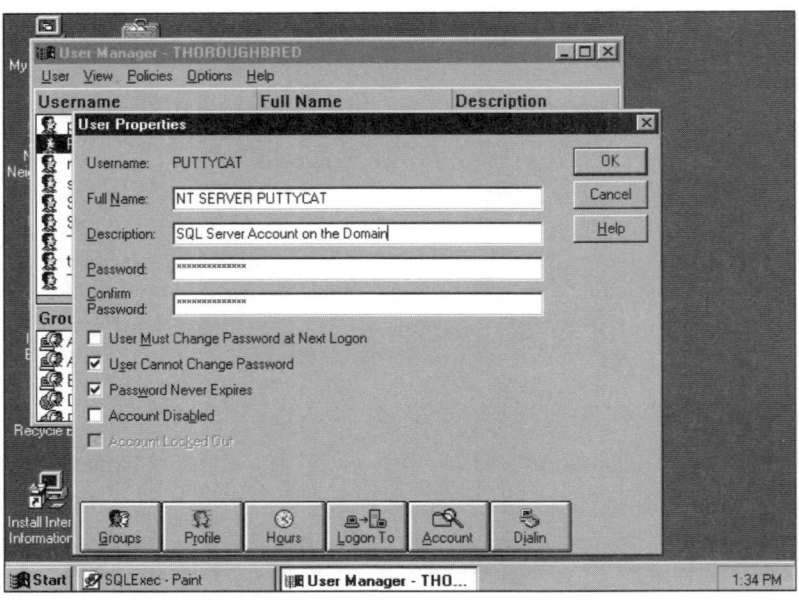

User Properties dialog box showing the SQL Server account settings.
Figure 2.2

Option	Value
User name	MySQLServer
Full name	SQL Server Account
Description	SQL server and mail account for this server
Password	[Choose something secure here.]

Table 2.1 Example SQL Server service settings.

2. Clear the User Must Change Password at Next Logon checkbox.

3. Select the User Cannot Change Password checkbox.

4. Select the Password Never Expires checkbox.

5. Click the Groups button.

6. In the Group Membership dialog box add this account to the Administrators group.

7. Click OK to close this window. Click Add, then Close to complete this user account

Granting Service Rights

Next you should grant these accounts the ability to log on as a service right. If you forget to do this step, you can use the Control Panel to grant this option when you specify which account to use for service startup. To allow these accounts to access the server regardless of whether someone is logged on to the server, follow these steps:

1. In User Manager For Domains, select Policies|User Rights.

2. Select the Show Advanced User Rights checkbox.

3. In the right pane, select Log On As A Service Right.

4. Click Add to display the Add Users And Groups dialog box.

5. Click the Show Users Button, find the SQLExec account, and click Add.

6. Find the MySQLServer account and click Add so both names appear in the Grant To list.

7. Click OK to close the dialog box and exit User Manager For Domains.

Installing Microsoft Exchange Client

Installing mail client software for this server should be done according to the specific directions associated with the mail system you use. In this example we will use

Microsoft Exchange Client. Because Microsoft SQL Server uses the profile that you specify when configuring SQL Mail, you should follow these instructions carefully. All three of our example servers will use the same settings, and none of the configuration options here would be different for any of the machines.

1. Go to the Microsoft Exchange server and set up a new mailbox for the SQL Server account created in the previous tutorial. If you have Exchange configured to create a mailbox for each new user on the domain, a mailbox should be created for this account automatically. You should, however, check that the mailbox is complete.

2. Now on the SQL Server machine, log on to Windows NT Server using the same user account created above.

3. Run the Microsoft Exchange Client Setup program and follow the screen prompts and instructions to install and configure the Microsoft Exchange Client on the SQL server machine.

4. Test the Microsoft Exchange Client by verifying that you can send and receive mail.

 Before you configure Microsoft Exchange Server, read the SQL Mail and Microsoft Exchange Server Configuration Requirements section of SQL Server Books Online.

Running Setup

When installing Microsoft SQL Server on the actual machines, you must choose the correct hardware platform directory from the CD-ROM. The I386 directory is where the Intel-based installation software resides. Follow these steps to install Microsoft SQL Server on our example Intel platforms:

1. Place the CD-ROM for SQL Server into the drive.

2. Locate the setup program in the architecture-specific directory. (In our example systems, we will select the I386 directory.)

3. Run setup.exe in that directory. The setup program will walk you through the installation step by step. The preinstallation checklist in the Practical Guide section of Chapter 1 provides the information needed to answer the prompts presented to you in Setup. For illustration purposes, I'll supply the answers to the prompts for each of the three types of servers discussed in this chapter where they apply differently. Most of the initial installation settings are identical for each server.

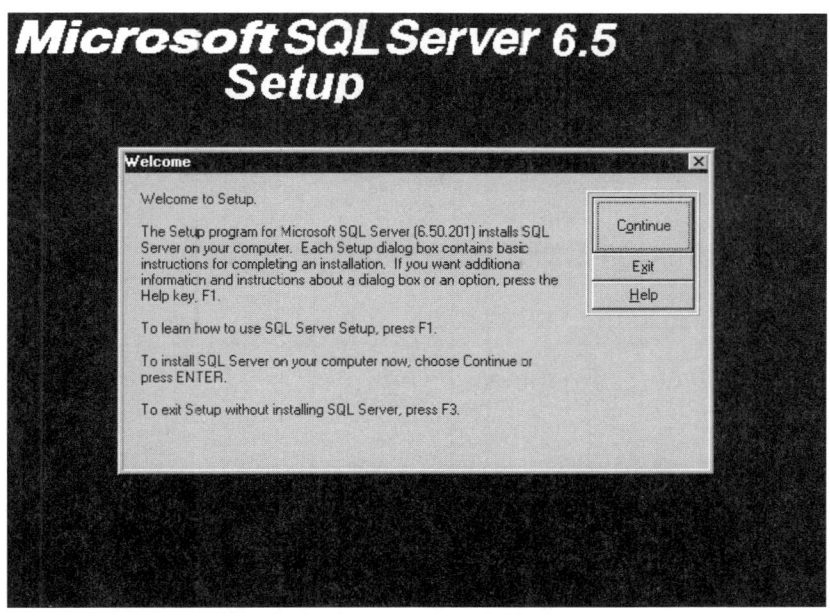

The Welcome dialog box on the Microsoft SQL Server Setup screen.
Figure 2.3

4. Figure 2.3 shows the first prompt you will see after launching setup.exe. This Welcome dialog shows the current version you are about to install (or upgrade). Select Continue to proceed.

5. Figure 2.4 shows the Enter Name And Organization dialog box. The product ID number is located on the back of the CD-ROM case. After you have filled in all three blanks, select Continue.

6. The Verify Name And Organization dialog box, shown in Figure 2.5, is used to confirm the information provided in the previous screen. If you have made a mistake, select Change. Otherwise, select Continue.

7. The Options dialog box, shown in Figure 2.6, presents your setup options. Since you can run Setup to perform configuration and option changes, you will become very familiar with this screen. In this example, we will select the Installing SQL Server And Utilities default by pressing Continue.

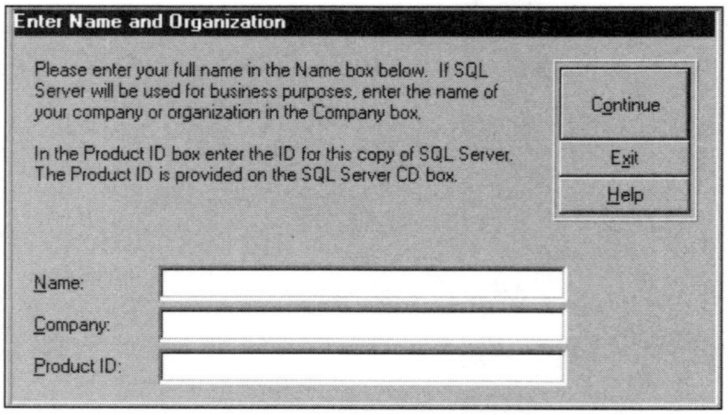

The Enter Name And Organization dialog box.
Figure 2.4

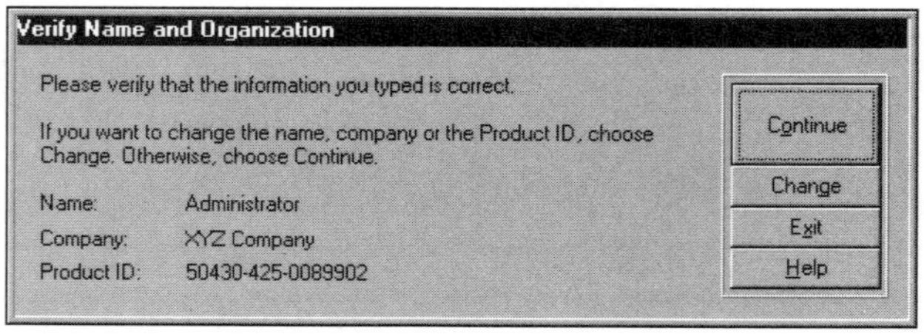

The Verify Name And Organization dialog box.
Figure 2.5

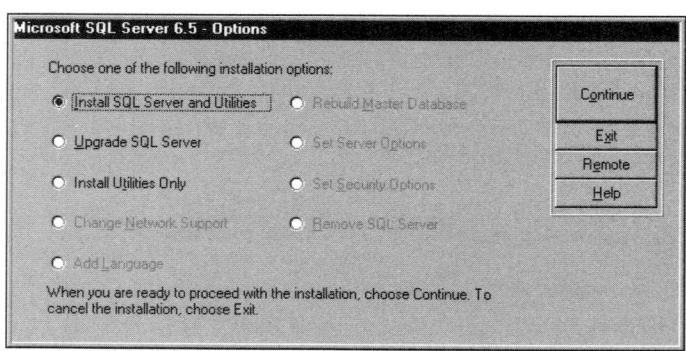

The Options dialog box.
Figure 2.6

8. In the Choose Licensing Mode dialog box, shown in Figure 2.7, you must indicate how you will manage the licensing of your server. By choosing the Per Server option, you are agreeing to handle the licensing for this server by the number of user connections that can be made to the server at any one time. (This option is very similar to that used by the Novell operating system to license network clients.) The more users you will have connected at the same time, the more licenses you will need.

    If you prefer, you can choose the Per Seat option. This is by far the easier of the two to keep legal, but it can be more expensive to maintain. If you choose per-seat licensing, Microsoft SQL Server does not check the number of connections against the number of licenses. Each client machine is assumed to have a valid license to connect to the server. Therefore, if you have 40 workstations, you will need 40 licenses.

    If you think you will have only 25 of the workstations accessing the server at any given time, you might want to choose the Per Server option. Recognize, however, that as needs grow, you will have to purchase more licenses and change the configuration of your server to match the purchase of additional licenses. The choice here depends on what you think best fits your organization. In our example, we will choose the Per Seat option.

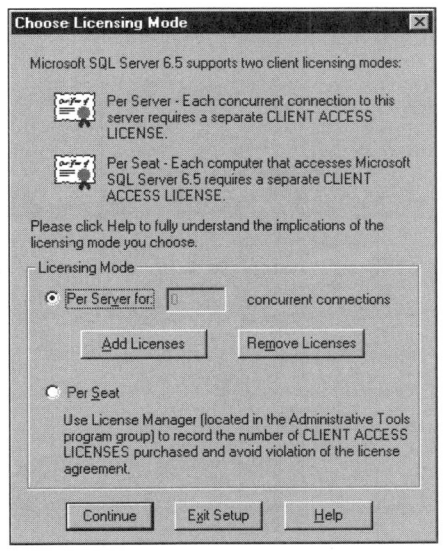

The Choose Licensing Mode dialog box.
Figure 2.7

There is always—and should be—a price to pay for someone's skills. Whether you want low prices now or high fines later is your choice. Staying legal is your responsibility, and it is something you should take very seriously. Like many programmers, I write software for sale and distribution to the public. Paying for the software written is the only way we can continue to support our products, keep prices down, and maintain the focus on development—not on security against piracy. Enough said.

9. The Per Seat Licensing dialog box, shown in Figure 2.8, is for client license verification. Select the I Agree checkbox and click OK.

10. The next prompt asks where you want Microsoft SQL Server installed on the disk (see Figure 2.9). This is the first step in the Setup program for which your answer depends on the layout of your hardware. If you have only one hard drive, then leave the default drive selected. Otherwise, select the disk on which you want to install your server. See Table 2.2 for our example server configurations.

11. The MASTER Device Creation dialog box, shown in Figure 2.10, asks where to place the master device and how large it should be. Your choice depends on the platform you are installing to. I recommend making this a 30MB choice at minimum and slightly larger if the system will be larger than average. See Table 2.3 for examples of the settings for this dialog box on our example servers.

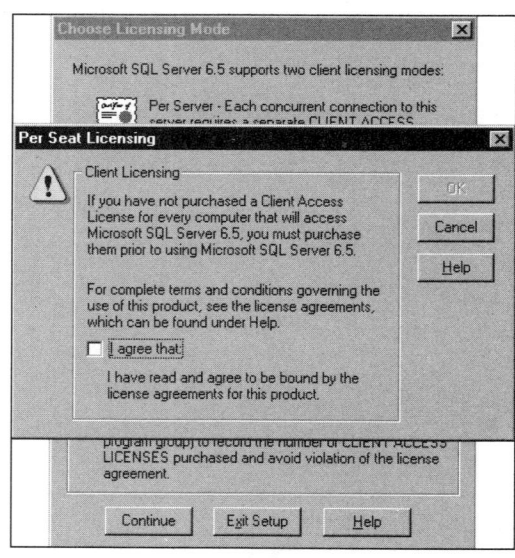

The Per Seat Licensing dialog box.
Figure 2.8

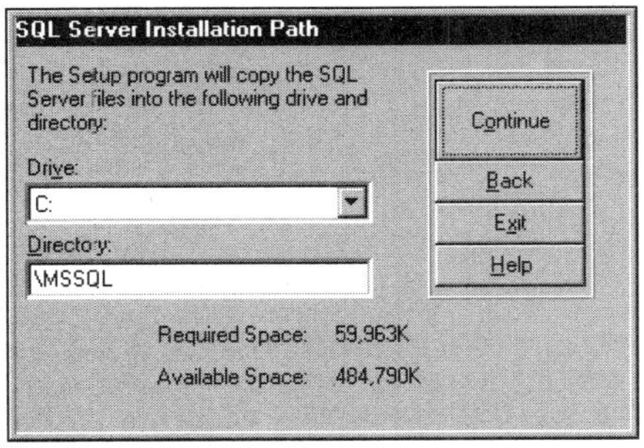

The SQL Server Installation Path dialog box.
Figure 2.9

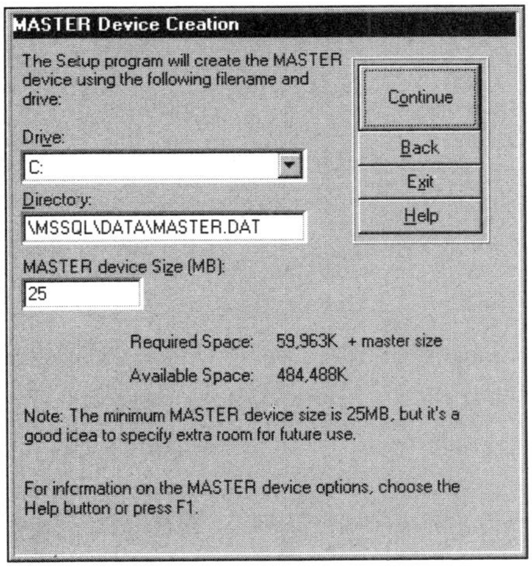

The MASTER Device Creation dialog box.
Figure 2.10

Server	Drive
SQL Server A	C:\
SQL Server B	D:\
SQL Server C	E:\

Note: SQL Server C assumes a duplexed boot drive. Select the drive letter of your RAID subsystem.

Table 2.2   Installation paths for our example servers.

Server	Size Of Master Device
SQL Server A	30MB
SQL Server B	30MB
SQL Server C	35MB

Note: Make sure the drive letter matches the previous step.

Table 2.3 Microsoft SQL Server settings for the master device on our example servers.

12. The next dialog box, shown in Figure 2.11, asks you how to install SQL Server Books Online. I strongly recommend placing it on the hard drive. I find myself looking things up almost daily, and having it on the machine makes access to information faster and more convenient. I install it on my workstation as well, for the same reason.

Great care should be taken not to make SQL Server Books Online accessible to the average user. These books are the keys to your kitchen, and with these keys users who don't know what they are doing could destroy the pantry. There is a lot of great information in these books; guard this resource from meddling hands.

13. The installation options for character set and sort order are displayed next (see Figure 2.12). Be sure to select both Auto Start checkboxes if you want the machine to automatically recover from power failures. Then click the Networks button.

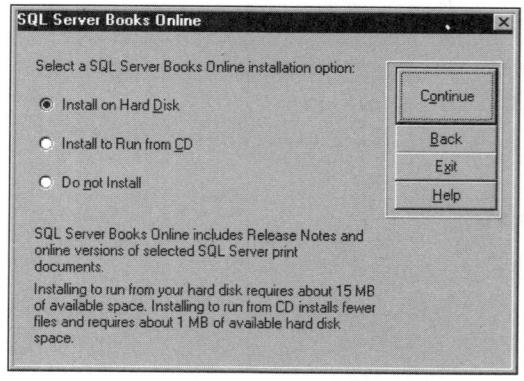

The SQL Server Books Online dialog box (choose the default when possible).
Figure 2.11

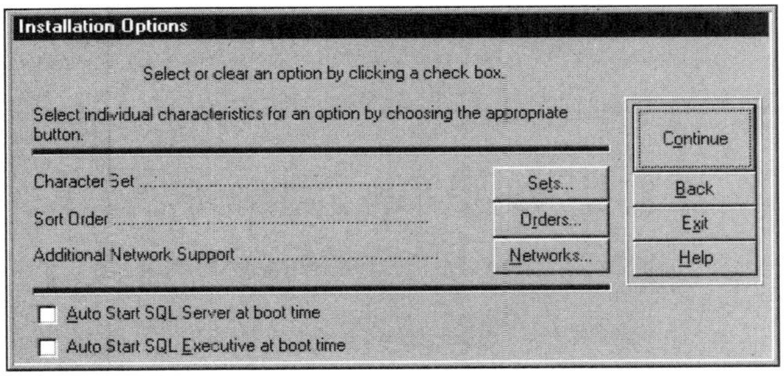

The Installation Options dialog box for character set, sort order, and network support.
Figure 2.12

14. The Select Network Protocols dialog box appears next. Because our example servers run on a TCP/IP network with NetWare clients, we will select the checkboxes for both IPX/SPX and TCP/IP support. (See Figure 2.15 for a screen capture of this window.) Click OK, then Continue.

15. The Select Character Set dialog box, shown in Figure 2.13, appears next. As mentioned in Chapter 1, your decision of whether to select an extended character set depends on whether you will be doing business in other languages. For most businesses, the default 128-character set is sufficient; however, you should review Chapter 1 before making a definitive decision. For our purposes, we'll go with the default. Select OK and proceed.

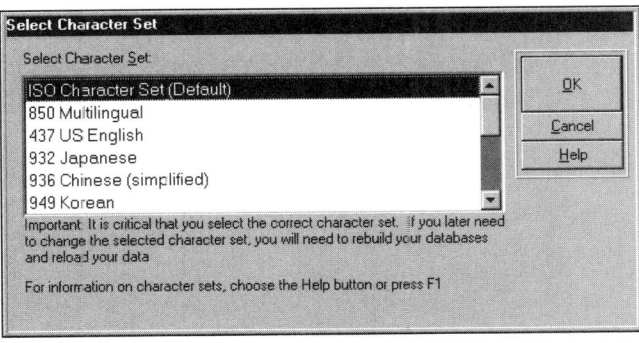

The Select Character Set dialog box.
Figure 2.13

Installation 55

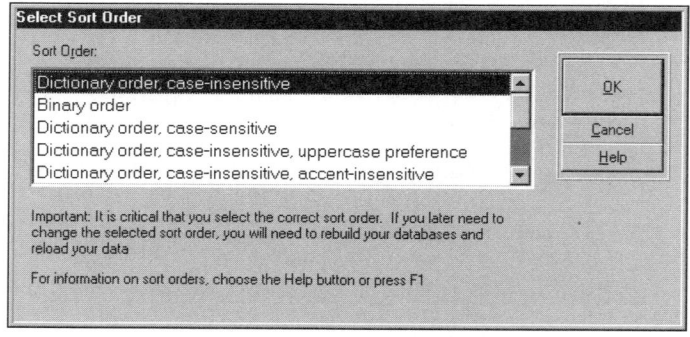

The Select Sort Order dialog box.
Figure 2.14

16. The Select Sort Order dialog box appears next, as shown in Figure 2.14. For most businesses, the default of dictionary order, case-insensitive is the best choice. Chapter 1 explains in detail the implications of choosing a different sort order than the default. Refer to that chapter before selecting a different sort order.

17. The Select Network Protocols dialog box, shown in Figure 2.15, appears next. Here you indicate which network protocols you want installed. In our example servers, we will also check the IPX/SPX and TCP/IP options in this dialog box in addition to Named Pipes.

18. Next, fill in the user account information we entered when we created a user account for the MSSQLServer to run under. Be sure to insert the fully qualified domain name (Domain\User) in the Account field. Type in the password you supplied for this account

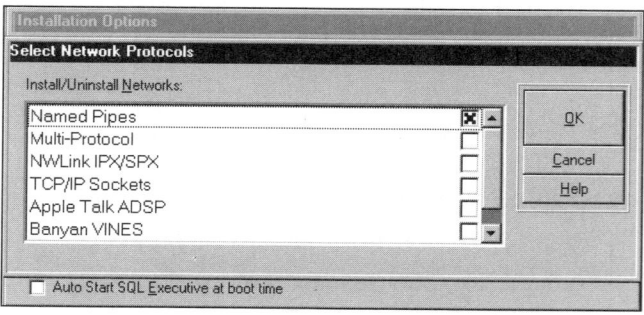

The Select Network Protocols dialog box.
Figure 2.15

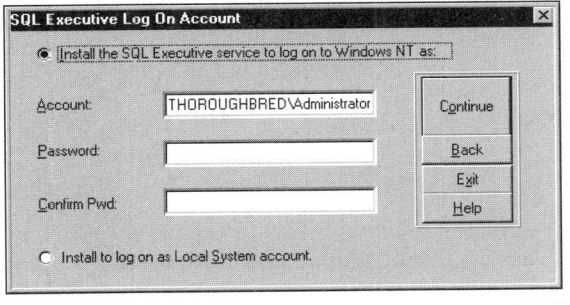

The SQL Executive Log On Account dialog box.
Figure 2.16

in User Manager For Domains in both of the fields and click Continue. See Figure 2.16 for the SQL Executive Log On Account dialog box.

19. The next dialog box, shown in Figure 2.17, asks you whether you want to use multiprotocol encryption. I usually leave this alone until I am certain I require this option. If I do need to add this, it can be done later without much problem.

20. Since SQL Server supports NetWare, Setup asks you for a name for the Novell bindery service, as shown in Figure 2.18. The default here is fine. Select Continue to proceed.

21. Next, the TCP/IP Socket Number dialog box appears, asking you about the port number to use for TCP/IP requests (see Figure 2.19). The default of 1433 is fine. This port number can be used by other remote processes to connect to the server via this port. Select Continue to move on.

22. You are now presented with a File Copy In Progress status bar, shown in Figure 2.20. We are now in the homestretch and have worked through the majority of installation

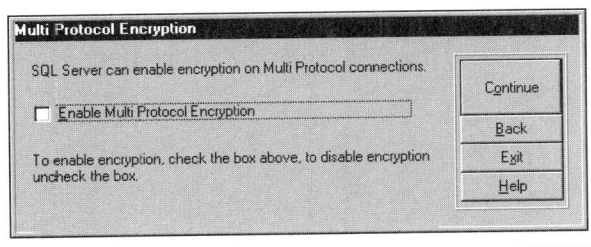

The Multi Protocol Encryption dialog box.
Figure 2.17

Installation 57

The Novell Bindery Service Name dialog box.
Figure 2.18

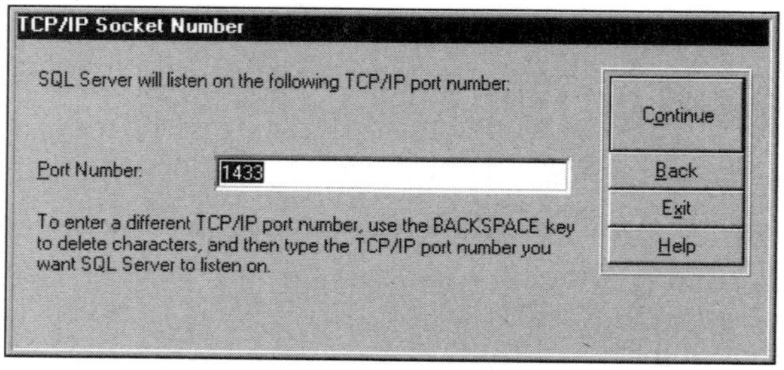

The TCP/IP Socket Number dialog box.
Figure 2.19

issues. Allow this procedure to complete without interruption. Do not try to start any other application or process during this time.

23. After the Copy operation is finished, the screen shown in Figure 2.21 appears. This screen tells you that you may perform other tasks while the installation continues. The hourglass icon fills with sand many times. I recommend not doing anything else on the machine until this screen goes away. Although I have tested this multitasking feature and have found that it works, I trust the installation more by playing it safe and letting this process run its course.

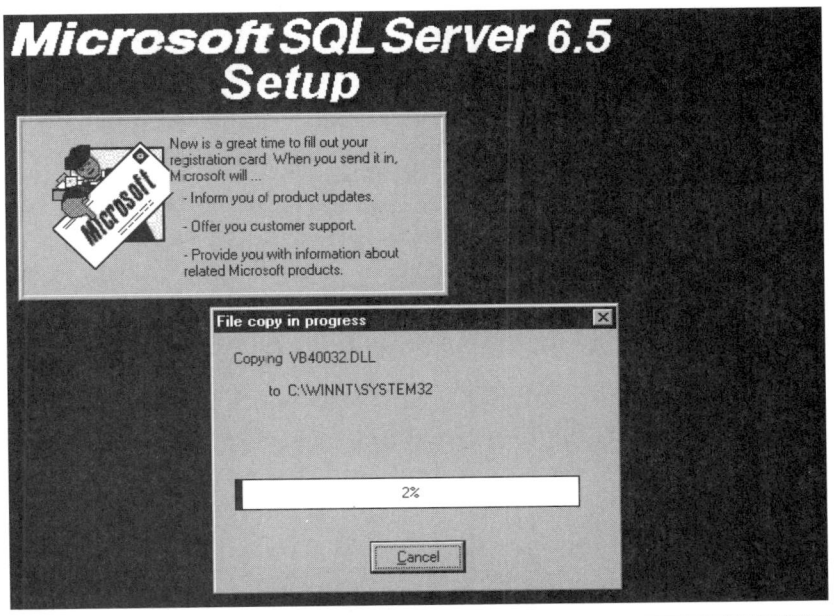

The File Copy In Progress status bar.
Figure 2.20

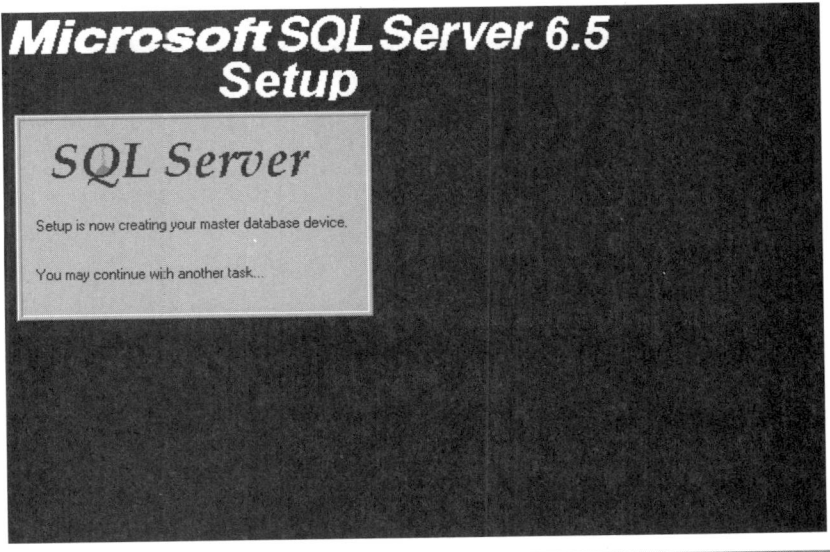

The Setup keep-alive screen.
Figure 2.21

A Quick Tour Of The SQL Server Program Group

Now let's take a brief tour of the SQL Server program group, shown in Figure 2.22. The ISQL/W icon represents the graphical query tool that allows your query tables on the server. This tool is similar to many popular manual code entry query tools. ISQL/W has some nice features that I will discuss as we progress through writing queries and optimizing code later in the book.

The yellow question mark next to ISQL/W is a Help file that answers some questions and holds some key information about accessing Microsoft SQL Server with **ODBC**. I highly recommend this tool to anyone developing ODBC clients.

The next icon displayed is only available with version 6.5 and above. This is a **RQBE** tool that many of your users might be used to using. Microsoft Query uses ODBC to connect to the server and allows you to build queries graphically by clicking on the fields you want and selecting the order through its interface. This is a good tool for testing any ODBC connection since the server is accessed in this manner.

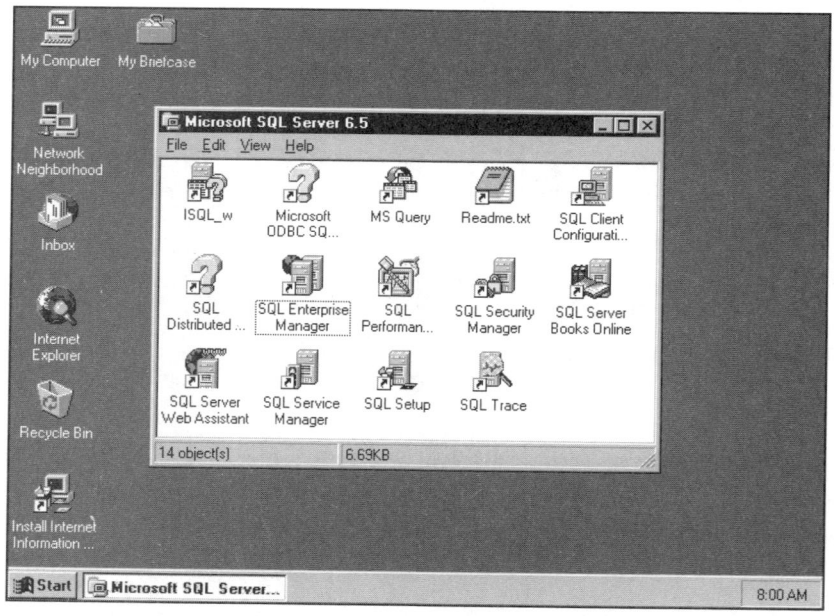

The Microsoft SQL Server program group.
Figure 2.22

60   Chapter 2: Practical Guide

The readme file contains release notes for running some SQL files installed on your server to expand your management abilities. This file also contains some Distributed Transaction Coordinator notes that you should read before configuring DTC services on your server.

The SQL Client Configuration utility is perhaps the most overlooked program you install. This utility should be run any time you have connection problems with the server. Remember that the Enterprise Manager is also a client program, even though it runs on the same machine as the server itself. This is the first place I send people who call me and tell me they cannot connect to the server with a client or the Enterprise Manager.

The next yellow question mark is a Help file that explains the distributed management objects (DMO) at the root of this system. These objects can be used by client applications to perform many tasks without having to log on to the server as the administrator. I strongly recommend that client developers become familiar with the DMO structure outlined in this file.

Next is the Enterprise Manager. This is a client utility that can be run on the server or remotely to administer your entire enterprise. This tool does an excellent job of showing you the remote management abilities of your servers (using the DMO). I will go into more detail on the Enterprise Manager as we progress through the book; for now, just note that this tool performs many tasks that you can add to your client applications for increased management of your server.

The SQL Performance Monitor icon represents a standard set of Windows NT counters saved in a file that you can open to test the performance of not only your SQL server, but the operating system and network as well. This tool warrants a book unto itself; I will cover some of its uses in Chapter 11.

The SQL Security Manager is a small but powerful application that allows you to easily map NT user accounts to SQL server login IDs and databases. This tool is a huge timesaver and should not be overlooked when configuring users and their ability to connect to the server.

The SQL Server Books Online icon is next, and second only to the Enterprise Manager, this is probably the most-used icon in the group. This calls a TechNet CD-type search engine that holds all the information and documentation that ships with Microsoft SQL Server. This resource will help you troubleshoot 85 percent of your problems without having to open a book (well, except for maybe this one).

In the bottom row is the SQL Server Web Assistant. This utility allows you to publish static HTML pages to your Web site. I have found the tool easy to use and fairly powerful when coupled with stored procedures. If you need dynamic data access to the Web, you will still need to use the IDC or ADC features of your Web server for interactive database query capabilities. This Web utility gives you good basic reproducible results with little effort.

The SQL Service Manager is a utility that performs the same actions as the Services icon in the Control Panel. This is an easy way to stop and start SQL Server-related services.

The SQL Setup icon allows you to run the setup program while Microsoft SQL Server is running. This allows you to change configuration options or network support through the setup program. Keep in mind that some changes you make in this program require you to restart the MSSQLServer service before they take effect.

Last is the SQL Trace utility. This tool is crucial to monitoring the use of your server and determining what raw SQL is being passed to your server by its clients. I will walk you through this utility in Chapter 11.

Post-Installation Issues

To properly finish the installation process, you'll need to check the following items. If you have other SQL Server-based applications to install on this server, you should check these items first before moving on to any other software.

Configuring The Server Service

From the Control Panel, open the Services application and configure the MSSQLServer service to run under the same Windows NT user account that Microsoft Exchange is set to use. Start or restart the MSSQLServer service. This change will not take effect until you restart the service. This particular setting is considered to be static during the current session that Microsoft SQL Server runs under.

Changing The Memory Setting To Reflect The Hardware

The next task is to properly configure the amount of memory the server will be using. Microsoft SQL Server does not automatically access whatever memory is available on your machine. You must establish the amount of RAM for the server to use. This step refers to the preinstallation checklist from the previous chapter, in which we calculated what value to place in the memory configuration option.

The memory setting can be set through the call of a stored procedure or through the Enterprise Manager. I will focus on the graphic method here to help illustrate where to find other configuration options and settings. Many of the options you see in the configuration screen will be discussed in Chapter 11 and should not be changed from their original value until you know without the slightest doubt that the option should be changed. Microsoft SQL Server will choose either 8MB or 16MB of memory at installation depending on the amount of physical RAM it detects when the installation program is run. Beyond the initial setting, you should change the memory configuration option setting to match your hardware, following the steps listed below:

1. Open the Enterprise Manager.
2. Right-click on the icon representing your server.
3. Choose the Configure menu option.
4. The Server Configuration/Options window appears with the Server Options tab selected; choose the Configuration tab.
5. Scroll down the list of options until you find Memory.

Note the amount of memory you are currently running under. By clicking on the Memory line in the display, you will see the description at the bottom of the Server Configuration/Options dialog, based on the line selected. The description also indicates whether you must restart SQL Server for the changes to take effect or if your changes take effect immediately. The dynamic and static configurations of the server determine when a change takes effect.

6. In the Current box, place the value from item 5 on the preinstallation checklist. (Refer to Figure 1.2 or preinstall.doc on the CD-ROM.)

7. Select OK, then Close to exit the Enterprise Manager.

8. Open the SQL Service Manager from the SQL Server program group.

9. Make sure the MSSQLServer service is selected.

10. Double-click on the red light.

11. After the service has stopped, double-click on the green light.

12. Once the service has started, close this program.

You can now repeat the configuration steps above to check that the server is running under the new amount of memory that you have specified. See Table 2.4 for the example servers' memory settings.

Testing SQL Mail

Open SQL Enterprise Manager, and if you haven't already, register your server. Select your server, and from the Server menu choose SQL Mail/Configure, or right-click the SQL Mail icon below the selected server and choose Configure. Type the profile name you used to configure the Microsoft Exchange Mail Client software. You do not need to provide a password for Microsoft Exchange; it uses the account and password configured for the MSSQLServer service.

Server	2K Amount
SQL Server A	17408
SQL Server B	55926
SQL Server C	115712

Table 2.4 Microsoft SQL Server memory settings on example servers.

In SQL Enterprise Manager, choose SQL Mail/Start from the Server menu, or right-click the SQL Mail icon and choose Start. The SQL Mail icon will become green if SQL Mail has started successfully. If mail does not start (or does not turn green) look up "Troubleshooting Mail" in the Microsoft SQL Server Books Online. To test this mail ability, perform the following steps from within the Enterprise Manager:

1. Go to the Server menu and select the Alerts/Operators item.
2. The Manage Alerts and Operators window opens.
3. Select the Operators tab. (The red firefighter hat becomes active.)
4. Click the New Operator button on the toolbar (left icon in center group).
5. In the ID box, type the name of an operator who will receive messages.
6. Press the Tab key twice. This should place you in the E-Mail Name field.
7. Type the mail system name to map this operator to (whatever you would type in the To box of the mail client; you can click the "…" button to look up an email address).
8. Click the Test button. (Always test this feature to ensure proper mail abilities.)
9. Select OK to close the window.

You have now successfully installed Microsoft SQL Server. Now, last but not least: *Back up the master database!*

Chapter 3

Development Versus Production

- Registering Servers
- Transferring Objects
- Warning Messages
- Pitfalls

Administrator's Notes...

Chapter 3

When management is faced with configuring a development environment, their latitude often depends on the size of the operation. Larger MIS departments usually have the resources and backing to provide a development server that mirrors the production machine fairly closely. Small- to mid-sized shops tend to have tighter budgets and fewer resources with which to accomplish this task. With Microsoft SQL Server's lower cost of ownership, this does not have to be the case any longer.

Microsoft SQL Server gives you the freedom to be creative when approaching the development process. In planning and budgeting the development environment for Microsoft SQL Server, you have many freedoms that some other systems do not allow. You can place a test server into your environment at a very reasonable cost. By scaling your SQL server, you can simulate many production environments. Microsoft SQL Server lends itself to scaling very well.

I have found that even on inexpensive machines, Microsoft SQL Server can play a very productive role in the development process. For some environments, I have recommended having multiple SQL servers in the development environment to lower the impact of the development process.

Setting Up The Development Environment

For many projects, having many programmers simultaneously developing client applications to run against a server is common. In most cases, one or two database programmers can support the needs of even a mid-sized MIS department. That is not to say that each project shouldn't be considered on a case-by-case basis. I have found that using a multiple-server development environment provides the greatest flexibility when creating stored procedures, triggers, and data modeling.

One benefit of using multiple servers is the isolation your SQL code development can enjoy. Your database programmers can write and test code against their development server, then copy tested and debugged code out to the server being used by the client development team. I have used a lightweight machine similar to the example Server A in the previous chapter to facilitate just such an environment.

In the event you cannot use this concept, you might want to install Microsoft SQL Server on your own workstation. Providing you have enough RAM to meet the minimum requirements and you install Microsoft Windows NT Server as your operating system, you would then have a machine you can develop on without impacting other programmers' productivity.

This type of development is a sharp contrast to the databases running in the UNIX environment. You are no longer forced to develop on the same machine as everyone else. One important note is to take additional care to ensure the correct version of the objects you develop and deploy. With the Enterprise Manager client provided with Microsoft SQL Server, you can effectively migrate or transfer your fully debugged objects to other servers rather painlessly.

Third-Party Tools

With the increased popularity of client/server development, many good third-party tools have become available. Embarcadero Technologies, for instance, has developed a series of excellent tools for developing SQL-based client/server solutions. The DBArtisan product is very similar in feature and function to the Enterprise Manager and will run against many servers other than Microsoft SQL Server. In a multiple-vendor product environment, having a single product to interface with your data servers can be a great benefit. I have included demo copies of each of these tools on the CD-ROM accompanying this book. You can also reach Embarcadero on the Internet at www.embarcadero.com.

The amount of thought and planning that has gone into these products is impressive. As with other tools of this type on the market, you will experience a short learning curve. Throughout the book I will mention where the Embarcadero products have proven useful. The use and methods of third-party applications are not the focus of this book; I will use them in examples where possible, however, because tools like these do provide significant benefits.

Most of these third-party modeling and development tools do a very good job at what they were designed to do. Take some time to learn what each target design is before committing to a purchase.

Data Modeling

When you begin the design process, good planning is essential. Pay particular attention to the underlying data structures and the end user's needs. I have been contracted to fix many systems that were written by and for programmers and the user was the first on the list of considerations. Many projects start with the user's needs in mind, but that focus soon shifts to the method of supplying the user with what they really need and the system requirements to meet those needs. When faced with the task of actually implementing the methods, programmers (myself included) will always take the path of least resistance. This path will cause you to stray from your focus of providing the user with a working product. The user is the focus of any project a developer undertakes. Users pay for our services with patience and feedback, as well as with money. The projects we develop are evaluated as to how well the user can perform the tasks we seek to automate with our creativity.

To keep myself on the right path when developing systems, I try to view the database objects as entities for as long as possible. Just as the term *entity* suggests, I give each order, load, or message a human-like attribute—a "personality." If you think in these terms, you can treat each entity and how it relates to other objects or processes in a very complete, well-thought-out manner; you can spend more time planning and less time fixing.

I like to model either at the physical or conceptual layer a bit longer than most developers. I have found that by spending more time at these levels, less revision time is required down the road. Use the data-modeling technique as a road map. Follow the design as closely as you can, but keep in mind it is only a guide. When making changes to your data structures, update your data model to reflect your modifications. Plan a few hours a month for keeping your data model as current as possible, whether it needs it or not.

Many of the third-party modeling tools available support designing and modeling of your data. Most have a base set of features that can aid you in staying current as long as possible. There will come a time when you lose the connection between your model and your data structure. Many things can cause this separation. Typically, problems arise when you use a tool for data modeling that does not allow you to create all the objects that your design requires. I have used most of the major modeling applications on the market today and have found limitations to each one. You'll need to overcome each of these. Be creative; use scripts to create or modify the objects that you cannot create with the modeling tool. Spending the time keeping your model current is time well spent.

When choosing a data-modeling tool, research each tool thoroughly. Keep in mind that these tools are not cheap. Look for a tool that allows you to model at either the conceptual and physical layer, and that allows you to create views and triggers. These components are crucial to taking advantage of your server's ability to implement security and data integrity. The tool you choose should support modifying triggers and views beyond the basic cascading INSERT, UPDATE, and DELETE statements.

Whether development or production, all systems have two levels of configuration that need attention: server-level parameters and application parameters.

Server-Level Parameters

Server-level parameters should be checked and verified when you install the server. When creating a mirrored server to your production environment, you can use these server-level parameters to help tune or scale your server to react to queries in the same way.

One important point to mention here is that some server-level parameters are dynamic and some are static. Dynamic parameters can be changed on the fly programmatically or through the Enterprise Manager. Other parameters are static, which is to say that you must stop and start the MSSQLServer service in order for the changes to take effect. Check the Microsoft SQL Server Books Online for details of each of these parameters before making any changes.

Let's take a moment to look at a few of the more important server parameters.

User Connections

The User Connections parameter should be configured after installation to allow for the number of users on your system. You should set this value equal to the number of expected connections to your server.

Keep in mind that one client may have more than one connection to the server at any given time. When a multithreaded application connects to Microsoft SQL Server for data access, the client may open several connections. In addition, the SQL Executive and the other management-type accounts on your server will use between five and seven connections.

The maximum value you can set for this option is a theoretical limit of 32,767. This limit assumes you have the hardware and memory to support that kind of burden. Each connection will take a small amount of memory away from the amount of memory that Microsoft SQL Server will use.

In some of its documentation, Microsoft recommends approximately 37K per user for each user connection. In other Microsoft documentation, however, I have seen 40K and 42K used as the magic numbers for calculating the amount of memory user connections will take. To be safe, I assume 42K per user connection. By choosing the 42K amount, I am allowing a small bit of memory to spill over into the caches for each user. That way, the most you can be off is a net of 5K. Although that may not seem like much, using the 42K value does give you a cushion.

Tempdb in RAM

Tempdb in RAM is another setting that can get you into trouble. There are some good reasons to place Tempdb in RAM, but in all cases, you should test the move to RAM thoroughly and make sure it really is providing an improvement. As a general rule, if you do not have at least 64MB of RAM in your server, you should leave Tempdb on-disk. When deciding whether to place Tempdb in RAM, research this option very thoroughly in the Microsoft SQL Server Books Online.

Sort Pages

Next is Sort Pages, which specifies the maximum number of pages that will be allocated to sorting query output on a user-by-user basis. On machines that execute large sorts, increasing this number can improve performance. Since additional sort pages will deplete your server's available memory, you may need to adjust the amount of memory dedicated to SQL Server.

Resource Timeout

Resource Timeout is used by Microsoft SQL Server to determine the number of seconds to wait for a resource to be released by another process. The default setting for this parameter is 10. Increase this value only if the SQL Server error log has a lot of logwrite or bufwait timeout warnings in it.

 I recommend that the DBA of Microsoft SQL Server check the server error log and the Windows NT event log on a daily basis. Checking these logs each day can help you proactively troubleshoot events that occur on your server. Remember that your server's load will fluctuate and grow over time. I have not found a system yet that you can set up and forget.

Read-Ahead Optimization

This subject will be covered in more detail later in Chapter 11. Most of the parameters in the RA section should be changed only if you are instructed to do so by a qualified support technician. Only two of the parameters are used for tuning the RA management for your server with any regularity: RA worker threads and RA slots per thread.

RA Worker Threads

The number of read-ahead worker threads you specify can impact the performance of your server. RA worker threads are used by Microsoft SQL Server to accommodate read-ahead requests. Microsoft recommends that this option be set to the maximum number of concurrent users on the server. (By the way, a warning will be written to Microsoft SQL Server's error log if the number of threads that request read-ahead scans exceeds the number of configured read-ahead slots.) Check the Microsoft SQL Server Books Online to find out more about how to interpret read-ahead settings.

RA Slots Per Thread

RA Slots Per Thread is another configuration option that should be approached with caution. The slots-per-thread option controls the number of simultaneous requests each read-ahead service thread will manage. The total number of worker threads multiplied by the number of slots equals the number of concurrent read-ahead scans that Microsoft SQL Server will support.

The default value of 5 should be fine. However, if your server has a very good disk subsystem, you might be able to increase the number of scans that a single thread can handle by adding to the default in small increments.

As with any change you make to your server, you should change options slowly and carefully. Write down the old value, then change one value at a time and test the impact on performance. Test and benchmark your changes and verify that they, in fact, did what you expected.

Priority Boost

You can increase the thread priority for SQL server within Windows NT by changing the Priority Boost option. Only change this option on a machine dedicated to SQL server, or you might find yourself being unable to launch other applications or tasks on your server. Be leery of this setting when you have a dual-processor machine as well. Setting this option can have a serious impact on your server's ability to service login requests and manage printer or file access.

Max Worker Threads

Max Worker Threads configures the number of threads Microsoft SQL Server has to service SQL Server processes. Microsoft SQL Server makes use of the native thread services of Windows NT Server. This is one reason why SQL Server is capable of such high performance—and why it only runs on Windows NT.

Instead of the database having to create and manage threads internally, the operating system shares threads with SQL Server. Other systems that are not tied to the operating system in this way must maintain their threads at the application level, thus slowing the application down (even a small amount) by adding additional overhead.

By changing this option, you control the number of threads allocated to the user pool. When the number of user connections is less than the worker threads setting, one thread handles each connection. However, if the number of connections surpasses the Max Worker Threads value, thread pooling occurs.

You might think that pooling threads would slow down the operation of your server and that this value should be set high. However, the default of 255 is too high for most systems. Independent third-party studies have discovered that setting this value to around 100 actually allows your server to operate much more efficiently. Check the white paper by Compaq Corporation (included on the CD-ROM) for more details.

Lock Escalation Parameters

Lock Escalation parameters is one of the hottest topics being discussed in newsgroups on the Internet today (and probably for a long time to come as well.) This set of options can lead you down the path of eternal server adjustments if you do not look at all the reasons you are having locking issues on your server in the first place.

It is easy to assume that you need to modify one of these parameters to thwart deadlocks and hung processes. In some situations, the source of your problem is in fact a misconfigured locking scheme, but in reality, most locking problems are the result of questionable query methods and database design.

The Lock Escalation Threshold Maximum is intended as an upper boundary for the server to use. The server will hold this maximum value of actual 2K page locks per statement executed before attempting to escalate the lock to a table lock. The lower boundary (the Lock Escalation Threshold Minimum) is used to help keep SQL Server from locking a small table with only a few rows in it every time a query is run against it. The minimum is used in conjunction with the Lock Escalation Threshold Percentage to control this situation and keep locks from getting out of hand.

All of these options can be overridden on a statement-by-statement basis with optimizer hints. Including hints in your SQL statements will cause these thresholds to be ignored. Great care should be taken when overriding the Query Optimizer. The only hint I supply with any regularity is the NOLOCK hint, which tells SQL Server not to lock any pages with this query at all. (The use of optimizer hints is covered in Chapters 5 and 6.)

Fill Factor

Fill Factor is a parameter that you should learn about almost as early as opening the shrinkwrap on your software. Changing this value affects how indexes will be rebuilt, as well as how the space on your server is used. See Figure 3.1 for the effects of using different fill factors on your databases. Both examples show the same index, yet the bottom set of 2K pages actually requires more disk space, due to the limit of filling the page only halfway.

The default for SQL Server is 0, or 100 percent. I usually change this to 80 or 90 percent, depending on the type of server that I am configuring. When you change this server option to a lesser value, the effect on your existing data is not apparent until you rebuild your indexes.

When an index is created on your SQL server, the fill factor is used to leave space available on pages for your index to grow into. This growth is what the fill factor allows to happen without fragmenting your index and slowing response down. When a page is filled, any other data that should be placed on that page has no place to go.

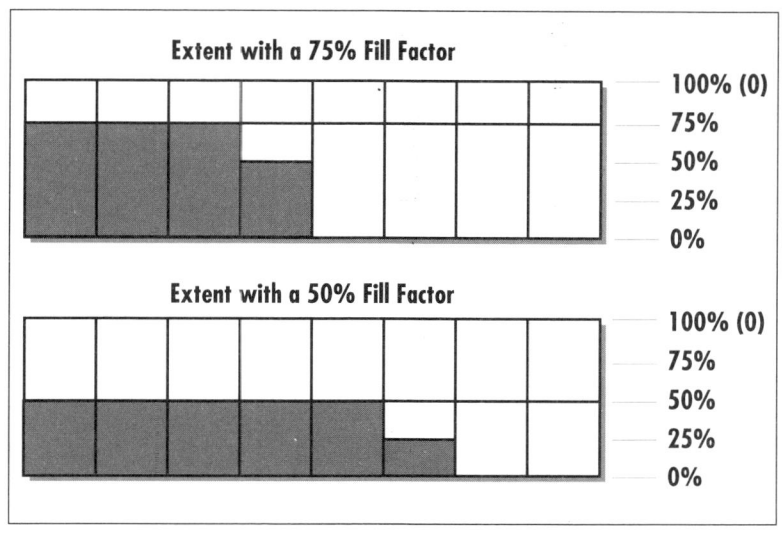

Fill factor's impact on disk space used for an index.
Figure 3.1

Therefore, the data must be split and placed in other pages or even other extents. (*Extents* are eight contiguous 2K pages stored in your database.) When a page split or an extent switch occurs, you're spending extra time moving the disk head for read operations or write operations.

I have seen some messages on the Internet that recommend using a 50 percent fill factor or even less, to help keep performance up on a system. This is fine if you have a lot of disk real estate and are not concerned with the amount of space you are losing to indexes. I recommend keeping this value as high as possible and using specific indexes with lower-than-normal fill factors to lessen the impact on your disk space.

The only time I use a fill factor of 100 percent is for read-only data or for data that will be modified or changed so rarely that the impact on performance is not an issue. The fill factor is only checked when you build or rebuild an index. When you add data to an index, the fill factor is ignored.

These are the main server parameters that you should concern yourself with at this point in the process. That is not to say, however, that your project won't require one or more of the other parameters to be configured differently from SQL Server's default setting. You should become aware of each parameter and its function on your server. The more you know about these parameters, the more you can understand why things happen the way they do on your server.

Application Parameters

Application-specific parameters represent the second level of configuration. Microsoft SQL Server does not allow you to configure global client variables; therefore, you should develop a table-driven approach to application parameters.

DBCC PINTABLE

A good technique for using table-driven parameters is the DBCC PINTABLE option. This option allows you to place the table containing your parameters into the data cache and keep it from being flushed, thereby increasing performance of queries against this table.

DBCC PINTABLE marks a table, once it is used, to remain in the data cache until "unpinned." DBCC PINTABLE does not read the table into cache; instead, as the table is queried, the data pages are put into cache, then marked so they do not get flushed later. Once the table is pinned, changes to the data are logged, and the table can be recovered in the event of a media failure.

Use this feature with caution. If you pin a large table, it will consume your available data cache and impact the performance of queries against all your other tables. When storing your application variables on your SQL server, beware of creating a table that is high maintenance and low return-on-investment. Create only the indexes needed and do not create a huge, wide, and hard-to-understand table structure.

Registry-Type Tables

There are two good methods for using server-based client application parameters. First is the creation of a registry-type table. This table allows you to store a broad range of data in a very flexible format. The Windows NT or Windows 95 Registry can be used as a model for this kind of table. Beware, however, of registry pitfalls. You have seen what can happen to a machine running Windows 95 or Windows NT when applications write to the registry in a haphazard way—disasters and the dreaded blue screen of death. Clean up after yourself and pay attention to keeping the data and keys clean and up-to-date. Remove unused keys and perform maintenance on this table regularly. Store only single-value data in this type of structure.

A registry-type table does not lend itself to relational or set-based data queries. Using a list-type table structure to return result sets to your client application is much more efficient.

List-Type Tables

A list-type table can be joined with other tables or used to return rows to a client application. One possible use of this kind of information might be a current user table. This table may store such information as the key values of the records the user is accessing and permission variables on those objects. By storing this information in a table, users can very easily be guided back to where they were last working, making the application appear to be smart and intuitive. Indexes play an even greater role in performance with this kind of table than with a normal data structure.

Beware of multiple indexes on this kind of table. Look at the queries that run against it and determine the minimum index configuration required. Updates are usually more frequent against this kind of table, and therefore the index values will need to be updated often.

Setup Scripts

A script is simply a file containing SQL commands that is executed against your SQL server to create, modify, or manipulate data or objects. Most large systems require you to run some sort of configuration scripts to prepare the system for operation. Very few good data-modeling tools are available that let you create a finished structure that takes into account revisions of objects and changes to permission structures. These types of issues are easily handled with scripts.

For example, scripts can be used to add the user-defined error messages for your application to the SQL server. Although these error messages can be configured by hand on a case-by-case basis, doing so lends itself to human error and inaccurately typed messages. Creating and executing a script file is much faster and allows you to configure two or more servers with exactly the same options. In fact, most data modeling tools allow you to create script files to run against your server for object creation.

When writing scripts, you should keep a few ground rules in mind:

1. A script is broken down into batches. These batches are designated by the word *GO*.
2. If an error occurs in a batch, that batch will not execute. Other batches in the script will still run, however.

3. You cannot create and reference an object in the same batch. You also cannot drop and create an object with the same name in the same batch.

4. SET statements take effect at the end of a batch.

5. Be sure to use a lot of comments in your scripts.

Although I will not go into writing SQL statements in detail until Chapter 5, these tips should be committed to memory. The above list will help you troubleshoot performance problems when executing scripts.

Sample Server Setup Script

In Listing 3.1, I've provided a sample setup script for adding or modifying user-defined messages. Notice that I have commented extensively in this script, even though it will be run only once in a while and should not change often. This allows other programmers to read and understand quickly what I was attempting to do with the script.

The /* and */ must be placed at the beginning and end of comments. Notice that the formatting shown here is for legibility only. Each of the EXEC lines is continued on the next line in this text (as indicated by indention) but should be on the same line in your script. See the sample scripts included on the CD-ROM for the actual text file.

Listing 3.1   Sample setup script.

```
/*
---------------------------------------------------------------------
Name         : Server Message Init
File Name    : ServerMsgInit.sql
Dated        : 08/17/97
---------------------------------------------------------------------
Description
---------------------------------------------------------------------
Create user-defined error messages to be called by SQL statements and
stored procedures with the system. Drop any existing messages in range
to meet my needs.
---------------------------------------------------------------------
*/

/* Must be called within the Master Database                        */
USE MASTER

/* Add new messages to SQL server                                   */
/* The TRUE option enables NT event logging                         */
/* The REPLACE option will overwrite existing message numbers       */
```

```
/* General SQL Error                    */
EXEC sp_addmessage 60000, 10, "General SQL Error in <%s>. This will be logged
   in the Windows NT Eventlog.", us_english, TRUE, REPLACE

/* Business Rule Violation              */
EXEC sp_addmessage 60001, 10, "<%s> has violated business rule <%s>.
   This will be written to the Windows NT Eventlog, and E-Mail will be sent.",
   us_english, TRUE, REPLACE

/* Missing E-Mail Address               */
EXEC sp_addmessage 60002, 10, "There is no defined E-Mail recipient for
   Business Rule <%s>. This will be written to the Windows NT Eventlog.",
   us_english, TRUE, REPLACE

/* SQL Error In Procedure (Logged)      */
EXEC sp_addmessage 60003, 10, "SQL Error %s in function ['%s']. Attempting
   to %s.", us_english, TRUE, REPLACE

/* SQL Error In Procedure (Non-Logged)  */
EXEC sp_addmessage 60004, 16, "SQL Error %s in function ['%s']. Attempting
   to %s. This error can occur due to %s and will be ignored.", us_english,
   FALSE, REPLACE

/* Finished                             */
PRINT 'Finished.'
GO
```

Setup scripts can be executed from a graphical interface or from the DOS Query tool provided with SQL Server. To use this sample script, you open the text file with any of the available text-based query tools, then execute it. The following is the sample output from this script when executed:

```
Replacing message.
New message added.
Replacing message.
New message added.
Replacing message.
New message added.
Replacing message.
New message added.
Replacing message.
New message added.
Finished.
```

This sample is intended only to illustrate what a script looks like. I will explain in later chapters how to write scripts to perform different tasks on your server. Scripts are a very powerful tool that can be used to save a lot of time and ensure consistency among servers.

Another method of creating these scripts is to let SQL Server's Enterprise Manager create them for you. Although Enterprise Manager cannot script user-defined error messages, it can generate scripts for just about anything else.

Scripting Objects

You can use SQL-DMO (SQL Data Management Objects) and the SQL Enterprise Manager to generate scripts of objects that exist on your SQL server. You can select pre-existing objects in the Enterprise Manager and have the script created that would be necessary to drop and re-create the object on your server or any other SQL server. This can be very beneficial when you need to modify an existing object quickly.

Figure 3.2 shows the dialog box that appears when you select an object in the Server Manager window, then select the Object menu and the Generate SQL Script option. This is a very useful feature in a development environment. You have the ability to generate scripts for groups of objects, as well as for specific objects. Notice the Object Creation and Object Drop checkboxes. These options allow you to drop and re-create objects from the script or scripts you generate.

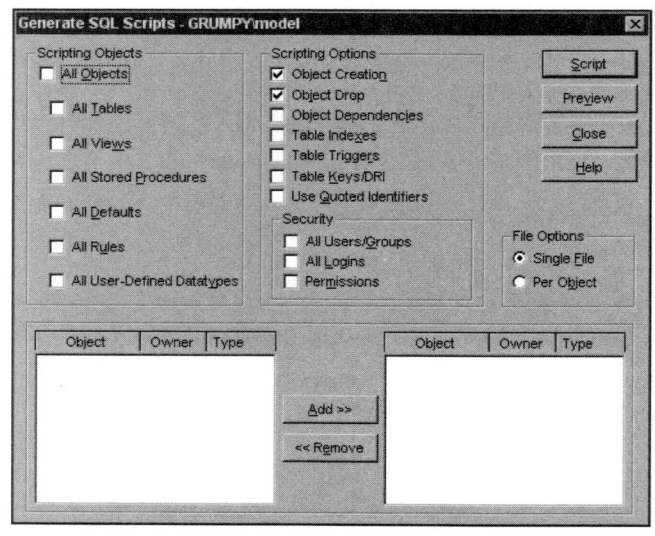

The Generate SQL Scripts dialog box.
Figure 3.2

You might want to generate scripts to document the objects created by any third-party vendor's software residing on your server. To do so, you could create a file with all the code essential to running other people's software on your server. Remember that the Enterprise Manager will generate scripts that will drop and re-create objects, but it will not generate a script to migrate data from one structure to another. The only option available with the Enterprise Manager is the Transfer utility, accessed by right-clicking on a database and selecting the transfer item. I will go through this process in detail later in this chapter.

Third-Party Management

DBArtisan and the other utilities on the CD-ROM provide you with a few options for creating scripts. Embarcadero's DBArtisan allows you to do a thorough job of scripting objects using the Extract button on the speed bar. This tool gives you an alternative system-management tool for your Microsoft SQL Server.

DBArtisan is designed to manage multiple servers of various manufacturers from a single utility. This can be a great advantage over the Enterprise Manager. Some options listed and displayed may not be available for Microsoft SQL Server, so take the time to learn what can and cannot be accomplished with each tool. See Figure 3.3 for a sample of what the DBArtisan product can offer you. Open the Microsoft SQL Server Enterprise Manager to compare features and functionality.

Rapid SQL, also from Embarcadero, provides a fast scripting option that allows you to use objects in a list as a base for building your scripts. Point-and-click graphic interfaces allow you to quickly select the objects you wish to modify or to create custom scripts with very little effort. Even if you are comfortable writing SQL in the standard text editor-like environment, these tools used by themselves or in conjunction with one another will provide you with the rapid development toolset that today's MIS departments require.

Figure 3.4 shows the result of double-clicking on a table in the Table List window. Note the formatted and easy-to-read text.

Transferring Objects

One of the most common tasks in developing on a separate machine is the transfer of your created objects and any supporting data to your production environment. In a multiple development-server environment, this transfer process becomes even more

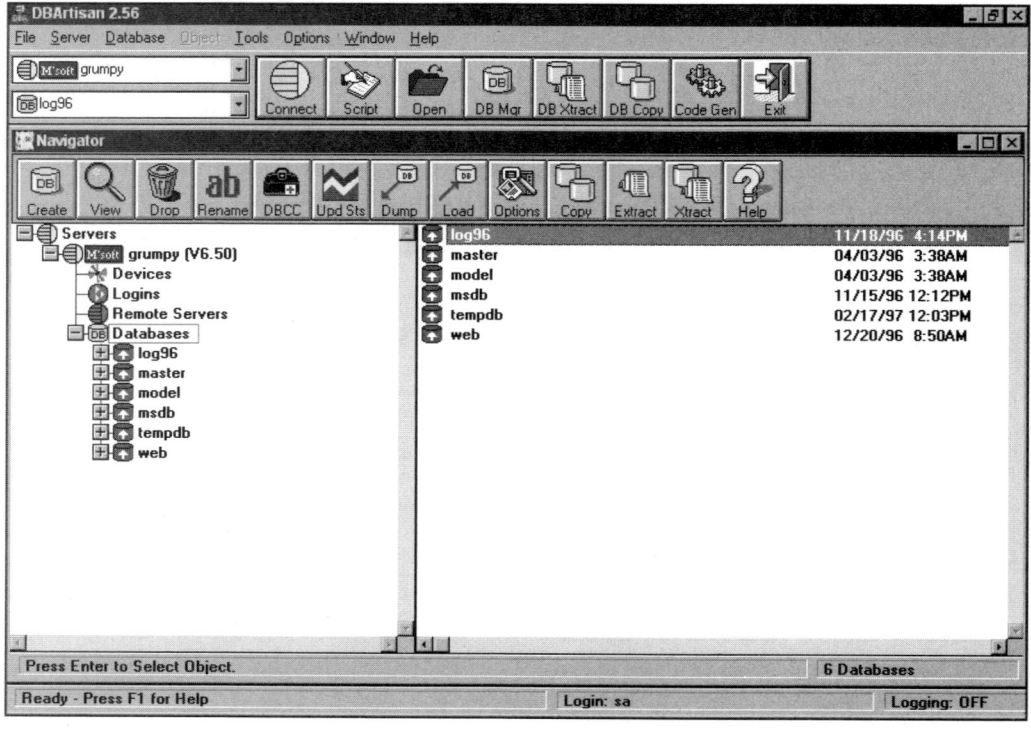

The DBArtisan work area.
Figure 3.3

significant. Ensuring that the correct version of each object is in place can be a daunting task. Confusion can surround the process of actually putting your changes in place on another server. In a development environment, you typically have the luxury of making backups of your data and applying your changes without the pressures of the production machine. However, there will come a time when your work must be migrated to another server as quickly and painlessly as possible.

Microsoft SQL Server provides you with a transfer utility, shown in Figure 3.5, to transfer objects—including data and permissions—from one server to another. This tool is much less error-prone in version 6.5 than it was in previous versions. One drawback is that the transfer utility does not allow you to remap old structures to new.

The Transfer Manager is a handy tool to move new objects to a production machine. (It does, however, fall on hard times when you must change an existing structure

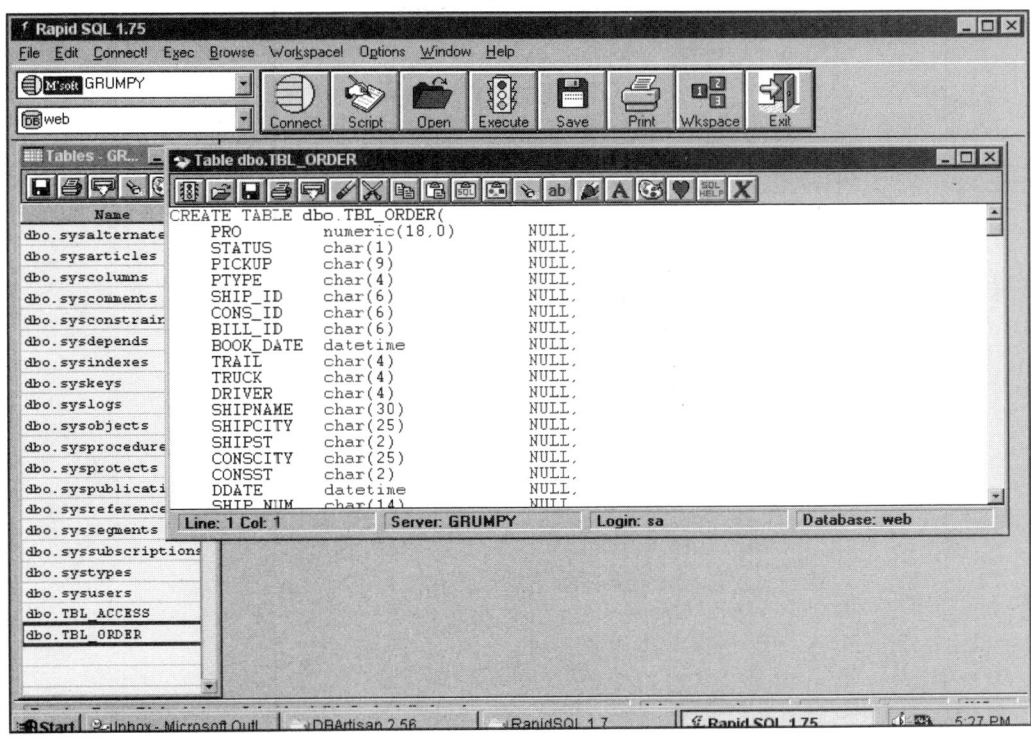

The Rapid SQL work area.
Figure 3.4

that contains data.) To the credit of Microsoft, the Transfer Manager does a wonderful job of copying a complete structure, including data, from one database to another empty container. It allows you to copy an existing production database to a development server with one easy step. Including the data in the transfer allows you to take a snapshot of your production server and place it on another server quickly and easily.

Keep in mind, however, that not all development servers have sufficient disk space to hold a complete database transfer; you might have to get creative and transfer everything but the data, then use scripts to grab smaller subsets of the larger tables.

When you are migrating existing data, it is a good practice to rename your target tables. (Typically _BAK is used at the end of the names for easy identification of the tables.) There is a stored procedure in SQL Server 6.5 that allows you to rename a

Development Versus Production

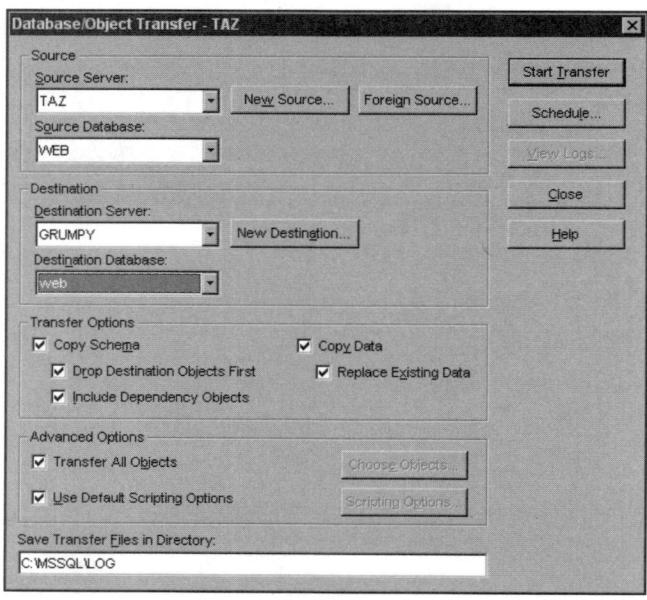

The Database/Object Transfer dialog box.
Figure 3.5

table without losing the data. Look up "sp_rename" in the Microsoft SQL Server Books Online for syntax and remarks about the use of this system-stored procedure. Once you have created the new table, you can remap the columns by using a script to migrate and convert data types and allow for new columns.

Transferring Data

The actual process of transferring data can be accomplished in many ways. I find that a few preliminary steps can make the process smooth and reduce frustration:

1. Plan your migration and test it locally first.

2. Create another container that is not under the load of production and test your transfer to ensure you have not missed anything.

3. Test run the data or schema transfer to uncover any potential problems with your process.

There are three main methods that I use to allow for the transfer or migration of objects and data from one container to another:

1. BCP is a DOS-based utility that allows you to move data from one location to another in either native file format or ASCII text.
2. An INSERT/SELECT query is another method that I use very frequently. You have control over the column data types and remapping of existing data through a script that can be run whenever you need to move your data.
3. DBArtisan has a table edit utility that is easy to use. DBArtisan actually lets you modify the structure of an existing table with data and create a single script that will rename the existing table, create the new structure, map the old data to the new table, and re-create any dependent objects that rely on the target table.

Let's look at each of these methods more closely.

BCP

The BCP (Bulk Copy Program) utility is perhaps the most under-documented utility in the Microsoft SQL Server arsenal. I have talked with many people who wish there were a graphic interface for this utility; by the time this book is printed, I am certain someone will have written one. I anticipate that Microsoft is also working on a graphic BCP utility for release in future versions of Microsoft SQL Server.

BCP must be run through the DOS prompt. I typically use a batch file that I can type into and run repeatedly for testing purposes. Some developers incorporate BCP batch files with the scheduled events in Microsoft SQL Server to allow for unattended bulk loading of data into or out of Microsoft SQL Server.

The following syntax for BCP from Microsoft SQL Server Books Online illustrates some of the many parameters used in BCP. The entire command goes on a single line, with a versatile list of options. Notice that the BCP utility can be used for moving data in and out of your SQL tables or views. See Table 3.1 for descriptions of each of the parameters.

```
bcp [[database_name.]owner.]table_name {in | out} datafile
[/m maxerrors] [/f formatfile] [/e errfile]
[/F firstrow] [/L lastrow] [/b batchsize]
[/n] [/c] [/E]
[/t field_term] [/r row_term]
[/i inputfile] [/o outputfile]
/U login_id [/P password] [/S servername] [/v] [/a packet_size]
```

Table_name	Source or destination of the data, depending on the direction of the operation.
In | out	Direction of the Copy operation.
Datafile	The name, including full path, of the source or target file.
Maxerrors	(/m) Maximum limit of the number of errors that will be allowed until the operation is canceled.
Formatfile	(/f) Name of the format file that can be used to control the mapping of data to specific columns.
Errfile	(/e) Name of the file, including full path, for any rows that cannot be processed.
Firstrow	(/F) First row in data file to process. Default is first row.
Lastrow	(/L) Last row in data file to process. Default is last row.
Batchsize	(/b) Number of rows to process per batch. Default is all rows in one batch.
/n	Microsoft SQL Server native file format.
/c	Character data type (ASCII text). Default column separator is a tab (\t), and the new line character is (\n).
/E	Designates that there are identity columns in the file that should override the identity values currently in the table.
Field_term	(/t) Field terminator.
Row_term	(/r) Row terminator.
Inputfile	(/i) Name of a file that redirects input to BCP.
Outputfile	(/o) Name of a file that receives output redirected from the BCP utility.
Login_id	(/U) Login ID for the user account with permissions to perform BCP.
Password	(/P) Password for the user account provided to Microsoft SQL Server.
Servername	(/S) Name of the Microsoft SQL Server you wish to connect to.
/v	Reports the current DB-Library version.
Packet_size	(/a) Number of bytes per network packet sent to and from the server.

Table 3.1   Parameters used with BCP.

BCP is a powerful tool that can import hundreds of rows per second. This utility is commonly used for nightly transfers of data between non-SQL-based systems to Microsoft SQL Server. For more details on the use of the BCP utility, see the Microsoft SQL Server Books Online.

INSERT/SELECT

Another method of moving data between two locations is the INSERT/SELECT statement. With this tool, you have the ability to insert into one table the rows selected from another table. This method is used often in scripts and stored procedures that must archive data. The programmer must remap any conflicting data types and handle column order within their code, but the power of this type of statement is incredible. Using a SQL statement to re-order your columns or to handle data-type conversions is a capability that many third-party tools overlook. Scripts are a way to supplement conversions and upgrades.

The INSERT/SELECT statement can also be used to recover records that have been accidentally deleted from a system. In some situations, users delete records without realizing their importance. As a DBA, you do not want to restore an old backup and lose data that had been entered over the past few days, so you can use this alternate method of getting the records back. You would restore the backup file to a temporary device and database container. Once the restoration to the temporary database is successful, you can then select the old missing record or records from the temporary table and insert them into the production database.

With some care and planning, you can use this method to restore most records without affecting production. I explain the use and syntax of the INSERT/SELECT statement in Chapters 5 and 6.

DBArtisan

Figure 3.6 shows the DBArtisan Database Copy dialog box. This is another very useful tool for migrating not only structures, but also data from one location to another. DBArtisan's graphic interface makes moving objects from one server to another very easy for the DBA. You just select the source and destination containers, then pick the items you want to copy.

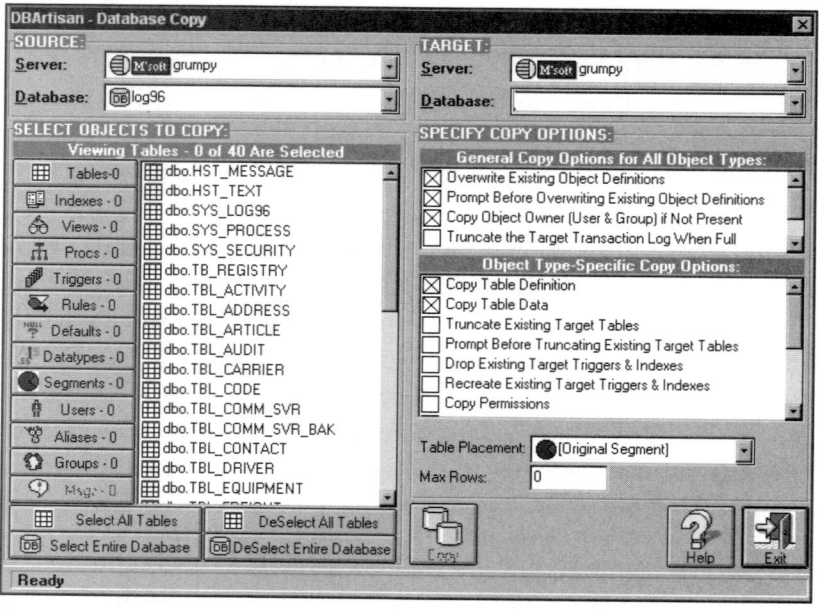

The DBArtisan Database Copy utility.
Figure 3.6

Permissions

The issue of permissions is perhaps the one stumbling block many DBAs and database programmers experience on a regular basis. Most of the transfer tools described here allow you to copy an object's permissions along with the object when you move it. In most development environments, not all users of the production database are fully mapped on the development server. Some shops require that a small percentage of actual users be mapped on the development system for test purposes. The best approach is to have a handful of "users" mapped on the development machine for test purposes, and then any developers.

As long as you develop a good strategy for managing permissions, you should have little problem keeping unwanted users out of your server. I have found that using views and data modification through stored procedures provides a great deal of flexibility in the development environment while still keeping the production machine secure.

Microsoft SQL Server deals with data access on a database-by-database basis. Through the use of groups and group membership, you can control access to your data. You are allowed to be a member of only one group other than Public on Microsoft SQL Server. This can cause you some problems in defining roles on your server.

Users And Groups

Users are defined as login IDs and passwords on your SQL server. Defining a user with a login ID and password does not give the user access to a database—*mapping* the login ID to a database user provides access to data. This login ID method allows many network users to connect to your server without being allowed any access to data. You can even use the Microsoft SQL Server Security Manager to automatically map Windows NT network users to SQL Server login IDs.

Assigning users to groups enables you to provide users who have similar functions the same amount of access to the database. The only real problem is that a user can be a member of no more than two groups at any given time. This seems like a serious shortfall for Microsoft SQL Server, but you can overcome it with special code that assigns "hats" to users to allow them to perform specific tasks. In other words, a hat is a group with permission to perform certain acts in the database. Users should be given the ability to change hats to another group if their role needs to change.

Summary

- Use multiple servers in your development plans.
- Research third-party tools thoroughly before purchasing.
- Data model at the conceptual and physical layers, and keep your models up to date.
- Know your server parameters and how they impact your server.
- Develop a table structure to support server-side parameters for client applications.
- Only use DBCC PINTABLE on small lookup tables.
- Become familiar with using scripts to configure and edit objects on your servers.
- Pay attention to permissions when transferring objects between servers.
- BCP is a powerful and potentially fast DOS-based utility.

- Use INSERT/SELECT statements to perform selective recovery of records.
- Security is implemented on a database-by-database basis.
- Users can be members of only two groups on Microsoft SQL Server (Public and one other group).

Practical Guide To Transferring Objects

The process of registering servers and transferring objects may be new to many users of Microsoft SQL Server. In this section, I will walk you through the steps of this process and cover the warning messages and pitfalls you should watch out for.

Registering Servers

In order to transfer objects between two SQL server databases or even two different servers, you must register both servers in the Enterprise Manager. See Figure 3.7 for the Register Server dialog box. Type the name, login ID, and password you use to connect to each server, then select the Register button when finished. Close the dialog box and make sure both servers are displayed in the Server Manager Window as shown in Figure 3.8.

If you fail to properly register both servers with a user ID that has permission on both servers to create objects, the transfer will not work properly. If you are unable to register a server with the Register Server dialog box, check your DB-Library setting to ensure your client connect is using the correct protocol.

Now you should make sure that the source server and database are correct, and that the destination server and database are correct. You can transfer objects from one location—for instance, a development database on a server—to another database on the same server. See Figure 3.5 for the Database/Object Transfer dialog box.

The checkboxes for configuring the transfer process are the next thing to consider. You have the ability to replace any existing data in the transfer by leaving the Replace Existing Data checkbox selected. If you uncheck the checkbox for transferring all

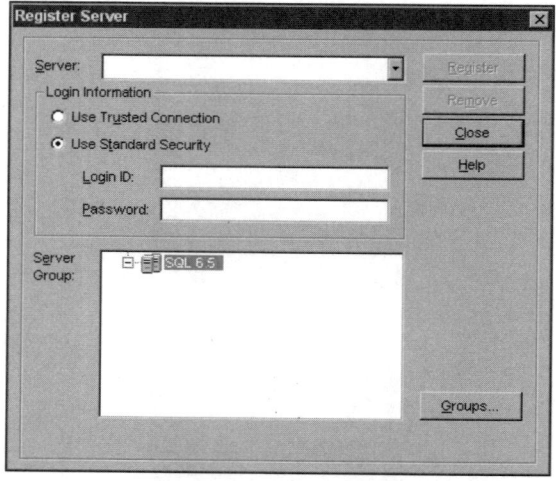

The Register Server dialog box.
Figure 3.7

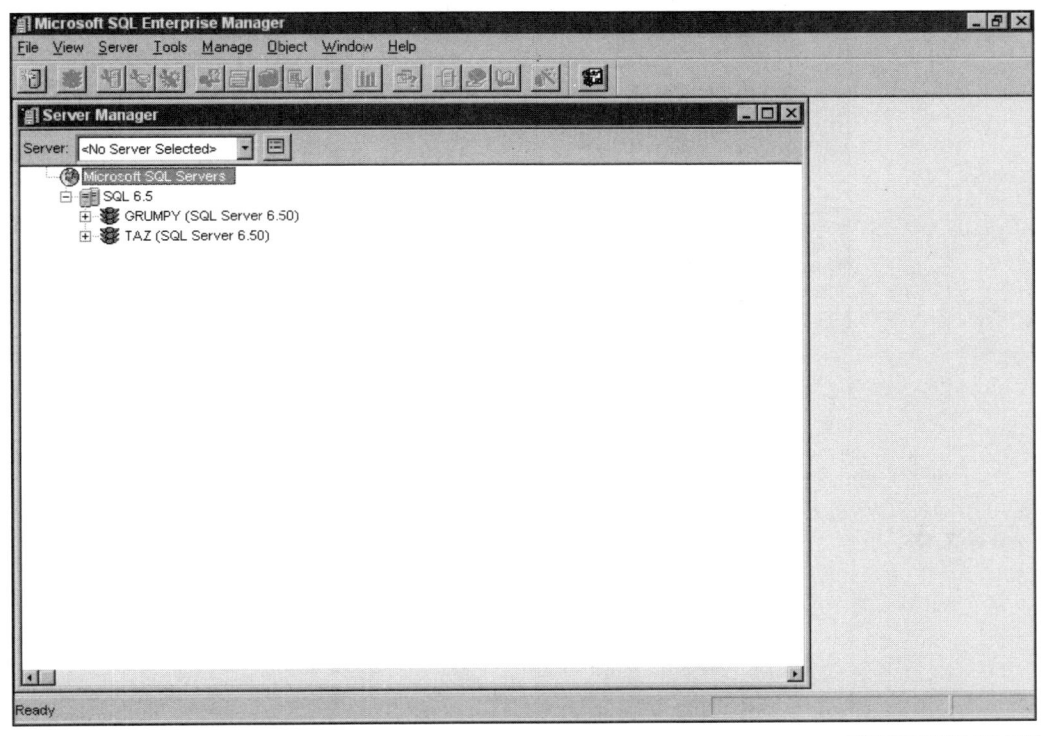

The Server Manager window.
Figure 3.8

objects, you can select the Choose Objects button to select only the specific objects you wish to transfer (see Figure 3.9). Beware of selecting the checkboxes that grab all the objects of a specific type; for instance, you might not want to move all tables in some situations. For an item-by-item transfer, use the bottom of the dialog box to select each object and place it in the right-hand list box.

If you should decide not to use the default scripting options, you can uncheck the Use Default Scripting Options box (see Figure 3.5) to enable the Scripting Options button. See Figure 3.10 for the resulting dialog box. This dialog box allows you to tune the transfer to meet your specific needs. Here you can specify the level of object scripting that will be performed as well as the security and permissions you wish to transfer to the new container. Passwords will be scripted as NULL, or empty, due to the encryption of the password. You should make a note of this and have a script prepared for assigning passwords to the transferred accounts.

The Choose Objects To Be Transferred dialog box.
Figure 3.9

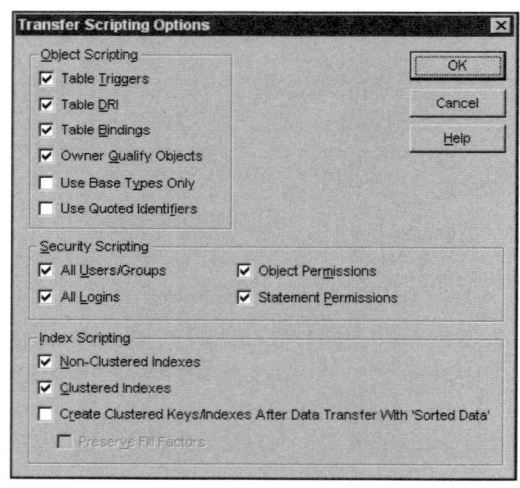

The Transfer Scripting Options dialog box.
Figure 3.10

Moving Objects From Server To Server

Once you have configured the transfer options presented in Figure 3.5, you simply click the Start Transfer button to begin the transfer. You have the option of scheduling the transfer to happen at any time you wish, including on a recurring basis. The scheduled transfer is basically a task that is created and run by the SQL Executive service, like any other scheduled task on the server. If you opt to transfer the objects now, you are presented with a set of progress bars showing the status of the transfer. The files created to perform this transfer are stored in the MSSQL\LOG directory by default.

Upon completion of the transfer, you are prompted with the results. If the transfer completed with no errors, you can simply select OK and move on.

Warning Messages

Most transfers that involve user manipulation will transfer with warning messages. If this occurs, select the View Logs button. Most of the entries should be warnings that the passwords were scripted with no password assigned. These warnings should not preclude the use of the transferred objects.

Do not assume that this type of message is the only message in the log files! Check each resulting log file completely before moving on.

You can open the resulting files in a text editor like Notepad or Microsoft Word by going to the \LOG directory on the server and opening each file independently. Always inspect these files after a transfer.

Pitfalls

I have found that over time I spend less time with the Transfer Manager and more time creating scripts to manipulate the server objects. Scripts allow much more control than the Transfer Manager. Providing you feel comfortable with SQL statements and can use a query builder tool like Rapid SQL or a set of generated scripts, you should be able to get a much more detailed and controlled transfer between your databases and servers.

Permissions are the one pitfall to any scenario. You should take great pains to ensure that user permissions are maintained on your servers. If users attempt to access a new or modified object without the proper permissions, they will get an error, leading them to believe that your software is faulty.

You can avoid this scenario by paying attention to detail when transferring objects, regardless of the method you choose. If you choose to schedule the transfer of objects or data on your system at off-peak hours, as many companies do, test the transfer as defined before assuming that it will work. Keep your development and production servers configured as identically as possible at all times. I cannot count the number of times that a small difference between server configurations turned into a long night of troubleshooting.

And, as always, *be sure to back up the master database.*

Chapter 4

Replication

- Installing The Distribution Database
- Setting Publication Options
- Creating Publications And Articles
- Setting Subscription Options
- Subscribing To A Publication

Administrator's Notes...

Chapter 4

Replication has become a popular topic of discussion within medium-to-large corporate MIS departments. Many systems have been developed in the past few years that focus specifically on replication of data between two or more sites. Not surprisingly, I am often asked how replication might work in practical applications. This chapter focuses on that issue as well as others dealing with distributed data with Microsoft SQL Server. I will cover the basics of what replication is, how it performs the tasks needed to move data, and how the scalability of Microsoft SQL Server replication can be used to fit many company requirements.

Data Distribution Models

Data replication is the result of companies needing to distribute data across a slow WAN link or online transaction processing, which requires that data on separate servers be synchronized at all times. Two models are used for this data distribution: the two-phase commit and replication.

Two-Phase Commit

A two-phase commit is possible with Microsoft SQL Server versions 6.0 and above, although in version 6.0, you must use the API functions and write some fairly advanced code. In version 6.5, the DTC (Distributed Transaction Coordinator) makes the two-phase commit easy to implement.

Two-phased commits are considered to be "tight consistency." In other words, there is no latency between data on the separate servers participating in the transactions. This is usually driven by the time-sensitivity of data and the requirement that it be synchronized 100 percent of the time. A common misconception among database administrators is that two-phased commits are the only way to keep multiple servers synchronized. This is simply not true. Replication also can achieve this purpose and, in some cases, other network-related issues as well, without any user intervention.

Replication Consistency

Replication is considered a looser consistency than the two-phased commit. This is, in fact, true, but it should not steer you away from using replication in your system design. The main difference between these two methods of moving data is that "real-enough" time data synchronization exists with replication. This means that, in replication, there is latency between the source and copy databases. The nice thing about replication is the tunable nature of the latency, coupled with built-in fault tolerance.

Microsoft SQL Server replication is a popular method of maintaining report servers, decision-support servers, and distribution of read-only copies of price lists or similar information across many divisions of a company. By distributing the load across many different servers, you are able to disseminate data across your enterprise quickly and reliably.

Microsoft SQL Server can effectively replicate data with as little as 32MB of RAM. Although Microsoft states that you can publish data with as little as 16MB of RAM, I do not recommend this minimum.

Replication is implemented through the transaction logs contained on your Microsoft SQL Server databases. The beauty of this concept is that only the changes to the database are replicated to the other servers. This reduces traffic on the network and provides a fault-tolerant method of distributing your data. While this method requires both servers participating in replication to be synchronized before you begin the process, the end result is the same as a two-phased commit, with much less traffic.

Terminology

Before we get into too many of the details about replication, let's cover the basic terminology involved in Microsoft SQL Server replication. If you are familiar with these terms, you might want to skim this section just to pick up the finer points. Some of the terms mean exactly what you might expect; others might be a little confusing.

Publisher

The publisher is the server that contains the source data you wish to distribute to other servers. This is analogous to the publisher of a magazine, who presides over one central location, putting all the copy, photographs, advertisements, and artwork together into one issue. The publisher then distributes the data to all shippers to put the magazine in the hands of the people who have subscribed to it.

Subscriber

The subscriber is the server that receives the data from the publishing server. Multiple servers can subscribe to multiple publications in any combination your company requires. For a clear picture, compare this to a magazine subscriber, who can subscribe to many magazines—from one publisher or from many different publishers at the same time.

Distribution Server

The distribution server collects all the publications and disseminates them to any servers that have subscribed to any of the publications. This server can be the same server as the publication server, or it can reside on a totally separate machine that performs the distribution tasks without affecting the publication or production server's performance. The distribution server can be related to a magazine distribution center. The publisher does not typically mail magazines directly to subscribers, but rather ships them in bulk off to a location that sends the magazines to retail stores and individual subscribers.

Transaction Log

Microsoft SQL Server uses transaction logs to perform many tasks, including replication. The transaction log stores only the changes made to data. Many people think transaction logs are some sort of text file that can be easily read and interpreted. This is not the case, however. The transaction log stores data in encrypted form in a table in the database.

The name of the table that stores the transactions in the database is *Syslogs*. For an example of what the transaction log looks like, run the following query against any database on Microsoft SQL Server:

```
SELECT * FROM SYSLOGS
```

Two columns will be returned from the query: the transaction data and an operation code that specifies the type of activity that occurred on this record. The resulting output should look something like the following:

```
xactid          op
--------------  --
0xd40a07001400  20
0x000000000000  17
0xd40a07001400  39
0xd40a07001400  9
0xd40a07001400  30
0x000000000000  17
0xd30a07001b00  39
0xd30a07001b00  9
```

Synchronization

Synchronization is the act of ensuring that both the source and target tables that participate in replication are *exactly* the same. Once the tables are the same, the transactions can then be applied to each table independently, and the tables will still be identical.

Horizontal Partitions

A horizontal partition of a table consists of the rows that you want to publish as articles to your subscribers. Horizontal partitioning is accomplished by using WHERE clauses in your SQL statements. By stating that you wish to publish only those rows that meet certain column values, you can increase replication speed. See Figure 4.1 for an example of a horizontally partitioned table.

Vertical Partitions

Vertical partitioning of a table is done by specifying in the SELECT statement of your query which columns you want to publish. If you want to publish only two columns of a table, you list only those columns in the SELECT statement. Because of the limited amount of data being passed between servers, vertical partitioning can greatly enhance replication performance. You can also use vertical partitioning to exclude certain types of columns—for instance, time stamp, nonuser, and system columns—from the replication process. See Figure 4.2 for an example of vertical partitioning.

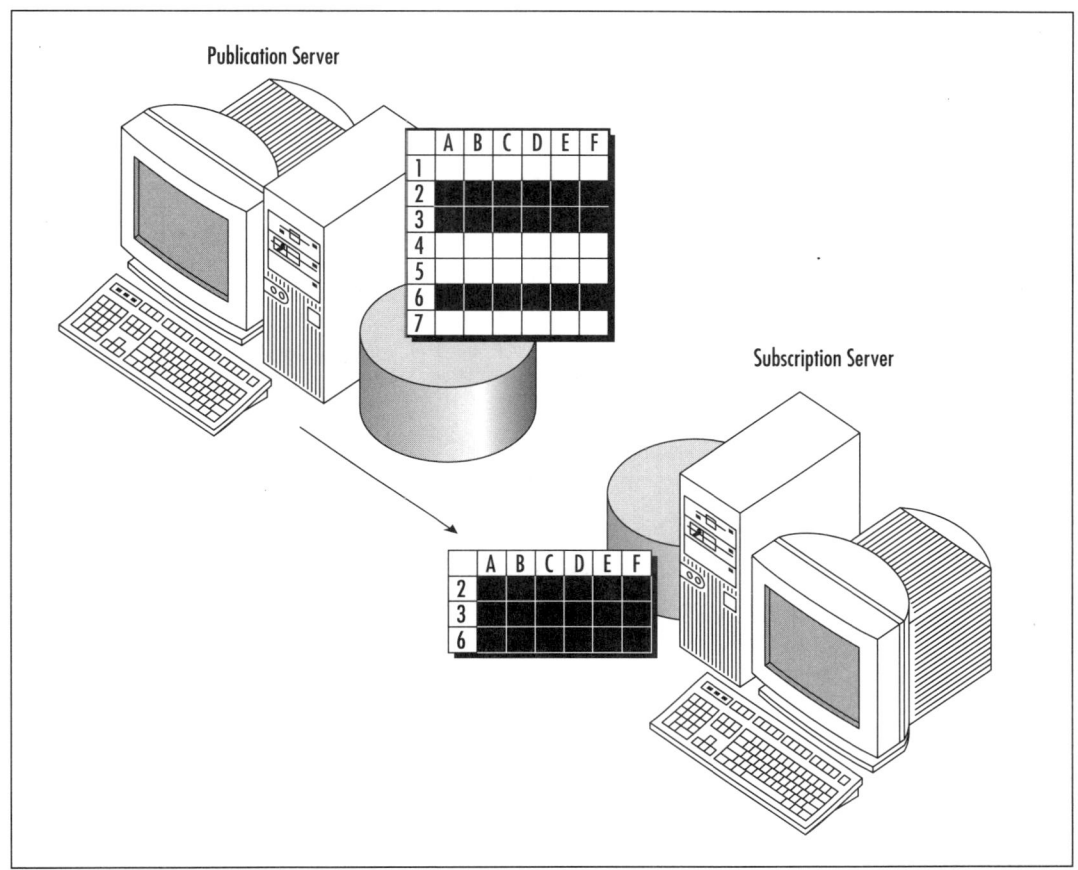

Horizontal partitioning.
Figure 4.1

Articles

In SQL, articles are analogous to the conventional meaning of the word. An article is the smallest unit that a subscriber may receive from a publication. In replication, an article is a specific horizontal and/or vertical partition of data found in a table or view. You can make a whole table an article, or you can parse it down, through horizontal and vertical partitioning, to just what the intended audience needs to see.

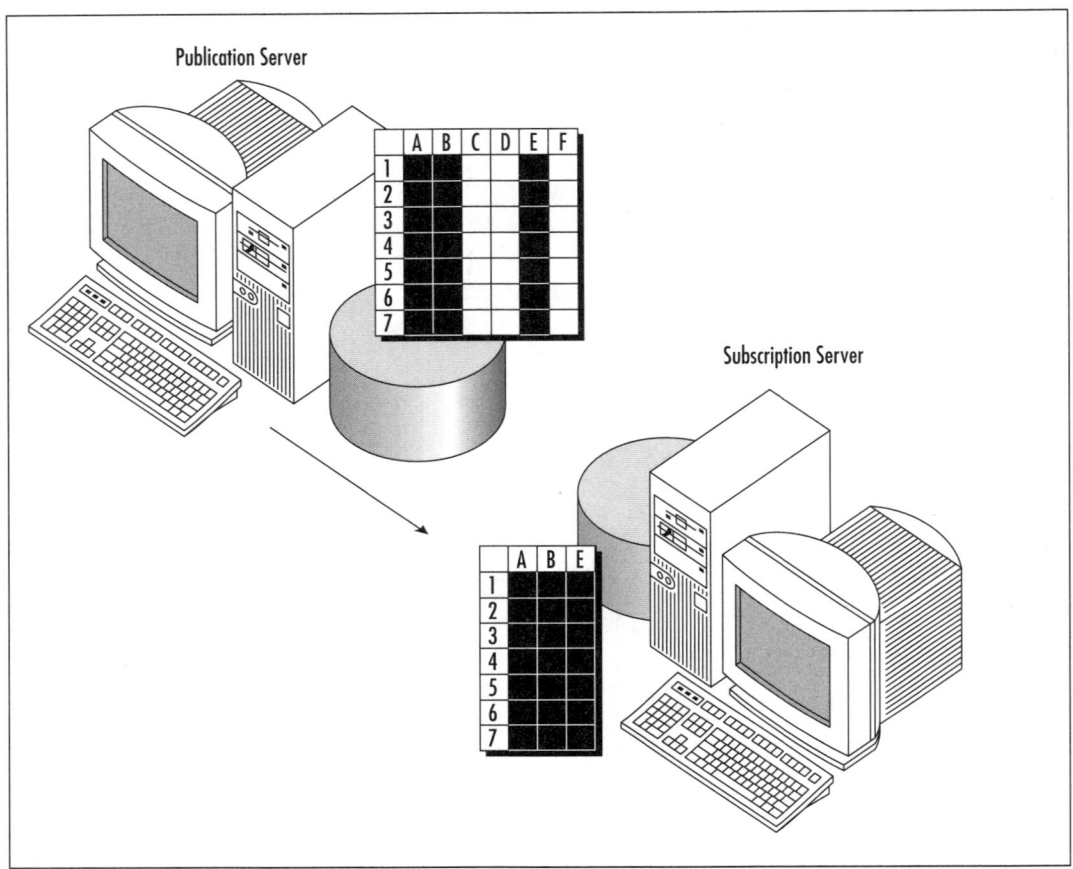

Vertical partitioning.
Figure 4.2

Publications

A publication is basically a group of one or more articles that is to be replicated between your servers. On a case-by-case basis, each subscriber can subscribe to the group of articles in a publication in whole or in part, depending on the needs of the organization. As with magazines, where you need to buy the entire issue even if you only want to read a few of the articles, the base unit of a subscription is a publication, not an article.

Push

The term *push* refers to the process of establishing a subscription to published information. A push subscription is initiated by the source server and controlled and created from that location. This subscription method is easy to manage because the server that has the data knows the structures of the articles and what the data should look like. Centralized management of your subscriptions is also a push-type subscription.

Pull

The opposite of push, a *pull* subscription is requested from a publisher by the subscriber. With this method of subscription management, users must ask for the correct information from the publisher, as opposed to the publisher telling users what they will get. Pull subscriptions are only convenient for organizations that want to publish information freely, without control over which publications are used by other organizations.

Server Roles

In the Microsoft replication model, SQL servers have three roles: publisher, subscriber, and distributor. These roles can be mixed and matched to suit your organization and budget. Companies wishing to take advantage of replication should be aware of all these roles and the scalability of each server performing each task.

Publisher Server

The publisher is the server where the source data is stored. When designing a system, many organizations begin with this server before moving on to the distribution or subscription of the data. This server is typically the production machine with the mission-critical data on it, as well as the load of performing production tasks.

Adding the publication tasks to a production server can usually be done without affecting performance. However, setting too tight a schedule for the replication process can place a burden on your production server. When deciding whether your publishing server should be your distribution server, look very closely at the existing load on your server to ensure that you won't overload your production machine. I recommend using the distributed server environment for replication whenever possible.

Data restrictions in the form of constraints or triggers should be placed on the publishing server since all changes should be applied here first, then replicated to the subscribing servers. This method allows for the centralized administration of the data that will be replicated. Subscribers should not be allowed to edit replicated data at their locations; edits should be applied to the publishing server so that the data remains consistent across the servers.

Subscriber Server

The subscriber is the server that receives data to be published for query and report purposes. The intent of the subscriber server is to provide a local, fast data source to run queries against. Microsoft documentation states that the subscriber server should not modify the data it receives through the replication process; the replication process requires both data sets to be synchronized in order to function properly.

It is very important to treat the data on subscriber servers as read-only. This is not to say that you should set the properties of the database to read-only; doing so would preclude any changes being written to the database by the publisher. Instead, you should make all your changes at the source of the data and allow the changes to be replicated to the subscribers. This will keep all the tables synchronized and up to date.

Updates to the data on a subscriber are received as either SQL commands that must be executed or as stored procedures. Using stored procedures can increase replication performance. However, do not try to implement replication through stored procedures to begin with—work up to it slowly. Take time to understand the process before you complicate matters. In addition, constraints and triggers placed on your data are enforced on the publication server and should be not be added to the subscriber server.

Distribution Server

The distribution server is the traffic cop of the replication process. The purpose of the distribution server is to make sure all servers receive the publications they have subscribed to in a complete and error-free state. The distribution server will continue to function if one or all of the subscribers happens to go offline. This fault tolerance is what sets Microsoft SQL Server replication apart from the two-phased commit.

Distribution processes and the concept of implementing a distribution server are directly in line with the Microsoft distributed server concept. As the load for any process becomes too much for a server to handle, simply increase the amount of disk, memory, or processor power you have on that server. Replication benefits from this concept by placing the distribution tasks on a dedicated server that can keep track of the publishers and subscribers and whether they are up to date.

Another huge benefit of using the distribution server is the fault-tolerance it provides your distributed data scheme. If a WAN/LAN connection goes down, the distribution server maintains a list of the information that must be passed to the subscriber when it becomes available again.

Scenarios

In this section, I'll focus on five scenarios: Central Publisher, Central Publisher With Remote Distribution, Publishing Subscriber, Central Subscriber, and Multiple Publishers Of A Single Table. You can borrow from one or a few of these scenarios and mix and match the features you require for your organization. Because your servers can perform many roles, you have great flexibility.

Considerations

Before we begin with the actual scenarios, let's run through the major items you should consider when setting up servers for replication.

Planning

Plan your replication on paper before trying to implement any portion of the process. Failing to plan your model can cause you many headaches. If you can't get the process to work on paper, you won't get it to work on Microsoft SQL Server.

Limiting Traffic

When you design your model, pay particular attention to how much data you plan to push or pull between your servers. Keep the amount of extra traffic to a minimum. You will save a lot of time and keep the performance of your system at its highest possible level if you send only what is required across the LAN/WAN connections. Be sure to create the databases that will store the publication data before you set up the replication process.

Granularity

Replication can be applied to units as small as subsets of data in a single table. This level of granularity requires a key value in a table to represent an entity to which replication tasks can be applied. This finer level of replication can be used to maintain information in a single table that multiple locations can view and modify; yet each location can only modify its own data locally. Implementing multiple editors of a single table is the most difficult scenario to program and get working.

More attention to detail must be paid when using granularity, but it can help you get past some of the design issues for your enterprise. The rules that should be applied at the table level are the same, so I will illustrate everything at a higher level of detail. See *Central Subscription* later in this chapter for more on the single-table requirements for replication.

What Cannot Be Published

A few things cannot be published with Microsoft SQL Server. With version 6.5 the list has shrunk a bit, but first let's talk about version 6.0. You cannot publish your system catalog or the model, master, Msdb, or Tempdb. You also cannot publish any data from a table that does not have a defined primary key. In addition, three data types cannot be published: text, image, and time stamp. In most scenarios, these restrictions should cause only a small inconvenience and can be overcome through some creative programming.

Version 6.5 allows you to replicate text and image data between your servers. However, your text and image statements must be a logged operation. I do not recommend replicating binary large object blocks (blobs). Because of their size, the Scheduled Table Refresh method is preferable. Scheduled Table Refresh is another option for moving data to remote servers. This method involves a block move of the entire table on a schedule between servers. It is time consuming and is usually incorporated into systems that make nightly updates during off-peak hours.

Keep in mind that you can replicate data between version 6.0 and version 6.5 databases as long as the publisher and the distribution server are the same version.

ODBC

You can replicate to ODBC databases only with Microsoft SQL Server version 6.5. To do this, you must first create a system data source through the ODBC Administrator, then create the subscriptions using the push or the publishing server controlled method. You will have no administrative control from the subscribers of replicated data through an ODBC connection. All administration must happen from Microsoft SQL Server.

Be careful of quoted identifiers with ODBC subscriptions. Some query tools do not like tables created with quoted names. Check your query tool to make sure it supports quoted identifiers before you end up chasing your tail and find you cannot view replicated data on your subscriber.

Central Publisher

The Central Publisher is the most basic scenario to implement. In Figure 4.3, notice that the publisher and distribution processes are located on the same server. This is adequate for enterprises that can put up a production server with a lot of horsepower and are not tasking the production machine heavily. For most of my consultations that concern replication, I recommend a separate distribution server—if not from the beginning, then as soon as budgets permit—to help balance the load across many servers.

Servers A, B, and C in the illustration are all subscribing to the data that resides on the publisher. Each subscriber can be connected over different types of LAN/WAN

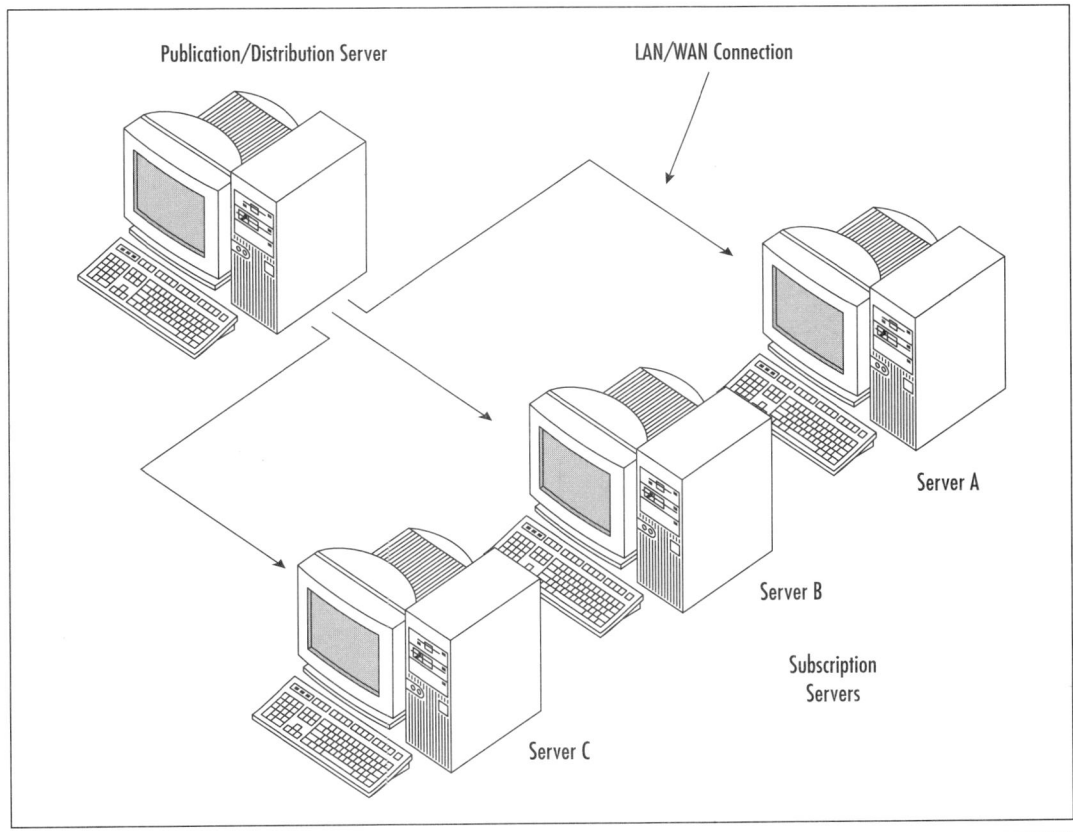

The Central Publisher scenario.
Figure 4.3

Replication 113

connections at various speeds without slowing down the entire replication process. This is where Microsoft SQL Server shines in data distribution. If the connection between Server A and the publisher goes down due to a hardware failure, the other servers can continue to receive up-to-date information without waiting for the communication failure to be resolved. When your link between Server A and the publisher is reestablished, the distribution process will make sure all modifications are applied to Server A until it reaches the same state of synchronization as Servers B and C.

Some of the possible real-life scenarios this model supports are executive management systems, report generation, ad hoc query databases, and distribution of price lists from a main office. One of the best features of this scenario is that, unlike a two-phased commit, it will continue to work during a communication failure.

Central Publisher With Remote Distribution

I frequently recommend this model for companies that want to test replication to see if they would benefit from it. This scenario places a modular, balanced load on your system, which will make it easier to manage and configure. This configuration of servers is the natural progression from the Central Publisher.

Although similar to the Central Publisher model, the distribution process is off-loaded to another server, as shown in Figure 4.4. This distribution server can be far smaller than your production server. You can configure it with 32MB of RAM, and it will still keep up with replication tasks quite nicely.

One important point to note is that many different publishers can use a single distribution server. In addition, many distribution servers can be used if your distribution load gets too high. This flexibility allows you to place as many subscribers online as you wish without an putting an extra load on your production server.

Publishing Subscriber

The next step up the ladder of complexity is the Publishing Subscriber scenario. This configuration can be used to push data across a slow link to a remote system, then re-publish and distribute the data to many subscribers without using all your available bandwidth for replication. See Figure 4.5 for an example.

This scenario has all the benefits of other replication scenarios, yet it can support a slow communication link much better. Say, for instance, your company wants to open an office and several stores across the country from its current location. You can establish a 56K link between your two offices and replicate data across that link, then

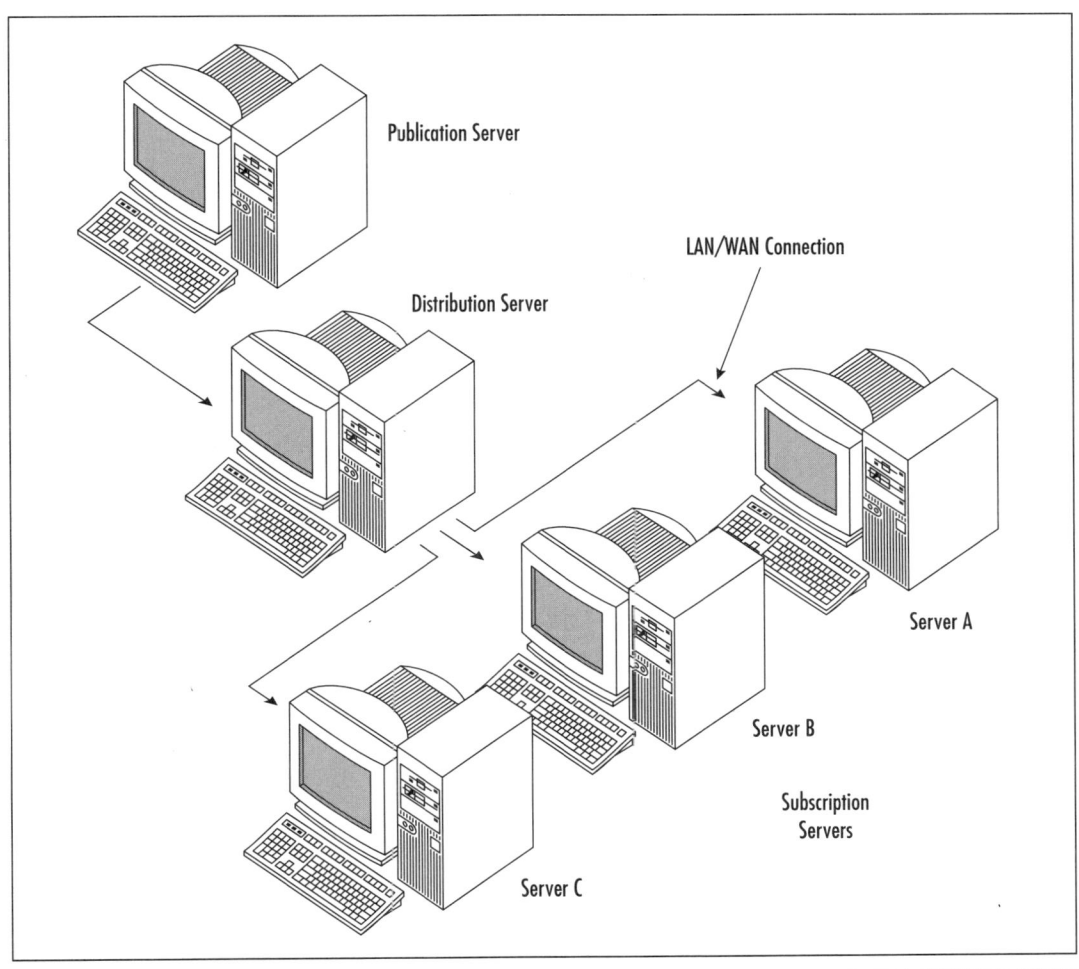

The Central Publisher With Remote Distribution scenario.
Figure 4.4

distribute the price lists or ad hoc query data to the stores as they open throughout the remote state. This will reduce network traffic and communication costs.

Central Subscriber

Now let me confuse you for a minute with a rather complex model. The Central Subscriber scenario is used commonly when a company has autonomous business divisions that must maintain local contact lists or inventory and report this information to a central office. This scenario is achieved on Microsoft SQL Server through

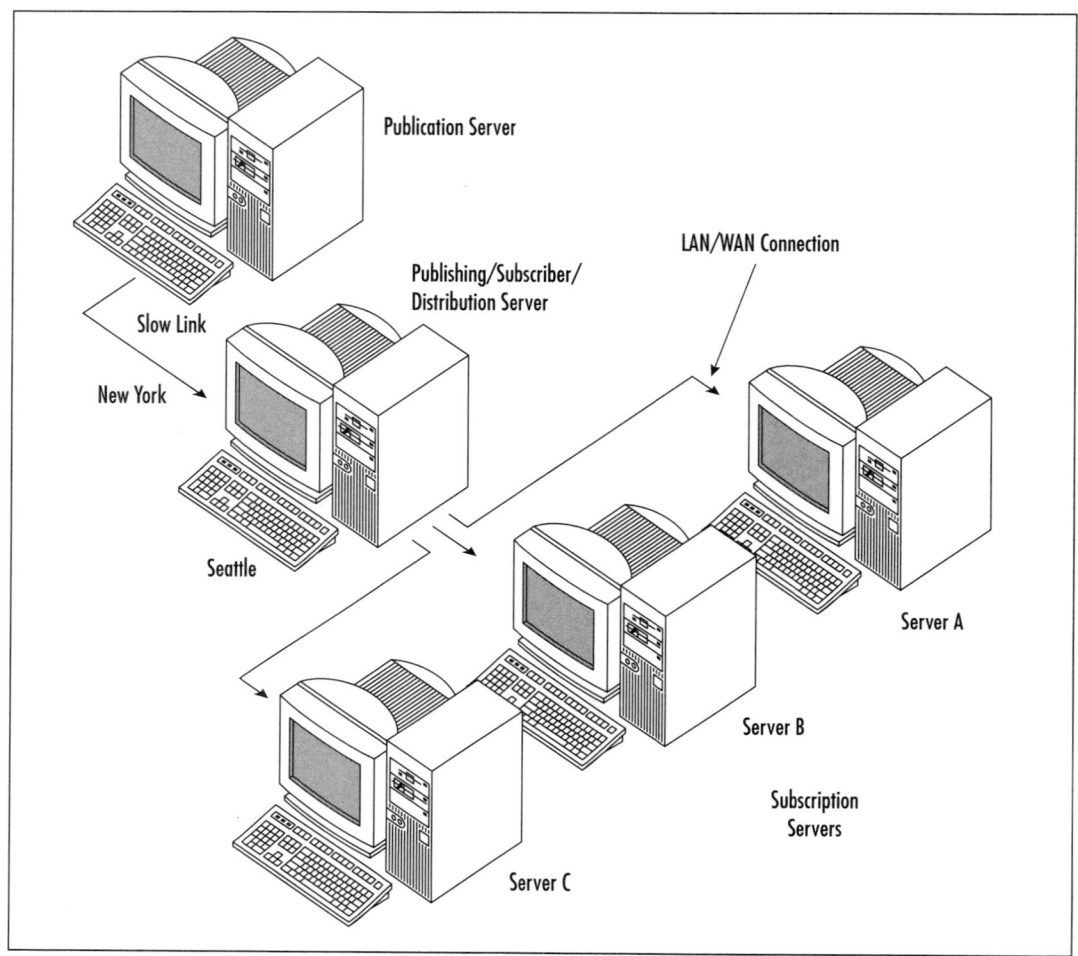

The Publishing Subscriber scenario.
Figure 4.5

the use of a location-specific key in the main office table that stores the "rolled-up" data from all the divisions. These regional keys separate the data and segment it in a single table so that effective queries can be written to analyze amounts or trends in one location.

This scenario, illustrated in Figure 4.6, requires manual synchronization at the beginning of the process. The key is not to get into a replication loop at the main office. A replication loop occurs if you make changes to the data at the main office

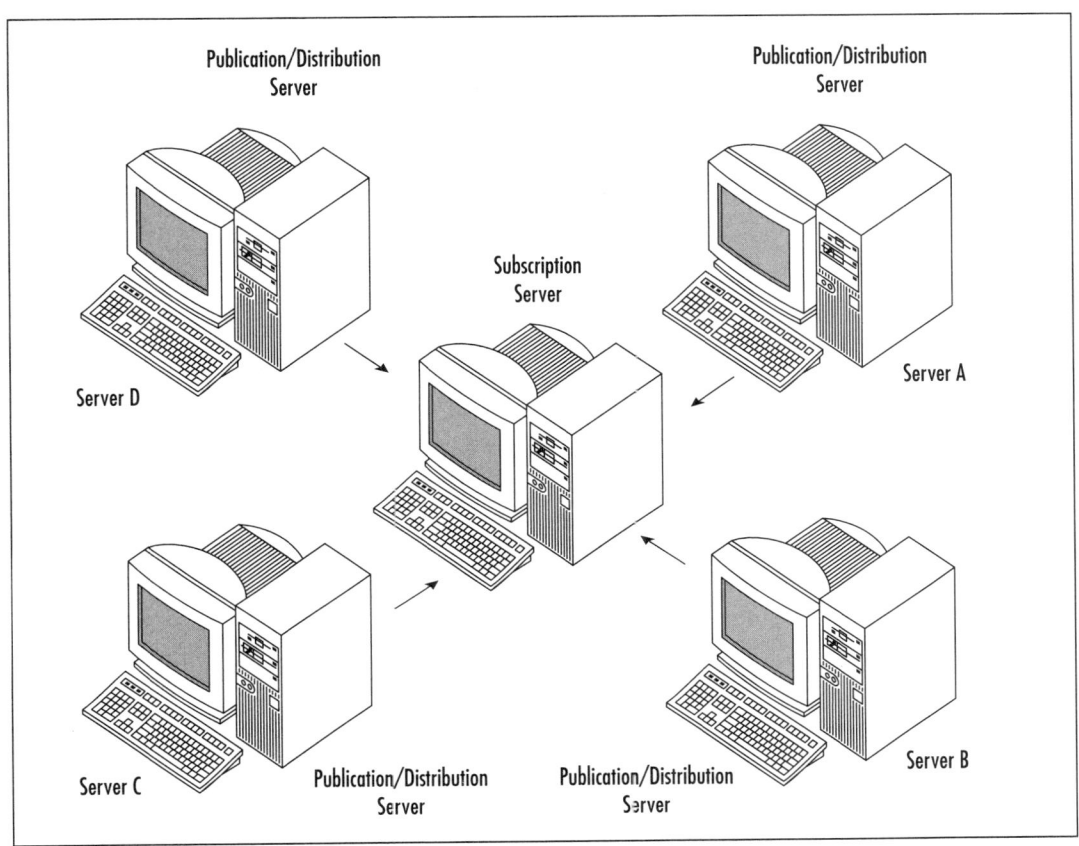

The Central Subscriber scenario.
Figure 4.6

and replicate the data back out to the satellite offices. The insertion of replicated data at the satellite offices would trigger the replication process back up to the main office and would continue to create more replication tasks until your server was brought to its knees.

Modify the data only at the source. If the main office needs to make a change to a piece of data, it should do so through remote procedure calls to the satellite offices, then allow the data to be replicated back up to the central office. This is a bit more difficult to program, but it allows you to modify your data.

Figure 4.7 shows how this data segmentation can be accomplished. Administrators at each of the remote servers can modify their data all they want without affecting each

Replication 117

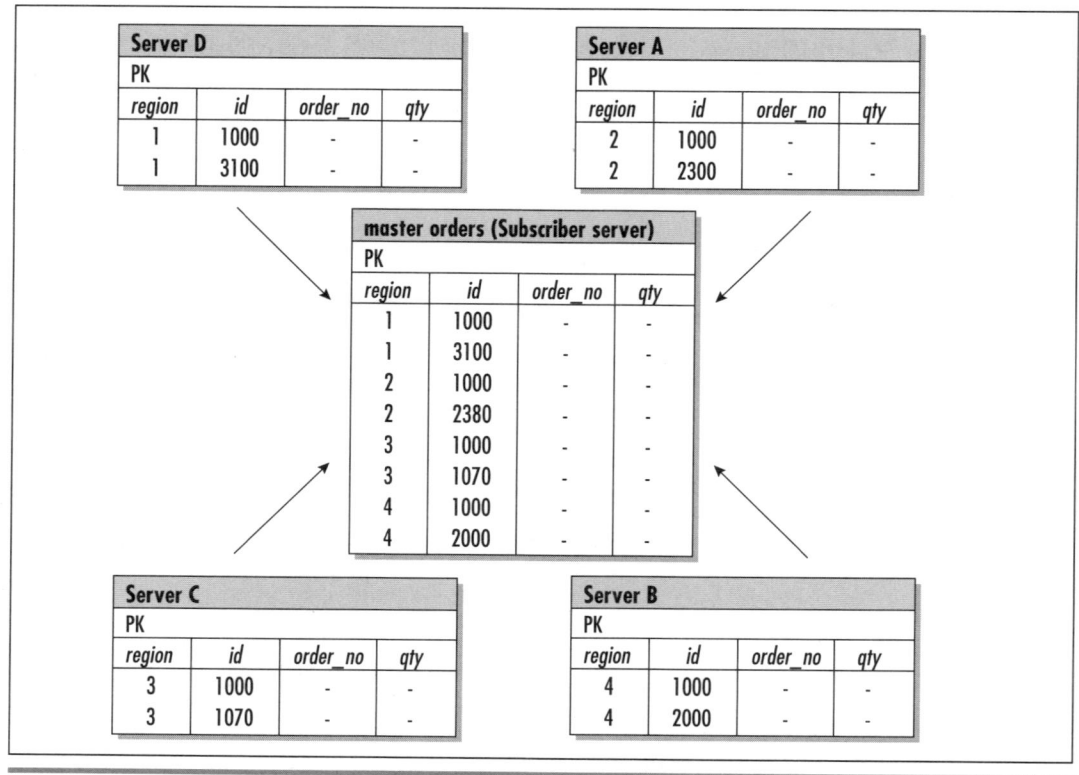

Spreadsheet example of a replicated table.
Figure 4.7

other's systems. The changes are replicated to the central subscriber and placed in a table that contains a primary key consisting of a region code and a part ID. The primary key in this example is a combination of region and ID so that there will be no redundant data in the table. You could then write some queries or stored procedures that run periodically to check inventory levels and alert someone if certain thresholds are exceeded or if a business rule is violated.

Multiple Publishers Of A Single Table

This scenario is the one I see most often discussed among Internet news groups. For some reason, everyone wants to publish the same thing over and over again. The only way to share data between servers is to provide a primary key that is location-specific, set up replication tasks that horizontally partition the data by region, and publish only the data they control.

See Figure 4.8 for the server configuration and how it differs from the other models we've discussed. This scenario is best used to show data across a decentralized company, multiple warehouse inventory systems, airline reservation systems, or regional order-processing systems. The only drawback is the amount of synchronization needed, since all sites contain both local and remote data.

Publishing a table multiple times can be accomplished with some of the same techniques just covered in the Central Subscriber scenario—with one small twist. In Figure 4.9, notice that only the data each server has control of is published. Each of the two other servers would subscribe to the other two servers' published data to make their lists complete. With this configuration, you still should not modify the data of remote systems locally. Use remote stored procedures to make the changes at the source of the data and allow the changes to be replicated normally.

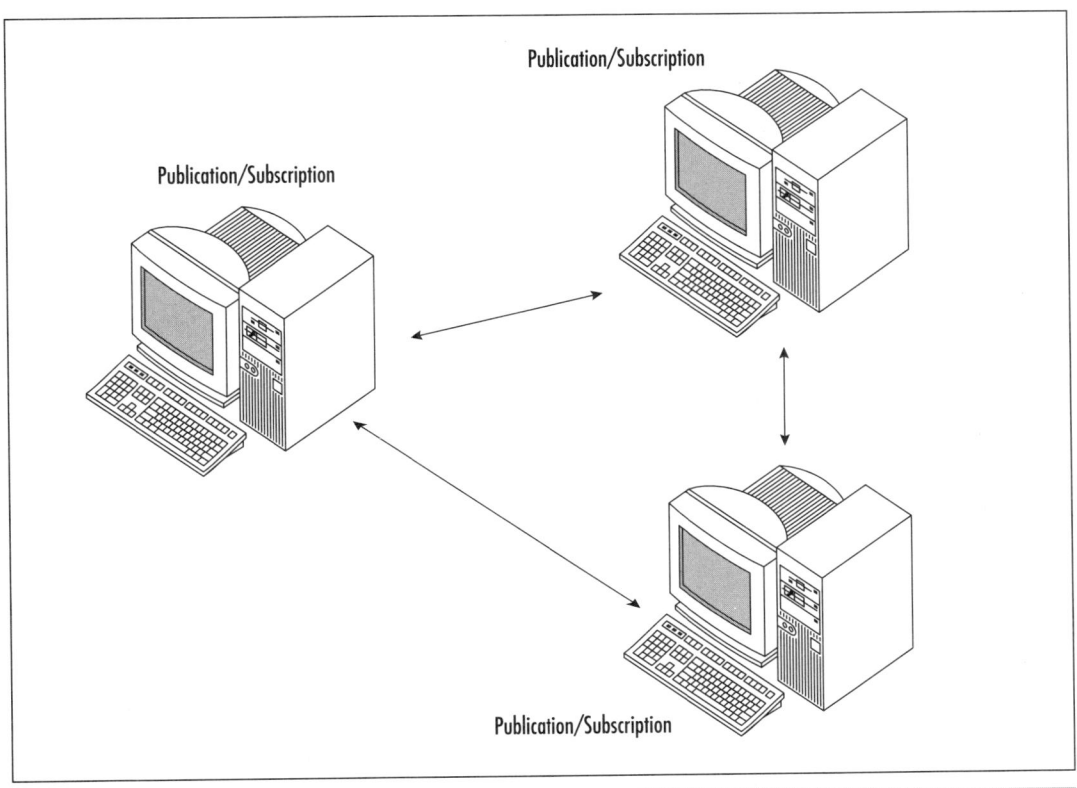

The Multiple Publishers Of A Single Table scenario.
Figure 4.8

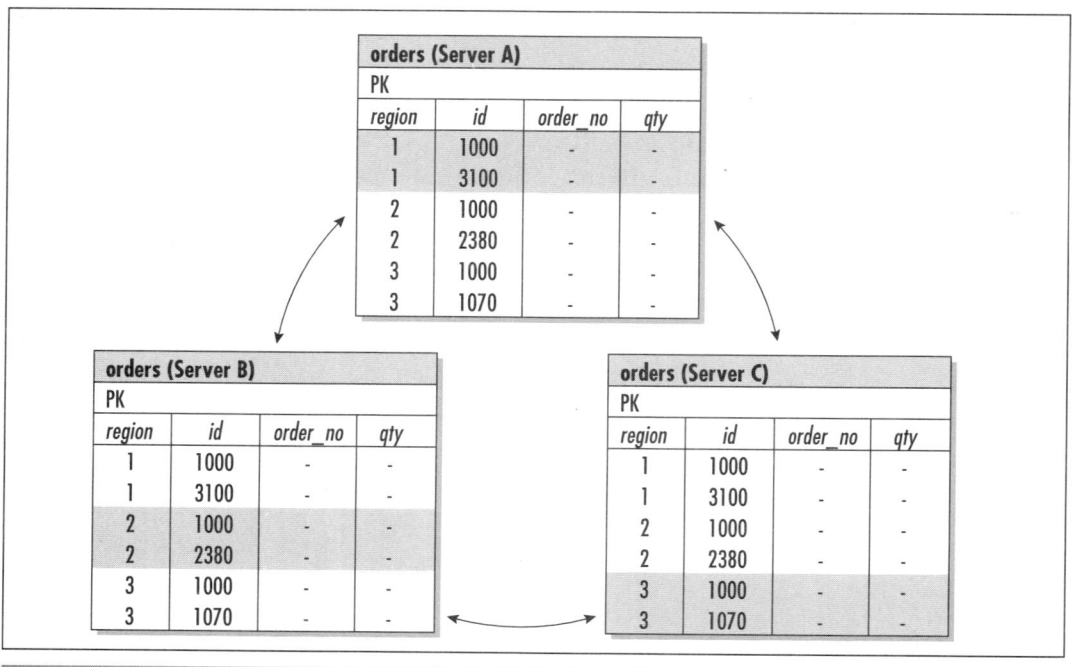

Single Table Publication spreadsheet.
Figure 4.9

Events And Processes

Now that we have covered the terminology and basic models, let's go behind the scenes. As mentioned, replication is transaction log–based. The major components of replication are the published databases themselves, the administration of the transaction log for any replicated database, the log reader task, and the synchronization process. A distribution database and the actual distribution process are also needed.

Log Reader Process

When a database is marked for replication, the transaction log is flagged so the log reader process knows to replicate these changes. Once you have completed a transaction in a replicated database, the actual transaction log entries are not removed until the log reader process moves them to the distribution database. This causes your transaction log to fill a bit faster than a nonreplicated database with the same number of transactions. Once the transactions are moved to the distribution database, the entries in the publishing database transaction log can be flushed through the normal checkpoint process in Microsoft SQL Server.

The log reader process does not run continuously; it is an interval-based process that is added to your server's scheduled task list. Keep in mind that the SQL Executive service must be running for replication to work properly.

Synchronization Process

Synchronization can be done manually or through the Enterprise Manager. To perform manual synchronization, you would create an *exact* copy of the schema on the subscriber database and load the table or tables with *exactly* the same data as the publisher. If you select manual synchronization, Microsoft SQL Server assumes that both publisher and subscriber are identical. If you miss any records or some structural element, the replication process will generate errors.

If you choose automatic synchronization, Microsoft SQL Server will generate scripts that will create the structures for you on your subscribers and a BCP task to load the existing data into the new structure once it has been successfully created. Upon completion of the BCP into the new structure, the distribution database is notified that the new subscriber is ready for any new transactions to be applied. Remember that transactions are applied on the subscriber in the same order as they were applied on the publisher to maintain the integrity of the data.

Replication Distribution Process

As mentioned, replication distribution is best described as the traffic-cop process in replication. The distribution process keeps a list of the transactions that are to be replicated to subscribers, which subscribers have received the transactions, and whether the transactions were applied to each table successfully. No transactions are purged from the distribution lists until all subscribers have successfully received and applied their changes.

In a multiple-server environment that merges two or three of the scenarios described in this chapter, the distribution of replicated data can get fairly difficult to manage. Take the time to test your configuration and make sure you have published your data only as much as needed to meet the requirements of replication.

Publish your data only one time. If your process requires that a particular piece of data be used in many different locations, publish it as an article one time and subscribe to it many times. Do not create a new publication of the same data each time it is used. If you fall into this trap, you will bring your system to its knees unnecessarily.

Do not forget to have a good backup strategy for the distribution server in your replication scenario. The transaction log and database should be backed up regularly and frequently. Should this server go down, your subscribers will not receive any transactions until you can bring it back online.

Communication Failures

Failures to communicate can cause problems in any environment. I have not found a system yet that does not require solid communications in order to function well—although Microsoft SQL Server comes close with regard to replication. If your link between publisher and subscriber fails for some reason, Microsoft SQL Server will basically cache the transactions that need to be applied to each of the subscribers until they can be contacted and successfully applied. Even the link between publisher and distribution server can be lost for a short period of time, and once reestablished, the publisher will still have the transactions in the transaction log for distribution. Using a distribution server with processes whose only function is to keep servers synchronized is a very fault-tolerant method of distributing data.

Should your link between publisher and distribution server be lost, be careful of the transaction logs in any database marked for replication. Keep in mind that transactions in logs marked for replication are not purged until they are successfully written to the distribution server. If the transactions have nowhere to go, they will not be purged by the checkpoint process in Microsoft SQL Server.

As a rule, always back up your transaction log more frequently than normal if it is part of a database participating in replication. Do not allow the log to get more than 75 percent full before making a backup.

Prerequisites For Replication

Your server and data probably already meet most of the prerequisites for replication. Most replication problems occur when people forget one of the minor limitations of replication and do not address the problem until they want to start replicating data. Read the next few paragraphs carefully. Take time to understand the requirements before trying to implement replication.

Memory

As mentioned, Microsoft's documentation states that a dedicated publishing server can have as little as 16MB of RAM and still operate. While this might be true, you won't be happy with the performance of your machine. Use 32MB as a minimum on any server. RAM is cheaper than any other upgrade to your server, and it gives the most gain for your dollar. Don't be stingy with RAM. Always put a bit more into the machine than you think you will need. You'll be glad you did in the long run.

Working Directory

Make sure that the working directory (\REPLDATA is the default) is available in the publication server. The replication synchronization tasks will write scripts and place the data files that will be bulk-copied to subscribers in this location.

Same Character Set

Make sure that the publisher, distribution server, and all subscribers participating in replication use the same character set. If you want query results to appear in the same order on all the subscribers, you should use a single sort order across all servers as well.

Protocol

You should set the default network protocol on the servers participating in replication to Named Pipes or Multiprotocol. The security mode you have configured—whether standard, integrated, or mixed—will work with replication. The trusted connection that will be established between the servers requires one of these protocols.

Trusts

If your servers are in separate Microsoft domains, prior to setting up replication you must ensure that adequate trust relationships exist. If your servers are not using the Microsoft domain model, you do not need to worry about trusts.

Disk Space

Make sure you have enough disk space for the transaction log for each database containing published data. You should also have the transaction logs on separate devices from the databases. This separation allows you to better manage disk usage and to monitor the size of the transaction log independently from the data. Usage monitoring versus actual storage requirements is critical in managing your replication servers.

Do not forget the distribution server; be sure to configure it the same way as your other servers. Each subscriber will be receiving data that is not generated locally. If you create a database to hold replicated information that is only 10MB in size yet will be receiving 30MB of data from the publisher, you'll have a problem. Calculate the size of the base data set you will be synchronizing, then add the amount of data to be added by normal transactions to come up with a figure that realistically represents the amount of disk space you require on each server.

SQL Executive

If you have not done so already, you should set up a user account for the SQL Executive service to use on the network. This account should be a member of the Administrators group, granted the Log On As A Service right, with the User Cannot Change Password and Password Never Expires options selected. This service is critical to the proper operation of replication tasks.

User Connections

You should increase the number of user connections on the servers to allow for replication tasks. The publishing server should have one connection added for each database that has published data in it. The subscriber servers should also have one user connection added for each database that will receive published data. This increase is not a client access license increase; it is simply an increase to the number of user connections that Microsoft SQL Server allows. Remember that each user connection will take from 37 to 42K per connection out of the available memory pool. You might have to reevaluate your memory setting if you are publishing or subscribing to many databases.

Primary Key

Each table that will publish data requires that you declare a primary key. You can add a primary key to an existing table by using the ALTER statement or you can create your tables with a declared primary key from the beginning. This is required for replication to function and cannot be ignored.

Your primary key can be a single column or a combination of columns in the table that will make each record unique. A primary key will mean that no duplicate values will be allowed in the key, and that NULL values will not be allowed. This might pose a small problem to existing data if you have not had data integrity checks in place before creating the primary key. Resolve any data integrity issues before trying to publish the data through replication.

Summary

- Publisher servers are the source of the data (publications and articles).
- Subscriber servers are the clients of the data (publications and articles).
- Keep traffic between servers to a minimum. Only replicate what is required.
- Plan your replication scenario on paper first.
- Use a minimum of 32MB of RAM in your servers participating in replication.
- Define a primary key on any table being published.
- Resolve any data integrity issues before trying to replicate your data.

Practical Guide To Replication

This section will walk you through the steps of setting up and configuring a Microsoft SQL server for participation in data replication.

Installing The Distribution Database

For the sake of illustration, I will set up a distribution database on the same server as the published data. The only real difference in the local distribution database and the remote database is that you must configure and set up the remote database prior to setting up publication on your production server. The steps for creating the distribution database to run on an independent server are the same.

One distribution server can serve as the distributor for many publications. The only requirement is that the distribution server have enough disk space and memory to handle multiple publishers and subscribers.

You can set replication manually by calling all of the stored procedures and executing all the scripts yourself. The method is outlined very well in about 14 pages of Microsoft SQL Server Books Online. Before trying this method, you should have a thorough understanding of Microsoft SQL Server.

I have had to resort to a manual configuration only one time since version 6.0 came out. It works, but I would not want to make a living doing it this way. The Enterprise Manager does a very good job of masking the complexity of configuring replication for you. Use the graphic, user-friendly method; you will be grateful if you have ever had to set replication by hand. To configure your server either for publication or to install the distribution database, follow these steps:

1. From the Enterprise Manager, select the Server menu.

2. Choose the Replication Configuration option, and from the drop-down menu, choose Install Publishing. The Install Replication Publishing dialog box appears (see Figure 4.10).

3. To configure this server to be either a distribution server or a publisher/distributor server, make sure the Local option is selected. (If you were using a remote server for distribution, you would choose Remote and specify that server here.)

4. Fill in the name of the distribution database (the default is Distribution). You can leave the default for clarity.

5. In the Data Device box, choose the data device from the drop-down list box. If you have not created the data device yet, you can select <New>, and Microsoft SQL Server will take you through creating that device now.

6. Next, select the log device for the transaction log. If you have not created the device previously, you can select <New> from the drop-down list and create it now.

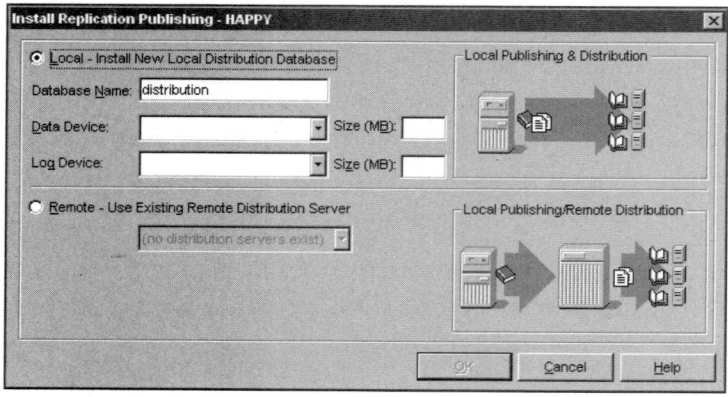

The Install Replication Publishing dialog box.
Figure 4.10

 The initial size of the data device and log device should be adequate to store the volume of transactions to be distributed. Microsoft suggests a value of 30MB for the database and 15MB for the transaction log. Consider setting up the transaction log closer to the same size as the data device for safety. You should monitor the sizes and usage of these devices closely.

7. Select OK to build the distribution database. This process might take some time, so don't worry if nothing appears to happen for a few minutes.

8. When the creation sequence is completed, you are presented a prompt asking whether you want to create publications now. Selecting Yes takes you to the next section, Setting Publication Options; selecting No returns you to the Enterprise Manager. If you are setting up this machine as a distribution server only, select No.

Setting Publication Options

Now that the distribution server is configured, you can publish information. You do this by selecting the database from the Replication Publishing dialog box, shown in Figure 4.11. After you have flagged the database as one that will be published, you should define a publication, as follows:

1. From the Enterprise Manager, select the Server menu.

2. Choose the Replication Configuration option, and from the drop-down menu, choose Publishing. The Replication Publishing dialog box appears. See Figure 4.11.

3. Select the subscribing server you wish to allow to subscribe to any publications in the Replication Publishing dialog box.. The Distribution Options dialog box appears. Notice that you can add subscribers in this dialog box as well as set the distribution options on a server-by-server basis (see Figure 4.12). The schedule and rate of replication is defined in this dialog, as well as any ODBC connections through which you will replicate.

4. Select the checkbox next to the database you wish to publish and select OK. You have now configured your server for publishing.

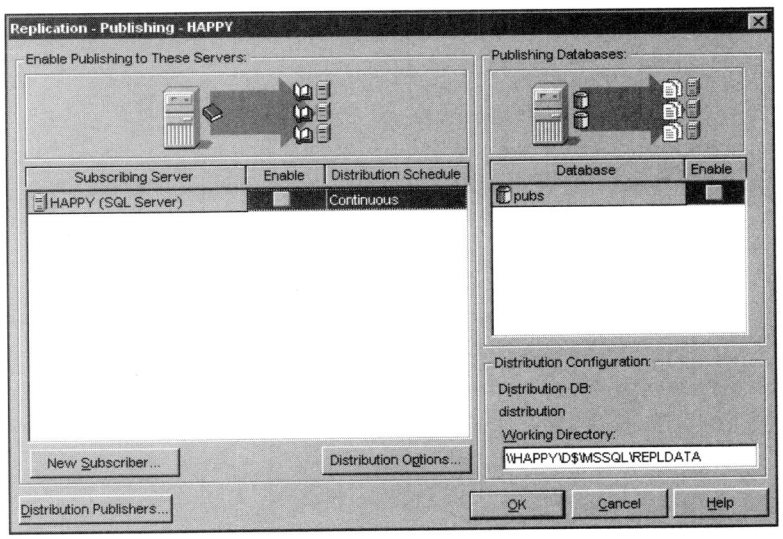

The Replication Publishing dialog box.
Figure 4.11

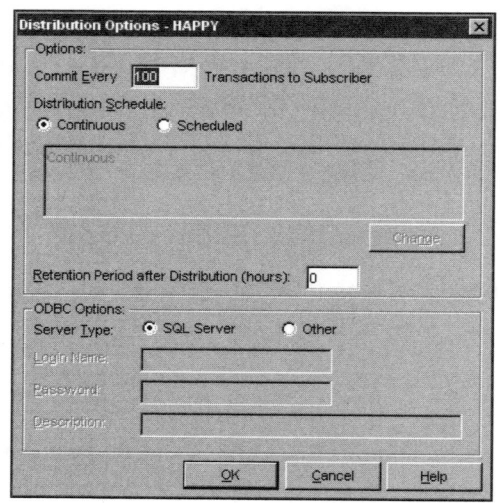

The Distribution Options dialog box.
Figure 4.12

Creating Publications And Articles

Now that you can publish data on your server, you must create a publication with at least one article in it. You cannot have an article without a publication. One thing to note, however, is that you can have multiple articles in one publication.

To create a publication, follow these steps:

1. In the Enterprise Manager, go to the Manage menu and select Replication. The resulting drop-down menu displays two options: Publications and Subscriptions. Choose Publications. The Manage Publications dialog box appears, as shown in Figure 4.13.

2. Click the New button. The Edit Publications dialog box appears, as shown in Figure 4.14. This is where you manage your publications in the Enterprise Manager.

3. Enter a descriptive title for your publication. (Remember that other database administrators might have to decipher what is in this publication from the name.) Add a good description and select the table you want to include in the article.

4. You may also change the replication schedule from Transaction Based to Scheduled Table Refresh in this dialog box. This is good for data that contains text and image data or that only requires a daily refresh.

5. Synchronization method and time frame can be adjusted through the Synchronization tab, and any security restrictions can be set on a server-by-server basis through the Security tab at this time.

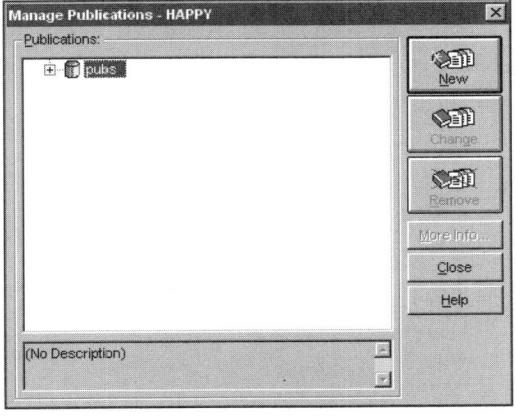

The Manage Publications dialog box.
Figure 4.13

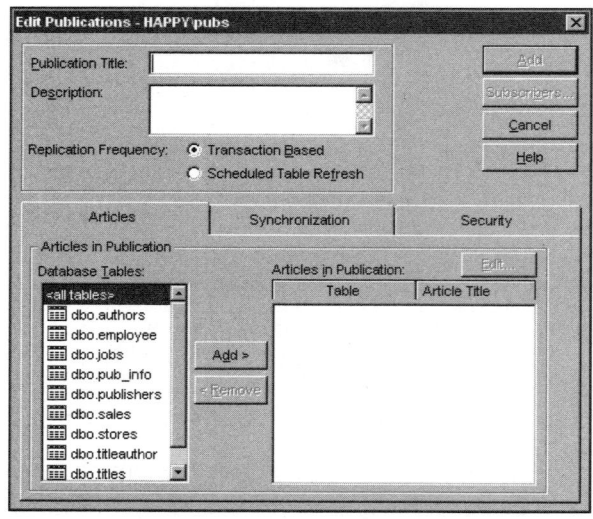

The Edit Publications dialog box.
Figure 4.14

6. To partition your article either horizontally or vertically, select the Edit button with one of the articles highlighted in the Articles for Publication box. This brings up the Manage Articles dialog box, shown in Figure 4.15.

7. You can limit the columns being replicated by deselecting the checkbox next to each column name in the list. (You must replicate the key column.) Use the Restriction box to specify what rows you wish to include in your article. You can modify any of the information in this dialog box as long as there are *no* subscriptions to an article. Once an article has been subscribed to, it cannot be modified.

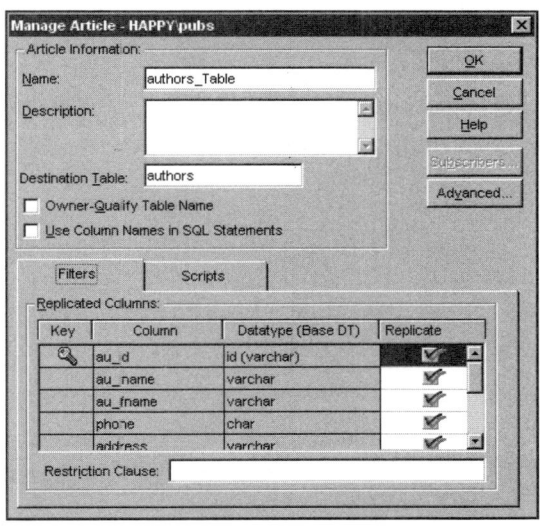

The Manage Articles dialog box.
Figure 4.15

8. Use the Scripts tab of the Manage Articles dialog box to specify any stored procedures you wish to use instead of the standard INSERT, UPDATE, and DELETE statements.

9. Once you are happy with your article, select the Generate button on the page under the Script to create the initial script for creating the subscribers' table structure.

10. Select OK, then Add. Your publication and article are now listed on your server. You are now ready to set up a push subscription to another server or have a subscriber pull a publication from you.

Setting Subscription Options

This section is very simple. Once you have been through the above steps, you have one thing left to do to enable your server to subscribe to publications: You must allow other servers to subscribe to your publications. You accomplish this by following these two steps:

1. In the Server menu, select Replication Configuration. Select Subscribing from the drop-down menu.

2. The Replication Subscribing dialog box appears, as shown in Figure 4.16. Simply check the Enable checkbox next to the database from which you wish to allow subscription and click OK. You are now ready to subscribe on this server.

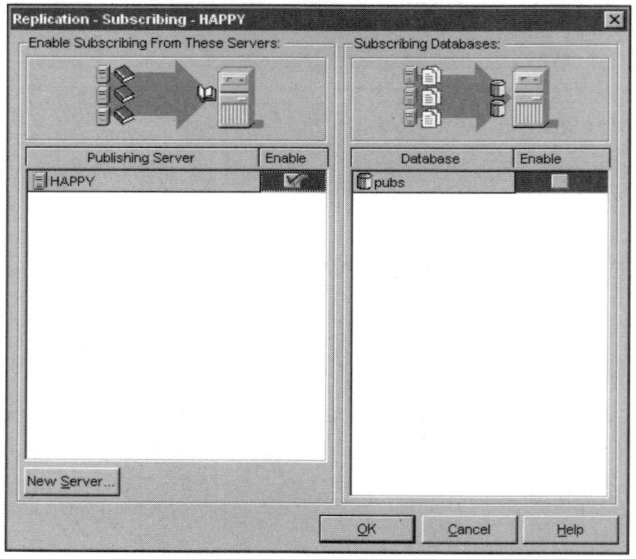

The Replication Subscribing dialog box.
Figure 4.16

Subscribing To A Publication

This part of the replication sequence is straightforward as well. Follow the steps below and you will have no problems whatsoever. You must select a publication and specify where the subscribed data should reside. (Remember to allow enough disk space for the new data.)

1. Select Manage from the Enterprise Manager menu. Scroll down and select Replication. In the resulting drop-down menu, select Subscriptions. The Manage Subscriptions dialog box appears, as shown in Figure 4.17.

2. The tree view on the left side of the Manage Subscriptions dialog box lists any registered servers and their publications. As you highlight each article or publication, the description for that item is displayed. This feature makes selecting a publication or article much easier.

3. Once you have found an article, click the Subscribe button. The Subscription Options dialog box appears, as shown in Figure 4.18.

4. Now specify where you want the publication to be placed and what synchronization method you wish to employ. Clicking the More Info button displays the publication information as it was entered on the publishing server. When you have selected the appropriate items, select OK.

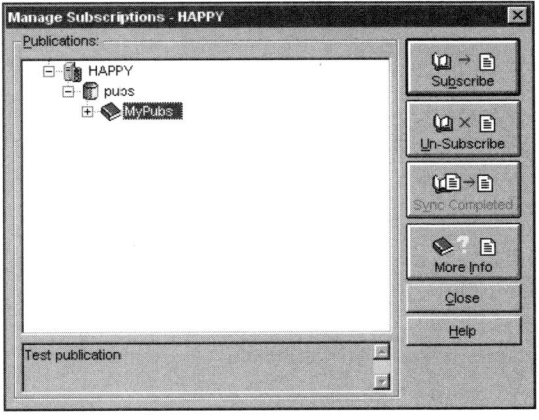

The Manage Subscriptions dialog box.
Figure 4.17

The Subscription Options dialog box.
Figure 4.18

You can now view the status of the synchronization in the same tree view in the Manage Subscriptions dialog box. Your information will show up here as not synchronized until the schema has been created and the structure filled with data. Depending on the options you have selected, this could occur in a few minutes, or not until that evening during off-production hours.

Once your tables have been synchronized, query both the source and the subscription to test that the same data exists in both tables. Keep in mind that if you are replicating data every 100 transactions, a simple insert of one row into the source table will not trigger the replication process.

And now for that helpful reminder: *Back up the master database!*

Chapter 5

Structured Query Language (SQL)

- Schema Changes
- Backing Up Data
- Renaming Objects To Be Modified
- Scripting Objects
- Converting And Inserting Old Data
- Cleaning Up The Environment
- A Word On Constraints

Administrator's Notes...

Chapter 5

There are as many ways to access data as there are ways to write programs. Each database has its own unique method of getting to the data stored on disk. Over time a standard has evolved that has come to be known as the Structured Query Language (SQL).

This standard is still being defined today, but it is by far better than it was 15 years ago. When looking back at early forms of databases, especially smaller systems, you will find that a proprietary language was the order of the day for most programmers. SQL was considered a second-class language compared with most programming languages available.

Even today, many true programmers look at SQL as a script language that is too simple to be as fast as what can be compiled and executed. Although SQL is not Pascal or C++, it is a very powerful language that takes data access to a higher level than either of those programming languages.

ANSI-Compliant SQL

SQL has been developed to provide a uniform method for accessing data stored in a database. Even the desktop and shared-file applications like Microsoft Access and Microsoft Visual FoxPro support SQL queries against their database files. In 1992 the American National Standards Institute (ANSI) published a set of standard SQL statements that should be supported by database applications. This standard was intended to provide functionality that can be depended on to run on many different platforms. Microsoft SQL Server, as well as other databases, supports this standard at some level or another.

If you write your SQL code to follow this ANSI standard, you will be able to run your scripts and queries against a broad range of databases without modifications. This ability has thrust database development into the forefront of application development in today's businesses. Coupled with the development of ODBC, your client applications can now take advantage of the features of many large database systems without your having to change client code.

Microsoft SQL Server is ANSI-SQL 92-compliant and will support ANSI queries. In addition, extensions to this ANSI standard allow you more freedom in your code. These extensions, along with different syntax that can be used to write queries, are available on Microsoft SQL Server and may not be available on all systems you run your code against. Be careful if you use non-ANSI standard queries in your code. You might have to modify your code slightly to run on another system.

I will focus on the Microsoft SQL Server version of SQL (Transact-SQL), since that product is the focus of this book. For the differences in syntax, check Microsoft SQL Server Books Online.

In addition, some very good quick-reference guides for writing ANSI-compliant code are available, including *SQL Instant Reference* by Martin Gruber, published by Sybex. This manual is a desktop reference all DBAs should own. It illustrates the differences between ANSI 89 and 92 SQL and has very good code examples for writing most any query you require.

Now back to *this* book. In this chapter, I'll walk you through the process of writing queries, from the simplest to the most advanced queries written against multiple tables with complex formatting and output. As an example, I'll use the Pubs database installed on your server. You can run the queries I have given you here against your own system to test them and determine if they are useful. Most production systems will not have the Pubs database installed; in this case, run the queries against a development system for test purposes.

Syntax

SQL is a very readable language once you get to know the different statements involved. You'll find the basics of SQL easy to memorize, but the more elaborate statements and functions require a quick lookup in Microsoft SQL Server Books Online.

Comments

Do not fall into the trap of leaving comments out of your code. Comment your code in blocks so that at a minimum you can look back on it six months later and remember what you were trying to do.

Comments are placed in your code in two ways: using the forward slash and asterisk (/*) at the beginning of a comment and an asterisk and forward slash (*/) to close the comment out; or beginning and ending inline comments with a dash, dash (*SQL code--comment*). Whether you use the slashes or the dashes, you will be doing yourself a favor by having good notes in your code for later.

The slashes will comment out a single line of code or multiple lines of code, similar to other major programming languages. Dashes are used for inline comments. Use a style that makes sense to you and stick with it. Adopting a standard for comments in a production environment can save many hours of work.

SQL statements ignore white space. You can therefore use spaces freely to make your code more legible. As you go through this chapter, you will find places where I have lined different sections of code up with other sections in the code. This is done for clarity. You do not have to follow this convention; however, some kind of standard should be adopted in a multiple-programmer shop for consistency and easy understanding. When you wish to see all columns in a table, use an asterisk (*) in place of each column name. This can make it easy to get all columns back in a query. Keep in mind, however, that this method can also cause problems. If a client software package expects five columns to be returned from a query and uses the asterisk to get the columns, a schema change can break the client. As a rule, specify the names of the columns you wish returned with your queries.

Pubs Database

We'll start our tour of SQL with a quick look at the Pubs database. I'll use a few of the tables in Pubs to illustrate the data manipulation techniques you need to write effective queries. These tables are loaded automatically by the installation program and are placed inside the master device along with the master database.

Authors

Let's first look at the Authors table, shown in Table 5.1. This table has nine columns and two indexes. Like any other entity-tracking table, the Author table holds address information. Microsoft has populated this table with sample data. Upon installation of SQL Server, 23 rows are in this table.

Sales

Next is the Sales table, shown in Table 5.2. This table has six columns and two indexes. The Sales table holds sales information for each title sold for a particular store. Microsoft has populated this table with sample data. Upon installation of SQL Server, this table contains 21 rows.

Titleauthor

Of the example tables, the Titleauthor table is probably the most confusing. Shown in Table 5.3, this table has four columns and three indexes. There is one record for each title that each author has written. It does not hold a lot of meaningful data,

Column	Data Type
Au_id	VARCHAR(11)
Au_lname	VARCHAR(40)
Au_fname	VARCHAR(20)
Phone	CHAR(12)
Address	VARCHAR(40)
City	VARCHAR(20)
State	CHAR(2)
Zip	CHAR(5)
Contract	BIT

Indexes are on the au_id column and the au_lname and au_fname columns.

Table 5.1   Authors table schema.

Column	Data Type
Store_id	CHAR(4)
Ord_num	VARCHAR(20)
Ord_date	DATETIME
Qty	SMALLINT
Payterms	VARCHAR(12)
Title_id	VARCHAR(6)

Indexes are on the title_id column and the store_id, ord_num, and title_id columns.

Table 5.2 Sales table schema.

except that each book can have many authors and each author is responsible for a percentage of each title's royalties. This table holds the ID values for each author and title. Microsoft has populated this table with sample data. There are 25 rows in this table when you install Microsoft SQL Server.

SELECT Statements

SELECT statements do not modify data in any way. They are simply a method of looking at the data stored in a single table or in many related tables. SELECT statements do not generate a transaction in Microsoft SQL Server either. We'll use the Authors table to illustrate some SELECT statements. See Listing 5.1 for the syntax.

Column	Data Type
au_id	VARCHAR(11)
title_id	VARCHAR(6)
au_ord	TINYINT
royaltyper	INT

Indexes are on the au_id and the title_id columns, and another index that combines the two columns au_id and title_id.

Table 5.3 Titleauthor table schema.

I recommend spending a few minutes in Microsoft SQL Server Books Online to become familiar with all of the clauses in a SELECT statement. This time can mean the difference between hours and minutes trying to get a query to perform the way the user needs.

There are three keywords to keep in mind when retrieving data through SQL: SELECT, FROM, and WHERE. The SELECT list is the list of columns that you wish to return from the query. Depending on your query, these columns can be from one table or multiple tables. You can return all of the column values or manipulate the column to return a computed value, or you can combine column values to create something totally new. The FROM statement specifies the table, tables, or views from which you want to retrieve the data. The WHERE clause specifies which rows to include or exclude for your query's output.

Omitting the WHERE clause will return or manipulate all rows in the table. Be careful to use this feature only when you really intend to query the entire table or view. Omitting WHERE places an extra burden on the server, so in production queries, always use a WHERE clause.

Listing 5.1 SELECT statement syntax.
```
SELECT [ALL | DISTINCT] select_list
    [INTO [new_table_name]]
[FROM {table_name | view_name}[(optimizer_hints)]
[[, {table_name2 | view_name2}[(optimizer_hints)]
[..., {table_name16 | view_name16}[(optimizer_hints)]]]
[WHERE clause]
[GROUP BY clause]
[HAVING clause]
[ORDER BY clause]
[COMPUTE clause]
[FOR BROWSE]
```

Listing 5.2 shows some basic queries. The first four example queries return the same columns and number of rows. As shown in Query 5, I can change the order of the columns or which columns are included to affect what the query returns. I prefer to use some formatting to help keep things clear and easy to change. With each column specified in the SELECT list, I can easily change the column order or add and remove columns with little problem. Notice in Query 2 that the long line of code, even with this basic query, is harder to read than the stacked code in Query 4. Use formatting to clarify your code.

Listing 5.2 Basic SQL queries.
```
/* Query 1 */
SELECT * FROM authors

/* Query 2 */
SELECT au_id, au_lname, au_fname, address, city, state, zip,
phone, contract FROM authors

/* Query 3 (Formatted) */

SELECT *
  FROM authors

/* Query 4 (Formatted) */
SELECT au_id,
       au_lname,
       au_fname,
       address,
       city,
       state,
       zip,
       phone,
       contract
  FROM authors

/* Query 5 (Formatted) */
SELECT au_fname,
       au_lname,
       address,
       city,
       state,
       zip
  FROM authors
```

I can use some string functions to manipulate the output to read exactly the way I need it to. For example, Listing 5.3 shows a basic query (Query 1) that will return the first name, last name, and phone number for each of our authors. Let's apply some string functions and formatting to make this list a bit easier to read. For the sake of this example, we'll assume that we want the list to show first initial and last name, with the area code of the phone number in parentheses.

Listing 5.3 Phone list example.
```
/* Query 1 (name and phone number) */
SELECT au_fname,
       au_lname,
```

```
          phone
    FROM authors

/* Query 2 (first initial, name, phone) */
SELECT UPPER(SUBSTRING(au_fname,1,1)) + '.',
       au_lname,
       phone
    FROM authors

/* Query 3 (first initial, name, formatted phone number) */
SELECT UPPER(SUBSTRING(au_fname,1,1)) + '.',
       au_lname,
       '(' + SUBSTRING(phone,1,3) + ') ' + SUBSTRING(phone,5,8)
    FROM authors

/* Query 4 (finished output with formatting and titles) */
SELECT 'Name' = UPPER(SUBSTRING(au_fname,1,1)) + '. ' + SUBSTRING(au_lname,1, 15),
       'Phone' = '(' + SUBSTRING(phone,1,3) + ') ' + SUBSTRING(phone,5,8)
    FROM authors
```

Query 2 of Listing 5.3 shows the syntax. The UPPER function will convert the text to uppercase and the SUBSTRING function will return text beginning with the first character of the first name and including only one character. Notice the period after the first initial is added by using the string concatenation operator '+'. This allows for good formatting and user-friendly output. We are still only returning three columns' worth of data to the client.

For more detailed explanation of these or any other functions, check Microsoft SQL Server Books Online.

Our next task is to format the phone number. This is accomplished the same way as for the first name, with a bit more string manipulation. Query 3 in Listing 5.3 shows the phone number formatting required. Now we'll tell SQL Server that we wish to combine the first two columns into one column and restrict the length to a good value to limit wasted white space and change the titles displayed for each column to a user-friendly title instead of the column name in the table.

Functions and string manipulations are common in SQL code. These functions are very fast and make the output easy to read. See Listing 5.4 for the sample outputs for Queries 1 and 4 from Listing 5.3 to compare the reports. You can copy these queries and run them on your system to make sure the results match.

Listing 5.4 Sample output.

```
Query 1
au_fname           au_lname           phone
----------------   ----------------   ------------
Johnson            White              408 496-7223
Marjorie           Green              415 986-7020
Cheryl             Carson             415 548-7723
Michael            O'Leary            408 286-2428
Dean               Straight           415 834-2919

Query 4
Name               Phone
----------------   --------------
J. White           (408) 496-7223
M. Green           (415) 986-7020
C. Carson          (415) 548-7723
M. O'Leary         (408) 286-2428
D. Straight        (415) 834-2919
M. Smith           (913) 843-0462
A. Bennet          (415) 658-9932
```

WHERE Clause

Staying with the same example data, we'll now look at restricting the number of rows returned by our queries. This horizontal partitioning is done with the WHERE clause. Let's assume for the sake of this example that we want to see only the authors that live in the 415 area code. As shown in Query 1 of Listing 5.5, we would add a WHERE clause to our query.

WHERE clauses use comparison operators to check the value of a column against another value to determine if it should be returned in the query. Using negative operators should be avoided since the Query Optimizer has a difficult time knowing if a record is *not* something. NOT is *not* optimizable! Most queries can be rewritten to take advantage of equalities rather than nonequalities.

Notice the same **SUBSTRING()** function is used, along with an equal sign and 415 in quotation marks. We could use a column name instead of the string function if we only wanted the authors in California. Or we could use Query 2 of Listing 5.5 to return just those records where the author lives in California. Notice in Query 2 that the WHERE clause uses a column that does not exist in the SELECT list. Listing the column in the SELECT list is not always required in your queries. However, it is required when using aggregate functions; we'll cover these functions later in this chapter.

Listing 5.5 Horizontal partitioning of data.
```
/* Query 1 (only 415 area code) */
SELECT 'Name' = UPPER(SUBSTRING(au_fname,1,1)) + '. ' + SUBSTRING(au_lname,1, 15),
       'Phone' = '(' + SUBSTRING(phone,1,3) + ') ' + SUBSTRING(phone,5,8)
  FROM authors
 WHERE SUBSTRING(phone,1,3) = '415'

/* Query 2 (California authors) */
SELECT 'Name' = UPPER(SUBSTRING(au_fname,1,1)) + '. ' + SUBSTRING(au_lname,1, 15),
       'Phone' = '(' + SUBSTRING(phone,1,3) + ') ' + SUBSTRING(phone,5,8)
  FROM authors
 WHERE state = 'CA'
```

When you execute these queries, you will notice different records returned that are still formatted by the functions in the SELECT list. These interchangeable WHERE clauses allow you to view the same data from a table, while restricting the row-matching and shortening the list considerably. See Listing 5.6 for the results of these two queries.

Listing 5.6 State and area code query sample output.
```
Query 1
Name                  Phone
------------------    --------------
M. Green              (415) 986-7020
C. Carson             (415) 548-7723
D. Straight           (415) 834-2919
A. Bennet             (415) 658-9932
A. Dull               (415) 836-7128
C. Locksley           (415) 585-4620
A. Yokomoto           (415) 935-4228
D. Stringer           (415) 843-2991
S. MacFeather         (415) 354-7128
L. Karsen             (415) 534-9219
S. Hunter             (415) 836-7128

(11 row(s) affected)

Query 2
Name                  Phone
------------------    --------------
J. White              (408) 496-7223
M. Green              (415) 986-7020
C. Carson             (415) 548-7723
M. O'Leary            (408) 286-2428
D. Straight           (415) 834-2919
A. Bennet             (415) 658-9932
A. Dull               (415) 836-7128
```

```
B. Gringlesby     (707) 938-6445
C. Locksley       (415) 585-4620
A. Yokomoto       (415) 935-4228
D. Stringer       (415) 843-2991
S. MacFeather     (415) 354-7128
L. Karsen         (415) 534-9219
S. Hunter         (415) 836-7128
H. McBadden       (707) 448-4982

(15 row(s) affected)
```

With these simple queries, there are no real mysteries as to what should be indexed on the table. If you were selecting only certain states, you would want to place an index on the state column to get the fastest results. I will cover index strategies in Chapter 11. WHERE clauses are one of two critical areas for indexes. Depending on your WHERE clause, the Microsoft SQL Server Query Optimizer may decide that an indexed search for matching records would be faster; it would then create a temporary table to support your query. When your query is finished, Microsoft SQL Server will drop the temporary table because it is no longer needed.

You can imagine what happens to servers without proper indexes when a query is run over and over again. This is where performance typically is affected the most.

The second and most critical area for index placement with regard to SELECT statements is the ORDER BY clause.

ORDER BY Clause

Now we will take our phone listing a bit further by alphabetizing it. The output of Query 2 in Listing 5.5 can be rearranged to follow the last name in ascending or descending order by adding an ORDER BY clause. See Listing 5.7 for the new query with an ORDER BY clause and the resulting output.

Listing 5.7 Phone list with an ORDER BY clause.

```
/* Phone list in alpha order (CA) */
SELECT 'Name' = UPPER(SUBSTRING(au_fname,1,1)) + '. ' + SUBSTRING(au_lname,1, 15),
       'Phone' = '(' + SUBSTRING(phone,1,3) + ') ' + SUBSTRING(phone,5,8)
  FROM authors
 WHERE state = 'CA'
 ORDER BY au_lname
```

```
Output
Name                    Phone
------------------      --------------
A. Bennet               (415) 658-9932
C. Carson               (415) 548-7723
A. Dull                 (415) 836-7128
M. Green                (415) 986-7020
B. Gringlesby           (707) 938-6445
S. Hunter               (415) 836-7128
L. Karsen               (415) 534-9219
C. Locksley             (415) 585-4620
S. MacFeather           (415) 354-7128
H. McBadden             (707) 448-4982
M. O'Leary              (408) 286-2428
D. Straight             (415) 834-2919
D. Stringer             (415) 843-2991
J. White                (408) 496-7223
A. Yokomoto             (415) 935-4228

(15 row(s) affected)
```

Notice that only the column name is used for the ORDER BY clause. We also could have used the area-code substring to further sort the resulting list. Another, more cryptic option would be to list the number of the column in the SELECT list. I seldom use this method because of the hard-to-follow 'order by 2' or 'order by 2,3' in the SQL statement.

ORDER BY clauses are the first place I look for matching indexes. Anytime I write an ordered or sorted query, I verify that a corresponding index exists on the table I am querying. A clustered index on the ordered column or columns helps guarantee that the server will not create a worktable for this query. Keep in mind that you can have only one clustered index on each of your tables. Microsoft SQL Server will almost always need an index to perform an ORDER BY statement efficiently.

You can sort by as many as 16 columns with an ORDER BY statement, although for performance reasons, I do not recommend this. Offline reporting and overnight processes are the only place I have seen ORDER BY statements with a great number of columns. On larger tables with queries that return large result sets, you can run out of space in Tempdb very quickly. Remember that worktables are placed in Tempdb while in use. Everyone shares this space for in-process query manipulation. If you place a large ordered worktable in Tempdb and others need to use that space, someone will get an error message that space in Tempdb cannot be allocated. This is not something you want to happen.

GROUP BY Clause

Now let's group our data in the Authors table so that our authors are listed in alphabetical order, grouped by state. First we'll need to add the state column to the SELECT list and list the other displayed columns in the GROUP BY clause. See Listing 5.8 for this grouped query and the corresponding output. Note that there is no ORDER BY in this list but that the names returned are in alphabetical order. The GROUP BY will sort in the order we wish to group columns.

Listing 5.8 Phone list grouped by state.

```
/* Query 1 Phone list grouped by state */
SELECT 'Name' = UPPER(SUBSTRING(au_fname,1,1)) + '. ' + SUBSTRING(au_lname,1, 15),
       'State' = state,
       'Phone' = '(' + SUBSTRING(phone,1,3) + ') ' + SUBSTRING(phone,5,8)
   FROM authors
 GROUP BY state, au_lname, au_fname, phone

Output
Name                State Phone
------------------  ----- --------------
A. Bennet           CA    (415) 658-9932
C. Carson           CA    (415) 548-7723
A. Dull             CA    (415) 836-7128
M. Green            CA    (415) 986-7020
B. Gringlesby       CA    (707) 938-6445
S. Hunter           CA    (415) 836-7128
L. Karsen           CA    (415) 534-9219
C. Locksley         CA    (415) 585-4620
S. MacFeather       CA    (415) 354-7128
H. McBadden         CA    (707) 448-4982
M. O'Leary          CA    (408) 286-2428
D. Straight         CA    (415) 834-2919
D. Stringer         CA    (415) 843-2991
J. White            CA    (408) 496-7223
A. Yokomoto         CA    (415) 935-4228
M. DeFrance         IN    (219) 547-9982
M. Smith            KS    (913) 843-0462
S. Panteley         MD    (301) 946-8853
I. del Castillo     MI    (615) 996-8275
R. Blotchet-Halls   OR    (503) 745-6402
M. Greene           TN    (615) 297-2723
A. Ringer           UT    (801) 826-0752
A. Ringer           UT    (801) 826-0752

(23 row(s) affected)
```

GROUP BY can be used for much more than I have illustrated here. Calculating summary data and reports with sectional summaries and grand totals can come into play as well. See Listing 5.9 for a sales grouping query from the Sales table. This query uses GROUP BY and HAVING clauses, which are frequently used together.

I also use the aggregate functions **SUM()** and **MAX()** for the first time in Query 2 to add each sale together into one record in the result set and to display the last date of a sale for that title. We'll cover aggregate functions later in the chapter. For more information on GROUP BY statements and HAVING clauses, see Microsoft SQL Server Books Online.

Listing 5.9   Sales report query.

```
/* Query 1 Listing of sales with no grouping */
SELECT title_id,
       ord_date,
       qty
  FROM sales
 ORDER BY title_id

/* Query 2 Volume sales > 20 */
SELECT 'Title ID'        = title_id,
       'Last Sale Date'  = MAX(ord_date),
       'Total Sales'     = SUM(qty)
  FROM sales
 GROUP BY title_id
HAVING SUM(qty) > 20
 ORDER BY SUM(qty) DESC

Output Query 1
title_id  ord_date                     qty
--------  -------------------------    ------
BU1032    Sep 14 1994 12:00AM          5
BU1032    Sep 14 1994 12:00AM          10
BU1111    Mar 11 1993 12:00AM          25
BU2075    Feb 21 1993 12:00AM          35
BU7832    Oct 28 1993 12:00AM          15
MC2222    Dec 12 1993 12:00AM          10
MC3021    Sep 14 1994 12:00AM          25
MC3021    Sep 14 1994 12:00AM          15
PC1035    May 22 1993 12:00AM          30
PC8888    May 24 1993 12:00AM          50
PS1372    May 29 1993 12:00AM          20
PS2091    Sep 13 1994 12:00AM          3
PS2091    Sep 13 1994 12:00AM          75
PS2091    Sep 14 1994 12:00AM          10
```

```
PS2091    Sep 14 1994 12:00AM         20
PS2106    May 29 1993 12:00AM         25
PS3333    May 29 1993 12:00AM         15
PS7777    May 29 1993 12:00AM         25
TC3218    Jun 15 1992 12:00AM         40
TC4203    Jun 15 1992 12:00AM         20
TC7777    Jun 15 1992 12:00AM         20

(21 row(s) affected)

Output Query 2
Title ID  Last Sale Date              Total Sales
--------  --------------------------  -----------
PS2091    Sep 14 1994 12:00AM         108
PC8888    May 24 1993 12:00AM         50
MC3021    Sep 14 1994 12:00AM         40
TC3218    Jun 15 1992 12:00AM         40
BU2075    Feb 21 1993 12:00AM         35
PC1035    May 22 1993 12:00AM         30
BU1111    Mar 11 1993 12:00AM         25
PS2106    May 29 1993 12:00AM         25
PS7777    May 29 1993 12:00AM         25

(9 row(s) affected)
```

Some special conditions are associated with the GROUP BY and HAVING clauses:

- ANSI-SQL requires that every column (nonaggregate) in the SELECT list be mentioned in your GROUP BY statement.

- Columns in a HAVING clause must have one and only one value. This requirement precludes subqueries that return more than one row.

- Any query with a HAVING clause must contain a GROUP BY clause.

These requirements are usually not hard to meet and should pose little problem to you as a programmer.

Microsoft SQL Server has added Transact-SQL extensions: GROUP BY statements can include expressions, and GROUP BY ALL displays all groups, even those that would be filtered out by the WHERE clause restrictions.

Join Conditions

Now we'll need to put some information together from more than one table so that the title ID can show the name and author for each sales report line in our new report. We'll use the same basic query from above and add a join condition to it so that the server connects the data. See Listing 5.10 for the new query and the sample output.

Microsoft SQL Server supports ANSI join syntax and Transact-SQL syntax (Microsoft SQL Server extended SQL). Use of inner, cross, and outer joins is supported fully on Microsoft SQL Server. The syntax for ANSI joins is slightly different than for Transact-SQL, so a trip to Microsoft SQL Server Books Online would be prudent. Transact-SQL uses join operators instead of actual text to perform the join in a WHERE clause. In the following examples, Transact-SQL methods are used.

Query 1 in Listing 5.10 displays what is in the Titleauthor table. This data is a collection of key values used to join together related pieces of information. Not all databases need this type of table, but good relational database design will produce a similar table in most situations.

Query 2 joins the Sales, Titleauthor, and Author tables. You specify the tables in a comma-delimited list in the FROM clause. In the SELECT list, you use the table.column reference to specify each column independently of the others. This allows you to use data from many tables and present it to the user as if it were from one table.

Hiding the complexity of the database structure is very important to your users. If a column name is unique to all tables involved in a query, such as qty in the Sales table, you can list the column without the table reference. The Optimizer will not choke on it because it knows there is only one qty column in all three tables.

I use the table.column reference in all my join queries to keep myself in check and to track which column comes from which table.

Listing 5.10 Sales by author join example.

```
/* Query 1 titleauthor table */
SELECT *
  FROM titleauthor
 ORDER by title_id

/* Query 2 Volume sales > 20 by author */
SELECT 'Author'        = UPPER(SUBSTRING(authors.au_fname,1,1)) +
                         '. ' + SUBSTRING(authors.au_lname,1, 15),
       'Total Sales'   = SUM(sales.qty)
  FROM sales, titleauthor, authors
 WHERE sales.title_id = titleauthor.title_id
   AND authors.au_id  = titleauthor.au_id
```

```
    GROUP BY authors.au_fname, authors.au_lname
   HAVING SUM(sales.qty) > 20
    ORDER BY SUM(qty) DESC

/* Query 3 Volume sales > 20 by author */
SELECT 'Author'      = UPPER(SUBSTRING(a.au_fname,1,1)) +
                      '. ' + SUBSTRING(a.au_lname,1, 15),
       'Total Sales' = SUM(s.qty)
   FROM sales s, titleauthor ta, authors a
  WHERE s.title_id = ta.title_id
    AND a.au_id   = ta.au_id
  GROUP BY a.au_fname, a.au_lname
 HAVING SUM(s.qty) > 20
  ORDER BY SUM(s.qty) DESC
```

Output Query 1

au_id	title_id	au_ord	royaltyper
213-46-8915	BU1032	2	40
409-56-7008	BU1032	1	60
267-41-2394	BU1111	2	40
724-80-9391	BU1111	1	60
213-46-8915	BU2075	1	100
274-80-9391	BU7832	1	100
712-45-1867	MC2222	1	100
722-51-5454	MC3021	1	75
899-46-2035	MC3021	2	25
238-95-7766	PC1035	1	100
427-17-2319	PC8888	1	50
846-92-7186	PC8888	2	50
486-29-1786	PC9999	1	100
724-80-9391	PS1372	2	25
756-30-7391	PS1372	1	75
899-46-2035	PS2091	2	50
998-72-3567	PS2091	1	50
998-72-3567	PS2106	1	100
172-32-1176	PS3333	1	100
486-29-1786	PS7777	1	100
807-91-6654	TC3218	1	100
648-92-1872	TC4203	1	100
267-41-2394	TC7777	2	30
472-27-2349	TC7777	3	30
672-71-3249	TC7777	1	40

(25 row(s) affected)

```
Output Query 2
Author              Total Sales
------------------  ----------
A. Ringer           148
A. Ringer           133
A. Dull             50
M. Green            50
S. Hunter           50
M. O'Leary          45
S. MacFeather       45
M. DeFrance         40
S. Panteley         40
C. Carson           30
C. Locksley         25

(11 row(s) affected)
```

Notice that in the WHERE clause of these queries I have had to place a join condition for each of the tables in my list. The Sales table has a title_id column that matches a title_id column in the Titleauthor table. By saying that these two columns are equal, you allow the server to add the information in the Titleauthor table to the list of available columns you can choose from. The Titleauthor table has an au_id column that corresponds to the au_id column of the Authors table. A good rule of thumb is that for each table that you wish to join, there should be one join condition in the WHERE clause.

The formula $N = T - 1$ should come to mind when joining tables. T is the number of tables in your FROM clause and N is the number of join conditions you should have. The wrong number of join conditions can return incorrect result sets to the user.

Aliases

In Query 3 of Listing 5.10, I have introduced aliases to each of the table names in the FROM clause. I do not have to do this, but it prevents me from typing things over and over again. In addition, aliases enhance readability of the code.

Notice in Query 2 the long lines of code, with the table reference repeated many times. Repeating the table name is not bad; it's just costly in the amount of typing you must do. Queries 2 and 3 return the same results, yet Query 3 is about 55 characters shorter. This might seem insignificant, but when you have to pass queries over a network or modems many times during the running of an application, it can save time in the communications between client and server. (I do not typically pass a query string from client to server; instead, I use stored procedures, which keep the requests as short as possible. See Chapter 6 for more on stored procedures and their benefits.)

To use aliases, add a space after each of the tables in the FROM clause and the character or characters you wish to refer or connect to each table. The Query Optimizer checks for the alias in the FROM clause first; then it uses those aliases to parse the SELECT list and WHERE clauses, respectively.

Aggregates And Functions

No system would function without some kind of standard set of functions that can be used to simplify queries. The aggregates and functions in Microsoft SQL Server are no different than their counterparts in other, more refined programming languages.

We'll spend a moment looking at some of the more useful aggregates and functions. You should also look each one up in Microsoft SQL Server Books Online to reinforce what we discuss here.

Try keeping a weekly task list that includes a reminder to look up a new function or feature in Microsoft SQL Server Books Online. This will help you stay on top of the many functions out there and how they can make programming easier.

These functions support nesting and are data type-sensitive where needed. They can return values to a query or to a local variable for manipulation in other parts of a script or stored procedure. For the syntax of each function, check Microsoft SQL Server Books Online.

SUM()

The **SUM()** function returns the total of a column's values. In the examples, I used the **SUM()** function to add the quantity column for each title sold. Depending how you use this function, it will work on an entire table or on a group of records.

Keep in mind that the columns must be numeric for this function to work properly. You can use the **CONVERT()** function to change numbers stored as text to the proper data type nested inside this function as well.

MAX()

This function returns the maximum value for a column in a table or set of rows returned in a query. In the examples, I used this function to return the greatest date value in the Sales table for each title listed. This was accomplished through the grouping of the rows by title and applying the aggregate function for each row. This function works with text as well as with dates and numbers.

MIN()

MIN() is the opposite of **MAX()** in every regard. The same rules and features apply to this function as to the **MAX()** function. Remember that the lowest value returned for text will depend on sort order and case sensitivity.

AVG()

Many reports depend on averages to keep track of trends over time. The **AVG()** function calculates the average value of a column in a table or in a set of rows, depending on how it is used. Only numeric values can be passed to the **AVG()** function. You can use the **CONVERT()** function nested inside of the **AVG()** function to return the numeric value of a number stored as text to get around the numeric restriction of this function.

COUNT()

This very common function returns the count of rows in the query that match a particular WHERE clause. The number of rows in a table can be returned to a variable for testing purposes very effectively. **COUNT()** returns the number of non-NULL values indicated by the WHERE clause in any query. You can pass the asterisk to the **COUNT(*)** function to get a row count from a query. **COUNT()** is useful in triggers and stored procedures for determining not only the existence of rows but the exact number of rows you are dealing with. The return value for this function is numeric.

CONVERT()

I use this function frequently in SQL code to ensure that I have the correct data types to perform an operation. This versatile function converts one data type to another so that a number of operations can be performed. You just specify the data type to which you wish the existing column or expression to be converted.

Microsoft SQL Server will attempt to convert like data types to the proper type automatically when it can. If Microsoft SQL Server cannot process a function or query with the data passed to it, the server returns an error message that suggests the use of the **CONVERT()** function to solve the problem. See *Calculated Values* later in this chapter for an example of the **CONVERT()** function.

GETDATE()

The **GETDATE()** function returns the current date and time from the server's system clock. This function can be used to automatically insert date values into columns or to find out the current date for comparisons in WHERE clauses. Audit trails and tracking tables benefit greatly from this function and the **CURRENT_USER** function.

DATEDIFF()

You can use this function to compare and return the difference between date items such as days, weeks, minutes, and hours. When this function is used in a WHERE clause, you can return records that meet a range of dates, or that meet certain timespan intervals. Make sure you specify the arguments to this function in the correct order, or the value returned might be the opposite of what you expected.

DATEPART()

This function returns a value equal to the part of a date that you specify. If, for instance, you need to know the day of the week of a particular date, you can use this function to quickly pull that data out of a column or variable.

SOUNDEX()

This function converts a string to a four-digit code that represents the string. If two strings are very close to the same spelling, they will have the same **SOUNDEX()** value returned. This function can be used to find a list of potential matches for a string in a set of rows.

I think of this as the "sounds like" function. If the strings sound alike, the number returned by this function will be the same. This can be useful for finding data when the user does not know the exact spelling. **SOUNDEX()** is critical to creating a full-featured Find for database records.

SUBSTRING()

The **SUBSTRING()** function is used many times throughout this book. Any string manipulation can be accomplished with this function in conjunction with a few string operators and some other basic string functions.

Another useful string function you should take a moment to look up in Microsoft SQL Server Books Online is the **STUFF()** function. **STUFF()** and **SUBSTRING()** in combination are useful for building strings on the fly in your SQL code. See *Calculated Values* later in this chapter for more on **SUBSTRING()** and its uses.

UPPER()

UPPER() converts the string passed to the function into all uppercase characters. You can use this function to maintain the data integrity of text columns in your tables without the user or client intervening. Some client software always assumes this function to be bound to a control with very little overhead, so I seldom use this for much more than making sure I pass uppercase characters where needed.

CHARINDEX()

This function can be used to search for a match for a string in a column. If you want the character offset of a string within a string, this function returns the corresponding numbered offset of the start of the match. If you use this function to search an entire table, it will return a result set with a non-zero value for each row that contains a string.

CHARINDEX() does not allow wildcard characters. If you need to search for a string containing wildcards, use the **PATINDEX()** function instead.

RTRIM()

RTRIM() removes any trailing blanks from a string or column. In some situations, this helps keep formatting and reporting working the way your applications expect. **RTRIM()** is most useful in text reports generated from raw SQL.

System Functions

Similar to the functions we have been covering so far, system functions return server-based values or perform functions that would require a great deal of code. These functions are typically used to give your scripts and stored procedures more intelligence and function.

You could write SQL queries to return most of the values returned by these functions, because almost all the data returned by these functions exists in system tables on the server. However, using these functions is faster and more convenient.

For more information on these and other very useful system functions, look up System Functions in Microsoft SQL Server Books Online and choose Item 6 from the Results list.

ISNULL()

You can replace NULL values in your result sets dynamically with the **ISNULL()** function. Specify what value you wish to have returned if the corresponding column contains a NULL value, and this function checks for you on the fly. This can be a very handy function in reports and daily run queries written out to text files. See **NULLIF()** for a reciprocal type of function to **ISNULL()**.

USER_ID()

This function takes a name string and returns the current database ID for that name. The **USER_ID()** function is useful when you are accessing the system tables and need to check names against group membership or permissions values.

USER_NAME()

USER_NAME() is the opposite of the **USER_ID()** function. You pass it a valid database user ID, and it returns the name for that user. As with **USER_ID()**, this function is good for on-the-fly checks of permissions or memberships. It is also useful in error handling. When an error occurs, you can return more specific information from an error-handling routine by getting the user's name and writing it to a log or to a procedure for error escalation.

DATALENGTH()

This function returns the length of the data stored in a variable or in a column. The **DATALENGTH()** function works on all text data types and is very handy for reporting and string manipulation routines. It works with text and image data types, as well as with character data.

COL_LENGTH()

COL_LENGTH() returns the defined length of a column in a table. This function works well with most data types. With it, you can determine whether the data you wish to insert into a column will fit.

Calculated Values

Calculated values are created when you perform math functions on columns to generate an average or some other derived piece of data. These calculations can be created on the fly to avoid using up storage space in your databases, yet still be presented so they appear to be stored in a table someplace. A lot of calculated values are needed for the day-to-day operation of any system. We'll focus on the methods to get these values to the user.

As a general rule, I do not store calculated values in a table when I can display the value to the user another way. Calculated values work best for items of data that are built from pieces of other data in a corresponding record. If you need to change data that is calculated, you must change the underlying data anyway, so why change it more than once?

To clarify this method, we'll use the tables I have defined already to create a new unique author ID. The existing ID is the author's social security number. If for some reason you cannot use the existing ID number, you would need to display some kind of unique key to identify each author in your system. See Listing 5.11 for the query that displays the new author ID from the stored values in the Author table. For this example, we'll use a part of the author's social security number and his or her initials, state of residence, and contract status.

Listing 5.11 New author ID key.

```
/* New author ID query */
SELECT 'Old Author ID' = au_id,
       'New Author ID' = UPPER(SUBSTRING(au_fname,1,1)) +
                        UPPER(SUBSTRING(au_lname,1,1)) +
                        '-' + SUBSTRING(au_id,1,3) +
                        '-' + UPPER(state) +
                        CONVERT(CHAR(1),contract),
       'Name'          = UPPER(SUBSTRING(authors.au_fname,1,1)) +
                        '. ' + SUBSTRING(authors.au_lname,1, 15)
  FROM authors
 ORDER BY au_lname

Output
Old Author ID  New Author ID   Name
-------------  -------------   ------------------
409-56-7008    AB-409-CA1      A. Bennet
648-92-1872    RB-648-OR1      R. Blotchet-Halls
238-95-7766    CC-238-CA1      C. Carson
722-51-5454    MD-722-IN1      M. DeFrance
712-45-1867    ID-712-MI1      I. del Castillo
427-17-2319    AD-427-CA1      A. Dull
213-46-8915    MG-213-CA1      M. Green
527-72-3246    MG-527-TN0      M. Greene
472-27-2349    BG-472-CA1      B. Gringlesby
846-92-7186    SH-846-CA1      S. Hunter
756-30-7391    LK-756-CA1      L. Karsen
```

```
486-29-1786    CL-486-CA1    C. Locksley
724-80-9391    SM-724-CA1    S. MacFeather
893-72-1158    HM-893-CA0    H. McBadden
267-41-2394    MO-267-CA1    M. O'Leary
807-91-6654    SP-807-MD1    S. Panteley
899-46-2035    AR-899-UT1    A. Ringer
998-72-3567    AR-998-UT1    A. Ringer
341-22-1782    MS-341-KS0    M. Smith
274-80-9391    DS-274-CA1    D. Straight
724-08-9931    DS-724-CA0    D. Stringer
172-32-1176    JW-172-CA1    J. White
672-71-3249    AY-672-CA1    A. Yokomoto

(23 row(s) affected)
```

If the author ID were used to join tables in queries, you would naturally need to store this key value in a column. If it is used for display purposes only, as file or case numbers sometimes are, this type of query would display the number exactly the way it needs to be useful, without being stored in another column in the table. In the event you change the file numbering system or outgrow the existing ID scheme, you would simply modify the query; you wouldn't need to rebuild any underlying data. This technique is much more efficient than reworking the entire table structure to allow for a new numbering method.

Notice in Listing 5.11 that the **UPPER()** functions are used to ensure that the text portions of the result set are formatted correctly, and the bit data type is converted to a single character. This way, the string operators can be used without error. This technique of displaying an expression as real data to the user saves disk space without affecting performance. Because this data appears to the user as a static piece of data that can be modified as business rules dictate, this method is very useful in production environments.

Some of you might be saying to yourselves, "What if the underlying data changes?" or "What about incomplete data?" You do have to be very careful when building this kind of data. However, I have seen tons of disk space chewed up on data servers storing information that could have been displayed with this very technique with no problem. At the same time, I have seen other systems where this won't work as well. You have to use data that is stable and has some built-in integrity. Try this only if you're sure the data is stable and none of the needed pieces of data is going to change.

Optimizer Hints

You have the ability to tell Microsoft SQL Server that you wish a certain action to be performed without the optimizer using its normal methods. This is good in some cases and a disaster in others. Use optimizer hints with great caution. Many years of programming have gone into the design and optimization of your queries in the built-in optimizer. Although no tool is perfect, the Query Optimizer checks many things on the fly each time a query is run. In most situations the Query Optimizer will choose the correct plan based on the existing state of your tables and indexes.

I use optimizer hints in two situations. The first is when I am reading data that is highly fluid. I use the (NOLOCK) option in my SELECT statements to be sure that I am not locking pages in my queries when someone else is trying to do something. See Listing 5.12 for an example of a query with the NOLOCK optimizer hint.

Listing 5.12 Reading data without locking pages.

```
/* Select ID and Name without locking */
SELECT 'Author ID' = au_id,
       'Name'      = UPPER(SUBSTRING(authors.au_fname,1,1)) +
                     '. ' + SUBSTRING(authors.au_lname,1, 15)
  FROM authors (NOLOCK)
ORDER BY au_lname
```

The results are the same as they would have been without the hint, but we have avoided the risk of creating a deadlock or wait state on the server. At least every other day I find a message among Internet newsgroups about locking, hanging, or slow queries. In some of those situations, this hint would solve the problem.

Highly active data benefits from the NOLOCK hint because the query will not attempt to place any shared locks on the pages SQL Server must access for the query. If a client does not read all the records it has requested from the server, Microsoft SQL Server will hold those pages with a shared lock until the last record has been returned to the client. Shared locks can cause problems with very active data.

The second situation in which I use optimizer hints is when I want to lock data sets or a table. I will specify a table-level lock to reduce overhead and ensure I have the whole table when I need it. See Table 5.4 for a list of optimizer hints and their uses in your queries.

Hint	Intended Use
NOLOCK	Does not lock any data pages for a given query on the specified table. No shared locks will be issued to Microsoft SQL Server and exclusive locks will be ignored. This statement basically means to perform a "dirty read" of exactly what is in the data pages at the time of query execution.
INDEX =	Specifies which index to use for this query. Forcing the index may not improve performance of your queries. You can also specify a table scan with this hint.
HOLDLOCK	Holds the lock on data pages until the transaction is completed. You cannot use HOLDLOCK in SELECT statements that include FOR BROWSE.
UPDLOCK	Issues update locks instead of shared locks when reading data. Holds locks until the end of transaction or statement execution.
PAGLOCK	Forces single shared page locks when a table lock may have been issued.
TABLOCK	Places a single shared lock on the entire table until the transaction is completed.
TABLOCKX	Requests an exclusive lock of the table. This lock will be held until the transaction is completed.
FASTFIRSTROW	The optimizer will use a nonclustered index to honor the ORDER BY statement, if one exists, to return the first row of a query as fast as possible. This method is not always faster overall for larger result sets. Look up FASTFIRSTROW in Microsoft SQL Server Books Online before issuing this optimizer hint. I do not usually use this hint on production systems.

Table 5.4 Optimizer hints and their uses.

Subqueries

To improve the intelligence of your code, you can nest a query inside your queries to return information to the outer query. Any place an expression is valid in a query, you can place another query to evaluate and return a value for use in your SQL code. INSERT, UPDATE, DELETE, and SELECT statements support expressions in many places. In many situations, a subquery can be rewritten as a join condition to return the same results. In some situations, a join condition can actually perform your query faster than a subquery. Triggers can be made more intelligent through subqueries as well.

I write a lot of table-driven stored procedures that will run with only a few parameters but may query many user or system tables to actually perform the tasks internally. By reducing the amount of data required to perform a given task, this can substantially simplify the client code.

There are two types of subqueries: noncorrelated and correlated. An example of a noncorrelated subquery is one that will run before the outer query to return its results to the outer query for execution. This nesting is very similar to the execution of a function call in your code. A correlated subquery references the outer query internally and will be executed one time for each of the matching rows in the WHERE clause of the outer query. This might sound confusing at first, but it makes sense if you think about what actually happens.

When the outer query executes, it might only have five rows of a thousand-row table returned. If the inner query must be executed one time for each of the thousand rows checked, the process will be slow. By referencing the outer query's WHERE clause in the inner query, you are telling the optimizer to first filter out the thousand rows and perform the subquery five times instead of a thousand.

A subquery uses the same syntax as a regular query. You must, however, adhere to a few restrictions when using subqueries. A subquery is always enclosed in parentheses. It can only specify one column name of any data type except text and image. Any DISTINCT option will be maintained inside the subquery only. If you are testing for equality, you can only return a single item. If you are using a subquery in a WHERE clause and use the IN option for a list, the subquery can return more than one row. See Listing 5.13 for an example of a subquery and its syntax.

Listing 5.13 Subquery example.

```
/* Percentage of total sales by quantity */
SELECT 'Title ID'  = title_id,
       'Sales'     = qty,
       '% of Total' = CONVERT(NUMERIC(5,2),
                             (CONVERT(NUMERIC,qty) /
                             (SELECT SUM(qty) FROM sales)) * 100)
  FROM sales
 ORDER BY qty DESC

Output
Title ID Sales  % of Total
-------- ------ ----------
PS2091   75     15.21
PC8888   50     10.14
```

```
TC3218   40   8.11
BU2075   35   7.10
PC1035   30   6.09
MC3021   25   5.07
PS2106   25   5.07
PS7777   25   5.07
BU1111   25   5.07
TC4203   20   4.06
TC7777   20   4.06
PS2091   20   4.06
PS1372   20   4.06
PS3333   15   3.04
BU7832   15   3.04
MC3021   15   3.04
PS2091   10   2.03
MC2222   10   2.03
BU1032   10   2.03
BU1032    5   1.01
PS2091    3   0.61

(21 row(s) affected)
```

Union

You can use the union operator to combine two or more result sets into a single result set. This operation is used in many systems to provide for the combination of current and historical data. If your system archives data into a history table, to keep the current working set of data smaller and more manageable, the union operator could be used to combine your current data and historical data when performing statistical analysis or archive look-up queries.

By default the union operator will remove any duplicate rows, which can be very useful when combining data from more than one source. An important issue with the union operator is that the SELECT lists for both queries must match exactly. Number of columns, data type, and order are very important in performing a union between two queries. If your query contains an ORDER BY statement, the entire final result set will be sorted based on your ORDER BY statement.

The output result set will pull the column headings from the first query. If you wish to replace the default column headers with legible English, you must modify the SELECT list of the first query. The WHERE clauses do not have to match in either query. You can also use placeholders for missing columns in a union to fill in any missing information in one table or another in your queries. For more on the use of unions in your SQL code, see Microsoft SQL Server Books Online.

INSERT Statements

Up to this point, I have focused on the retrieval of data. In a client-server environment, you have two real processes for which you must program: the presentation of data to the user and the modification or creation of data on the server. Presenting data to the client applications does not typically modify data or create transaction log entries. Modification of data will place entries into the Syslogs table and generate transactions on your server.

I have saved discussion of these statements until now because, as shown in Listing 5.14, much of the syntax is identical to that of the SELECT statement. You must specify the table into which you wish to insert data and the columns for which you are passing data. You are not required to pass data for all columns. Any column for which you have a default value defined or that allows a NULL value can be omitted from the column list.

Notice that you can use a SELECT statement to query for the values you wish to insert into a table. In the Practical Guide section of this chapter, I will walk you through using an INSERT/SELECT statement to populate a table with data from another source.

Listing 5.14 INSERT statement syntax.
```
/* Insert Statement */
INSERT [INTO]{table_name | view_name}
            [(column_list)]
{DEFAULT VALUES | values_list | select_statement}
```

INSERT statements typically involve a single row (unless an INSERT/SELECT is used) and will place the data you specify into the table and update any indexes with the appropriate values. This is important. The more indexes you have on the table, the longer an insert will take. If you are performing a nightly insert process of many rows with little activity on the table otherwise, you might consider dropping the indexes prior to the insert operation and rebuilding them when you are finished. This method would result in better performance and would increase the integrity of your indexes.

On occasion, Microsoft SQL Server generates some index/insert-related error messages. By using INSERT/SELECT statements when inserting many records after dropping any existing indexes, you can reduce the possibility of this type of error. If you have not applied Service Pack 2 for Microsoft SQL Server 6.5, you should do so as soon as possible, because it contains some fixes that are index- and insert-related.

Listing 5.15 shows how to insert records into a table. I have created a record in the Authors table with my information as an example. This information is provided as an example only—it will not exist in your table unless you run this query on your table.

Listing 5.15 Sample insert into the Authors table.
```
/* Sample insert into Authors table (not formatted)*/
INSERT INTO authors (au_id, au_lname, au_fname, phone, address,
city, state, zip, contract) VALUES ('123-45-6789', 'Dalton',
'Patrick', '502 555-1234', '123 Main Street', 'Shepherdsville',
'KY', '40165', 1)

/* Same Query formatted in line */
INSERT INTO authors
   (au_id, au_lname, au_fname, phone, address, city, state, zip, contract)
VALUES
   ('123-45-6788', 'Dalton', 'Patrick', '502 555-1235', '456 Main Street',
   'Shepherdsville', 'KY', '40165', 1)

/* Formatted in column form */
INSERT INTO authors
VALUES
   ('123-45-6787',
   'Dalton',
   'Patrick',
   '502 555-1236',
   '789 Main Street',
   'Shepherdsville',
   'KY',
   '40165',
   1)

/* If you execute all 3 queries, 3 records will be inserted into the
Authors table. */
```

Notice that I omitted the column list from the third query. I can do this because I am supplying all the values in the exact order they are specified in the table schematic. I could have reordered the columns any way I wanted, as long as the column list and the values list are the same. You can pass string literals, variables, or explicit NULL values in an INSERT statement. INSERT statements return the number of rows affected to the client and to the global variable **@@rowcount**. You must select the row again to view the data after it has been inserted.

INSERT statements affect one table at a time and cannot be combined to add rows to multiple tables at once. You must issue a separate INSERT statement for each table you wish to modify.

Identity Columns

In Microsoft SQL Server the identity column generates a unique number for a record when that record is inserted into the table. This identity can be incremented or decremented by 1 or any other number and maintained automatically by Microsoft SQL Server. You do *not* supply a value for this column when you insert records. Should you wish to override the automatic generation of the next number for an identity column, you can set a property for the table called "identity insert." See Microsoft SQL Server Books Online for more information on the identity column and its uses.

Stored Procedures

Stored procedures can be used to optimize SQL code execution and the methods of communication between client applications and Microsoft SQL Server. Stored procedures can have parameters with specific data types passed to them for execution of SELECT, INSERT, UPDATE, and DELETE statements. Return codes and output parameters are also useful in developing client interfaces to Microsoft SQL Server. To use a stored procedure in your scripts, you would use the EXECUTE statement preceding the stored procedure and parameter list. See Chapter 6 for more information on the use and syntax of stored procedures.

Triggers

INSERT statements cause any defined insert trigger to be fired each time the INSERT statement is issued. If you are using INSERT/SELECT, you will place multiple rows into the virtual table that is "inserted." The inserted table is used for and by the triggers that are placed on a table. The schema of the inserted table matches the structure of the target table exactly and will contain any records that are to be inserted into the target table containing a trigger. A trigger fires one time for each insert, not one time for each row.

UPDATE Statements

UPDATE statements are only slightly different than INSERT statements in that they are set-based and can affect the entire table. UPDATE statements use a WHERE clause with the same restrictions and functionality as a SELECT statement to determine which rows of the table to affect. See Listing 5.16 for a sample UPDATE statement.

Listing 5.16 Sample UPDATE statement.

```
/* Change my phone number in the Authors table */
UPDATE authors
   SET phone = '502 555-4321'
 WHERE au_id = '123-45-6789'
```

In Listing 5.16, the SET statement involves one column. In SET statements involving multiple columns, the columns and values are delimited by commas. The WHERE clause determines what row or rows in the table will be changed by this query. If the WHERE clause evaluates to more than one row in the table, each matching row will be changed by the query.

If you omit the WHERE clause from an UPDATE statement, the entire table will be updated on the columns specified. This can be useful. For example, if you wish to place a price increase across the board for your product line, you would use an UPDATE statement with no WHERE clause on your inventory tables that contain a price column. However, be careful not to omit the WHERE clause unless you intend to.

The only way to safeguard against accidental modification of your data is to use transactional processing (even from query tools), then check that the modification was what you intended before committing your changes.

UPDATE statements support subqueries to return data for an update operation. Be careful to return one and only one value when using subqueries in an UPDATE statement. Multiple rows returned by a subquery will generate an error upon execution.

UPDATE statements utilize two virtual tables when a trigger is applied to a table for updates to records: the same "inserted" table the INSERT statement used and the "deleted" table Microsoft SQL Server will place the record prior to the changes into the deleted table and the new record with the applied changes into the inserted table. Triggers can then use the original data and the changes when carrying out their functions. Beware of multiple-row UPDATE statements in your triggers. You must cycle through each record in the inserted table and match it to a deleted record (typically with a cursor) in order to manipulate multiple rows inside a trigger.

The UPDATE statement is executed once for each table and affects a row one time during execution. The same row is never updated twice by a single UPDATE statement. You can use join conditions to optimize your UPDATE statements. Refer to Microsoft SQL Server Books Online for more information on the UPDATE statement.

DELETE Statements

This is the most dangerous statement in your SQL arsenal. You can remove a record from a table permanently with the DELETE statement. Like SELECT and UPDATE statements, DELETE statements use the WHERE clause. Once a record has been deleted, it no longer exists in a recoverable state in any location other than a backup of either the transaction log or database. I always use transactional processing when deleting records. If an error occurs in the execution of the command, I can roll back the deletion and restore my records.

If you omit the WHERE clause from your query, the entire table will be cleaned out; each and every record will be removed. This is a logged operation, so if your table has many rows, you will generate a lot of traffic in the transaction log. If you are trying to remove all the records in a table and no longer need to log the transactions, use the TRUNCATE TABLE statement instead of DELETE. TRUNCATE TABLE is not logged and gives you the same results much faster than DELETE. For more information on the TRUNCATE TABLE statement, see Microsoft SQL Server Books Online.

Both statements leave the schema of a table intact and do not drop existing indexes from the target table. Use this feature with great caution. At least once a month I get an email asking me to explain how to recover from a situation like this without affecting other tables and the relational integrity within a database. You *can* recover from it, but it takes time and disk space, and necessitates a sound backup of your data. See Listing 5.17 for a sample DELETE statement.

Listing 5.17 Sample DELETE statement.
```
/* Remove myself from the Authors table */
DELETE FROM authors
 WHERE au_id = '123-45-6789'
```

Batches

An *SQL script* is a file that contains one or more batches of SQL code that you wish to run against your server. SQL statements are inherently implied transactions and will be executed one by one unless you specify otherwise. A *batch* is a section or grouping of SQL statements that you wish to execute together and treat as a unit of execution. They are not transactions, although you can use transactional processing inside of batches to maintain the integrity of data.

Up to this point I have used single statements executed one at a time. If I wanted to insert, display, or modify data, I could create a text file with a batch in it and open that to run when needed. I create many of these for installation of systems, day-to-day reports, or troubleshooting.

A script can contain many batches. A batch is delimited by the word GO on a line by itself. See Listing 5.18 for a sample batch of SQL code. For clarity, I have used queries that you have already seen.

Listing 5.18   Sample batch script.

```
/* Sample batch to add remove and display authors */
/* Dated : 07/15/97                                */

/* Batch 1 - insert                                */
BEGIN
  BEGIN TRANSACTION

  INSERT INTO authors
  VALUES
    ('123-45-6789',
     'Dalton',
     'Patrick',
     '502 555-1234',
     '123 main street',
     'Shepherdsville',
     'KY',
     '40165',
     1)

  IF (@@error <> 0)
  BEGIN
/* We have a problem, Houston!                     */
/* Place any error handling here                   */
    ROLLBACK
  END
  ELSE
  BEGIN
    COMMIT TRANSACTION
  END

/* Display the record to verify insert             */
  SELECT *
    FROM authors
   WHERE au_id = '123-45-6789'
END
GO
```

```
/* Batch 2 - Update new record                    */
BEGIN
/* Declare any local variables                    */
  DECLARE @oldPhone CHAR(12), @newPhone CHAR(12)
  DECLARE @tmpString VARCHAR(255)

  BEGIN TRANSACTION
/* Get the current phone number                   */
  SELECT @oldPhone = phone
    FROM authors
   WHERE au_id = '123-45-6789'

/* Change the phone number and contract status    */
  UPDATE authors
     SET phone    = '502 555-4321',
         contract = 0
   WHERE au_id = '123-45-6789'

  IF (@@error <> 0)
  BEGIN
/* We have another problem, Houston!              */
/* Place any error handling here                  */
    SELECT @tmpString = 'Error performing update!'
    ROLLBACK
  END
  ELSE
  BEGIN
    COMMIT TRANSACTION
    SELECT @tmpString = 'Old Number : ' + @oldPhone + CHAR(10)
    SELECT @tmpString = @tmpString + 'New Number : ' + '505 555-4321'
  END

  PRINT @tmpString
END
GO
```

I have introduced some control-of-flow statements here with local and global variables to help illustrate just what can be done with batches. Local variables are only available inside a single batch, so be careful not to use them across batches without re-initializing them and assigning new values to them. The IF, BEGIN, and END statements help define the conditional nature and flow of my code. I do not have to use the BEGIN and END statements in all the areas, but I do it out of habit and for clarity. The only time I have to use BEGIN and END statements is after a conditional or looping statement that has more than one line of code.

I also used some string manipulation again to illustrate how to build a string inside your code. The **CHAR()** function evaluates *10* to be the new line character for me and places that in my string. The use of the global **@@error** variable to check for an error state is standard practice. **@@error** holds the return value for the previous SQL statement only. A value of zero means successful execution with no warnings or errors.

The GO statement at the end of the batch tells the server that I am finished and want this section of my code to be executed as a group. I have included some transactional processing in these batches to show how you can "undo" a modification or group of modifications in the event of an error on the server. For more information on batches, control-of-flow statements, and variables, see Microsoft SQL Server Books Online.

Cursors

This is the subject most SQL programmers master last. Using cursors requires intimate knowledge of your table structures and the ability to visualize what is happening with your code on the server. Cursors are very powerful and provide a great deal of flexibility.

Cursors are very versatile. From overnight processes to table-driven procedures and queries, their usefulness covers many areas of a production environment. Cursors allow you to manipulate data on a row-by-row basis rather than with result set-based queries. This method of processing is in most cases slower than result set-based queries are, and it typically takes up more memory on the server. Depending on your needs, you can implement cursors at the client or at the server. I will focus on the server-side cursors here since each client has different requirements.

Cursors require you to use local variables for each column value that you load into a cursor. They also require the definition and manipulation of the cursor as if it were a pointer definition. When you use cursors in your scripts or stored procedures, five keywords will play important roles: DECLARE, OPEN, FETCH, CLOSE, and DEALLOCATE. See Table 5.5 for the purpose of each of these keywords.

On any system that places structures into memory, it is a good idea to properly dispose of those structures. The CLOSE and DEALLOCATE statements should be issued when you have completed the manipulation of data. Leaving them open holds those resources and limits others' ability to perform tasks on the server.

Microsoft SQL Server Books Online contains a very good example of how to use a cursor to perform an update of the statistics. See Listing 5.19 for the code from

Word	Use
DECLARE	Defines the cursor through a SELECT statement that shows the columns and defines the rows that will be included in this cursor. A standard SELECT statement is used after the cursor name and type is given. Allocates memory for the cursor on the server. Must be supplied before an OPEN statement can be issued.
OPEN	Physically opens the cursor and gets the defined record set as it exists in the table at the time of the statement execution.
FETCH	Retrieves the specified record and places the column values for that row into local variables for further manipulation.
CLOSE	Closes the cursor and releases any locks that may have been placed automatically on any data pages due to the cursor definition.
DEALLOCATE	Removes the data structure from memory on the server. You may reopen a cursor after it has been closed, but not after deallocation. You must redefine the cursor once it has been released with this statement.

A cursor can also be created through SQL-passthrough and ODBC function calls. See Microsoft SQL Server Books Online for more details.

Table 5.5   Keywords for cursors.

Microsoft SQL Server Books Online. I have modified and formatted the code only slightly, in accordance with my preferences. Previously, there was no CLOSE statement at the end of the run, just a DEALLOCATE statement. While this will still run okay, it is against my practices to assume things will always work as advertised. Better safe than sorry.

In addition, I have added the SET statement to turn off the display of the number of rows affected by the query. This is strictly for personal preference and could be removed at no cost to the actual performance of the procedure.

Listing 5.19 introduces the syntax needed to create a stored procedure. We'll cover stored procedures in detail in the next chapter, but I just want to illustrate here that in some situations, code in Microsoft SQL Server Books Online can be both copied and pasted right into your server and be highly useful. If you would like to copy this procedure instead of the one in the online documentation, see the upd_all_stats.sql document on the CD-ROM accompanying this book.

Listing 5.19 Microsoft SQL Server Books Online code illustrating cursor uses.

```
CREATE PROCEDURE update_all_stats
AS
/* This procedure will run UPDATE STATISTICS against */
/* all user-defined tables within this database.     */

/* Turn display text off                             */
SET NOCOUNT ON

/* Declare local variables                           */
DECLARE @tablename varchar(30)
DECLARE @tablename_header varchar(75)

/* Declare the cursor                                */
DECLARE tnames_cursor CURSOR FOR
  SELECT name
    FROM sysobjects
   WHERE type = 'U'

OPEN tnames_cursor

FETCH NEXT FROM tnames_cursor INTO @tablename

WHILE (@@fetch_status <> -1)
BEGIN
  IF (@@fetch_status <> -2)
  BEGIN
    SELECT @tablename_header = "Updating : " + RTRIM(UPPER(@tablename))
    PRINT @tablename_header
    EXEC ("UPDATE STATISTICS " + @tablename)
  END
  FETCH NEXT FROM tnames_cursor INTO @tablename
END

PRINT " "
PRINT " "

SELECT @tablename_header = "*************  NO MORE TABLES" +
       "  *************"
PRINT @tablename_header

PRINT " "
PRINT "Statistics have been updated for all tables."

CLOSE tnames_cursor
DEALLOCATE tnames_cursor
GO
```

The key to using cursors well is understanding the FETCH statement. You can fetch rows in any direction as well as absolute positions into variables for manipulation. The global variable **@@fetch_status** tells you if there are no more rows to be returned and helps you control flow within the WHILE loop construct. Fetching NEXT or PREVIOUS inside of a loop allows you to move through the records one at a time and exit the loop when finished. Beware of missing that FETCH statement and variable check when writing your code. You can place yourself in a continuous loop with no exit point if you are careless and miss a logic check.

You can nest cursors inside other cursors to add to the feature and function of your code. Nesting cursors requires a bit of planning and some good naming conventions with regard to your local variables. Tackle nested cursors only after you have become comfortable with a standard cursor and can visualize what is being done on the server. You can add PRINT statements to your cursors to check the values of variables at different stages in the cursor.

The PRINT statement will only allow character data types, so use the CONVERT statement to change any noncharacter data to text before printing. You cannot use functions or expressions inside a PRINT statement. Load a local variable with the string you wish to print, then print that string.

Summary

- Comment your SQL code clearly.
- Specify the name of the columns you wish returned in your queries.
- Always use a WHERE clause in production-based queries.
- NOT is *not* optimizable!
- Joining tables requires $N = T - 1$ join conditions in the WHERE clause.
- Use the (NOLOCK) optimizer hint on highly active data for read-only queries.
- Use transactional processing when modifying data for safety and recoverability.
- Do *not* omit the WHERE clause from an SQL statement unless you intend to affect an entire table.
- Use PRINT statements inside your cursors to debug your code.
- Use Microsoft SQL Server Books Online to familiarize yourself with SQL and troubleshooting your queries. It is very useful—get in the habit!

Practical Guide To SQL

This section provides an example of the creation of SQL scripts for use with Microsoft SQL Server. We will change a column data type and move data from one table to another.

Schema Changes

SQL does not support the changing of a data type in a table directly. Some third-party tools accomplish this task through the generation of scripts that go through the process of creating a new table with the requested schema change and copying the data to the new table. DBArtisan is one such product, included on the CD-ROM, that does a good job of masking the user from the complexity of changing the data type of a column in an existing table with data already in it.

We'll go through the process step by step. For our example, we'll use the Authors table we have become so familiar with in this chapter.

The existing table schema for the Authors tables is in Table 5.1, shown earlier. We'll change the data structure so that the contract column will be an integer, and we'll change the size of the zip column to support the zip plus four address. This example should show you the concepts involved in changing your existing table structures in the future.

The steps are as follows:

1. Back up your data before running any structure modification routines.
2. Rename the objects to be modified.
3. Re-create the object with the intended data structure.
4. Put the old data into the new table while converting at the same time.
5. Clean up the environment so that all data integrity, view, and stored procedures will work with the new table.

Now let's take a closer look at each step.

Backing Up Data

Before running any structure modification routines, your first step should always be to back up your data to protect yourself from human or hardware error. There is a single script, table_change.sql, on the CD-ROM to put all the SQL into a single file. For clarity, I'll break that file up into sections in the Practical Guide.

Renaming Objects To Be Modified

The next step is to rename the existing table so that we may use the current name again within the database. Duplicate names within a database are not allowed. We accomplish this with the sp_rename stored procedure found in the master database. See Listing 5.20 for the syntax of sp_rename and its use in the table_change.sql script.

Note that this procedure, new to Version 6.5, allows you to rename a column. This is helpful in applying a good naming convention to existing data structures on your server. Be sure that all column references are changed to look for the new name as well, or you will be asking for broken code.

Listing 5.20   Sp_rename from the master database.

```
Syntax
EXEC sp_rename oldname, newname [, COLUMN | INDEX | OBJECT | USERDATATYPE]

Script
/* Change the name of the existing table           */
IF NOT EXISTS (SELECT *
                 FROM sysobjects
                WHERE id = OBJECT_ID('dbo.authorsbak')
                  AND sysstat & 0xf = 3)
BEGIN
/* Sysstat is the object type in the table         */
  EXEC sp_rename 'authors', 'authorsbak'
END
ELSE
BEGIN
/* Script will error due to existing backup        */
  PRINT 'Sorry, cannot run this script with out removing authorsbak.'
  RETURN
END
```

To avoid unintentionally overwriting data, it's a good idea to check if the backup table already exists in case there is data sitting out there already. If the table already exists, I simply return out of the script with a message.

Scripting Objects

The next step is to re-create the table with the new name. I have already placed the code into the script file for you. See Listing 5.21 for this section of code. If you have not created the scripts for each of your objects already, you can generate them again. Refer to Chapter 3 for details on how to generate an object's scripts through the Enterprise Manager.

Listing 5.21 Object re-creation section of script.

```
/* Create the new structure                            */
/* Drop authors if it already exists                   */
/* This will drop indexes as well                      */
IF EXISTS (SELECT *
             FROM sysobjects
             WHERE id = OBJECT_ID('dbo.authors')
               AND sysstat & 0xf = 3)
BEGIN
/* Sysstat is the object type in the table             */
  DROP TABLE dbo.authors
END
GO

/* Re-create authors with new columns                  */
CREATE TABLE dbo.authors (
   au_id    id              NOT NULL ,
   au_lname varchar (40)    NOT NULL ,
   au_fname varchar (20)    NOT NULL ,
   phone    char (12)       NOT NULL ,
   address  varchar (40)    NULL ,
   city     varchar (20)    NULL ,
   state    char (2)        NULL ,
   zip      char (10)       NULL ,
   contract INTEGER         NOT NULL
)
GO
```

Again, always check for the existence of an object before dropping it to keep errors from popping up. In the Create Table section, I have specified the structure changes for the new table. The zip column now has a width of 10 characters, and the contract column is now an integer. We could have used a TINYINT data type here, but to keep with the example we'll use an integer. The GO statement at the end of this batch will create the new object so that it exists before moving on in the script to the next batch.

Converting And Inserting Old Data

Now that the new schema structure exists, the next step is to get the old data into the new structure. You cannot reference an object before it has actually been created, so the previous GO statement will ensure that the INSERT/SELECT statement shown in Listing 5.22 will not generate an error. The INSERT/SELECT statement actually performs the task of converting the data and inserting the resulting changes into the new structure.

Listing 5.22 INSERT/SELECT section of script.
```
/* Get the old data from the bak table for new one   */
INSERT INTO authors
SELECT au_id,
       au_lname,
       au_fname,
       phone,
       address,
       city,
       state,
       zip + '-0000',
       CONVERT(INTEGER,contract)
  FROM authorsbak
```

In this statement, I have padded existing data to have four zeros at the end. This was not really needed, but it will help with the look of the old data when compared to the new data on reports or when passed back to a client application. We'll use the **CONVERT()** function to change the existing bit data type to an **integer** before inserting it into the new table. We'll use a single statement here to perform a block move of the records to the new table. We could also have used a cursor and moved and inserted each record one at a time. The cursor method would still get the job done, but it would require more code and error-checking and take longer to run.

Cleaning Up The Environment

Now we must clean up the environment to make sure all data integrity, views, and stored procedures will work with the new table. The renaming stored procedure changed the references for the constraints bound to this table so they pointed to the new backup table. We now need to add the lines of code to clean up and restore those items. See Listing 5.23 for the cleanup SQL code from the script file.

Listing 5.23 Clean up code from script file.

```
/* Re-apply the indexes to the new data        */
 CREATE INDEX aunmind ON authors(au_lname, au_fname)
GO

/* Check the data                              */
SELECT *
  FROM authors
GO

/* Handle the existing constraints             */
ALTER TABLE titleauthor
DROP
CONSTRAINT FK__titleauth__au_id__1312E04B
GO

/* Drop the backup table later after verified  */
DROP TABLE authorsbak
GO

/* Add new constraints                         */
ALTER TABLE authors
ADD
CONSTRAINT UPKCL_auidind PRIMARY KEY CLUSTERED ( au_id )

ALTER TABLE titleauthor
ADD
CONSTRAINT FK__titleauth__au_id__1312E04B FOREIGN KEY
  ( au_id ) REFERENCES authors ( au_id )
```

 **A Word On Constraints**

I have not covered constraints or views in this book yet, so some of the terms here may a bit confusing. We'll cover them in detail later in the book, but I need to mention them briefly here because of the nature of their function. Views will not be dropped when you drop an underlying table, so if they exist, they must be dropped and re-created in the cleanup section of this script. The Authors table does not have a view defined, so it does not have any code in the script. You would have to add the code to drop and re-create the view yourself.

Constraints, on the other hand, will not let you drop an object or create a new constraint if the existing name already exists in the database. So we must drop the constraints that point to this new structure before continuing on in the code and dropping the backup object. For clarity, return the new data to the client so that the modifications can be tested. You have modified the column in an existing structure without losing any data or functionality in your system. Should you want to restore the old structure, that script file appears on the CD-ROM as well; the table_restore.sql file will return the Authors table to its original state.

And now, once again, that helpful reminder: *Back up the master database!*

Chapter 6

Stored Procedures

- Parsing A String
- Redundant Code
- Reduced Network Traffic
- Calling Procedures Within Procedures

Administrator's Notes...

Chapter 6

Helping you create a well-rounded production server has been the primary focus of this book. We have covered the installation, configuration, and precautionary steps to building a good foundation for your production server. Chapter 5 focused on SQL and writing scripts; this chapter will show you how to increase your SQL skills and apply those skills to stored procedures.

Stored procedures are supported in one form or another on most major database platforms. Microsoft SQL Server supports stored procedures in many forms. We'll cover custom procedures, system procedures, remote procedures, and external stored procedures at some length.

While the last chapter was not a comprehensive tutorial for writing SQL scripts, it highlighted some of the crucial features in writing good SQL. This chapter will take the same path, explaining the important points and pointing you to sources of more information about each of the topics. Because of space limitations, I won't attempt to explain every detail of SQL or stored procedures. Instead, I'll cover the issues that arise most often in news groups and in production environments.

Many of the procedures and related topics covered in this chapter are on the certification exam for both Microsoft SQL Server Administration, and Database Design and Implementation. I strongly recommend studying each topic in this chapter before taking either exam.

Consistent Data Manipulation

Programmers have struggled for years to provide a bulletproof method of manipulating data. This endeavor has brought about many changes in the way applications are written and designed. While each application takes a slightly different approach to managing data, one methodology remains constant for all applications: Use a consistent procedure for access, additions, modifications, or deletion of data. You will have far fewer problems in the long run.

Enter Stored Procedures

Adopting a standard method of data access is not difficult. Each company may choose a different path, but all have the same end result in mind. Use one way to do things, with as few "special-case" changes as possible. Following the same procedures for inserting data or error checking across all your code ensures that anyone looking at the code can easily figure out what must be done to add data to one of your systems. As long as every programmer follows the guidelines that you have established for that particular system, he or she will not create problems for other applications or processes running in your production environment.

Most of the standards presented here are gleaned from production environments I've encountered. I am, of course, not the absolute authority on your system, nor is anyone else that does not have a thorough understanding of your specific needs. Take what I have to say here with a grain of salt. Apply what will work for you and put the remaining things into memory for later consumption. After working with these for a while and seeing what standards can do for you, you might find that you can come up with standards and methodologies that meet your needs precisely.

Establishing Standards

At this point you're probably asking, "What standards are you talking about?" Any standard you can come up with will probably work, and each enterprise has unique requirements that would cause one that I might suggest here to be invalid. I will offer a set of standards here; however, you must decide for yourself whether to adopt them in whole or in part.

I use standard naming conventions with database objects, just as I do with programs that I write. The naming conventions help me recall the function or purpose of the object if I have not looked at it for a few months. I also use standard methods for manipulating data. Using a certain method to edit data ensures that consistent client manipulation is used across all programs.

Getting Data

When a client application needs data, whether in a true client/server environment or in a multitiered system, the act of reading data usually is different than the act of making changes or additions. Therefore, for getting data to client applications I use a stored procedure.

These procedures usually are called something like CP_GETMESSAGE, CP_GETORDER, or CP_LOOKUPRECORD. The CP is used for a few reasons. First, in an alpha list, these names would show up before any system or external procedures, since these latter procedures are prefaced with SP and XP, respectively. Second, each of these objects, along with many others, exists in many system tables on your server. You can distinguish easily between a stored procedure and another object by looking at the prefix.

It is well worth the time to develop a good naming convention for all your server objects. Having a standard prefix for each object in your system and publishing them among all programmers will avoid any potential confusion and can be a lifesaver. In a multiple-programmer environment, consistent naming conventions are practically a requirement. See Table 6.1 for some sample naming conventions. Keep in mind that these are only suggestions; they should be thought out thoroughly before being adopted in any environment. If your enterprise has an existing naming convention in use, try to mirror that as closely as possible to reduce confusion.

Another benefit of using stored procedures to transfer data between client applications is the security associated with stored procedures. Users or groups of users can be granted permission to run only those procedures to which they need access. If no permission is granted, the data is protected from access. I rarely recommend giving users direct access to query tables or views on production systems. Because ad hoc query tools make maintaining data security much more difficult, using stored procedures as a method of accessing data is invaluable. If a user is only allowed to call a procedure to read the data, you are protected from any accidental user modification.

For performance reasons, I typically do not allow general queries to run against tables. If I write the queries that are getting the data from the server and allow others to run that code through stored procedures, I am ensuring that no long-running or system-resource-killing query can be introduced while production is running its queries.

Object	Prefix
Table	TBL_
View	VIEW_
Clustered Index	CIDX_
Unique Index	UIDX_
Index	IDX_
Cursor	CUR_
Local Variables	TMP_
Stored Procedure	CP_
Insert Trigger	INST_
Update Trigger	UPDT_
Delete Trigger	DELT_
Rules	RUL_
Defaults	DEF_

Table 6.1 Some server naming conventions.

I can better spend my time tuning the queries for speed and maintaining data integrity. Most client applications that use stored procedures to get data need to know only the name of the procedure and the data type of any parameters required to execute the procedure. If I change the underlying code of the procedure without changing the parameter list or names, I can update and improve my stored procedures without having to rebuild any client applications. Improving performance without changing or affecting client code is an important reason to use stored procedures instead of standard SQL in a client/server environment.

Modifying Data

All systems must have the ability to add, change, or delete records on an ongoing basis. Stored procedures are valuable in this area as well. They provide two types of security: the additional security of not allowing anyone who doesn't have permission to run a particular procedure to modify data, and the built-in integrity of each client utilizing the same method to perform any modification task.

In addition, stored procedures allow you to mask from your client applications the complexity of the underlying data structure. If a procedure requires derived or table-driven data to complete a task, you can look up what is needed in your stored procedures without the user ever having to know what is happening. Concealing the complexity of your data structure from the user and client application has many benefits. It typically reduces the amount of traffic between the client and the server and gives you much more control over potential locking issues.

Modular Programming

Stored procedures not only provide the client developer with a standard method of dealing with the server, that they also give the SQL programmer the ability to write modular code. For instance, in many systems you will need to develop a standard set of string functions. The method of parsing tokens from a string could be written as a stored procedure and called from both the client applications and other stored procedures.

By analyzing your existing stored procedures or SQL statements and looking for redundant code that performs the same task in many places, you usually can find candidates for utility functions. In this situation, consider writing a stored procedure that performs the task with as few parameters as possible while returning a standard response. Once you have created the new procedure, you can easily replace the redundant code with a call to the new procedure.

Using stored procedures can greatly reduce the amount of actual SQL code you have to write because you can call other stored procedures to perform like functions. This feature appears in all popular programming languages and allows for more reliable, error-free SQL code.

Once a procedure is written and tested, you can call that procedure from many places and it will work the same way in each case. If you need to enhance the feature set of the stored procedure, you make the change in one place, debug the change, and you're done. In addition, stored procedures can cut the development cycle of your applications dramatically. A library of standard stored procedures can be developed once and reused many times by many different client applications.

Reduced Client Processing

There is one feature of stored procedures that even hard-core, talented client programmers often miss. In earlier applications, the programmer was responsible for determining all the related and supporting code for modifying data. Primary keys, lookup tables, and calculations were maintained by the applications individually. With server-side processing becoming more a requirement, stored procedures can reduce the amount of client-side processing by looking up data and maintaining key values and internal integrity.

Server-based stored procedures allow you to develop "thin" client applications—applications concerned only with displaying data in a manner that meets the user's needs. Very little data logic is needed in client applications with strong server-side processing. With the speed and power of database servers today, we can offload the time-consuming tasks to the server, while letting the users perform the tasks.

Network Traffic

Network bandwidth is typically in the 10- to 100-megabit range in most enterprises. Unless you are developing an application for modem dial-up connection to the database, you will have plenty of throughput to support your applications. If you do support modems or Internet access to your applications, the amount of traffic that goes across the pipe is very important.

If we analyze the amount of characters that must be sent to a server for a typical SELECT statement, you will begin to see the difference that a stored procedure can make. See Listing 6.1 for a standard SELECT statement of 206 characters, including formatting, and approximately 170 without spaces.

Listing 6.1 Regular SELECT statement.
```
/* Phone list in alpha order (CA) */
SELECT 'Name' = UPPER(SUBSTRING(au_fname,1,1)) + '. ' + SUBSTRING(au_lname,1, 15),
       'Phone' = '(' + SUBSTRING(phone,1,3) + ') ' + SUBSTRING(phone,5,8)
  FROM authors
 WHERE state = 'CA'
 ORDER BY au_lname

/* Same data returned through a call to a stored procedure. */
EXEC CP_GETAUTHORLIST 'CA'
```

The last line is a call to a stored procedure. EXEC tells SQL Server to execute the procedure named CP_GETAUTHORLIST with a parameter of the two-character state code for added flexibility. I can call the stored procedure in this manner and allow it to return any state I wish to specify as the parameter in the call. Although the result list for these queries would be identical, by using the stored procedure, I would be passing only 26 characters across the network.

If this query is called by 50 different client applications 20 times per day, I would see a reduction of 180,000 characters in character-based traffic on my network. Although you would still have the same traffic volume return from each query, you would see reduced traffic with regard to the actual request.

Now if we add the modem or even a full T1 bandwidth to the equation, you can begin to see the impact. Remember that a full T1 line can reach a speed of just over 1 megabit per second and that even a fast modem can reach only 28,800 bps. In tested dial-in modem access, by using stored procedures and a well-designed client application, I have seen client/server applications attain speeds almost equal to those of a regular network application.

Keep in mind that to get that level of performance across a modem, you must keep network traffic to a minimum. The benefit of this kind of application is that it responds very well over your network compared to fat client applications that pay no attention to how much traffic is passed between client and server.

Calling A Stored Procedure

As Listing 6.1 shows, a call to a stored procedure is not complicated. The EXECUTE, or EXEC, statement followed by the stored procedure name and any parameters is about all you need. You can return a result set or a single record with a stored procedure. The beauty of stored procedures is that the code is hidden from the client application. The client developer does not need to know much about SQL to use them in his or her applications.

For more information on the many uses of the EXECUTE statement, see Microsoft SQL Server Books Online. EXECUTE can be used in many ways to create powerful SQL scripts and stored procedures.

Stored procedures can be nested and call other stored procedures to return the results to the client. In fact, you can even use recursion in a controlled environment to make your code more useful. I have developed stored procedures called with no parameters that literally processed hundreds of records in many separate tables to return a single value to the client. Cursors and control-of-flow language features can be used in your stored procedures for added functionality.

Query Optimizer

Microsoft SQL Server uses a cost-based query analyzer that determines the best method to return the data that you request to the client. Indexes, join conditions, WHERE clauses, ORDER BY statements, and optimizer hints all come into play when determining the best way to access the data. You should look for any known resource-intensive item in your queries to help reduce the amount of time it takes for the Query Optimizer to determine the best plan for retrieving data. Whenever possible, you should avoid the following items when writing queries:

- Large results sets
- IN, NOT IN, and OR queries
- <> (not equal)
- Row aggregate functions such as SUM, AVG, MAX, etc.
- Local variables, expressions, or data conversions in WHERE clauses
- Highly nonunique WHERE clauses or no WHERE clause at all
- Complex views with GROUP BY or ORDER BY statements

Remember that the Query Optimizer will look at the current state of the indexes and data distribution to choose the best plan possible. If you do not keep the statistics and integrity of your data current by periodically rebuilding indexes and updating statistics, the Optimizer will recognize this and create worktables even when there are indexes that should have been used to return the data faster.

Query Plan

For each query, SQL Server creates a query plan that includes all the information required to return the data effectively to the client. If the query is a stored procedure, this plan is stored in cache so that it can be used again when needed.

Understand that when stored in cache, these plans can be accessed by only one user at a time. If two users request the same query plan for a stored procedure, SQL Server will create a new, second plan and store it in cache as well. This second query plan might even be different than the first due to the integrity of the available indexes and data at the time of execution.

To better understand how query plans work, let's look at the steps in executing a query. When your SQL statement is first loaded by SQL Server, it performs the following steps:

1. Parses the raw SQL code to determine if there is any syntax error to be reported.
2. Checks for alias references in the FROM clause for use later in the process and checks for valid object references (SELECT LIST, FROM, and WHERE clauses).
3. Generates the query plan based on available data statistics and indexes (sometimes referred to as the "optimization step").
4. Compiles the query and places it into cache if it is a stored procedure.
5. Executes the compiled query plan and returns the data to the client.

Once the query plan for a procedure is cached, it will remain in cache until it is pushed out by other, more active procedures. If a procedure's query plan is pushed out of the cache on SQL Server, it will be recompiled and a new query plan created the next time it is called. If the procedure is in cache, the user requesting data through a stored procedure must have the parameters used in the procedure checked and then have the plan reexecuted to return data. This reduces the amount of overhead on the server for the process of returning data to the clients. In many situations where a standard set of procedures is used and constantly cached, the users will see marked improvement over raw SQL code execution.

Stored procedures also enhance performance with regard to object references. In raw SQL, every time a query is executed, each object reference is checked when it is passed to the server. With stored procedures, the objects are checked when compiled, and stored in the query plan. Each subsequent call to the stored procedure does not trigger the object reference check on the server, thus reducing overhead.

In addition, permissions are handled differently with stored procedures. When a stored procedure is written, the security context of the author is used. Access to all objects is based on the author's permissions. Once the stored procedure is created, anyone calling the procedure assumes the permissions of the author inside the stored procedure. This way, the users of a stored procedure can be granted permission to run a procedure, but not to do anything else to the data. Users are not able to see or change the code within a stored procedure—so the underlying objects and data are protected—and users are allowed to perform only the tasks specified. Stored procedures can greatly reduce the occurrence of security problems on your SQL server.

Parameters

The maximum number of parameters you can use in a stored procedure is 255. I have never written a stored procedure that even came close to this limit, but I imagine someone will test this at some point. When possible, I limit the number of parameters by using table lookups internally in the stored procedure to get the data I need. This reduces the amount of parameter traffic on the network and keeps the client application as "thin" as possible. Parameters are data type-specific and should be defined to the correct size and precision as needed inside the stored procedure. You can use the CONVERT() function to change any data types once they are passed into a stored procedure.

You also can use output parameters with stored procedures. These parameters are passed into the procedure marked as output parameters, modified internally within the stored procedure, and returned in the modified state to the client. This can be useful with complex client applications that require multiple return values from a stored procedure as well as with result sets.

Variables

Another great feature of stored procedures is the ability to use local variables and access-to-server global variables. You can create as many local variables as needed with stored procedures, providing you have enough memory on the server set aside for Microsoft SQL Server. Local variables are designated by the @ sign, preceding the variable name. You must declare all variables before they are referenced and use data type-specific declarations so that Microsoft SQL Server knows how to use the variables.

To be consistent, I typically use the tmp lowercase prefix when naming my variables. With this method, I can distinguish easily between variables and column names. For a list of global variables you can access from within your SQL code, see Table 6.2. Note that this is a partial list of variables. See Microsoft SQL Server Books Online for complete information on variables. Global variables have an @@ prefix to distinguish them from local variables.

Many of the variables listed in Table 6.2 can be combined with queries against the system tables in Microsoft SQL Server to create an intelligent set of stored procedures. I

Variable	Use Or Value
@@CONNECTIONS	Contains the number of logins since SQL Server was last started.
@@CPU_BUSY	Holds the amount of time the server has spent executing SQL statements since the last time SQL Server was started. (Data is in ticks, which are one three-hundredth of a second, or 3.33 milliseconds.)
@@ERROR	Holds the return code or status of the last SQL statement executed on SQL Server. This variable is maintained on a per-connection basis. (A value of 0 means success.)
@@FETCH_STATUS	Contains the result of a cursor's FETCH command. This will be 0 if the FETCH is successful, −1 if the FETCH failed or the row was beyond the record set for the cursor, and −2 if the row fetched is missing.
@@IDENTITY	Holds the value of the last identity value generated by an INSERT statement. Identity values are generated automatically by SQL Server for each table that has an identity column and will be unique for each record in that table. This value is maintained on a connection-by-connection basis.
@@IDLE	Specifies the amount of time, in ticks, that SQL Server has been idle since it was last started.
@@IO_BUSY	Contains the time, in ticks, that SQL Server has spent performing input and output operations since it was last started.
@@MAX_CONNECTIONS	Holds the maximum count of simultaneous connections that can be made with the server at one time. This is not the amount of client licenses that you have purchased. One client can acquire more than one connection in a multithreaded application.
@@NESTLEVEL	Holds the current count of how many levels you are nested within your stored procedures. The maximum nesting level is 16. If you exceed the maximum level, your transaction will be terminated.
@@PROCID	Holds the stored procedure ID of the current stored procedure.

(continued)

Table 6.2   Global variables available on Microsoft SQL Server.

(continued)

Variable	Use Or Value
@@ROWCOUNT	Specifies the number of rows affected by the immediately previous statement. Set to 0 (zero) for statements such as IF or control-of-flow statements. Caution should be taken when relying on this variable for the number of rows returned by queries. Local variable assignments can set this value to another number and mislead you.
@@SPID	Holds the server process ID number of the current procedure. This value can be used for looking up information about a stored procedure in the SYSPROCESSES system table.
@@TRANCOUNT	Specifies the number of currently active transactions for the current user. This value is maintained on a connection-by-connection basis.

Table 6.2 Global variables available on Microsoft SQL Server.

often find that to create a stored procedure to perform a highly complex task, using variables can save me hours of programming. Spend some time in Microsoft SQL Server Books Online and view some of the sample code to become more familiar with how local and global variables can be used in your code.

You cannot create a global variable on Microsoft SQL Server programmatically. We have discussed using tables on your server to store parameters or even runtime variables that must be shared between client connections to simulate server-based global variables (see the section on application-level parameters in Chapter 3).

NT Server Registry

When you require server-based global variables that are static with regard to the server operation, you have one other option: the Windows NT Registry on the server itself. This location is a static repository many client applications use on each local machine for startup and runtime parameters. I recommend this option only for experienced programmers with a good knowledge of the Windows NT Registry and how it works.

You can make calls to the Windows NT Registry by using external stored procedures available with Microsoft SQL Server (see Table 6.3). If you use the Windows NT Registry on your server, you should adopt a very strict standard of writing, reading, and deleting these values so that you do not leave a lot of stray entries floating around in the Registry.

Name	Function
XP_REGREAD	Reads a key value or data from the Registry.
XP_REGWRITE	Writes a key value or data to the Registry.
XP_REGDELETEVALUE	Removes a key from the Registry.

Table 6.3 External procedures used to access the Windows NT Registry.

Note that the procedures listed in Table 6.3 are not documented in Microsoft SQL Server Books Online. You can pick up bits and pieces and the syntax from looking up XP_REGWRITE and finding a related topic with some examples.

As with any other application, adopting a standard of using a specific key value structure is a good idea when using these procedures. Typically, the directory structure that falls under the MSSQLSERVER key in the Registry is where you should place all your subkeys. Use well-thought-out, descriptive names for your keys. This makes finding your custom Registry entries with an application like REGEDT32.EXE easier. See Listing 6.2 for an example of how to add a key, read the new key, and remove the key within an SQL script or stored procedure.

Listing 6.2 External procedures for accessing the Windows NT Registry.

```
/* Sample Registry script    */

SET NOCOUNT ON

/* Local variables           */
DECLARE @tmpAuthorID    VARCHAR(11)
DECLARE @tmpMichiganID VARCHAR(11)

/* Get a Michigan author     */
SELECT @tmpAuthorID = au_id
  FROM authors
 WHERE state = 'MI'

/* Write to Registry         */
EXEC master.dbo.xp_regwrite 'HKEY_LOCAL_MACHINE',
    'SOFTWARE\Microsoft\MSSQLServer\Global_Keys',
    'Michigan',
    'REG_SZ',
    @tmpAuthorID

/* Return the Registry value */
EXEC master.dbo.xp_regread 'HKEY_LOCAL_MACHINE',
```

```
        'SOFTWARE\Microsoft\MSSQLServer\Global_Keys',
        'Michigan',
        @param = @tmpMichiganID OUTPUT

/* Display the Registry value  */
PRINT @tmpMichiganID

/* Remove the key              */
EXEC master.dbo.xp_regdeletevalue 'HKEY_LOCAL_MACHINE',
     'SOFTWARE\Microsoft\MSSQLServer\Global_Keys',
     'Michigan'
```

Notice that each EXEC line in Listing 6.2 references the stored procedure with the database, owner, and name of the stored procedure separated by periods. This allows you to be in the Pubs database and run a procedure stored in another database without changing the current active database.

Each procedure lists the sample syntax to perform the basic tasks of getting things into and out of the Registry. You can use these samples as a template and modify them for your environment by replacing the key values and the data types of the keys on a case-by-case basis. The listing is provided only to illustrate the use of these stored procedures to create pseudo-global variables on your server. This method can be used to store many things, such as server-error state or the steps of a long-running process.

The only real drawback to using the Registry in this manner is that you are creating additional disk I/O for each call. Also keep in mind that these procedures are not documented well at all in Microsoft SQL Server Books Online.

Maintenance

Stored procedures allow you to centralize your code management. You can easily maintain and/or debug your SQL code on the server and be sure that all the clients that call the stored procedures are not going to run into SQL errors or introduce problems in the server environment. I typically print out each of my stored procedures and keep a hard copy around for developers to use when writing client applications. I can change to a stored procedure in one location to provide additional features to all the clients that use my stored procedures.

Periodically you should recompile each of your stored procedures to ensure that the underlying data structure and query plans are all up to date and error-free. You cannot recompile or change a procedure that is in use.

When performing maintenance on your procedures, you might occasionally see an error message saying that you cannot change a stored procedure that is in use. Do not be alarmed—this is normal. To solve this problem, make sure you are not the one with the procedure loaded in another window, and try to recompile the procedure again. Users do not have to disconnect for you to replace or rebuild a stored procedure. However, they must not be accessing it at the time of recompile. Remember that users load the procedure into cache the first time it is called and use the cached information from that point on until it is purged from cache or recompiled with the RECOMPILE option.

Finally, as far as procedure maintenance goes, I usually create a master script file containing all my procedures for a database, and then back it up on tape or disk. This allows me to re-create all my stored procedures in a single step on the same server, or on another server should the need arise. The only prerequisite to running the master script is that all the underlying dependent objects that are referenced in the procedures exist prior to running the script.

Return Codes

Stored procedures can return result sets and return codes to signal the success or failure of the execution. The RETURN statement terminates the execution of a stored procedure and optionally returns an integer value that can be checked by the client application or another stored procedure.

Another useful method of returning values to calling procedures or clients is the use of output parameters. You can specify that a particular parameter in a stored procedure is an output parameter, then modify the value of the parameter passed into the stored procedure with SQL statements. The resulting changes can be viewed by the calling procedure. This is a powerful and often underutilized feature. For more information on return status and output parameters, check Microsoft SQL Server Books Online.

Additional Rules

Following are some additional rules to keep in mind when creating stored procedures:

- CREATE PROCEDURE statements cannot be combined with other SQL statements in a single batch. This means that you cannot use multiple batches inside a stored procedure (only one GO statement is allowed per stored procedure).

- The CREATE PROCEDURE definition can include any number and type of SQL statements, with the exception of the CREATE VIEW, TRIGGER, DEFAULT, PROCEDURE, and CREATE RULE statements.

- Other database objects can be created within a stored procedure. However, you can reference these new objects only if they are created before being referenced. (Take care that when doing this you do not generate errors in the stored procedure during execution.)

- Within a stored procedure, you cannot create an object, later drop it, and then create a new object with the same name. The compiler will return an Object Already Exists error.

- You can reference temporary tables from within your stored procedures.

- If you execute a procedure that calls another procedure, the called procedure can access all objects except temporary tables created by the first procedure.

- If you create a private temporary table inside a procedure, the temporary table exists only for the purposes of the procedure and will be released when you exit the stored procedure.

- The maximum number of local and global variables in a procedure is limited by the available memory on your server (not on the client).

- You can create private and public temporary stored procedures as you do temporary tables by adding # and ## prefixes to the stored procedure name.

Nesting And Recursion

Microsoft SQL Server supports nesting calls of stored procedures to a maximum of 16 levels. Say, for instance, you have a transaction that calls stored procedures, which will internally call other stored procedures, and so on. If the transaction exceeds 16 levels, Microsoft SQL Server will terminate the process and return an error (code 217). This is not usually a problem; most systems I have worked with nest procedures only three to six levels deep on average. However, be aware of this limitation when creating stored procedures and making internal calls to other procedures.

Transact-SQL supports recursion in a controlled manner. You are limited to the 16-level rule for stored procedures. In most situations, recursion can be used to process small amounts of hierarchical data in order to reduce the amount of code you must write.

I recommend using temporary tables or join conditions to reduce the recursion to a minimum. Recursive calls typically need to run many times to be effective and may cause the nesting level error to crop up in unexpected situations.

 Plan the use recursion with caution to make sure you won't violate the 16-level nesting rule.

System Stored Procedures

Microsoft SQL Server ships with literally hundreds of procedures designed to make your life as a DBA more pleasant. Many of these procedures perform specific tasks on your server that help in day-to-day server management. These stored procedures are located in the master database and can be viewed in the Enterprise Manager.

To view the list of procedures, go to the tree view of your server in the Enterprise Manager and click on the plus sign next to your server. Repeat the process of clicking on the plus signs for the databases folder and for the master database. Next, click the plus sign again to open the objects, and then open the stored procedures folder. Double-click on any of the procedures in the list to open the Manage Stored Procedures window (see Figure 6.1).

You will notice that each of the stored procedures in the database can be accessed through the window's drop-down list. This allows you to check stored procedures one by one and compare the code in each procedure. By selecting <new> from the list, you can create a new stored procedure in this window as well. The green Play button compiles the stored procedure and checks it for any errors. If the compiler finds an error, it gives you a line number or a close reference to help you find the problem in the SQL code.

All procedures for each database are stored this way. You can also create a stored procedure in the model database so that each time a new user database is created, it will contain the stored procedures you have defined. In addition, you can print each of the procedures through this window by selecting the Printer button on the title bar.

Each of the procedures on the server has a CREATE PROCEDURE statement and GO statement that delimit the bounds of the stored procedure. If you scroll to the bottom of the list, you will also see any permissions granted for this procedure. This can help you determine who can run a procedure.

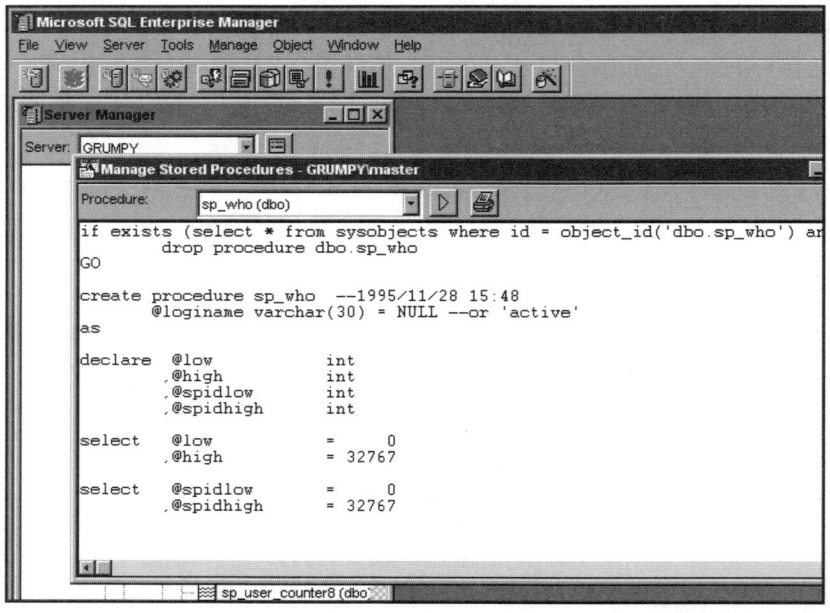

Manage Stored Procedures window.
Figure 6.1

All of the code within a stored procedure is written in standard SQL control-of-flow statements. Stored procedure code appears in this easy-to-read format unless you encrypt it with the WITH ENCRYPTION option in the CREATE PROCEDURE statement. (See Microsoft SQL Server Books Online for more on encrypting stored procedures. The set of procedures that ships with Microsoft SQL Server can also serve as templates for future stored procedures.)

You can even modify the behavior of existing stored procedures to better suit your environment. I *strongly* recommend making a copy of an existing system procedure and modifying the copy. Call the new copy to perform your tasks and leave the original intact so that you do not accidently change a procedure that the server uses and break some critical process.

Many of the system procedures in the master database are covered on Microsoft certification exams; therefore any DBA who works with Microsoft SQL Server should be familiar with those procedures. See Table 6.4 for a list of the most important system procedures and their uses. While space limitations prevent me from covering

Name	Use
SP_ADDEXTENDEDPROC	Adds the name and dynamic link library of an extended stored procedure to SQL Server's SYSOBJECTS and SYSCOMMENTS tables. Once registered with SQL Server, an external procedure can be called from within your SQL code and used to extend the functionality of your server. Only the system administrator can run this procedure.
SP_ADDLOGIN	Adds a network user to the list of users who can log in to SQL Server and gain connection to the server. This procedure does not grant any user permission to data. Only the system administrator can run this procedure.
SP_ADDMESSAGE	Can be used to add user-defined messages to your server. (See Listing 3.1 in Chapter 3 for an example of how SP_ADDMESSAGE can be used.)
SP_ADDUSER	Adds a user to the database and allows access to data. This procedure does not allow the user to connect to the server. See SP_ADDLOGIN for granting server access.
SP_CHANGEDBOWNER	Changes the owner of a database in the event the user is no longer needed in that capacity. Only the system administrator can run this procedure.
SP_CHANGEGROUP	Changes the group membership of a user within a database. A user is allowed to be a member of only two groups in SQL Server—the Public group plus one other. To get around this restriction, you can change group memberships programmatically, providing you have permission within the database to do so.
SP_COLUMNS	Displays the columns of a single object, either a table or a view that can be queried in the current environment. This procedure is useful in determining what columns are available for a custom query builder or a user-definable query tool.
SP_CONFIGURE	Displays or changes current SQL Server options. Note that some options are dynamic and can be changed without stopping and starting the MSSQLServer service, while others are static and can be changed only by restarting the SQL Server.

(continued)

Table 6.4   System stored procedures.

(continued)

Name	Use
SP_DATABASES	Lists any databases available through your connection with SQL Server.
SP_DBOPTION	Displays or changes the options for a database on SQL Server.
SP_DROPEXTENDEDPROC	Removes the reference to an external procedure from the server. Only the system administrator can run this procedure.
SP_HELP	Reports information about any database object in the SYSOBJECTS table. A DBA must become thoroughly familiar with this procedure above all others. Along with other Help stored procedures, a lot of information can be gleaned from SP_HELP.
SP_HELPDB	Returns information about a single database or all databases on SQL Server.
SP_HELPDEVICE	Displays information about a single device or all devices on your server. Useful for third-party applications installed on your server without proper device documentation.
SP_HELPROTECT	Reports security and permissions by database object or by user.
SP_HELPSQL	Can be used to return the proper syntax for an SQL statement.
SP_HELPSTARTUP	Displays a listing of startup procedures for the server.
SP_HELPTASK	Provides useful information about a scheduled task on SQL Server.
SP_LOCK	Reports information about locks on the server. Individual process ID numbers can be passed to this procedure for more detailed lock reporting.
SP_MONITOR	Displays 13 different server diagnostic variables used to track statistics on the life cycle of the current session on SQL Server.
SP_RECOMPILE	Flags a table in such a way that all triggers and stored procedures associated with that table are recompiled the next time they are requested by a user. This is a useful tool for rebuilding the query plans of stored procedures after any index maintenance on a table has been performed.

(continued)

Table 6.4   System stored procedures.

(continued)

Name	Use
SP_RENAME	Changes the name of a user-defined object in a database.
SP_SPACEUSED	Can be used to compute and display the current usage of space by a table or an entire database on SQL Server.
SP_STATISTICS	Returns a list of all indexes on a particular table in a database.
SP_STORED_PROCEDURES	Displays a list of all current-environment stored procedures, with information about the owner, names, and database.
SP_TABLES	Returns a list of all database objects and their type that can be queried in the FROM clause of an SQL statement.
SP_WHO	Reports information about all current database users and their processes.

Table 6.4 System stored procedures.

all 240 stored procedures, be sure to throughly review the list in Table 6.4 before taking the Microsoft SQL certification exam. Each of these procedures has related procedures that are covered in depth in Microsoft SQL Server Books Online.

Most of these procedures can be combined into a server management report stored procedure or used in nightly scheduled tasks to report on the state of your server. Create a proactively managed server with messages and, in some cases, even pages to warn yourself of any potential problems before they become critical.

All the procedures listed in Table 6.4 are valuable to your enterprise in one form or another. You might find that one or a few of these procedures are almost exactly what you need—but not quite. In that case, make a copy of the procedure and edit it to perform the way you need. I do not recommend changing existing server-supplied stored procedures.

Custom Stored Procedures

You can create your own custom stored procedures based on the needs of your particular environment. Almost any SQL script can be modified to run as a stored procedure. As mentioned earlier, to select queries as candidates for stored procedures, look for redundant SQL code. If you are running the same queries repeatedly, you should consider using stored procedures to improve the performance and portability of your queries.

Listing 6.3 shows a query for returning a list of authors based on a match of a string passed to the procedure as a parameter. I check to see if the parameter is NULL; if so, the entire table contents will be returned to the client rather than just the specified record. In some situations you might want to let the user know that some kind of value must be supplied for the parameter by making the appropriate changes to the conditional check for good data. I have used the LIKE operator instead of the equal sign operator to allow a partial author ID number to be passed in. If I only wanted to allow for exact matches and desired a bit more speed in the query, I could replace LIKE with an equal sign (=).

Listing 6.3   CP_GETAUTHORS example.

```
CREATE PROCEDURE cp_getAuthors @tmpString    VARCHAR(12) = NULL,
                               @tmpSearchBY VARCHAR(10) = 'ID'
AS
/* Check for good data coming in              */
IF (@tmpString = NULL)
BEGIN
/* Return all rows for this example           */
  SELECT @tmpString = '%'
END
ELSE
BEGIN
/* Add wildcard to string for LIKE assignment */
  SELECT @tmpString = @tmpString + '%'
END

/* Check search criteria param for where clause */
IF (@tmpSearchBY = 'ID')
BEGIN
/* Get the row or rows                         */
  SELECT 'ID'         = au_id,
         'Last Name'  = au_lname,
         'First Name' = au_fname,
         'Phone'      = phone
    FROM authors
   WHERE au_id LIKE @tmpString
END
ELSE
BEGIN
  IF (@tmpSearchBY = 'STATE')
  BEGIN
```

```
/* Get the row or rows                              */
    SELECT 'ID'         = au_id,
           'Last Name'  = au_lname,
           'First Name' = au_fname,
           'Phone'      = phone
      FROM authors
     WHERE state LIKE @tmpString
  END
  ELSE
  BEGIN
/* Add any other columns for search                 */
    PRINT 'Unknown search column.'
  END
END
GO
Syntax
EXEC cp_getAuthors '724', 'ID'

Returns
ID            Last Name    First Name  Phone
-----------   ----------   ----------  ------------
724-08-9931   Stringer     Dirk        415 843-2991
724-80-9391   MacFeather   Stearns     415 354-7128

(2 row(s) affected)
```

The stored procedure returns two rows to the client with formatted headers for enhanced readability. This type of query would be useful in a Find or Search dialog that required the user to enter a value for a set of authors and an optional parameter, based on the value of the @tmpSearchBY parameter, to change the search results. If you prefer, you may omit the second parameter from the EXEC line. I have assigned a default value for each parameter so that if one is left off, the procedure will still run.

Always try to provide default values for the parameters in your stored procedures. Default values give you the flexibility to use the stored procedure in many different ways without having to call multiple copies of the same code for different procedures.

Each enterprise will have its own needs for stored procedures. Look at your applications from the standpoint of the server and ask, "Could this data be provided faster by having the body of code on the server and simply passing a parameter?" Practically every system I have encountered has benefited or could have benefited from server-side stored procedures. For more information on custom stored procedures, check Microsoft SQL Server Books Online.

External Stored Procedures

In every application, you will at some point require the system to do something that it normally cannot perform. If modifying SQL code and recompiling a stored procedure to enhance the functionality of a program is possible, you have an easy out to this dilemma.

Throughout my career, I frequently have found myself wanting to push the envelope of database applications. This has meant learning how the host applications interact with DLLs and creating a huge library of custom program snippets to attach to my applications. Over time, most systems have matured into well-rounded, robust applications with features and functionality that I could not have expected. In the old days, to enhance functionality I would have to write a complex program in a higher-level language, compile it as a dynamic link library (DDL), and attach it to the application. While the same is true today, most applications require fewer custom DLLs and can usually use third-party DLLs to accomplish virtually any task.

If you want to create your own libraries to run as external procedures with SQL Server, you should be able to write your DLLs as you would any other applications. Attach the DLLs to SQL Server by registering them with the server, and call them in a similar fashion to the other external procedures available with SQL Server.

I have already mentioned a few external procedures in this chapter in the section on variables and writing to the Windows NT Registry. These functions were written to perform a task that Microsoft SQL Server was not necessarily suited to do well or efficiently. A few other external procedures are equally important. See Table 6.5 for some of the most useful ones that ship with Microsoft SQL Server. This is only a partial list; for a more complete one, check out Microsoft SQL Server Books Online.

Remote Stored Procedures

You also can call stored procedures on other SQL servers you have defined as remote servers. By specifying the server name before the database name, you tell SQL Server that it should run the procedure on the remote server and return the results through your current server to the client. This process allows a client application to gain connection to a single server and retrieve and modify data on multiple servers in an enterprise. See Listing 6.4 for an example of calling a remote stored procedure. The server name SERVERX is added to the database, owner, and procedure name to let the local server know that this procedure should be run on another server.

Name	Use
XP_CMDSHELL	Runs an application or command line utility from SQL Server. This external can run executable programs or batch files that perform a wide range of tasks. Keep in mind that any command shell application must not require user interaction or be a modal window that requires user input.
XP_SENDMAIL	Sends query results, messages, and automated reports with XP_SENDMAIL to any MAPI-compliant email system. As long as you have configured the SQL Mail Client on your server and have a functioning mail system that is MAPI-compliant, you can use this procedure to warn you proactively of system problems or send reports to email recipients through SQL code. This is the most powerful and useful external procedure shipping with SQL Server.
XP_LOGININFO	Reports login and account information pertaining to your server.
XP_DISKFREE	Returns the amount of free space available on a specified hard drive to an output parameter that can determine if there is enough free space to extend a device or create a new one on the server. This procedure can be found in the XP.DLL library and must be loaded into SQL Server before it can be used.
XP_LOGEVENT	Writes a message to the SQL Server error log and/or the Windows NT Application log.

Table 6.5 External stored procedures.

Listing 6.4 Calling a remote stored procedure on another server.
```
DECLARE @tmpStatus INTEGER
EXECUTE @tmpStatus = SERVERX.pubs.dbo.checkcontract '409-56-4008'
```

Keep in mind that remote stored procedures and external stored procedures are not within the scope of any user transactions and do not follow the transactional paths that local SQL transactions do. Great care should be taken when utilizing these features in your transaction-based client applications. For more information on how to configure your local server to communicate with other servers, consult Microsoft SQL Server Books Online and look up the keyword **remote**.

Startup Stored Procedures

As mentioned earlier, you can set certain procedures to be executed each time you restart the MSSQLServer service. By default, the stored procedure SP_SQLREGISTER is the only startup procedure installed by the setup application. To view a list of the startup procedures for your server, execute the SP_HELPSTARTUP procedure.

In many production environments, you need to cache certain tables or create or run certain reports to notify someone of the state of the server or to perform a maintenance task automatically. To do this, simply write the stored procedure(s) to be run at startup and then use the SP_MAKESTARTUP stored procedure to add it/them to the list of startup procedures for your server.

Each procedure that is run as a startup uses one connection to the server unless you create a master procedure that calls a list of other procedures from the one procedure. If you require sequential or step-by-step startup procedures, use the single-master-procedure approach to control the order of each startup procedure on your server.

Prior To Production

Before placing any stored procedure into production, you should test it against a reasonable data set and client load to be sure you have not created a resource hog. In a test environment, a procedure might run without error hundreds of times on a development server; but under a load, it can cause locking and performance problems in production.

Check the size of your SQL server's procedure cache before adding any new procedures to production. By default, the cache is set to 30 percent of memory available after SQL Server starts and allocates the memory needed to open objects and respond to user connections. If your cache is already close to full with the existing load, you might want to add more memory to the server or adjust the procedure cache setting on the server. Without the extra memory, you might experience performance problems.

Print out each stored procedure and keep a hard copy around for client developer reference. While your system on the whole might be striving to become paperless, don't forget that good documentation can save hours in development. Comment your code as if you were going to have a first-year intern make all modifications. All developers appreciate good comments.

Summary

- Comment your SQL code very clearly.
- Specify the name of the columns you want your queries to return.
- Use stored procedures to provide security when reading or manipulating data.
- Try to limit ad hoc query abilities whenever possible.
- NOT is *not* optimizable.
- Stored procedures are faster than raw SQL because their query plan is cached.
- Copy any existing system stored procedure before making any changes. Edit the new procedure so you do not create any unexpected problems on your server.
- External and remote procedures do not fall under transactional rules.
- Stored procedures can be nested up to 16 levels before causing an error.

Practical Guide To Stored Procedures

This section will walk you through the creation of a stored procedure for use with Microsoft SQL Server—a string manipulation procedure that will take a tokenized string and return items to the client application or another procedure.

Parsing A String

One of the most common tasks in dealing with text data is string manipulation. SQL allows for string operations to accomplish most tasks involving text. In this Practical Guide example, we'll create a stored procedure to accept a string variable and remove a token from the string while reducing the working string to reflect the removed item.

In many applications, you need to manipulate a list of items in some sort of grouped fashion. A token list provides a method for passing a single string list as a parameter to a stored procedure and letting the procedure work through the list and parse items out internally. Token lists reduce network traffic and increase the speed with which your client applications can respond to list-type edits.

Redundant Code

Our example script will create a stored procedure that updates the author's contract status to the value passed in. While this is rather simple, it does illustrate how the process can be changed for list-based modifications.

The first procedure, shown in Listing 6.5, creates CP_SETSTATUS. This procedure must be called one time for each author that needs a contract-status update.

Listing 6.5 CREATE stored procedure to modify contract status.
```
CREATE PROCEDURE cp_setStatus @tmpAu_ID   VARCHAR(11) = NULL,
                              @tmpStatus BIT          = 0
AS
/* Change the contract status of the author passed in */
UPDATE authors
   SET contract = @tmpStatus
 WHERE au_id    = @tmpAu_ID
GO

Syntax
EXEC cp_setStatus '172-32-1176', 0
```

If you want to update the entire table, you could use a single update statement. But what if only a portion of the table needed to be updated? You could use the method shown in Listing 6.6 to update each of the seven authors. Your client application would have to make seven calls to the stored procedure. If the client already has the list of authors and could pass it as a comma-delimited string to the procedure, only one call would be required.

Listing 6.6 Updating seven authors.
```
EXEC cp_setStatus '172-32-1176', 0
EXEC cp_setStatus '213-46-8915', 0
EXEC cp_setStatus '238-95-7766', 0
EXEC cp_setStatus '267-41-2394', 0
EXEC cp_setStatus '274-80-9391', 0
EXEC cp_setStatus '341-22-1782', 0
EXEC cp_setStatus '409-56-7008', 0
```

Reduced Network Traffic

By placing each of the author's ID strings one after the other, you reduce the number of characters passed across the network connection to the server. You also shorten the overall response time for this transaction, because the client does not have to wait for each call to return a status of execution before sending the next update call.

Listing 6.7 shows the SQL code needed to pass a list into the procedure and loop through the list until there are no more tokens before exiting. This code uses control-of-flow statements to direct what occurs within the procedure and some built-in string functions to loop through the list and reduce the list by the appropriate amount during each pass through the loop.

Listing 6.7 List-based status update.

```
CREATE PROCEDURE cp_setStatus @tmpIDList    VARCHAR(255) = NULL,
                              @tmpSeparator CHAR(1)      = ',',
                              @tmpStatus    BIT          = 0
AS
/* Change the contract status of the authors passed in */

/* Local Variables                                      */
DECLARE @tmpID VARCHAR(11)

/* Pad with an ending comma for while loop              */
SELECT @tmpIDList = @tmpIDList + ','

WHILE (CHARINDEX(@tmpSeparator,@tmpIDList) > 0)
BEGIN
/* Get the first token from the list                    */
   SELECT @tmpID = SUBSTRING(@tmpIDList, 1, (CHARINDEX(@tmpSeparator,
      @tmpIDList)-1))

/* Trim current ID from the list                        */
   SELECT @tmpIDList = SUBSTRING(@tmpIDList, (CHARINDEX(@tmpSeparator,
      @tmpIDList)+1), 255)

   UPDATE authors
      SET contract = @tmpStatus
      WHERE au_id  = @tmpID

END
GO
```

Although this procedure is more efficient than the first one, it still lacks some portability. I cannot use this method in other stored procedures without copying and pasting the code from one procedure to another. Copy and paste is not a bad solution, but there is a better way. By creating a totally separate string procedure called CP_GETOKEN, I can use this method in many other stored procedures without copying all the code. See Listing 6.8 for an example of the stored procedure code for the string procedure CP_GETOKEN.

Listing 6.8 SQL code for creating CP_GETOKEN.

```
CREATE PROCEDURE cp_geToken @tmpList      VARCHAR(255) = NULL OUTPUT,
                            @tmpSeparator CHAR(1)      = ',',
                            @tmpItem      VARCHAR(20)  = NULL OUTPUT
AS
/* String token utility function                           */

/* Pad with a separator for while loop                     */
IF (RIGHT(@tmpList,1) <> @tmpSeparator)
BEGIN
SELECT @tmpList = @tmpList + @tmpSeparator
END

/* Get the first token from the list                       */
SELECT @tmpItem = SUBSTRING(@tmpList, 1, (CHARINDEX(@tmpSeparator, @tmpList)-1))

/* Trim current ID from the list                           */
SELECT @tmpList = SUBSTRING(@tmpList, (CHARINDEX(@tmpSeparator, @tmpList)+1), 255)
GO
```

Calling Procedures Within Procedures

The final piece to this puzzle is to modify CP_SETSTATUS to call the new stored procedure. I can now call CP_GETOKEN from any procedure to remove the leading token from a string for manipulation purposes. Notice that in Listing 6.9 I use a parameter for the token separator. I could have hard-coded that into the procedure, but doing so would have limited the use of this utility.

Listing 6.9 Code for modified CP_SETSTATUS.

```
CREATE PROCEDURE cp_setStatus @tmpIDList   VARCHAR(255) = NULL,
                              @tmpStatus   BIT          = 0
AS
/* Change the contract status of the authors passed in */
/* Local Variables                                      */
DECLARE @tmpID VARCHAR(11)

WHILE (CHARINDEX(',',@tmpIDList) > 0)
BEGIN
/* Call CP_GETOKEN for string trim and variable        */
  EXEC cp_geToken @tmpIDList OUTPUT, ',', @tmpID OUTPUT

  UPDATE authors
     SET contract = @tmpStatus
   WHERE au_id    = @tmpID

END
GO
```

I called the subroutine with both parameters designated as output parameters so that I could get the modifications of the strings passed back and forth without worrying about storing data into temporary variables. The number of lines of code shrank from the original due to the multiple variable assignment by CP_GETOKEN. I eliminated the item separator in the stored procedure to illustrate what a hard-coded solution might look like. Even though the token routine takes any separator, the new status procedure assumes that commas separate the list being passed in.

You can pass multiple strings into a stored procedure using this same methodology to update sets of data based on a tokenized list. The power of this kind of function really surfaces when you look at your client processes from the server's standpoint.

And now for the obligatory reminder: *Back up the master database!*

Chapter 7

Views

- Determining Column Needs
- Partitioning And Combining Data
- Checking Index Coverage
- Modifications

Administrator's Notes...

Chapter 7

Many data models created to run on larger database systems tend to become too wide and denormalized with regard to table layout. This may be the result of upsizing an existing desktop database to Microsoft SQL Server or of prototyping and running applications against sample data while in development.

Most new systems do not have the luxury of an extended design cycle to address the data structure and normalize the data to provide best disk utilization. This is not usually a problem until the server begins to slow because of extra-wide tables, or disk space is depleted due to redundant stored data. In most cases, a consultant is called in to troubleshoot the problem, or more disk space is added to take care of the symptom rather than solve the problem.

A well-planned, normalized data structure can save huge amounts of disk space and provide very good performance across many of the queries run against the system. Index usage is key to high normalized data performance. Many people take the normalization step only as far as is needed to get some kind of data out on the server so that developers can start writing code against it. This approach can cause problems for most any database, Microsoft SQL Server notwithstanding.

Syntax For Creating Views

As with all the objects stored in the database, a view is created through the use of the CREATE statement with some specialized code. See Listing 7.1 for an example script that creates a view. Notice that you can encrypt the view definition for more security for the underlying objects on which the view is based. All users have the ability to access system tables, and the definition of the view is stored in the Syscomments system table.

One other option shown in the syntax section of the script is the CHECK option. This option allows the view to check that all modifications to data will fall within the scope of the view. If a modification will cause an included record to be removed from the result set, the query will generate an error. This option is useful for departmental views that must restrict user modifications to a clearly defined data set.

Listing 7.1 Sample view creation script.

```
/*
Syntax
CREATE VIEW [owner.]view_name
    [(column_name [, column_name]...)]
    [WITH ENCRYPTION]
    AS select_statement [WITH CHECK OPTION]
*/

CREATE VIEW titleview
AS
SELECT title,
       au_ord,
       au_lname,
       price,
       ytd_sales,
       pub_id
  FROM authors, titles, titleAuthor
 WHERE authors.au_id   = titleAuthor.au_id
   AND titles.title_id = titleAuthor.title_id
```

The titleAuthor view is a sample view supplied with Microsoft SQL Server. This view joins the information in three tables into a single representation against which the client application can run queries or stored procedures.

Normalized Data

The key to successfully normalizing your data is to look closely at each entity that is defined and determine if any data represented as an attribute of that entity is potentially stored many times across record sets without change. Locating redundant data is a great first step in normalizing your data. When analyzing your data, make sure you look at it from a level more comprehensive than that of an individual table; look for redundant data in multiple tables that could be combined into a single related table.

For instance, if you are storing the address of an author and the address of a store in two separate tables, you might want to combine both of the addresses into one table. This method saves disk space and makes managing your data much easier. The Pubs database provided with Microsoft SQL Server has been normalized to some degree so that you can use it as an example data structure. In some cases, Pubs may be normalized a bit too much for practical usage, but on the whole it is a good example of normalized data.

The purpose of this chapter is not to illustrate normalization nor to advise you to which level you should apply normalization techniques to your data. Many schools offer whole classes on normalization and data modeling. For more information on normalization, refer to Microsoft SQL Server Books Online.

Writing queries for certain complex data models can prove to be very difficult. These models are typically overnormalized and can be reverse-engineered a bit to improve performance and to make writing queries easier. If you find you are constantly joining two tables together, you might want to consider combining them. There is no one right way to normalize your data, and no one is going to become an expert at normalization without having a good working knowledge of the application design and features that the data model must support.

A few of the benefits of normalization are as follows:

- Faster sorting of data and index creation and re-creation (due to tables being narrower)
- More clustered indexes, increasing overall performance
- Narrower and more compact indexes
- Fewer indexes on a per-table basis, aiding in the execution speed of INSERT, UPDATE, and DELETE statements
- Fewer NULL values and less redundant data, reducing the amount of storage space your data takes up on the disk
- Improved performance when executing DBCC diagnostics because the table locks affect less data

Once you have normalized the data in your data model, you must present the data to the client application or the user in an easy-to-understand format. This is where views come into play. You can provide column titles and formatting, or convert the data into what the user expects to see rather than the most logical way to store it on the server.

Partitioned Data

One useful feature of a view is that the end user sees only those columns and rows to which you wish to allow access. If, for example, you want to allow queries against the Authors table but disallow the Contract Status column, you could create a view similar to that in Listing 7.2. This view defines which columns to include in the view and keeps the data protected from the user.

Listing 7.2   Example of Authors view.
```
CREATE VIEW view_Authors
AS
SELECT au_id,
       au_lname,
       au_fname,
       address,
       city,
       state,
       zip
  FROM authors
```

By allowing users to query the view and not the table, you have in essence implemented a form of column-level security. While Microsoft SQL Server supports column-level security at the table level, using views to enforce access is much more efficient and consumes less overhead and system resources.

Vertical Partitions

Vertical partitioning of the data in a table structure, as shown in Listing 7.2, is accomplished by specifying the columns in the SELECT statement's column list. Modifying this view is as simple as adding or removing a column name and recompiling the view definition.

Horizontal Partitions

To restrict the rows that a view will contain, you would add a WHERE clause to the view definition (see Listing 7.3). This code example could be applied to divisional or regional data stored in a large table to limit the scope of departmental edits on subsets of records in the database.

Listing 7.3 Sample syntax for a California Authors view.
```
CREATE VIEW view_CA_Authors
AS
SELECT  'Author_ID'   = au_id,
        'Last_Name'   = au_lname,
        'First_Name'  = au_fname,
        'Address'     = address,
        'City'        = city,
        'State'       = state,
        'Zip'         = zip
  FROM authors
 WHERE state = 'CA'
```

You can combine horizontal and vertical partitioning to supply client applications or users of your data with clear, easy-to-read data. Notice that I have used new column identifiers to help with the user's understanding of the result set. Standard SELECT statement formatting and string manipulation can be used in the view definition to provide legible data sets to client applications.

Multiple Tables

You can combine data from more than one table into a single view that from the end user's perspective appears to be a single table. While the underlying tables can be as numerous as the maximum number of join conditions in your SELECT statement, I don't recommend combining more than three to four tables at a time in a view (or, for that matter, in a SELECT statement).

Tables are joined in the view definition through the use of join conditions in the WHERE clause of the SELECT statement.

I typically use views as the first level of security in my data model. I create the views based on how the client application needs to view the data and translate the underlying normalized data into functional views. I then grant query permission on the views and keep the underlying objects fully protected from client access. Stored procedures can run against the views to handle the data modification routines, so the complexity of data structure is masked from the client application and the users of the system.

Computed Values

As mentioned earlier, I seldom store computed values in a table. If, for instance, the user needs to see a winning percentage or batting average, I use the actual columns that store the source data for computing the values as the basis for creating a column in a view to represent the aggregate value.

By using stored procedures to modify the data presented to the user, I can break up the data modification statements into separate commands that will modify data in the underlying objects as needed without passing the complexity on to the client application. What does this mean in English? If a user sees an average of a particular expression, such as sales, he or she can call a procedure to modify that value (sales) because the stored procedure has the built-in intelligence to update the underlying columns; the user doesn't need to know where the columns are located or what the existing values are. When the user requeries the view, he or she will see the updated information and know that the changes took effect without realizing the scope of the update process itself.

Security

Views are a great first-line defense in data model security. By default, all objects within a database have permissions granted only to the owner. This allows the owner of an object to be selective in granting access to objects he or she creates. When a data structure is designed and normalized, maintaining relational integrity and enforcing business rules during the update process become significant issues.

To keep unwanted queries and data manipulation to a minimum, I use the view as the base level of user access in the data model. I usually use the view in read-only mode and control changes to the data through stored procedures. This method of implementing security has proven the easiest to maintain when a large, enterprise-wide system is placed into service. Keeping track of access to stored procedures and views is much simpler on an object-by-object basis than using column-level security and task-based access control.

Updates

Keep in mind that you can modify only one table at a time with an INSERT, UPDATE, or DELETE statement. This applies to views as well as tables. If a view is based on a single underlying table, and any columns not displayed in the view allow NULL values or have a default value assigned, you can issue data modification statements against the view as if it were a table.

If a view is based on multiple tables, you must break the data modification statements into separate statements that update only a single table's column list in the view or update the underlying tables individually within a stored procedure or SQL script. (See the *Restrictions* section later in this chapter for more ways you can use views to complement your data model.)

Underlying Objects

To present an easy-to-read record set to the client application and user, Microsoft SQL Server allows you to create a view based on another table or a group of tables, or create a combination of views and tables. You can even create a view of a view to further segment what a certain group of users can see.

Each time a view is accessed on Microsoft SQL Server, the query plan, underlying objects, and the query tree can be evaluated to ensure that the view is still valid and that it will provide accurate information to the requests Microsoft SQL Server processes. If an underlying object has been changed or deleted to render the view invalid, Microsoft SQL Server generates an error message when the view is accessed.

When dropping tables or views from Microsoft SQL Server, you will not be presented with a warning about dependent objects. When you drop a table from a database, the corresponding views are not removed and will generate an error code when accessed.

Performance

The single most important thing you can do to keep performance high with regard to views is to maintain good index coverage on the underlying tables. Pay particular attention to the join conditions in the view definition. Keeping the statistics up-to-date on those indexes greatly improves the chance that the Query Optimizer will use the index to return data instead of a worktable.

Many developers have been misled into believing that a view is actually a table. To keep this from happening, use a standard naming convention to identify your views within your data model. A view can mask performance problems by separating the index needs from the table and establishing a new requirement based on how the view will be accessed.

Views 231

Restrictions

When creating and using views on Microsoft SQL Server, follow these guidelines:

- CREATE VIEW statements cannot be combined with other SQL statements in a single batch. You must provide for the view object to be created before you reference the new object. Issuing the GO command causes the batch to be executed in a script; you can then access the view.

- You cannot create a trigger or an index on a view. The only way to change the sort of the result set in a view is to use ORDER BY clauses in your SELECT statements that run against the view.

- A view can contain up to 250 columns. For performance and system management reasons, try not to reach this limit.

- You cannot use the UNION operator within a CREATE VIEW statement. You can use the UNION operator to merge two views into a single result set.

- Modification statements (INSERT, UPDATE, or DELETE) are allowed on multitable views if the statement affects only one base table at a time.

- You cannot modify computed or aggregate column values in a view. You must make the modifications to the underlying data and allow the view definition to recalculate the values.

- INSERT statements are not accepted on a view if there are non-NULL columns without defaults in the underlying table or view. This allows for columns outside the column list to be filled by NULL or default values that the user does not have to supply. If a non-NULL column exists outside the scope of the displayed columns, an error will be returned for the INSERT statement.

- All columns being modified must adhere to any data type and rule issues as if they were executed directly against the underlying table.

- You cannot use READTEXT or WRITETEXT on text or image columns in views. You must access the underlying table or tables to use these commands.

- Data modification statements on views are not checked to determine whether the affected rows fall within the scope of the view. You can issue an INSERT statement on a view to add a row to an underlying table but not to add it to the view alone. If all modifications to data inside a view should be checked, use the WITH CHECK option in the CREATE VIEW statement.

- You cannot create a view on temporary tables.

Summary

- Use views to implement column-level security without the worry and overhead of using table-level column restrictions.
- Specify the name of the columns and the identifiers you wish displayed in your views.
- Use stored procedures to provide for security when reading or manipulating data.
- Pay attention to index coverage on views.
- Removing or modifying the underlying objects will cause views to return error messages when accessed by queries.
- Use views for data access in a read-only mode and use stored procedures to modify data for maximum control over the data integrity on your server.

Practical Guide To Views

This section addresses the creation of views to present the user or client application with an easy-to-understand data structure. Step by step, we will create a view similar to the titleauthor view and examine how to manipulate data in the view through stored procedures. For our example, we will create a view for use by a client application with a screen that displays the author's personal information and year-to-date sales. We will also provide the ability to change the author's address information.

Determining Column Needs

The columns needed for the client display are author ID, name, address information, and year-to-date sales. See Listing 7.4 for an example of the SELECT statement syntax used to return this information to a query window. I will use a query tool and write the SQL SELECT statement syntax for the view definition before actually creating the view within the database. This allows me to debug the definition until I am sure it is correct and returns what I need for the client application. After the script is tested, I can wrap the SQL code with the appropriate CREATE VIEW code to actually create the object on the server.

Listing 7.4 SELECT statement for Authors view.

```
/* Get the Authors info and YTD Sales */
SELECT  'Author_ID'   = a.au_id,
        'Last_Name'   = a.au_lname,
        'First_Name'  = a.au_fname,
        'Address'     = a.address,
        'City'        = a.city,
        'State'       = a.state,
        'Zip'         = a.zip,
        'YTD_Sales'   = (SELECT SUM(ytd_sales)
                           FROM titles t, titleAuthor ta
                          WHERE ta.title_id = t.title_id
                            AND a.au_id     = ta.au_id)
  FROM authors a
```

In Listing 7.4, I used a subquery to return the year-to-date sales column in the Titles table for each title, grouped by the join condition of the titleAuthor table and the Author table. (For the schematic and structures of these tables, see Appendix A.)

Partitioning And Combining Data

Notice in Listing 7.4 that a few subtle things have occurred with the query. First and most obvious, the column names are changed to make them easier to read. Second, aliases are used to refer to each of the three tables that return the data in the view. Third, a subquery that uses an aggregate function to total the value of the rows returned by the subquery is included.

The subquery I used here is somewhat unique in that it is considered a correlated subquery. In normal queries, the inside SELECT statement is executed first to return a list to the outer query to use in its process. This particular query is different in that I have a column in the inner query's WHERE clause that exists only in the outer SELECT statement. The inner query must get the data it needs to function from the outer query first. This causes only the rows that match the author's ID to be returned by the inner query. Most queries can be written in many different ways to get the same results. I used this example to show how a correlated subquery would work in a production environment.

To create the view we use in this exercise, we would have to wrap the SQL code shown in Listing 7.4 within the proper CREATE syntax, as displayed in Listing 7.5.

Listing 7.5 Create the actual view.
```
CREATE VIEW v_authorsSales
AS
/* Get the authors info and YTD Sales */
SELECT  'Author_ID'   = a.au_id,
        'Last_Name'   = a.au_lname,
        'First_Name'  = a.au_fname,
        'Address'     = a.address,
        'City'        = a.city,
        'State'       = a.state,
        'Zip'         = a.zip,
        'YTD_Sales'   = (SELECT SUM(ytd_sales)
                           FROM titles t, titleAuthor ta
                          WHERE ta.title_id = t.title_id
                            AND a.au_id     = ta.au_id)
   FROM authors a
```

Checking Index Coverage

Before moving on to modifying the data in any way, let's take the time to make sure the indexes match the columns we are relying on to support this object. Set the query options as shown in Figure 7.1 to see the query plan for a query running against the new view. Click on the yellow wrench button at the top of the query window to display the Query Options dialog box. The first selected checkbox, Show Query Plan, displays the output from the Query Optimizer so that you can see which indexes, if any, are being used to support this particular query.

The next checkbox, Show Stats Time, displays the time each step took to parse and compile the query. The third checkbox, Show Stats I/O, shows the number of scans and physical and logical reads that were required to service the query. See Listing 7.6 for the sample output.

Listing 7.6 Query Options output for selecting data from our sample view.
```
SQL Server Execution Times:
   cpu time = 0 ms.  elapsed time = 201510 ms.
STEP 1
The type of query is SELECT
FROM TABLE
authors
Nested iteration
Table Scan
FROM TABLE
Worktable 1
SUBQUERY : nested iteration
GROUP BY
Vector Aggregate
   FROM TABLE
   titleAuthor
   Nested iteration
   Table Scan
   FROM TABLE
   titles
   Nested iteration
   Using Clustered Index
   TO TABLE
Worktable 1
SQL Server Parse and Compile Time:
   cpu time = 20 ms.
(output rows…)
```

Let's take a moment to examine what this query is telling us. First, Listing 7.6 shows the parse time for the first part of the query, and the source of the query. Notice that

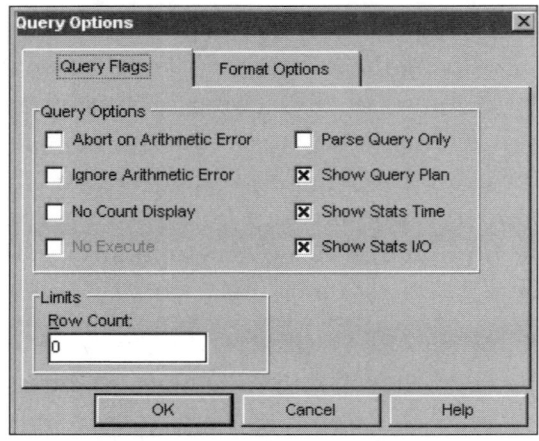

Query Options dialog box.
Figure 7.1

even though we executed the query against the view, the Query Optimizer references the underlying object. So the Authors table is the object really being accessed by this SELECT statement.

Next, you see the term *nested iteration*. This refers to the default method used to join tables or views that loop.

through the rows in a table and checks them against the search criteria in the WHERE clause. Next is the reference to the subquery and another nested iteration step. Note that the subquery is indented to show the nesting in the display.

As you move through the output, you see some table scan methods and one clustered index reference. The index reference means that the existing index on the Titles table will be used to return records to the worktable. Table scans, on the other hand, are used to return each row in the table one at a time and compare it to the conditions in the WHERE clause. This method is chosen when no matching index for the query is determined to be useful in satisfying the query plan.

Last, you see the compile time for the query plan. The output rows would follow. This plan can help point you in the right direction with regard to creating coverage indexes on your tables. Keep in mind that even though you are querying a view, your query is being passed on to the underlying tables to be resolved.

Modifications

Now we need to get a row from this view, and a method to optionally change a record or perform an INSERT of a new record into the list. To do this we will create two stored procedures. See Listing 7.7 for the creation code for each stored procedure.

Listing 7.7 Stored procedures for modifying data in the sample view.

```
CREATE PROCEDURE cp_getAuthorInfo @tmpID VARCHAR(11) = NULL
AS
/* Check for good data                  */
IF (@tmpID = NULL)
BEGIN
  PRINT 'USAGE : cp_getAuthorInfo <Author ID>'
  RETURN
END

SELECT *
  FROM v_authorsSales
 WHERE Author_ID = @tmpID
GO

/* Usage example                        */
EXEC cp_getAuthorInfo '486-29-1786'
```

The CP_GETAUTHORINFO stored procedure returns all the columns from the view that matches the row in the table containing the author ID being passed in as a parameter. This query could be modified to return the closest match or to allow for partial-string matches, adding flexibility later in the development cycle without changing the client code to run the procedure. This procedure retrieves a record for display on a client form and allows for edits to be made by the user and passed back to the server via another stored procedure. To see the changed data, you would have to apply the changes to the local client data or requery the GET procedure to return the changed data.

Listing 7.8 shows the creation code for the CP_UPDAUTHORINFO stored procedure. This procedure performs more than one task on the server, depending on the existence of a record with the matching author ID in the table. I also modify the underlying object inside the stored procedure. This allows me to take into account the ability of a column to accept a NULL or default value within my SQL code.

Listing 7.8 Create code for cp_updAuthorInfo.

```
CREATE PROCEDURE cp_updAuthorInfo @tmpID        VARCHAR(11) = NULL,
                                  @tmpLastName  VARCHAR(40) = NULL,
                                  @tmpFirstName VARCHAR(20) = NULL,
```

```
                            @tmpAddress    VARCHAR(40)  = NULL,
                            @tmpCity       VARCHAR(20)  = NULL,
                            @tmpState      CHAR(2)      = NULL,
                            @tmpZip        CHAR(5)      = NULL
AS
/* Check for good data                                              */
IF (@tmpID = NULL OR @tmpLastName = NULL OR @tmpFirstName = NULL)
BEGIN
/* Require these three columns before adding new records */
  PRINT 'USAGE : cp_updAuthorInfo <Author ID>, <Last Name>, <First Name>, [...]'
  RETURN
END

/* Determine mode based on existence of ID              */
IF EXISTS(SELECT Author_ID
            FROM v_authorsSales
           WHERE Author_ID = @tmpID)
BEGIN
/* Update the existing record                           */
  UPDATE authors
     SET au_lname = @tmpLastName,
         au_fname = @tmpFirstName,
         address  = @tmpAddress,
         city     = @tmpCity,
         state    = @tmpState,
         zip      = @tmpZip
   WHERE au_id    = @tmpID
```

```
END
ELSE
BEGIN
/* Insert a new one                                          */
   INSERT INTO authors
   VALUES (@tmpID,
           @tmpLastName,
           @tmpFirstName,
           DEFAULT,
           @tmpAddress,
           @tmpCity,
           @tmpState,
           @tmpZip,
           0)
END
GO
```

Modifying the sample procedures here allows you to pass a variety of information into a procedure and deal with the data modifications case by case inside the procedure through using control-of-flow statements. These two procedures illustrate one method of controlling access to data by using views and stored procedures. While these methods might not work in all enterprises, they have proven functional and easy to maintain in most environments.

One last thing: *Back up the master database!*

Chapter 8

Triggers

- Remove The Foreign Key Constraints
- Define The Business Rule
- Identify The Child Records
- Graphically Represent The Trigger Firing Order
- Write A Test Script
- Check The titleAuthor Table
- Create The Trigger
- Test The Trigger

Administrator's Notes...

Chapter 8

Database design is one area where programmers tend to learn by the seat of their pants. They make mistakes, fumbling with slow and cumbersome designs until they understand the way the database engine works and how to effectively integrate that functionality into their client applications. One significant factor that impedes this server-side development is the vast array of tools and methods the developer can use to give users what they expect.

I am no different than anyone else; I made lots of mistakes and created many poor implementations before I started to see the light. As my understanding of Microsoft SQL Server and other database systems grows, I am learning how to use these tools to better deliver applications that are fast and efficient. You will undoubtedly do the same with some time and practice using Microsoft SQL Server.

One difficult-to-master section of the client/server puzzle is the trigger. While not very difficult to program, triggers are sometimes hard to follow and debug. You are not required to use triggers in your data model; however, once you have read this chapter, you will gain an understanding of how they might be applied to your enterprise to save you time and headaches.

Data Integrity

The most important reason I can give for using triggers in your data model is data integrity. I have been asked to analyze many data structures to make sure that they will function and serve the application to the best-possible end, with solid, dependable data. Let's face it—if the user believes that the data is full of holes or the reports don't make sense, the system has failed to achieve its goals.

In older shared-file or relational systems, you had to create client applications that took care of the security and validity of the data from the client perspective. Although this allowed many good programmers to be creative and write wonderful code, it also relied on each programmer to intimately understand the relationships of the data and the structure of the data model. This helped create "fat" clients that took every possible user issue with regard to validating data and screened each record before passing it on to the server.

This screening approach was not that bad, but the applications would have to be re-created each time a change was made to the database—a time-consuming and error-prone process. The copy-and-paste bug would work its way into the front-end applications and, over time, introduce a level of error into the integrity of the data. Enter client/server technology and the ability to bind rules and set actions to data directly.

With a true client/server application, whether a multiple-level application or simply a client application running against a server in standalone, placing rules that are bound to the data has proven to be a great step forward. By placing the rules for deleting records or establishing a set method of manipulating a key piece of information, you provide a more secure method of maintaining data integrity.

During one job for a client, I found that in some tables, over 30 percent of the records were useless to the system due to missing data or a lack of related records. These tables numbered in the millions of rows and took up huge amounts of storage space. Bad data integrity can cost money in terms of disk usage, processing time, and hardware upgrades.

One nice thing about using triggers to implement data integrity is that they are centrally managed. Regardless of changes to the client applications, or even any future applications that are written, the rules will protect the data. Even entry-level programmers can develop applications that run against a well-designed system with the knowledge that there are hooks built in to protect against errors. This allows the client developers to focus on providing a good application instead of worrying how many key values must be maintained for a particular type of record.

Another benefit of triggers is that you can run any application against the data, and the triggers will maintain the integrity of the data for you. This gives the DBA the power to modify records through a scripting tool without violating established rules pertaining to the deletion or modification of records in the system.

Syntax

The syntax for the creation of a trigger, shown in Listing 8.1, illustrates the ability to encrypt a trigger for security purposes. While encryption is not required for most systems developed in-house, you should note this ability when developing an application for resale. A trigger is nothing more than a stored procedure that is bound to a table so that it adheres to certain business rules you've established for changing data.

Listing 8.1 Trigger creation syntax.
```
CREATE TRIGGER [owner.]trigger_name
ON [owner.]table_name
[WITH ENCRYPTION]
FOR {INSERT, UPDATE, DELETE}
AS sql_statements
```

Microsoft SQL Server traps only three actions for trigger execution. Triggers will only fire in response to INSERT, UPDATE, and DELETE operations, listed in the FOR clause of the CREATE statement. Most of the SQL syntax and control-of-flow statements available in triggers match those of stored procedures. See Table 8.1 for a list of specific statements *not* allowed within the SQL statement section of the trigger definition.

You can define individual triggers for each of the three statements or combine them into one trigger. A trigger will fire only one time for each statement and will not be fired a consecutive time if you make any changes to the same table within a trigger. In other words, if you modify a record in a table that has a trigger bound to it, and the trigger makes a further modification (such as changing a column value without the user's knowledge), another instance of the trigger will not be fired as long as the action is the same as the one defined by the current trigger. If you change information in another table, however, you will set off that table's trigger automatically.

Say, for instance, you fire the INSERT trigger. That trigger performs an update on the table, which will cause any UPDATE trigger to fire as well. See Figure 8.1 for an example of what would occur and what triggers would be fired.

Statement	Notes
All CREATE statements	Databases, tables, procedures, or any other object stored in a database cannot be created as the result of a trigger firing.
All DROP statements	A trigger cannot dynamically drop objects within a database.
ALTER statements	You cannot modify the structure of a database or a table as the result of the firing of a trigger.
TRUNCATE TABLE	This operation is not logged and will remove *all* the data in the target table.
GRANT or REVOKE	You cannot modify a user's or group's permissions because data was modified.
UPDATE STATISTICS	This statement causes the key values and system information pertaining to your indexes to be updated. This is not allowed from within a trigger, because of the amount of traffic that would be generated by executing this statement for each record added, removed, or changed in a table by a given statement. You should execute this statement after manipulating data separately from triggers as a single call.
RECONFIGURE	You cannot change the settings of your server when records are added, removed, or changed in a table.
LOAD statements	You cannot restore from a backup while in a trigger. This process could effectively remove records from a table and would be dangerous.
DISK	DISK statements manipulate the hard drive of the server to create, delete, or modify the storage space SQL Server uses.
SELECT INTO	This statement creates an object (i.e., a table). You cannot create tables based on a trigger's action.

Table 8.1   Statements *not* allowed within a trigger.

Business Rules

One way to look at triggers is to analyze the data from the standpoint of the business as a whole. If a client owes your company money, you would not want to delete any records in the system that show how much money is owed or other pertinent details of the transactions. This is where triggers can come into play; they ensure that certain situations do or do not exist in the database before carrying out a requested command.

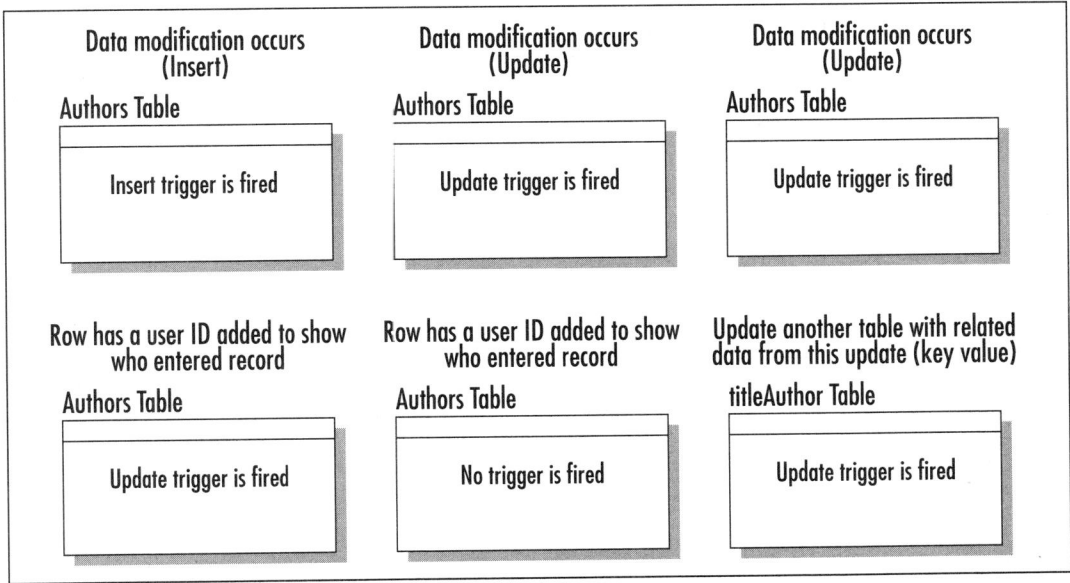

Trigger firing sequences.
Figure 8.1

Depending on your needs, you can program a very complex business rule into your triggers, or a very simple one. If you find that you are checking for a certain value or the existence of a record before performing an action in your code, chances are that check would make a good trigger.

Although default values for certain columns can be applied through triggers, other mechanisms, covered in the next chapter, do a much better job of assigning default values to columns. Triggers are typically used to maintain relational integrity and to enforce business rules.

Permissions

One interesting thing about triggers is that they function very similarly to stored procedures. You do not call a trigger directly from the client application; SQL Server does that for you. The permissions of the owner of the trigger are used to carry out the tasks internally. The only real permission issues occur if, when creating the trigger, you reference an object you do not have permission to access. This would become a problem only if you have a lot of different people creating tables in your data model.

User permissions are not an issue with regard to triggers and enforcing business rules and data integrity. Triggers are directly associated with tables, so you should be the owner of any tables for which you write triggers.

When a table is dropped, the related triggers are removed from the database as well. Be sure to save any definition of the triggers you might want to reapply somewhere in the future.

Nesting

Microsoft SQL Server supports an optional nesting of triggers that can be used to create some very elaborate and complex business rules. As with stored procedures, you can nest triggers up to a maximum of 16 levels. (Keep in mind, however, that nesting requires a very thoroughly thought-out design and strict coding.) You can change data in other tables that you would not normally expect to change when using triggers. Test your triggers completely before placing them into production. An untested trigger in a nesting environment can cause catastrophic damage before you realize it.

Another reason that you might want to avoid using trigger nesting is the need for a specified table modification sequence. Controlling the sequence of modifications in a chain of tables is sometimes difficult. If you modify one of the tables in the middle of the chain, how do you control the changes upstream? In the rare case when your system must be maintained in a sequential manner, you might want to turn off trigger nesting to ensure that unwanted modifications do not occur in your system. You can use stored procedures that perform sequential table maintenance with only single-table triggers.

You can turn off nesting on your server by changing the Nested Triggers server option in the Enterprise Manager or through the sp_configure system stored procedure:

```
EXEC sp_configure 'nested triggers', 0
```

More On Triggers

A trigger is fired one time for each of the three data modification statements and is considered a logged operation. This means that an entry will be written to the transaction log for the modifications that occur for each table regardless of the source. One option for keeping down the size of your transaction log is to use special nonlogged operation statements when you are going to perform mass manipulation of your data.

To insert a large number of rows into a table, I recommend using BCP when possible. This DOS utility will perform in a nonlogged state if you have set the correct options on the database and have dropped the indexes on the target table. Moving a huge amount of records can be done with standard SQL statements, but it can cause the transaction log to fill very quickly. If there are triggers bound to a table with a large number of rows being added, you are in essence creating multiple entries in the log for each new record. Try to move mass records in batches to reduce the amount of log space taken up by your transactions.

If you need to remove all the records in a table—for instance, to prepare for a special process—you might want to use the TRUNCATE TABLE statement to purge the table. This statement will not create transaction log entries for each record deleted, thereby saving a lot of transaction space.

Although a TRUNCATE TABLE statement is, in effect, like a DELETE statement without a WHERE clause (it removes all rows), it will not activate a trigger and it is not logged.

Keep in mind that performing nonlogged operations on a production system is not always advisable. If you will be performing any nonlogged operations on your data, you should perform a backup before you begin the transaction and after you have completed it. This way, you can restore your data in the event of a problem. In situations where the transactions are not an issue, using these statements can increase performance and decrease system overhead.

Virtual Tables

Microsoft SQL Server uses as many as two virtual tables for servicing triggers applied to a table. These virtual tables are identical in structure to the table to which the trigger is bound and are referenced as the Inserted and Deleted tables within the trigger.

As with Microsoft SQL Server, Oracle has the ability to define triggers for each of the three data modification statements. Oracle can have a before trigger and an after trigger defined for each of the actions performed on a table-by-table basis. On the other hand, Microsoft SQL Server uses the virtual table structure described here to allow you the same basic functionality with your triggers as other major databases.

These virtual tables exist in a cached state for each of the tables that have triggers defined. They will hold the records being added or deleted for comparison purposes in your SQL code. You can query these tables and use the same control-of-flow statements to add functionality to your triggers on Microsoft SQL Server.

Inserted Tables

The Inserted table will have the same rows that are added to the target table in a single structure for you to utilize in your triggers. This type of table can be queried to supply values for local variables for use within your trigger. The data in the Inserted table is always a duplicate of what is added to the target table. The rows will exist in both tables during the execution of the trigger.

Deleted Tables

The Deleted table created for each table having a defined trigger is used to store a snapshot of the records being removed from the target table. The rows in the Deleted table will no longer exist in the target table. The structure and use of this virtual table is identical to those of the Inserted and target tables, except that it does not hold the rows removed from the table during execution of the trigger.

Virtual Table Usage

These virtual tables are used by each of the triggers based on the need in each trigger. The INSERT statement will not remove any records, so there is no need to use the Deleted table in INSERT-related triggers. The DELETE statement will not cause the Inserted table to have any rows placed in it, due to the lack of new records.

A special case with these virtual tables involves UPDATE triggers. The UPDATE statement causes information to be placed in both tables and requires a bit more understanding to program properly. When an UPDATE statement is issued on a table that has a defined UPDATE trigger, the original unmodified data will be placed in the Deleted table first, then the updated row is placed in the Inserted table and applied to the actual target table itself. While in the trigger, you can reference both tables to test for certain conditions or perform any other related actions based on the data in both virtual tables.

Global Variables

There are some useful global variables that you should consider when programming triggers. See Table 8.2 for global variables that may come in handy when writing business rules or creating data integrity routines. Note that the @@ROWCOUNT variable should be checked first in the query so that the value can be stored in a local

Variable	Use
@@ROWCOUNT	Returns the number of rows affected by the last query statement.
@@IDENTITY	Holds the last identity column-generated value. This is a per connection value that would reflect the INSERT statement-generated value.
@@SPID	Holds the value of the current server process ID. This value can be used to query the system tables to find out which user or what process is making a data modification.
@@ERROR	Holds the result code for the preceding query.

Table 8.2 Global variables and their use in triggers.

variable. The execution of any SELECT statement inside the trigger will change the value of @@ROWCOUNT.

You can, and should, use local variables inside your triggers. In some cases you might want to use a cursor to process the records in a trigger. Having the virtual tables store the new and deleted records saves you from having to query a large table for the critical information you will need to process your trigger effectively. By combining local variables with the virtual tables, Microsoft SQL Server has given you a very powerful way to place solid rules directly into your data model.

INSERT Triggers

An INSERT trigger will fire anytime a record is added to table. If you are using an INSERT statement with a subquery to supply many records to a new table, then the Inserted table will hold many rows. For the syntax associated with an INSERT trigger, see Listing 8.2. Once inside the trigger, you can use standard SQL to create the tests and validations that make up your trigger.

Listing 8.2 INSERT trigger syntax.
```
CREATE TRIGGER [owner.]trigger_name
ON [owner.]table_name
FOR INSERT
AS sql_statements
```

One of the common tasks an INSERT trigger performs is to create any supporting child records with appropriate key values. You can use a trigger to insert records into many other tables based on the information contained in the Inserted table and any pertinent global variables. As with stored procedures, you can use standard control-of-flow statements inside a trigger.

UPDATE Triggers

While INSERT triggers handle new records being added to the table structure, UPDATE triggers perform probably the most important task in a data model with respect to business rules and data integrity. The UPDATE trigger helps you manage which columns can be modified in a table; it also determines column-level rules and how they are applied to your tables during UPDATE operations. In addition, UPDATE triggers ensure that if a value changes in one table, all related information is updated to match the change. This is critical to maintaining referential integrity in a large data model.

UPDATE() is a very useful function in INSERT and UPDATE triggers. See Listing 8.3 for the syntax associated with this tool. By passing a single column or multiple columns into the UPDATE() function, you can test for changes to specific columns in a table and handle those changes programmatically in your code. Note that the UPDATE() function can be used with an INSERT trigger as well as an UPDATE trigger. (Typically there is no need to check column values when deleting records.)

Listing 8.3   UPDATE trigger syntax with the UPDATE() function.
```
CREATE TRIGGER [owner.]trigger_name
ON [owner.]table_name
FOR {INSERT, UPDATE}
[WITH ENCRYPTION]
AS
IF UPDATE (column_name)
[{AND|OR} UPDATE (column_name)...] sql_statements
```

Remember that if you are inside an UPDATE trigger and you issue a new update of the same table, the trigger will not fire again. This allows you to add information to an UPDATE statement without getting the information from the client application. This method is especially useful in the creation of audit trails.

DELETE Triggers

DELETE statements can affect only one table at a time. Using triggers, however, you can create a cascading delete of information across many tables. Say, for instance, you want to make sure all child records for a particular parent record are removed when the parent is deleted. You would create a DELETE trigger on the parent table that would use the key value in the parent table to qualify and delete the child records in your data structure. This way, the child records do not become orphans.

Once a child record is orphaned by a parent deletion, it essentially becomes useless to the system and takes up valuable disk space. I have run into some database designs that had literally millions of orphan records; these would never show up in a query because the parent record no longer existed. Had a trigger been defined to maintain the relational integrity of the data, the disk space saved would have paid for the time it would have taken to write the triggers and test them.

By definition, databases grow; it's the natural progression and life cycle of a good data model. Professionals expect the database to use a large amount of disk space. This assumption should not be abused, however. If you can save space in the database, you are essentially prolonging the life of the hardware and saving money.

Limitations

There are limitations to what you can do in a trigger. As listed earlier in Table 8.1, certain statements cannot be executed inside a trigger. These statements typically manipulate objects within the server or database environment and would make a poor choice for being automatically called when a record is inserted, updated, or deleted.

Triggers afford you peace of mind; they are bound to the table and will fire regardless of the data manipulation statement source. This can be a blessing and a curse. If you need to change a large amount of data, due to a system upgrade or even a bug in your code somewhere, you should consider the trigger and the impact it will have on your changes. If you are not careful to follow all the paths that a trigger can take during execution (nesting especially), you might remove or modify records that are in fact fine the way they were. Beware of compounding your problems by ignoring triggers.

A good graphical representation of your trigger strategy will enable any programmer to understand the built-in data modification routines. A good flowchart works best. Graphical designs and maps of your triggers are also beneficial in that they increase the likelihood that you will catch any recursive or looping trigger actions.

Only the table owner can create and drop triggers for a table. This permission cannot be transferred to another user. This means that only the system administrator (SA) and the user who creates a table can create these objects in the database. (The SA has global rights on the server and can perform any task.)

Triggers cannot be created on temporary tables or views. A trigger can, however, reference a view or temporary table from within its code. I recommend, however, that you avoid using temporary tables for this task. Views are a bit more stable and are less likely to be dropped from the database structure than are temporary tables.

As a general rule, triggers should not return a value to a user in any fashion other than through an error handler. SELECT statements should be used only to fill local variables and supply lookup information, not to return information to a client application.

Multiple-Row Considerations

When writing your triggers, be very careful to take into account the possibility of handling more than one row of data at a time. The @@ROWCOUNT global variable is useful in testing for the existence of more than one row in a particular trigger sequence. See Listing 8.4 for an example of how you would trap for a multiple-row insert into the titleAuthor table. Note that this trigger serves no real function but is intended to illustrate the code needed. I use the *ins* prefix to remind myself that this is an INSERT trigger, and the table name helps me identify this trigger when I query the system tables for further information down the road.

Listing 8.4 Sample multiple-row trigger.

```
CREATE TRIGGER ins_titleAuthor
ON titleAuthor
FOR INSERT
AS
DECLARE @recCount INTEGER
SELECT @recCount = @@ROWCOUNT
IF (SELECT COUNT(*)
      FROM authors a, inserted i
     WHERE a.au_id = i.au_id) = 0
BEGIN
  PRINT 'No Author exists in the authors table.'
  ROLLBACK TRANSACTION
END
IF (SELECT COUNT(*)
      FROM authors a, inserted i
     WHERE a.au_id = i.au_id) <> @recCount
BEGIN
  PRINT 'Some of the Authors do not exist in the authors table'
  ROLLBACK TRANSACTION
END
/* Process the authors one by one after these checks */
```

The trigger illustrated in Listing 8.4 first declares and assigns the current value of the global variable @@ROWCOUNT to a local variable so that we know how many records are being inserted into the Authors table. Then I use an IF statement check to compare the count of records being inserted against any pre-existing records in a totally separate table to determine if this operation should continue. I then check to make sure that each of the author ID values exists in the related Authors table before allowing this operation to continue. The business rule for this would read something like: "No author's books can be added to the titles or to the titleAuthor table without a valid record existing in the Authors table first."

Performance

The overall performance of a trigger is dependent on a few factors. The associated overhead of a trigger is usually pretty low, because the virtual tables are in memory and are typically a much smaller set of data than an entire table. The location of any related table lookups will affect the speed at which a trigger fires. If a trigger references a table in a separate database, it will be slower than one that validates data in the virtual tables only.

If you place extended stored procedure calls inside triggers to perform certain actions, you will slow the trigger operation down. For instance, you might want to notify someone by email whenever a certain action occurs in a table, such as the count of new authors exceeding 5 within the last 10 days. Although this might seem farfetched, the point is to be careful how you write your queries. The extended procedure call to the email procedure may affect the performance of your trigger. If the need for an external procedure warrants the extra time that it will take to execute, it can be included as needed.

I typically write triggers with the functionality they require to perform the business rule or relational check, even if they run a bit slowly. This ensures that I will have good data instead of just fast data. If you find that a trigger is running slowly, remember that it is essentially an SQL statement and should be checked for index coverage and optimization just like any other query.

Summary

- Triggers are fast and cover any data manipulation regardless of the source.
- Only three triggers can be defined on a table (INSERT, UPDATE, and DELETE).
- Watch the size of the transaction log when manipulating large result sets against table with triggers; if they affect other tables, you might fill the transaction log without realizing it.
- Use global variables to make your triggers smarter.
- Remember the nesting rule (maximum 16 levels).
- Consider the possibility of multiple rows when writing your triggers.
- Create a graphic representation of your triggers to get a better understanding of what will happen when data is manipulated.
- When a table is dropped, the triggers are dropped as well.
- View business-rule triggers from a higher, more general level to ensure that you are covering the needs of the business and not just the data requirements.

Practical Guide To Triggers

In this section, I'll show you how to create a cascading delete of all records related to a parent record so that there are no orphan records left in the system. We'll also check to make sure that records are not deleted from the system if they are active. This ensures that only the intended records are removed with a single DELETE statement.

As with our previous examples, we'll use the Pubs database. The same process may be applied to your system with a little bit of modification to allow for table names and specific needs. This trigger is used for illustration purposes only.

The Authors table is a key table in the Pubs database. This table contains a list of all authors and the attributes that make each one unique in the system. One key piece of data for this exercise is the Contract column. To prepare for this Practical Guide, remove the existing foreign key constraints on the titleAuthor table before running these scripts. If you do not remove the constraints, the test phase of the Practical Guide will fail. Before removing the foreign keys, either create a backup of the Pubs database as it exists now or accept that all changes will be lost later when we re-create the database from scratch. If you do not want to lose any test objects, make a backup of the Pubs database before continuing.

Remove The Foreign Key Constraints

To remove the foreign key constraints from the titleAuthor table, you should open the Enterprise Manager and connect to the server. Click the plus sign next to the Databases folder, and in the list databases, select Pubs. On the menu bar select Manage Menu, then scroll through the list and select the Tables option.

A dialog box appears that allows you to graphically manage the tables inside the Pubs database. See Figure 8.2 for the Manage Tables dialog box.

Now you are ready to remove the foreign key constraints on the titleAuthor table, performing the following steps:

1. In the table drop-down list box, select the titleAuthor table to bring up the columns in the titleAuthor table. See Figure 8.3 for the resulting column list and how it should look in your display.

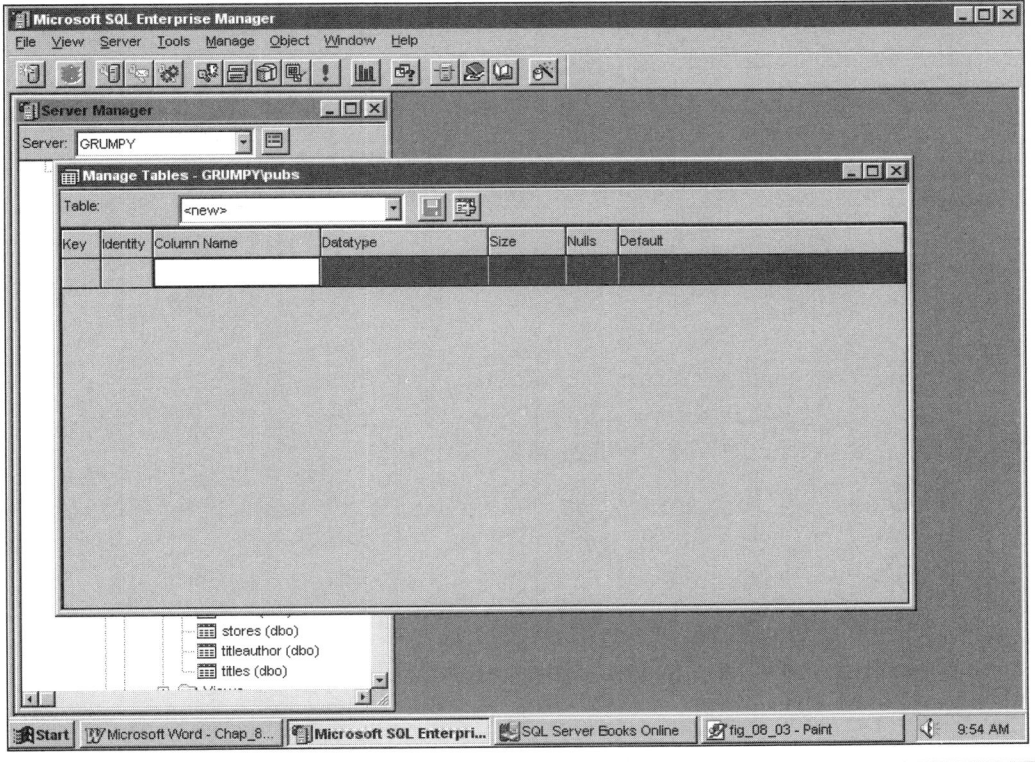

The Manage Tables dialog box.
Figure 8.2

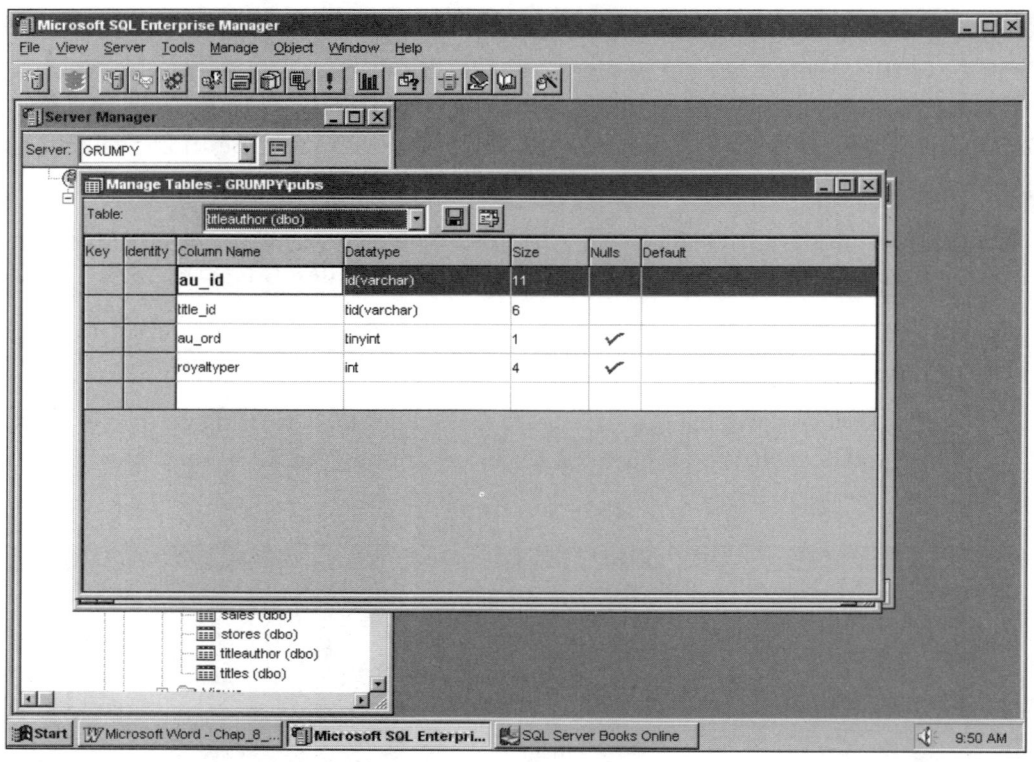

The Manage Tables dialog box with the titleAuthor table displayed.
Figure 8.3

2. Select the second button (Advanced Features) in the title bar to open the bottom section of the dialog box that allows you to manipulate constraints. See Figure 8.4 for the resulting change in the Manage Tables dialog box.

3. Select the Foreign Keys tab to change the foreign key constraints for this table. See Figure 8.5 for the resulting change in the dialog box. You are presented with a Foreign Key drop-down list box and a Referenced Table drop-down list box.

4. Select the Foreign Key box and note the two foreign keys in the list. Select each one in turn and click the remove button to drop the constraints.

5. After removing the constraints, click the Save button in the title bar of the Manage Tables dialog box. You can now close the dialog box and continue with the Practical Guide.

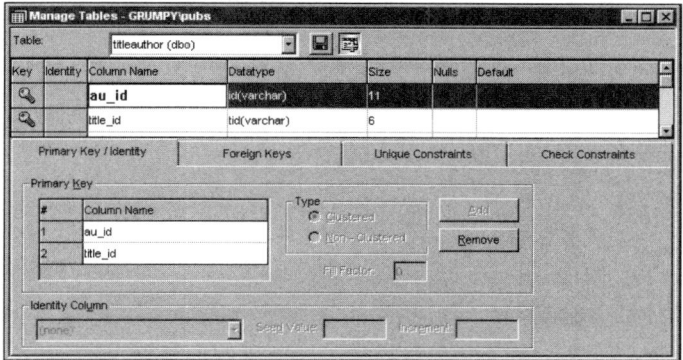

The Manage Tables dialog box with Advanced Features displayed.
Figure 8.4

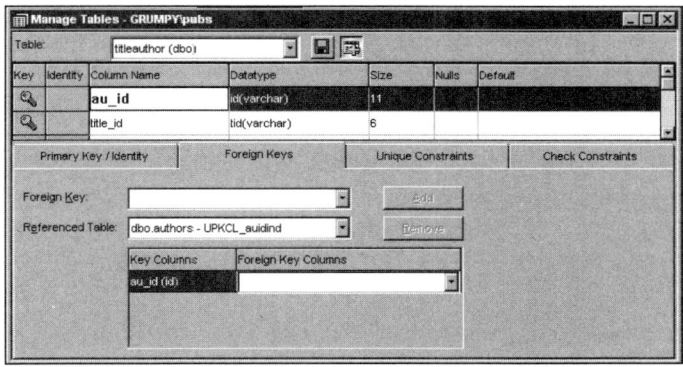

The Manage Tables dialog box with the Foreign Keys tab selected.
Figure 8.5

Define The Business Rule

In our fictitious company, we'll assume that no author can be removed from the system while still under contract. Therefore, we would first write a query similar to the one shown in Listing 8.5 to determine whether an author is under contract. (We could, of course, elaborate on this business rule more and add sales figures and other information before we allow the deletion of an author record, but I want to keep this simple and straightforward.)

Listing 8.5 Query to check an author's contract status.

```
/* Determine if an author is under contract */
IF (SELECT contract
      FROM authors
     WHERE au_id = '341-22-1782') = 0
BEGIN
  PRINT 'No contract.'
END
ELSE
BEGIN
  PRINT 'Under contract.'
END
```

I am only using the PRINT statements here to illustrate the logical structure behind the query. They are not needed and could be dropped from the query. You should focus on the IF statement, because that part of the query will be used with only minimal modification to test our business rule. The second business rule that applies is to remove all records for this author, including titles and royalty information. While this might not make much business sense, it allows me to show you how to remove records from other tables with a single DELETE statement.

Identify The Child Records
The next step in the process is to identify the tables that contain data related to this author record. In the Pubs database, two tables have records that match our business-rule requirements to remove title information and royalty records: the roySched table, which has a key field of title_id to be used by our trigger for deletion, and the titleAuthor table, which holds the au_id and title_id columns for our authors.

Graphically Represent The Trigger Firing Order

To completely understand this step, you should look for the key values and begin to get an idea of the join conditions or search criteria that you will use for your trigger. The Authors table will have the au_id column from the Deleted table to use as a key for looking up information in the titleAuthor table. The titleAuthor table holds both the au_id and title_id key values. To correctly remove the title information, we would have to use the key value from titleAuthor to remove the title record first, then remove the titleAuthor records. See Figure 8.6 for an example of how you might illustrate the trigger process before writing any SQL code.

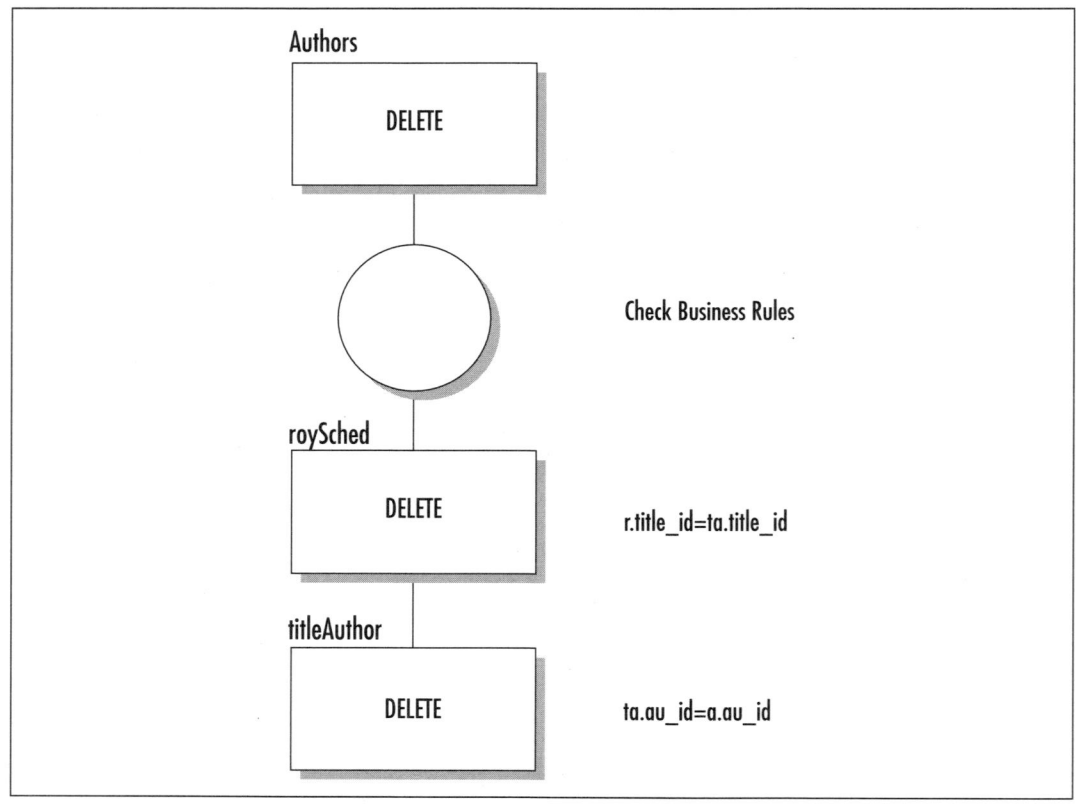

Sample deletion trigger for the Authors table.
Figure 8.6

I have not applied any real work to this trigger yet, but I know enough about the data model to plan what the trigger will do and where the data will come from. The flow of my SQL code in the trigger should follow the same logic I have applied in the graphic representation. I will enter the trigger through a DELETE statement, check the data in any related tables for business-rule violations, then remove the roySched table entries for any titles that the deleted author might have. To complete the process I then remove the titleAuthor records for this author.

Again, let me stress that this trigger would not really make sense, because the sales information and history would be lost. This is strictly for illustration purposes.

Write A Test Script

The next step in creating a trigger is writing a test script to make sure that the records you want removed are in fact those you are getting with your queries. SQL developers often overlook this step, but I highly recommend spending the time verifying your code to ensure that records are not accidentally removed.

A major portion of the SQL code from your script will plug right into the trigger, and you will have the peace of mind that the records you are manipulating are the correct ones. See Listing 8.6 for the sample script used to plan the actual execution of the trigger.

Listing 8.6 Sample trigger test script.

```
/* Author Deletion Script                  */

/* Temp variables for script               */
DECLARE @tmpID CHAR(11)

/* Load temp variables                     */
SELECT @tmpID = '213-46-8915'

BEGIN TRANSACTION
/* From this point on use a trigger format */

/* Determine if an author is under contract */
IF (SELECT contract
      FROM authors
     WHERE au_id = @tmpID) = 1
BEGIN
  RAISERROR('Author is still under contract.', 10, 1)
  ROLLBACK TRANSACTION
END
ELSE
BEGIN
/* Get any roySched records                */
  SELECT *
    FROM roySched r, titleAuthor ta
   WHERE ta.au_id = @tmpID
     AND r.title_id = ta.title_id

/* Check for an error                      */
  IF (@@ERROR <> 0)
  BEGIN
    RAISERROR('Unable to complete operation, roySched error', 10, 1)
    ROLLBACK TRANSACTION
  END
```

```
    /* Get any titleAuthor records         */
      SELECT *
        FROM titleAuthor
        WHERE au_id = @tmpID

    /* Check for an error                  */
      IF (@@ERROR <> 0)
      BEGIN
        RAISERROR('Unable to complete operation, titleAuthor error', 10, 1)
        ROLLBACK TRANSACTION
      END

      COMMIT TRANSACTION
    END
```

Now let's analyze what the script is doing so that we follow the flow of the trigger from start to finish before moving on to the next step. The first few lines of the script handle the task of assigning a value to a local variable for the script to use. This value would be provided by the deleted table's au_id column inside the trigger. Next I use a SELECT statement inside an IF check to determine whether the author is under contract. This check will raise an error if the author is under contract and should not be deleted. The ROLLBACK TRANSACTION statement will undo any changes made to the table and exit the trigger.

If the deleted author passes the business-rule check, I then move into the code that will handle the related table data. I have used SELECT statements in this script for a very specific reason. I can change the first line of the statement to DELETE and leave the WHERE clause intact to remove the records. This allows me to view what is going to be deleted without performing the actual delete.

I have included the code to check for any error performing the delete operation since I would not want to remove a record from the target table if I cannot successfully remove the related records. I have used the RAISERROR() function here to illustrate an error handler; however, you should substitute your own error handling inside the IF statement to properly log the error and handle the problem.

Check The titleAuthor Table

The next step is to check the titleAuthor table for any records and remove them as well. For consistency's sake, I still check the success of the statement and handle the error. The last statement, COMMIT TRANSACTION, is needed only in the script. I am simulating the implied transactional state that triggers run in. By simulating this in the script, I can put the proper code in place to handle any errors in the script instead of waiting until I place the SQL code in the trigger.

I have commented each line of code so that I can quickly understand each step. This will allow some other programmer (or even me) to look at this code later and follow the flow of what is going on in the trigger. In addition, this script provides me with the ability to plug an ID value into the script and determine what will happen in the trigger. If a user reports a problem with an author deletion, I can run this script with little change and see exactly what the trigger is trying to do. Keeping these kinds of scripts around in a directory somewhere can save you debugging time later. For the sample output, see Listing 8.7.

Listing 8.7 Sample output from test script.

```
(1 row(s) affected)

title_id  lorange  hirange  royalty  au_id
--------  -------  -------  -------  -----------
BU1032    0        5000     10       213-46-8915 …
BU1032    5001     50000    12       213-46-8915 …
BU2075    0        1000     10       213-46-8915 …
BU2075    1001     3000     12       213-46-8915 …
BU2075    3001     5000     14       213-46-8915 …
BU2075    5001     7000     16       213-46-8915 …
BU2075    7001     10000    18       213-46-8915 …
BU2075    10001    12000    20       213-46-8915 …
BU2075    12001    14000    22       213-46-8915 …
BU2075    14001    50000    24       213-46-8915 …

(10 row(s) affected)

au_id        title_id  au_ord  royaltyper
-----------  --------  ------  ----------
213-46-8915  BU1032    2       40
213-46-8915  BU2075    1       100

(2 row(s) affected)
```

The output from the test script tells me a few things. First the "1 row(s) affected" line tells me that I have successfully assigned a value to the temporary variable. The output from the first SELECT statement follows.

Notice the extra columns displayed in the output. I stated that I wanted to SELECT * (all) columns in my SELECT statement. This is interpreted to mean all columns from all joined tables, so I see the author ID value and the title ID value from the titleAuthor table in my output. This feature helps me know that I have the correct records selected by my WHERE clause. (I have truncated the output to fit the page.)

The second result set lists the titleAuthor records that match my ID value. I should be able to scan this output to determine if the logic in my script meets the needs of the trigger.

Create The Trigger

To actually create the trigger, I must wrap this SQL script with the CREATE TRIGGER statement. See Listing 8.8 for the script that will actually create my new trigger. I have added the code to test for a multiple-row delete so that this trigger will not break if a blanket DELETE statement is issued against the Authors table.

Listing 8.8 Trigger creation script.

```
CREATE TRIGGER del_authors
ON authors
FOR DELETE .
AS
/* Author Deletion Script                 */
IF (SELECT COUNT(*)
      FROM deleted) > 1
BEGIN
  RAISERROR('Remove one author at a time!', 10, 1)
  ROLLBACK TRANSACTION
END
ELSE
BEGIN
/* Determine if an author is under contract */
  IF (SELECT contract
        FROM deleted) = 1
  BEGIN
    RAISERROR('Author is still under contract.', 10, 1)
    ROLLBACK TRANSACTION
  END
  ELSE
  BEGIN
/* Get any roySched records               */
    DELETE FROM roySched
      FROM roySched r, titleAuthor ta, deleted d
     WHERE ta.au_id    = d.au_id
       AND r.title_id = ta.title_id

/* Check for an error                     */
    IF (@@ERROR <> 0)
    BEGIN
      RAISERROR('Unable to complete operation, roySched error', 10, 1)
      ROLLBACK TRANSACTION
    END

/* Get any titleAuthor records            */
    DELETE FROM titleAuthor
      FROM titleAuthor ta, deleted d
     WHERE ta.au_id = d.au_id
```

```
/* Check for an error                         */
    IF (@@ERROR <> 0)
    BEGIN
       RAISERROR('Unable to complete operation, titleAuthor error', 10, 1)
       ROLLBACK TRANSACTION
    END
  END
END
GO
```

For clarity, I used Transact-SQL syntax for the DELETE statements; this allows me to join tables in a similar manner to how a SELECT statement works. I only have to change the SELECT statement to DELETE and supply the table name for the new DELETE statement to work as I expect from the script example. When I run this creation script, it will create a DELETE trigger on the Authors table that protects me from deleting records for authors who are currently under contract, or are part of a multiple-row DELETE statement.

Test The Trigger

The only piece left to this puzzle is to test our trigger to make sure it functions as expected with a DELETE statement. I would normally use a stored procedure to issue a DELETE from a client application, but we'll use a script here to test that it is working. If there were a real-world application, I would create the needed stored procedures later. See Listing 8.9 for the test script used to examine the performance of our new trigger.

Listing 8.9   Sample test script for the authors trigger.

```
/* Test two authors for functionality */
/* 172-32-1176 is under contract      */
/* 341-22-1782 is not under contract  */

/* Test multiple row delete           */
PRINT 'Test 1 :'

DELETE FROM authors

PRINT ''

/* Test for active contract deletion  */
PRINT 'Test 2 :'

SELECT au_lname,
       contract
  FROM authors
 WHERE au_id = '172-32-1176'

SELECT COUNT(*)
  FROM titleAuthor
 WHERE au_id = '172-32-1176'

/* Test for real contract deletion    */
PRINT 'Test 3 :'

SELECT au_lname,
       contract
  FROM authors
 WHERE au_id = '341-22-1782'

SELECT COUNT(*)
  FROM titleAuthor
 WHERE au_id = '341-22-1782'

PRINT 'Done.'
```

Each of the queries in the test script performs a specific step to certify that the trigger is working properly. The first test will issue a DELETE statement with no WHERE clause. This will create a multiple-row Deleted table. The second test will attempt to delete an author whose contract status is 1, or active. A message should be returned that the operation could not be carried out. The additional SELECT in Test 2 provides me with proof that the DELETE statement was rolled back and the record was not deleted.

In the final test, we delete a record that has an inactive contract status. This query should work and remove rows as expected. The additional SELECT statement will verify that the related data was removed from the other tables. For the output of this test script, see Listing 8.10.

Listing 8.10 Sample output from test script.

```
Test 1 :
Remove one author at a time!

(23 row(s) affected)

Test 2 :
au_lname                    contract
-------------------------   --------
White                       1

(1 row(s) affected)


----------
1

(1 row(s) affected)

Test 3 :
au_lname                    contract
-------------------------   --------
Smith                       0

(1 row(s) affected)


----------
0
```

The final zero returned from the last SELECT statement tells me that the trigger is functioning properly and that we are finished creating our cascading delete trigger.

Although this is a simple example, it provides you with the template to apply this technique to your own data model.

To clean up after this Practical Guide, you should run the instpubs.sql script file in your Microsoft SQL Server Install directory to rebuild the Pubs database for the Practical Guide sections in later chapters. Any existing changes to Pubs will be lost. If you made a backup of the Pubs database before this chapter, you can skip the script file and restore from that backup now.

Once again: *Back up the master database!*

Chapter 9

Rules, Defaults, Constraints, And User-Defined Data Types

- Defining The Domains
- Creating The Scripts
- Printing Out A UDT Listing
- Building A Table Structure
- Maintenance And Troubleshooting

Administrator's Notes...

Chapter 9

By this point, you are most likely beginning to see that Microsoft SQL Server is a very useful tool for developing enterprise information systems. Currently I am involved in a few exciting projects that are putting Microsoft SQL Server to the test. In most cases, the systems being developed take advantage of the many features of SQL Server. In others, however, some features are being overlooked.

Many systems are developed under enormous time constraints resulting from the need to get a software package delivered and in place quickly and efficiently. When developers create solutions under pressure, they typically use the features required to get a package released—without looking at the best solution as a whole. This approach is not bad; however, some of the really good features of Microsoft SQL Server can be overlooked in the hurry to roll out a new product.

This chapter covers some of the features that may prove beneficial if you take the time to learn how to use them: specifically, rules, defaults, constraints, and user-defined data types. While these won't make or break a system, they can prove useful and save you time if they are used properly.

Rules

A *rule* is an object created and bound to a column or user-defined data type that checks the data being inserted or updated in a table. You can create a rule that checks for the existence of certain situations or value requirements before allowing the INSERT or UPDATE action to take place. This can be valuable in applications that allow for free-formed manipulation of data through query tools or free-formed SQL execution.

Syntax and structure requirements of rules are very similar to those for WHERE clauses. See Listing 9.1 for a few examples of rule-creation statements. Notice that after the AS section of the definition, there is a block of SQL code that could be placed just after a WHERE clause in a SELECT statement. Doing so would give you a clear picture of what you are testing for within the rule.

Listing 9.1   Sample listing for the creation of a rule.
```
CREATE RULE in_list
AS
@value IN ('1', '6', '8')

CREATE RULE check_pattern
AS
@value LIKE '[0-9][0-9][0-9]-_[0-9]'

CREATE RULE check_range
AS
@value BETWEEN 100 AND 1000
```

I have used a few different examples here to show the flexibility of rules and some of the potential uses for rules in a data model. Checking values or characters to make sure they meet certain conditions is specifically what rules are designed to do for you. The beauty of using rules is that they are objects that are created once in your database and are bound directly to the columns that require validation.

There are alternatives to rules, such as table- or column-level Check constraints. Your decision of which tool to use to validate the data being placed into a table column depends on how you wish to manage your data and the problems you are trying to avoid. We'll cover constraints later in this chapter and discuss the differences between rules and Check constraints. You should also refer to the section on the stored procedure sp_helpText in Microsoft SQL Server Books Online for information pertaining to rules.

A rule must be compatible with the defined data type of the column or user-defined data type it will be bound to. You will get data type errors when inserting or updating a column with a mismatched data type.

Creating Rules

As displayed in Listing 9.1, the CREATE statement is used to define the rule as an object within the database. The syntax is very similar to that of a stored procedure, view, or trigger. You create the rule with a name and supply the definition after the AS. Notice the local variable **@value**. This variable can be called anything you wish; the name I have used is totally arbitrary. I have used IN to illustrate the need for checking in a list to ensure that a value matches a pre-existing list. The BETWEEN and LIKE statements are also available in your rules and should be used to create and define the restrictions that are to be bound to the table columns.

The local variable that you use in a rule can be referenced many times to test for a great number of conditions. See Listing 9.2 for an example of a rule that uses a local variable more than one time. You can only use one variable to match the data being passed to the rule. The SQL statement essentially takes the column data that is being placed into a column and places the value into the local variable of the rule for processing. This is very similar to macro substitution or passing a parameter to a procedure for execution.

Listing 9.2 Rule with multiple local variable references.
```
CREATE RULE good_value
AS
@value > 50 AND @value <= 100
```

Binding Rules

Once a rule has been defined and created in a database, it can be bound to a column or user-defined data type. A rule is not automatically bound to a column. You must specify the binding manually one time. Then, until the rule is unbound, the rule will check any data being added or modified on that specific column or data type. The following is an example of the syntax used to bind a rule to a column:

```
EXEC sp_bindrule rulename, objname [, futureonly]
```

The optional **futureonly** parameter applies to user-defined data types. If supplied, this switch causes only new columns to inherit the rule without being applied to existing columns that have the matching user-defined data type. User-defined data types are covered later in this chapter. Be careful using the **futureonly** switch. If you don't want the existing columns to inherit the new rule, you might want to consider creating a separate rule for your new data types and leaving the existing columns and data types intact. Inevitably, when the **futureonly** switch is used, someone forgets whether the rule is applied to a column and you must go back and redefine your rules for clarity anyway.

Dropping a table that has rules bound to any columns in that table will not cause the rules to be removed from the database because they, the rules, are objects within the database. Rules must be dropped independently of the tables and data types with which they are associated.

Changing Rules

If you want to modify a rule you have created, you can call up the rule in the Enterprise Manager by selecting the database that contains the rule and selecting the rule item in the Manage menu. When the resulting dialog box appears, you must drop the existing rule and create the replacement rule. Figure 9.1 shows the Manage Rules dialog box.

You should check for any existing bindings in the Manage Rules dialog box before dropping a rule. If you try to drop a rule while it is bound to a column or data type, you will receive an error.

Dropping Rules

You can drop rules through the Enterprise Manager or programmatically with the DROP RULE statement, as shown in the following code:

```
DROP RULE [owner.]rule_name [, [owner.]rule_name...]
```

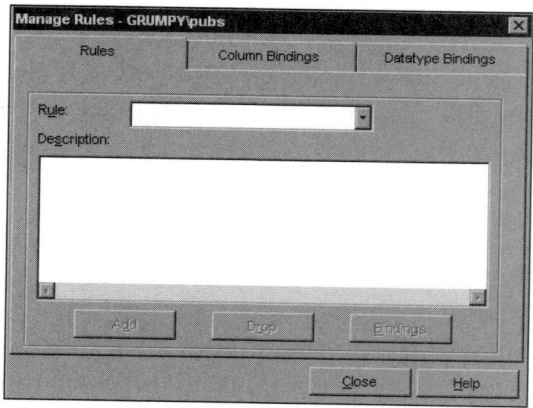

The Manage Rules dialog box.
Figure 9.1

Dropping rules does not affect the existing data in any of the columns to which they were previously bound. When you apply a new rule to a column or columns, the new rule will be applied to all new data statements applying changes to bound columns. Existing data is ignored and will not be changed or validated against the new rule.

If you are concerned about the existing data in a table for which you are creating a new rule, you should write a query to check the existing data. If you find any violations with the query, you can write a script that will change the existing data before applying the new rule.

Defaults

Although very useful, *defaults* are one of the most underused features of Microsoft SQL Server. Most developers create tables and views with a lot of care; however, they create indexes based on experience gathered from slow-running queries and seldom give much thought to how defaults can be used to streamline their processes. A default is just what you would expect: a value that is assumed when no other value is specified. Interestingly, in Microsoft SQL Server, the default is an object in the database, just like a table or a rule. Therefore, you can create defaults as objects and bind them to tables and user-defined data types.

Many defaults can be applied to any system to help with the repetitive tasks of the client application or even the stored procedures you have created for modifying your data. One way to tell where you should be considering defaults is to look through your SQL code and pay particular attention to the INSERT and UPDATE statements. These two statements are prime candidates for defaults.

In addition, any function call or system information that is supplied to these SQL statements should be considered for use as a default—for instance, the system's ability to write the current user or system date to a record when the user is changing or adding data to a table (audit trails). In this situation, you could apply a default to these columns at the database and be assured that the values inserted or updated in the table or tables are applied correctly.

For more on defaults, look up the stored procedure sp_helpText in Microsoft SQL Server Books Online.

Creating Defaults

Default values can be applied on a table-by-table basis to tables as they are created, or, in the case of default objects in the database, they can be created one time and bound to as many columns as needed. I prefer the second method, because it provides a bit more flexibility within the data model. The following syntax is used in creating a default object in your database:

```
CREATE DEFAULT [owner.]default_name
AS expression
```

Binding Defaults

After you have created a default, you must bind it to a column or user-defined data type. Once it is bound to an object, you can either omit the column reference and value from INSERT or UPDATE statements, or pass the keyword DEFAULT in either statement to have the default value applied to the table. This concept can be hard to get used to at first. Writing an INSERT statement that does not supply values to be inserted is a bit nerve-racking. If you have default values bound or defined for each column in a table, you can even specify an INSERT with *no* values and still get a fairly complete record.

Remember that you must bind a default to a column or user-defined data type just as you would a rule: either programmatically with sp_bindefault or through the Manage Defaults dialog box, shown in Figure 9.2.

Changing Defaults

The basic guidelines that apply to changing rules also apply to changing the values associated with a default object in your database. To change a default, you must drop

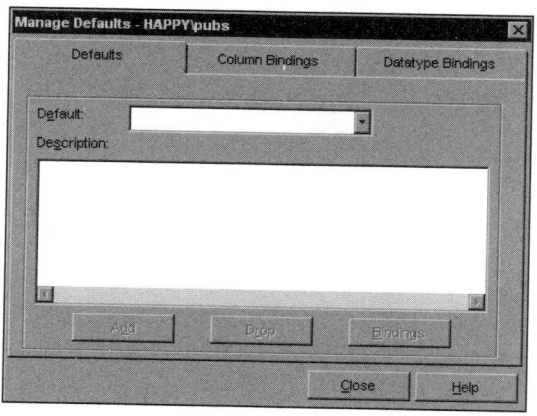

The Manage Defaults dialog box.
Figure 9.2

it first, then create a new one, rebinding the default to the appropriate columns. Keep in mind that you must unbind the default before dropping it or an error will be returned. You can perform this operation programmatically or through the Enterprise Manager.

Another common method of changing default values is to create a default with a new value and apply it (with a different name) to any new columns that require the new default value, leaving the old one in place or replacing it as time permits. Be sure not to keep old versions of defaults hanging around. After a month or two of being away from your data model, you will forget which default should be used where and Murphy will jump up and bite you in the ... well, you get my point.

Dropping Defaults

The syntax for dropping a default is shown below. Be sure to unbind the default from any columns or user-defined data types before issuing the DROP statement.

```
DROP DEFAULT [owner.]default_name [, [owner.]default_name...]
```

Do not confuse the default object with the declared default issued in the CREATE TABLE statement. A default applied to a column in a CREATE statement is considered declarative, or bound by declaration to a column in a table, whereas the default object is not. For more on the differences between these two kinds of defaults, consult Microsoft SQL Server Books Online.

Constraints

Constraints are another seldom-used and often-misunderstood component of your data model. Many data modeling tools, including the Embarcadero product on the CD-ROM enclosed with this book, create constraints based on the entity and relationships you define in your data model. A constraint can be column-level or table-level. (*Note:* This is a Microsoft SQL Server exam question!) Let's look at each constraint and how it is applied in Microsoft SQL Server.

Primary Key

Primary Key is the most commonly used constraint in data models today. It ensures that no duplicate records are inserted into the table to which it is applied. When you create a primary key, Microsoft SQL Server creates a supporting index that matches the column list in the primary declaration. You can supply optional index information or your own unique name for a Primary Key constraint.

Keep in mind that you cannot use NULL values in your primary key columns and that you can have only one Primary Key constraint defined per table. Primary Keys are used for implementing entity and/or relational integrity. You can supply the constraint creation code in either the CREATE or ALTER TABLE statements.

Unique

The Unique constraint is similar to the Primary Key in that it does not allow duplicate values to be entered into a column or group of columns in the table in which it's been created. Some systems refer to this constraint as a "Candidate" constraint, because it can replace the Primary Key in function, should the need arise.

Unlike Primary Keys, Unique supplies a NULL value for a column if it is part of a composite key or group of columns that make up the key value for the constraint. However, I do not recommend allowing NULLs into your Unique constraints because of the behavior of NULLs in sorting and output, and because a NULL value in a column would preclude the use of the Unique constraint as a Primary Key.

As with the Primary Key constraint, an index will be created to match the columns specified in the constraint definition. You have the ability to supply index-specific information through either the CREATE or ALTER TABLE statements.

Foreign Key

This constraint works in concert with the Primary Key constraint to supply you with the referential integrity that today's data models demand. The Foreign Key constraint is applied to the child table of a parent-child relationship, or the "many" side of a one-to-many relationship. This constraint does not create an index automatically. You should create an index that matches the join conditions used to relate the foreign key value with the primary key value. Missing an index on the column or columns specified in a Foreign Key can cause big performance problems for your queries.

Default

You can create a constraint that in essence works just like the DEFAULT object except that it is applied to the table and column directly through the CREATE or ALTER statements. The syntax is very similar to that of the DEFAULT object and follows the same SQL statement guidelines. This type of default is considered declarative since you must state the column and value at the time you create or alter the table object.

However, unlike the DEFAULT object, the default constraint does not need to be bound and unbound to columns. The DEFINE statement takes care of that step for you.

Check

This constraint is applied to one or more columns to ensure that a piece of data falls within a range or pattern. You can define multiple Check constraints to columns on your tables to take many different system requirements into account. Check constraints can be applied to columns where existing rules are applied.

These constraints can be administrated through the Microsoft SQL Server Enterprise Manager or through the SQL code. Unlike the reusable objects discussed in this chapter, when a table is dropped from the database, the constraints are also dropped. For more on these constraints, see Microsoft SQL Server Books Online.

User-Defined Data Types

In the data-modeling world, this section would be called "Domains." A *user-defined data type (UDT)* is a definition that is created using existing system data types and can be used to define column data types in table definition statements. For example, instead of defining a ZIP code column as a CHARACTER(10), you would create a UDT called ZIP and define its data type as CHARACTER(10). Then in all tables that require a ZIP code column, you would supply the ZIP data type in the CREATE TABLE statement. Sounds easy, doesn't it? Yet not many systems take advantage of this feature because most of the tables are already in place by the time the developers discover it.

You should look at user-defined data types as a possible solution for the table creation problems that arise in a multiple-programmer shop designing a major system from the ground up. Typically the more complex the data model, the more people involved in the creation process. Defining a standard set of UDTs for creating tables makes life a lot easier.

Entity Definition

Once you have identified the possible entities in your model, look for places where a standard definition of a data type might be helpful. I typically use UDTs for short strings, notes, first and last names, and address columns. It's hard enough to get two people to agree on how even one thing should be defined or the size it should be set to—let alone 40 or 50 columns distributed across 15 to 20 tables.

Next time you are in a room with four or five programmers, ask them each to define a table structure for storing employee information—address, phone number, spouse, pay scale, and so on. Don't compare any structures until everyone is finished. Most often, there will be as many solutions as there are programmers, which demonstrates the importance of user-defined data types in a multiple-programmer environment.

For the syntax associated with the creation of a user-defined data type, see Listing 9.3. In this listing, I am creating a UDT called **fName** and making it a variable-length character value that does not allow NULL values.

Listing 9.3 Syntax for the sp_addType stored procedure.

```
SYNTAX
sp_addtype typename, phystype [, nulltype]

EXAMPLE
EXEC sp_addtype fName, 'VARCHAR(20)', 'NOT NULL'
```

You can manage your user-defined data types through stored procedures or through the Enterprise Manager. See Figure 9.3 for the Manage User-Defined Data Types dialog box.

Create Table Statement

In order to understand how UDTs work, we'll build on the **fName** type from Listing 9.3. I can now create a table using the standard CREATE TABLE syntax, and where

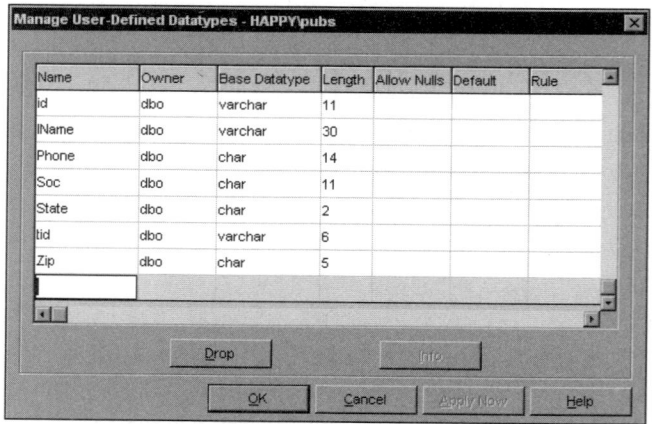

The Manage User-Defined Data Types dialog box.
Figure 9.3

the first-name column would be provided, I would type the line of code, as shown in Listing 9.4.

Listing 9.4 Sample CREATE TABLE statement.

```
CREATE TABLE testTable (
    SocSecNum    CHAR(11)      NOT NULL,
    F_Name       fName,
    L_Name       VARCHAR(30)   NOT NULL,
    Address1     VARCHAR(35)   NOT NULL,
    Address2     VARCHAR(35),
    City         VARCHAR(25)   NOT NULL,
    State        CHAR(2)       NOT NULL,
    Zip          CHAR(10)      NOT NULL)
```

Let's look at this table more closely for a moment and identify the additional columns that would make good UDT candidates. You could also define a standard data type and size for the social security number column, the other name column, and all the address information if needed. Creating a UDT for each column would probably be overkill. I'd use a UDT for the address columns, because it has usually been one of those columns that has bitten me in the past when I was trying to convert systems or upsize or integrate outside data.

You could also create a UDT for city if the city column exists in many other tables. State is most likely OK as a CHARACTER(2), but if you were storing the state in many tables, you might want to create a **ShortState** data type and a **LongState** data type for clarity when using state data. The ZIP code column is a good candidate if ZIP code information is stored in more than one table.

The data type rules I use are fairly simple. When determining a data type for a column or UDT, make sure that you are not storing more than you need. If you only care about the date and not the time down to the minute, use **smallDateTime** instead of **dateTime**. This uses half the space and holds the same information needed to generate reports.

Assessing when to use **character** data types is more difficult. As a rule, if the width of the data is static, **character** data types are probably good unless you have the possibility of lots of empty column values. For variable-length character data over 15 to 20 characters, I usually use **varchar** data types. These save storage space and only add a bit of overhead to the record stored in the table.

Dependency

I like to use UDTs when possible for two reasons: You can reuse them in more than one table, and you can bind a rule or default directly to them. This gives me a powerful tool for creating a solid data model and an easy-to-maintain system. Once you have created these data types, rules, and defaults in your system, essentially you have created an interdependent relationship among the objects in your database. Tables can be created with predefined data types with defaults and rules built in from the beginning of the data model's life cycle.

You can also define all the domains you are going to use in your table structure as UDTs and create tables based on your list of UDTs. This method might be overkill, but it does have some merit. You can then assign default values and rules to columns of similar type across the tables in your data model, providing a very strict data validation model that takes advantage of rules and default values. I have seen only a few systems developed that have taken constraints and UDTs to that level; a great deal of discipline and hard work is required to keep a strict model within that kind of scope.

Summary

- Rules can be used to help ensure data integrity.
- Default values can be created and bound to columns in your table on the fly or statically when the table is created.
- Constraints can be used to ensure the integrity of your data.
- Using constraints in conjunction with triggers provides an additional level of integrity within your data model.
- User-defined data types (UDTs) can reduce the amount of programmer error with regard to table creation in a multiple-programmer environment.

Practical Guide To Rules, Defaults, Constraints, And User-Defined Data Types

In this section, you will walk through the creation of user-defined data types and the process of applying UDTs to the table creation process.

Defining The Domains

The first step in creating effective user-defined data types is to define the domains that are present in your system. Phone numbers, names, ZIP codes, and ID values are good candidates for UDTs, as are any columns that could be interpreted as more than one data type or more than one length.

In this guide, we'll go through a typical human resources-type table. We'll store the information pertaining to our employees in a table and determine which columns could be used as user-defined data types. See Table 9.1 for the columns.

Each of these columns or domains could be defined any number of ways. The purpose here is not to convince you of which data type is best for, say, phone numbers; it is to illustrate how you can standardize the way you set up column widths and apply rules when creating tables in Microsoft SQL Server.

Domain	Possible Data Types, Lengths, And Rules
Social	CHAR(9), CHAR(11), NOT NULL, "Hyphens in right position"
First Name	CHAR(?), VARCHAR(?), NOT NULL, First UPPER()
Last Name	CHAR(?), VARCHAR(?), NOT NULL, First UPPER()
Address	CHAR(?), VARCHAR(?), NOT NULL
City	CHAR(?), VARCHAR(?), NOT NULL
State	CHAR(2), CHAR(?), VARCHAR(?), NOT NULL
ZIP	CHAR(5), CHAR(9), CHAR(10), NOT NULL
Phone	CHAR(7), CHAR(10), CHAR(15), VARCHAR(?)
DOB	DATETIME, SMALLDATETIME, CHAR(8), NOT NULL
DOH	DATETIME, SMALLDATETIME, CHAR(8), NOT NULL

Table 9.1 *Employee table columns.*

Creating The Scripts

The next step is to decide what system data type you will use for each of the user-defined data types. See Listing 9.5 for the stored procedure script that will create the data types for this exercise.

Listing 9.5 UDT creation script.
```
/* Create the UDTs */
/* Soc */
IF EXISTS(SELECT uid FROM SYSTYPES WHERE name = 'Soc')
BEGIN
EXEC sp_droptype Soc
END
EXEC sp_addtype Soc, 'CHAR(11)', 'NOT NULL'

/* First Name */
IF EXISTS(SELECT uid FROM SYSTYPES WHERE name = 'fName')
BEGIN
EXEC sp_droptype fName
END
EXEC sp_addtype fName, 'VARCHAR(25)', 'NOT NULL'

/* Last Name */
IF EXISTS(SELECT uid FROM SYSTYPES WHERE name = 'lName')
BEGIN
EXEC sp_droptype lName
END
EXEC sp_addtype lName, 'VARCHAR(30)', 'NOT NULL'

/* Address */
IF EXISTS(SELECT uid FROM SYSTYPES WHERE name = 'Address')
BEGIN
EXEC sp_droptype Address
END
EXEC sp_addtype Address, 'VARCHAR(30)', 'NOT NULL'

/* City */
IF EXISTS(SELECT uid FROM SYSTYPES WHERE name = 'City')
BEGIN
EXEC sp_droptype City
END
EXEC sp_addtype City, 'VARCHAR(30)', 'NOT NULL'

/* State */
IF EXISTS(SELECT uid FROM SYSTYPES WHERE name = 'State')
BEGIN
EXEC sp_droptype State
```

```
END
EXEC sp_addtype State, 'CHAR(2)', 'NOT NULL'

/* Zip */
IF EXISTS(SELECT uid FROM SYSTYPES WHERE name = 'Zip')
BEGIN
EXEC sp_droptype Zip
END
EXEC sp_addtype Zip, 'CHAR(5)', 'NOT NULL'

/* Phone */
IF EXISTS(SELECT uid FROM SYSTYPES WHERE name = 'Phone')
BEGIN
EXEC sp_droptype Phone
END
EXEC sp_addtype Phone, 'CHAR(14)'

/* DOB */
IF EXISTS(SELECT uid FROM SYSTYPES WHERE name = 'DOB')
BEGIN
EXEC sp_droptype DOB
END
EXEC sp_addtype DOB, 'SMALLDATETIME', 'NOT NULL'

/* DOH */
IF EXISTS(SELECT uid FROM SYSTYPES WHERE name = 'DOH')
BEGIN
EXEC sp_droptype DOH
END
EXEC sp_addtype DOH, 'SMALLDATETIME', 'NOT NULL'
```

I have included the logic in this script to check for the existence of a data type in the Systypes system table. Although this is not a requirement, it is good practice when creating scripts and data model modifying routines.

Printing Out A UDT Listing

Next, you should create a spreadsheet or some other form of document that lists the available user-defined data types, then distribute it to all the programmers and developers who have CREATE permissions within your data model. It would also be helpful to post this information over your desk or in the front of the scripts that create tables in your data model. Table 9.2 shows the sample UDTs.

UDT	Data Type And Nullability
Soc	CHAR(11), NOT NULL
fName	VARCHAR(25), NOT NULL
lName	VARCHAR(30), NOT NULL, First UPPER()
Address	VARCHAR(30), NOT NULL
City	VARCHAR(30), NOT NULL
State	CHAR(2), NOT NULL
ZIP	CHAR(5), NOT NULL
Phone	CHAR(14)
DOB	SMALLDATETIME, NOT NULL
DOH	SMALLDATETIME, NOT NULL

Table 9.2 User-defined data type list.

Building A Table Structure

The only real difference between creating a table using UDTs and using system data types is that your CREATE TABLE statement can use the new UDTs in place of system data types, as shown in Listing 9.6.

Listing 9.6 Sample table creation script using UDTs.

```
/* Create the NewEmployee Table */

CREATE TABLE NewEmployee (
Social      Soc,
First_Name  fName,
Last_Name   lName,Address1    address,
Address2    address,
City        city,
State       state,
Zip         zip,
Phone_Num   phone,
Birthday    DOB,
Hire_Date   DOH )
```

Although I did not have to specify any precision in this new table, I can open the new table in the Enterprise Manager to ensure it has been successfully created. For an example of the new table, see Figure 9.4. Notice that the size is still reported, as is the UDT information.

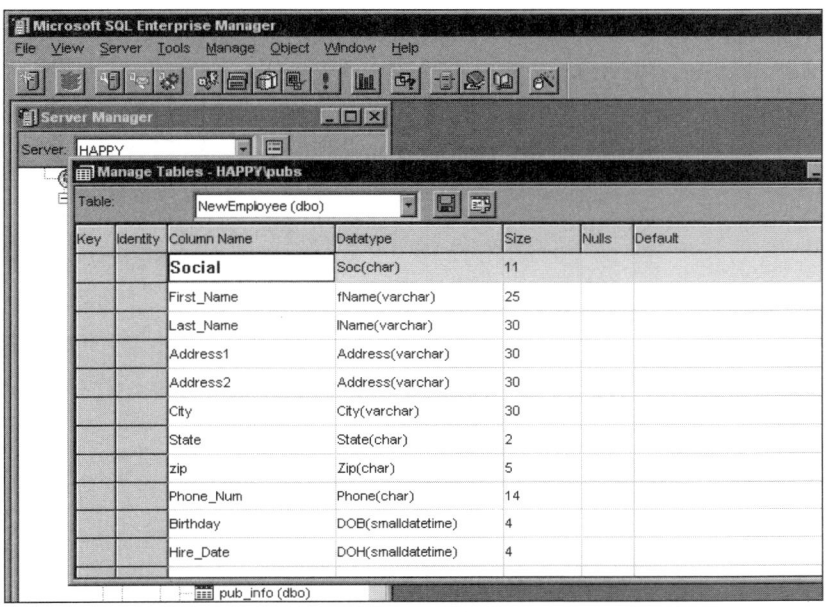

The Manage Tables dialog box showing the NewEmployee table.
Figure 9.4

Maintenance And Troubleshooting

The last thing to take into account is how often you'll need to remind people about using the UDTs you have defined in your data model. You'll hear the "I forgot" and "I was in a hurry" excuses more often than you can count. Be patient and supportive. The only way to effectively implement this type of data model is through established standards. Supporting and practicing these new standards may be more difficult than you anticipate.

One helpful technique is to place UDTs in the Model database, so that each user database created will inherit the predefined data types by default. Try using this in your environment for many common database objects that can be populated automatically with each CREATE DATABASE statement run against Microsoft SQL Server.

One last thing: *Back up the master database!*

Chapter 10

Error Codes

- Query/Connection-Based Errors
- Server Configuration Errors
- Connectivity Errors
- Transaction Log Errors
- Table And Index Errors

Administrator's Notes...

Chapter 10

Errors In Microsoft SQL Server

Although some in the industry consider SQL to be error-prone, when properly implemented, it runs reliably and consistently. Only a handful of errors of any significance have crept up in the last few years. As with any complex piece of software, however, Microsoft SQL Server does pose some challenges.

Errors occur for a number of reasons: poorly written code, server configuration issues, and so on. I have found that there are some problems with Microsoft SQL Server that require some fancy programming to get around. These errors can be overcome with some thought and planning and should not steer you away from using Microsoft SQL Server as the server-side data repository for your enterprise.

Over the last several months, I have logged some of the errors frequently discussed on the Internet, as well as some I have run across setting up production servers. This list, which appears in the Practical Guide, by no means comprises all the problems that you could encounter when using Microsoft SQL Server. Nor is it intended to point out the shortfalls of Microsoft SQL Server. More constructively, this list gives you a road map to deal with errors as they occur.

Method Or Madness

When you see an error, in most any situation you begin to question the product and its ability to perform the task. Most developers, myself included, do not like to find fault in the code we write. Our first instinct is to blame someone else or look for some other reason for the problem. The same is true when developing server-side procedures for managing your data. You might try your best to create a solid set of methods for manipulating data that takes every event into consideration, but there will come a time when you will miss something. It is human nature; we make mistakes.

I have found that most systems lack any kind of in-depth error handling. Client applications can usually be debugged very well and have good error-handling techniques, but Microsoft SQL Server needs to have some error handling as well. After all, you would not build a house without taking the time to make sure the foundation was solid, and error handling is the foundation of your server-side processes. I have had the opportunity to work on some fairly elaborate systems that needed some well-thought-out error handling built in to each procedure. This is not always the case with systems developed in-house or under a strict timetable.

Take the time to look at the way your clients and server-side processes handle errors. Try to keep errors from the user screen. Nothing fosters distrust more than repeated error messages notifying the user of a problem with the system. Trap and handle your errors and create a log so that you can trace the problems and find the answers without chasing your tail for hours.

Service Packs

While many people see service packs as a sign of weakness in an application, I see them as a response to the needs of users. Early on in the life cycle of the product, I uncovered a bug in Microsoft SQL Server 6.5 that would have caused serious system problems for one of my clients. I contacted the usual support channels (Microsoft Support, Knowledge Base, and newsgroups) and received adequate responses—including a "hot-patch" that was basically a beta of a service pack. With this, I was able get the development cycle back on track.

I have found service packs to be very timely considering the amount of operations and implementations that each service pack must be tested against. Some people have had trouble installing service packs correctly. My only advice is to *read the directions*. Microsoft can only test so many methods of applying an update. If you do not follow the directions to the letter, service packs can become unstable and unpredictable.

As of this writing, we are awaiting Service Pack 3 for Microsoft SQL Server 6.5 and are starting to hear rumblings about version 7.0 coming down the beta trail very soon. My suggestion is this: If you are having trouble with a particular error, check to see if a service pack has been released to fix it. If it has, apply the service pack before calling for support. Microsoft or any other service provider will recommend that first anyway.

Research

When asked to solve a problem, I first gather all the information so that I have a thorough understanding of what is happening. When under time constraints, after fixing the problem, I later go back and research the cause of the error so that I can head it off in the future.

I have found Microsoft SQL Server Books Online to be a good resource. It is not very descriptive, however, regarding the more obscure errors that can come up with Microsoft SQL Server. You can also turn to Knowledge Base articles on TechNet and on the Microsoft Web site. There you'll find some of the reasons and workaround solutions for most errors on Microsoft SQL Server.

To help keep up to date, I also spend an hour or so per day in the newsgroups pertaining to Microsoft SQL Server to see what others are encountering in their systems. If I see a problem for which I know a fix, I offer my solution. If I find an error I do not know about, I then look it up and see what I can learn about it.

This might seem like a lot of work, but it pays off in the end. You will spend less time fixing problems if you know why they occur.

Summary

- Know your limitations. Ask yourself whether the error is being caused by your approach or the software.
- Understand the product and how it works.
- Create error handlers for all your procedures, whether server-side or client-side.
- Realize that people are only human, and they make mistakes. Plan for those mistakes.

- Know why an error occurs, not just that it occurs.
- Apply all related service packs to your operating system and to Microsoft SQL Server when they are available and tested. This will reduce the number of errors that you see on your server.

Practical Guide To Error Codes

This section will walk you through some of the more common errors experienced in developing enterprise database systems with Microsoft SQL Server.

This Practical Guide focuses on some of the most common errors and how to get around them. I have used information available in Microsoft SQL Server Books Online, the TechNet CD issues, Internet newsgroups, and the Microsoft Knowledge Base. For each error, I cite the recommendations given by Books Online, the Knowledge Base, and Microsoft newsgroups. You may encounter errors that are not on this list; take the time to research your errors and understand not only that they happen but also why they happen.

Query/Connection-Based Errors

The majority of these errors are based on the code that you write to run against SQL Server. You should be able to troubleshoot many of these errors in your code with little outside help. Microsoft SQL Server Books Online and Transact-SQL Reference should provide you with the tools needed to fix just about any problem you run into with regard to this type of error.

Error 107

This error occurs when you attempt to create a view that contains a UNION clause and a correlated subquery. (For more on correlated subqueries, see Chapters 5 and 6.) This error can also be returned if you have mismatched table or alias names inside your query. Error 107 can be returned by more than one problem. Pay attention to the situation and take the action to fix the problem based on your individual situation. The error message is as follows:

```
The column prefix '%.*s' does not match with a table name or alias name
used in the query.
```

Books Online: No real useful information is available in Microsoft SQL Server Books Online for this error code. This error is typically related to a typo in your code and can be corrected by analyzing the error output to determine where the error is occurring.

Knowledge Base: In its Knowledge Base, Microsoft has confirmed that this is a problem with regard to views in Microsoft SQL Server versions 6.0 and 6.5. To work around this error, change your view definition and avoid using both a UNION clause and a correlated subquery. You can also fix this bug by contacting Microsoft Online or researching the latest volume of Microsoft TechNet for the service pack that fixes this problem.

Newsgroups: I have not often seen discussion of this error on the Internet newsgroups. This error occurs mostly in classroom environments and is usually easily fixed once the situation has been pointed out to the student.

Error 156

An error 156 message helps you find syntax errors in your code. You will see this error when writing pass-through SQL or creating stored procedures. Read carefully all the lines of your query near matching keywords returned by the error to find the problem with your code. This error is most often due to missing keywords or incorrect formatting of SQL code. (For examples of ANSI 92-compliant SQL syntax, check out *The SQL Instant Reference,* written by Martin Gruber and published by Sybex.) Following is the text of the error message:

```
Incorrect syntax near the keyword '%.*s'.
```

Books Online: As with many syntax-related errors, there is little in Microsoft SQL Server Books Online beyond explaining that you have a typo in your code.

Knowledge Base: Little in the Knowledge Base archives covers writing SQL statements.

Newsgroups: There are many questions in the SQL-related newsgroups with regard to this error code. I have seen many postings to the newsgroups for help with syntax for a particular query. The Internet is a huge repository of information from people willing to help you write better SQL code.

Error 1205

Error 1205 is perhaps one of the most feared errors in writing a client application or overnight process. This error is returned when your process encounters a deadlock. A deadlock occurs when two or more processes try to access a resource that another process has a lock on. Microsoft SQL Server automatically detects these deadlocks, terminates one of the processes, and rolls back any changes made by that process. The process chosen for termination will be the one with the least amount of active time on the server. In most cases, you can simply reissue the statements that were rolled back and should have no problems.

I highly recommend trapping for this error in all your procedures and client applications. Usually this error is generated by client applications that read or select a large amount of data from the server without returning the entire record set to the client. This means that Microsoft SQL Server cannot release the shared lock on the pages affected by the query. I have found that issuing a NOLOCK optimizer hint for my read-only queries greatly reduces the chances of deadlock and blocked processes. The message text for error 1205 is as follows:

```
Your server command (process id#%d) was deadlocked with another process
and has been chosen as deadlock victim. Rerun your command.
```

Books Online: This error is usually just a bit of bad timing. Books Online recommends that you cancel the batch you are currently executing and re-run your command. SQL Server does not always cancel the entire batch of commands being executed in a deadlock situation, however. If the entire batch is not canceled, any attempt to submit a new set of commands can result in DB-Library error 10038 (the general message "results pending") being returned from subsequent SQL code execution.

Newsgroups: I have found that most problems regarding deadlock reported in the Internet newsgroups are due to improper client-side processing of result sets. If a client requests data, even for read-only purposes, and does not get the entire result set back from the server, Microsoft SQL Server holds the shared locks on the pages affected by the query. Most developers believe they have locked up the server or a query has been "hung" and should be killed; in reality, however, they are running a blocked process.

Server Configuration Errors

These errors result primarily from improper configuration and tuning of your server. The solution to this type of error might require a bit more research or require you to restart the SQL Server service. Most of the configuration options that need to be changed as a result of these errors are static and take effect when the server is shut down and restarted. Check Microsoft SQL Server Books Online for more information on the configuration parameters discussed here and how any changes you make will affect the overall operation of your server.

Error 603

In researching this error, I found two causes and two different message texts returned. One cause of this error is insufficient memory, which limits the number of table descriptors available to a single query. (Remember that the number of open objects you have defined on your server is totally dependent on the system.) The other cause has to do with dumping or creating a backup of the database to a Digital Linear Tape device (DLT), and then subsequently restoring it on another server that has a different type of DLT device. Because the number of descriptors stored in the backup is different than that on the server you are restoring to, the restore will fail. You will have to look at what you have defined on your system and set your configuration options appropriately.

The error message text for error 603 is as follows:

```
There are not enough system session descriptors available to run this query.
The maximum number available to a process is %d. Split query and rerun.
```

To avoid backup-related errors, consider staying with a single brand of backup device across your data servers or using a network share point to write backups to and restore from.

Books Online: To fix query-related problems, split the offending query into smaller parts or increase the number of open objects on your server. If this error occurs often when you are running large queries, you should go into the Enterprise Manager or use sp_configure to increase the OPEN OBJECTS parameter on your server. This problem is a configuration issue and can be resolved by changing the SQL Server OPEN OBJECTS parameter.

When SQL Server starts, it builds a pool of descriptor data structures in memory that are used to reference database objects. The number of descriptors is equal to the number of open objects you have configured on your server. Once the free pool of descriptors has been used up, SQL Server will reuse inactive descriptors as needed. The first time a descriptor is reused, SQL Server issues the following message:

```
Warning: OPEN OBJECTS parameter may be too low; attempt was made to free
up descriptors in localsdes().

Run sp_configure to increase parameter value.
```

Remember that allocating too many descriptors to memory will steal from the available RAM on your server and may affect total system performance. Add descriptors sparingly and test any changes on your server to determine whether changing the amount of open objects has affected something else on your server.

Knowledge Base: If you dump a database to a DLT and restore through a different server or different DLT, the system will return an error 603. To avoid this error, the Knowledge Base advises you to dump the database to a disk dump device and copy the file to the other server across the network. If the network copy is not an option, use the Windows NT backup facility to back up and restore the disk dump file from the source server to the target server, then load the backup normally without getting the tape device involved in the actual restoration process.

Another possible approach is to use the Transfer Manager to copy the database from one server to another. Although this method takes more time, you could restore the backup on one server and migrate it to another across the network. Be careful of permissions and passwords with the Transfer Manager; it will script NULL for all passwords for the users it migrates from one server to another.

Microsoft confirms that this error occurs with Microsoft SQL Server version 6.0 and at the time this book was published, it was researching fixes and will be posting any service packs to the Internet as quickly as possible.

Newsgroups: I have only seen a few questions regarding error 603 on the Internet newsgroups. If you find you are getting frequent 603 errors, you might want to analyze the configuration of your server to see if you have properly accounted for enough open objects in your environment.

Errors 706 And 707

We'll look at these two errors together, because they are both related to insufficient SQL Server system memory. When records are accessed from the database with server-side cursors and not enough system memory has been allocated to SQL Server, error 706 or error 707 will be returned. The message text returned for error 706 is as follows:

```
Process %d tried to remove PROC_HDR 0x%1x that it does not hold in Pss
(Process Slot Structure).
```

Error 707 returns the following error message:

```
System error detected during attempt to free memory at address 0x%1x.
Please consult the Microsoft SQL Server error log for more details.
```

Books Online: If you receive error 707, Books Online suggests stopping and restarting Microsoft SQL Server. After startup, check the consistency of your databases by running the DBCC CHECKDB and NEWALLOC commands. Review your SQL Server error logs and look for any sign of hardware-related failures. This error is probably related to your server's memory configuration and should be corrected by stopping and restarting the SQL Server service.

Knowledge Base: The Microsoft Knowledge Base suggests the same fixes as Books Online but adds that after either error 706 or 707 is reported, it is often followed by handled access violations. As a result, SQL Server often locks up and becomes unusable with 100 percent CPU utilization. Microsoft has confirmed that this is a problem with Microsoft SQL Server version 6.5. It can be corrected with U.S. Service Pack 1 for Microsoft SQL Server version 6.5.

Newsgroups: This bug is familiar to some users in the newsgroups. Microsoft released Service Pack 1 to fix this and other problems related to Microsoft SQL Server 6.5. If you are seeing a lot of these errors, you should consider applying Service Pack 1 to your server.

Error 1105

This error is returned when you run out of available space inside a device or database. The action you are trying to perform has caused you to run out of room and the following message is returned:

```
Can't allocate space for object '%.*s' in database '%.*s' because
the '%.*s' segment is full. If you ran out of space in Syslogs, dump
the transaction log. Otherwise, use ALTER DATABASE or sp_extendsegment
to increase the size of the segment.
```

You typically see this error when your transaction log fills up. In addition, running out of room in Tempdb generates this error. If you have run out of room, you should look at the size of the result sets your queries are returning and adjust the space allocated to Tempdb to better suit your needs. Poor index coverage also will cause worktables for your queries to be created in Tempdb, and depending on the size of the table, can cause you to run out of room.

Books Online: Books Online provides a very detailed account of the causes of error 1105. The most common is that Tempdb has used all of its allocated space. Another cause of this error could be that the system has outgrown the space allocated at the user database level or in the master database. Once you have determined which object has run out of room, refer to Books Online for a step-by-step method of solving the problem.

Knowledge Base: The Knowledge Base suggests increasing the size of Tempdb and restarting SQL Server to clear any leftover temporary tables. You can, on occasion, create temporary tables in Tempdb that are not released properly by Microsoft SQL Server. Beware of using the EXECUTE statement in a situation that would cause multiple temporary tables to be created on the server.

Error 1108

Error 1108 is another message associated with Tempdb. This error is returned when SQL Server traverses the extent chain for deallocation and finds an extent that holds unexpected information. User databases utilize these chains for fast manipulation of data on an extent-by-extent basis. Recall that SQL Server allocates contiguous storage space as a single unit called an *extent*, which is made up of eight 2K pages. Each record is stored on the 2K pages. As each database table requires more space, SQL Server allocates additional extents to the object from within the device and database pool of allocation units. If an unexpected value is found, your table may be corrupted and should be rebuilt or repaired. The message text for error 1108 is as follows:

```
Cannot deallocate extent %Id, database %d. Object id %Id, index id %d,
status %d in extent does not match object id %Id, index id %d, status
%d in object being deallocated. Run DBCC CHECKALLOC.
```

Books Online: If you get this error in Tempdb, Books Online suggests shutting down and restarting SQL Server. Upon restart, increase the size of Tempdb. User databases that report this error need to be checked by the DBCC CHECKALLOC command.

Knowledge Base: The Knowledge Base suggests the same fix as Books Online. In addition, Microsoft has confirmed this to be a problem in Microsoft SQL Server version

6.5. This problem can be corrected with U.S. Service Pack 1 for Microsoft SQL Server version 6.5.

Newsgroups: All the newsgroup threads pertaining to this type of error recommend applying Service Pack 1 to your server to fix the problem.

Error 17809

Error 17809 usually occurs when SQL Server is not configured for enough user connections. You must define or configure the number of user connections that you will allow on each SQL server. Each user connection takes up some overhead and limits the amount of available memory left to service data cache and procedures on your server. User connections are *not* client access licenses. A single client application can have many user connections. This is seen especially in multithreaded applications that utilize multiple connections to improve client-side performance.

Changing this value should be one of the first things you do when installing SQL Server. The default (15 user connections for SQL Workstation and 20 for SQL Server) will almost always not be enough. The error message returned when trying to get a connection when none is available is as follows:

```
Unable to connect. The maximum number of '%d' configured user connections
are already connected. System Administrator can configure to a higher
value with sp_configure.
```

Books Online: Books Online suggests that you use the sp_configure system stored procedure to increase the number of user connections, or that you use the Enterprise Manager and change the configuration options for your server. To increase the number of user connections configured on your server, see the sample syntax below. By replacing the new number parameter with the number of connections you require, you can change this option programmatically through a script.

```
sp_configure 'user connections', new_number
go
RECONFIGURE
Go
```

For static options, you must restart SQL Server to activate the changes. For dynamic changes to take effect, issue the RECONFIGURE statement shown above.

Newsgroups: Once a week or so I run across someone who is setting up a server for the first time and misses this configuration option. It's easy to miss, and because in the development stage you typically do not need more than the default number of user connections, you might overlook this option until you place your server under a normal load. The fix for this is easy and fast and should not pose a problem once the cause of the error has been identified.

Connectivity Errors

Connectivity errors tend to baffle network administrators more than any other type of error. "Why can't I connect to the server?" or "What happened to my connection?" are often-heard questions in the client/server world. Most of these errors can be traced back to a client application being closed down improperly or a network connection being broken in a nonstandard way. Seldom does the server close connections improperly. Remember that client/server programs contain a step when the client application initiates a connection to the server. The server does not usually connect to the client. It is ultimately the client application's responsibility to properly connect and disconnect from the server.

Error 1608

Error 1608 is returned when the connection is lost between SQL Server and the front-end application while SQL Server is sending query results back to the client. This error is usually hardware-based or the result of a client machine being shut down while awaiting results from a query. The syntax for this error is as follows:

```
A network error was encountered while sending results to the front end.
Check the SQL Server error log for more information.
```

Books Online: According to Books Online, this error is returned when the front-end application either ended abnormally or was terminated. In other words, the front-end computer was turned off or restarted, a network failure occurred, and the network was shut down. Check all hardware connections and network error logs for possible causes.

Knowledge Base: No other solutions are offered in the Microsoft Knowledge Base for this error beyond what is listed in Microsoft SQL Server Books Online.

Newsgroups: This error usually can be debugged easily; few questions are posted to Internet newsgroups. From time to time, questions appear about how to properly trap for this kind of error, however, so you should occasionally check for postings regarding error 1608.

Error 17824

This error is similar to error 1608 in that it is due to an improper hardware connection or because the client's computer has been powered off and restarted, causing the write operation from SQL Server to fail. There can also be a network or a connectivity problem. The message text for this error is as follows:

```
Unable to write to server-side connection.
```

Books Online: Books Online suggests reviewing the Windows NT event and application logs for information that may indicate whether the problem is related to the server network protocol, network card, or system configuration. Also review the Microsoft SQL Server-specific entries in the Windows NT application log and the SQL Server error log for relevant network-related errors that occur along with this error. If this review does not provide enough information or if the problem persists, network-monitoring tools might be needed, along with a review of the client configurations.

Knowledge Base: The Microsoft Knowledge Base recommends the same review as Books Online but further suggests making sure the client does not power down his or her system or log off because of a long wait time for long queries. If the client does any of the above actions, the original connection is lost, and error 17824 is imminent.

Newsgroups: Most of the message threads regarding this error attribute the problem to a failure to use the proper Net-Library or to use a common access method to your server. If you mix and match protocols and drivers across many different applications, you are asking for headaches with connectivity. Keep it simple.

Error 17825

Error 17825 occurs when SQL Server attempts to close the network connection to the client. This error almost never happens by itself—it is often a sign of more serious errors. You should check all appropriate error logs for any connectivity-related entries. The message text for this error is as follows:

```
Unable to close server-side connection.
```

Books Online: Books Online suggests checking the SQL Server error log for other, more serious errors that occurred in the same time frame. You should focus on correcting the more serious errors first; in most cases, this error will then go away.

Error 17832

Error 17832 occurs when a client cannot successfully connect because of a client operating system or application failure. It also occurs when the network fails between the time a connection attempt is initiated and when it is completed. The exact syntax for error 17832 is as follows:

```
Unable to read login packet(s).
```

Books Online: Books Online suggests verifying that all clients connected to the affected SQL Server are using the latest version of all Microsoft SQL Server client components, including Net-Libraries, DB-Library, and/or ODBC drivers. Although the type of network library you use to connect to the server will vary, you should use current versions of Net-Libraries when connecting to Microsoft SQL Server. Make sure that both sides of the client/server connection are using the correct Net-Library.

Knowledge Base: Most information in the Microsoft Knowledge Base on this error is the same as what you will find in Books Online. You should be able to troubleshoot this error with your current documentation and a bit of common sense.

Newsgroups: This error gets more traffic in the non-SQL Server newsgroups than in the Microsoft SQL Server groups themselves. A number of client-specific groups are focusing on development of client applications that run against Microsoft SQL Server. Check out the newsgroups for the client development tool you are using to see what kind of message traffic is out there.

Transaction Log Errors

Users often ask me if they can turn off the transaction log on Microsoft SQL Server. The answer is basically *no*. You can truncate the log on each checkpoint issued by SQL Server, but the Syslogs table will always be used by the server to recover from errors or to resolve internal questions as to which processes are active and which can be written to disk. The following error is common to the transaction log in some form and should be researched thoroughly before placing a server into a "live" production environment.

Error 1511

Error 1511 may cause a LOAD TRANSACTION command to fail. If the transaction log being loaded contains the log records for a CREATE CLUSTERED INDEX on a large table (usually over 150MB), the transaction log may fail to load. The exact message returned for this error is as follows:

```
Sort cannot be reconciled with transaction log.
```

Books Online: Microsoft SQL Server Books Online contains little documentation on this error. You'll need to check the Microsoft Knowledge Base for articles related to this error.

Knowledge Base: The Microsoft Knowledge Base suggests dumping the database after a CREATE CLUSTERED INDEX statement on a large table. Microsoft has confirmed this is a problem with Microsoft SQL Server version 6.5. U.S. Service Pack 1 can be used to fix this problem.

Newsgroups: I have recommended to many users in the various newsgroups I frequent that they create backups of all user databases after any static object creation. If the CREATE statement does not trigger a backup of the database, you are asking for problems.

Table And Index Errors

Many of these errors are related to indexes and tables on your server. Some are documented well and some are not. You probably will not like most of the solutions for these kinds of errors; at times you'll even need to make a serious change to your data structure. Many of these errors have been fixed in Service Packs 1 and 2 for Microsoft SQL Server.

Error 605

This is a fatal error that occurs when a database is considered corrupt. The first thing you should do is run **DBCC CHECKDB** and **CHECKALLOC** to determine the extent of the damage. The exact error message is as follows:

```
Attempt to fetch logical page %ld in database '%.*s' belongs to
object '%.*s', not to object '%.*s'.
```

Books Online: According to Books Online, this error occurs when SQL Server detects database corruption. The second parameter specified in the message string (not to object '%.*s') is probably corrupt. This error can mask other errors. To determine the extent of the problem, you should run **DBCC CHECKDB** and **CHECKALLOC**. If these commands do not report additional errors, then the first parameter returned in the message string is not corrupt, and the second object listed should be restored from backup or re-created to fix the problem.

SQL Server detects database corruption when it traverses the page chain of an object and finds a page whose object ID does not match that of the object being accessed. If there is a damaged page chain or an invalid entry in the Sysobjects system table for that object, SQL Server will think that the object is corrupted. Also check the SQL Server error log for other errors that often accompany a 605 error.

Knowledge Base: The Microsoft Knowledge Base describes the same symptoms and fixes as Microsoft SQL Server Books Online.

Newsgroups: Occasionally a database becomes corrupted and cannot be used. Although the reasons for corruption are difficult to trace, this is not a common occurrence with Microsoft SQL Server. Having a good backup strategy in place and tested is a good safety net for this potential hazard. Another safety mechanism is to run DBCC CHECKDB on a regular basis to determine if the database structure is intact and has no major problems. One lesson that is hard to learn is that if you back up a corrupted file, it is still corrupt and there is nothing you can do about it. Check the consistency of your databases often, especially on highly volatile data that changes frequently.

I recommend to anyone who receives this error message that they read all the information in Microsoft SQL Server Books Online before proceeding with the fix for this problem. This error can point to a hardware failure or other failure that might bring the server down if left unchecked.

Error 803

Error 803 is returned when you insert data into a table with one clustered index and at least two nonclustered indexes when the clustered index does not have a unique key associated with it. This error is usually reported on a periodic basis on highly volatile data. I have found that when error 2610 problems (see below) were fixed with Service Pack 2 for Microsoft SQL Server 6.5, 803 errors appeared in their place. Although 803 errors are not impossible to fix, they take some work to overcome. The exact message string returned is as follows:

```
Unable to place buffer 0x%lx holding logical page %ld in sdes
(session descriptors)for object '%.*s'—either there is no room
in sdes or buffer already in requested slot.
The SQL Server is terminating this process.
DB-Library: Possible network error: Write to SQL Server failed.
Net-Library error 232: ConnectionWrite (WriteFile()).
DB-Library process dead - connection broken.
```

If you experience these errors and cannot build a unique clustered index, you can create an error handler that drops the indexes on the table, performs the data modification with no indexes, and rebuilds the indexes after a successful data operation.

Books Online: Books Online states that this error is rare, and therefore it devotes only a few lines to it. I have found that error 803 is not all that rare; when it occurs on your server, it should be treated with care. Dropping indexes to perform an operation causes increased overhead on the system and usually cannot be done on the fly without some complex programming. The queries that seem to cause this error are SELECT-based INSERT statements that move more than one row from one table to another. An example of one of these queries is as follows:

```
Insert into destinationTable
Select sourceTable.*
   from sourceTable
```

Knowledge Base: The Microsoft Knowledge Base suggests dropping all the indexes or the clustered index for the duration of the data insert, performing the operation that caused the error, and rebuilding the indexes. Microsoft has confirmed this is a problem with SQL Server version 6.5, and as of this writing, it is researching potential fixes for inclusion in service pack releases.

Newsgroups: Error 803 has a lot to do with the index coverage you place on a table and the method you use to add records to that table. Although not every situation calls for the same kind of index, a clustered unique index on a table can greatly improve performance and eliminate this error. If you cannot use a unique index and still need index coverage, try using a nonclustered index until Microsoft releases the bug fix.

I have written some fairly complex routines that trap for this error and establish an error state on the server, allowing me to drop any indexes on the affected tables and to retry the operation that caused the error. Then after an allotted time frame, I set the error state off on the server and rebuild the indexes on the affected tables. While this allows the server to continue processing, it might cause some performance issues for a short period of time. This kind of fix should be applied on a case-by-case basis after carefully determining if any other avenue is possible to correct the problem.

Error 806

This error is usually triggered by a hardware issue that creates a conflict at the system level with regard to read/write operations on your server. Make sure that the disk subsystem and controller are on the hardware compatibility list and that the controller is not incorrectly reporting write operations to Microsoft SQL Server. You should check the Windows NT event log for any hardware-related entries that may point to the source of the error. The error message text returned by SQL Server for error 806 is as follows:

```
Could not find virtual page for logical page %ld in database '%.*s'.
```

Books Online: The information in Books Online relates to a hardware problem that may be associated with this error. If a disk controller is going bad or is not reporting disk write operations correctly, Microsoft SQL Server generates this error. First, check the Windows NT event log for any possible disk subsystem errors. Next, run DBCC CHECKDB and CHECKALLOC commands on the database to make sure that the structure of the database is intact and makes sense. Review the output; if structural problems are reported, resolve any problems and monitor the system to verify that they are in fact fixed.

Knowledge Base: In the Microsoft Knowledge Base, error 806 is related to Microsoft SQL Server version 4.21a. This error comes from using a single DBPROCESS to read data and perform a DBWRITETEXT function. Refer to the "Programmer's Reference for C" for information regarding the use of DBPROCESS functions and how they are used to perform a valid DBWRITETEXT operation. Using a single DBPROCESS can be dangerous. All other entries pertain to hardware issues as described in Microsoft SQL Server Books Online.

Newsgroups: This error seems to crop up most in systems that are put together from components and built to suit a client's specifications. If you have not already checked all the components in your server against the hardware compatibility list, you should do so when you start seeing hardware-related errors. Caching seems to be the feature that causes most older disk controllers to fall on hard times. If Microsoft SQL Server is told that a particular piece of information is written to disk, it assumes that it has been and will move on. If a controller reports that it has successfully written to disk, yet has only cached the information, Microsoft SQL Server can get confused and generate errors.

Compaq has some good disk controllers that use caching in such a way that Microsoft SQL Server can function well within the restrictions of how the controller writes to disk.

Error 2506

Error 2506 occurs when SQL Server detects an inconsistency in the storage of the variable columns of a row and a page. This can happen after a fast BCP operation involving many variable-length columns. The exact message syntax returned for error 2506 is as follows:

```
Table Corrupt: The values in adjust table should be in ascending order
starting from the end of the table (page#=%1d); check adjust table in
this row.
```

Books Online: Microsoft SQL Server Books Online suggests the following steps to correct this error:

1. Make sure the Select Into/Bulkcopy option is set to True for the databases.
2. Save the index/trigger/constraint definitions for the problem table. You will need to re-create them later when you re-create the table.
3. Select the data from the problem table into a new one.
4. Drop the problem table.

5. Rename the new table, giving it the problem's name.

6. If applicable, re-create the indexes and triggers.

Newsgroups: Discussion of this error does not show up often in the newsgroups, but it can crop up in production environments that employ BCP to load data and a lot of variable-length columns in their tables.

Error 2610

This error was a mystery to most people until sometime close to Microsoft's release of Service Pack 2 for SQL Server 6.5. Most of the technical support calls regarding this error seemed to generate little response, leading me to believe that Microsoft knew of the problem and was trying to get a fix out as fast as it could. (I have noticed that when Microsoft Support is the quietest about a problem, it is preoccupied with fixing it.) There was a lot of traffic on the Internet newsgroups pertaining to this error, and of all the fixes suggested, only a few really generated any positive result. Your best bet for fixing this error is applying Service Pack 2 for SQL Server 6.5. The error message returned is as follows:

```
Could not find leaf row in nonclustered index'%.*s' that corresponds
to data row from logical data page %Id, row offset %d during update
index attempt after data page split.
```

Books Online: The documentation provided by Microsoft suggests that this error can usually be corrected by dropping and re-creating the index. Books Online considers this error to be rare and therefore has little documentation about it. The only suggested course of action is shown in Listing 10.1. (This script will be of little importance if you follow my recommendation of applying Service Pack 2 when you see this error.) Although the early notes on this error pointed to a corrupt system table entry, it has since been found that this is, in fact, a bug in Microsoft SQL Server 6.5.

Listing 10.1 Suggested course of action for correcting error 2610, from Microsoft SQL Server Books Online.

```
USE master
go
sp_dboption <db_name>,single,true
go
USE <db_name>
go
CHECKPOINT
go
sp_fixindex <db_name>,<system_table_name>,1
```

```
go
USE master
go
sp_dboption <db_name>,single,false
go
USE <db_name>
go
```

This script should *not* be used to correct error code 2610. I have included it here because it will show up when you query this error in Books Online. Although this will correct the problem, it is overkill to fix a bug instead of correcting the problem with the patch.

Knowledge Base: The accounts of this error suggest the following fixes: Make the clustered index unique, drop some or all of the nonclustered indexes for the duration of the insert, or drop the clustered index for the duration of the insert. Although these actions seem unacceptable in a production environment, they *do* provide a workaround for this error.

Newsgroups: This error generated a lot of traffic in the newsgroups. In particular, many messages pertained to the unacceptable fixes offered by the available documentation. It quickly became apparent that users had stumbled on an error and that Microsoft was trying to release a fix as fast as possible. It was just a few weeks later that a patch became available to resolve this problem. Error 2610 is easily the biggest problem I have run into with Microsoft SQL Server to date.

One final tip, as always: *Back up the master database!*

Chapter 11

Performance Tuning And Optimization

Using The Performance Monitor
- Opening The PerformanceMonitor
- Creating A New Chart
- Saving Charts To Files
- Organizing Charts

Using SQL Trace
- Overview Of SQL Trace
- Running SQL Trace

Administrator's Notes…

Chapter 11

I should have my head examined for including this chapter in the book. I could get off much easier writing about developing a good backup strategy or multiple database platform coexistence within your enterprise. But instead, I wrote about performance tuning and optimization because Microsoft SQL Server runs well out of the box for a limited number applications, and therefore a knowledge of tuning and optimization is critical. Also—as with any other major system—it takes "time on the pond" to understand how to troubleshoot well. Read this chapter carefully and make sure you understand *exactly* what to check and how to apply a solution before tinkering with your system.

> **note** *All systems are different and should be treated as unique entities. Do not assume that because you have identical machines with identical configurations you can set them up in the same way and achieve good performance.*

Microsoft SQL Server has been benchmarked and compared against all the major database players in the market and has held its own fairly well. I caution you to really understand what these benchmarks mean before you use them as criteria to judge the performance of any system. A benchmark will *never* be a representation of your system or your SQL code. Find out how the machines were configured before the benchmark was run. Make sure the benchmarks are comparing apples to apples and oranges to oranges. I have set up many different databases and seen some great things from each one. But none worked out of the box exactly the way I needed it to. I have always had to apply indexes and configure the hardware or the parameters of the database server to get the best results.

Microsoft SQL Server has been tested at execution speeds of over 300 transactions per second on some independent tests. The only system I know of that can achieve any sustained kind of throughput in that range is Oracle. This does not mean that Oracle is superior to Microsoft SQL Server, Sybase, Informix, or Progress. Each has its own niche and does a good job of meeting its customers' expectations.

These timed tests are designed to give the marketing people something to promote, and management a basis for making purchasing decisions. If you use these performance numbers for other decisions, you are going down the wrong path. Managers should look at support costs and reliability issues as well as price-versus-performance issues when purchasing a database product. The only other way that benchmarks are useful is to provide an indication of how well the hardware and server software are configured.

Also keep in mind that these tests are run on extremely high-level equipment. The only real-world system I have ever worked on with a sustained throughput of 300 transactions per second or better is a Cray supercomputer, but it doesn't fall within many companies' budgets. Most of the high-end machines that *are* more reasonably priced perform very well and achieve impressive throughput.

Many systems may come close to benchmark execution times for a particular type of query, but none has achieved this level of performance day in and day out. Benchmarks are run under exacting conditions that your system will never be able to match.

However, benchmarks *do* help you ensure that you have a well-tuned machine before placing production data on it. I use the TPC benchmark program available on the TechNet CD-ROM to test my basic configuration to determine if things will run correctly. I then take the benchmark stuff off, apply the real-world data, and move on.

What Is Performance?

The issue of performance is subjective. When called upon to troubleshoot a problem on a database server, whether Microsoft SQL Server, Oracle, or any other, I first determine what exactly the client means by *performance*. To clarify, let's look at a development contract I worked on recently that concerned a very specialized application for analyzing large amounts of data.

I was brought in to "tune" the system after others had attempted to configure the database to best support this new application. I looked at the data model and the timing of the different sections of the application and noted where things could be improved to obtain more speed. Although the application was a bit slow and cumbersome, it was well worth the processing time used, given the amount of behind-the-scenes work required.

After spending a few days coming to understand the scope and detail of the code running behind the client, I dove headfirst into tuning this beast. My first task was to correct the many problems with calculations, then to look at how the speed might be improved. I spent a day or so getting the initial runtime of critical sections of the application down to about 90 seconds on my test machine. Not satisfied yet, I spent a few more days tweaking things until I pushed the runtime down to about 58 seconds.

I wanted the process to run faster still—if possible, under 30 seconds. I brought this up with the project manager, and his response put the whole tuning issue into perspective for me: "The process you are working on currently runs in about 6 minutes on the old machine! What are you worried about?"

You can spend hours getting things to run faster and make only marginal gains. With some systems, those marginal gains may make a significant difference to the end result; with other applications, they will not. Each user's perspective on performance is different. Take the time to determine what *performance* means before spending time trying to fix something that's not really broken.

Establish realistic performance expectations early on in project development and continuously check yourself against those requirements to ensure you are meeting the user's needs—and not trying to fulfill your own.

I have been obsessed with speed since early in my career, when my colleagues and I spent countless hours getting things to run faster than anything currently available. We were keeping track of time in nanoseconds and celebrating even a thousandth of a second improvement as a great milestone. This need for speed drives me to learn more about how things work (and I suspect many of you reading this are nodding your heads in agreement). This chapter is geared toward the techno speed freaks out there.

Bottlenecks

The key to problem solving is breaking down problems into the simplest-possible form before getting involved in finding a solution. A process may be running slowly due to any number of things. If you lump all the issues into one hopper and try to solve the problem, you might find a fix that is only cosmetic. Find the exact place in the process where speed is an issue before looking for a solution.

I have been brought into situations where processes were running poorly because of the indexes (as it turned out), yet everyone was analyzing every component under the sun—network drive controllers, application code, and so forth—to find the solution. An index is the first thing you should check when attempting to solve performance problems. If you break things down and test for the most common violation of performance and tuning rules first, you can save time and money. Once you have identified the bottleneck to your performance, you can then address the problem with a permanent solution.

Now let's take a look at some products that will help you take advantage of the performance that SQL Server can provide.

Performance Monitor

The Windows NT Performance Monitor is one of the most useful tools for troubleshooting Microsoft SQL Server performance problems. In fact, an entire module in the Microsoft Windows NT certification program is devoted to helping students become familiar with the tool. See Figure 11.1 for the Chart view of the Performance Monitor. Included with Microsoft Windows NT, this utility is useful for troubleshooting all sorts of hardware, network, and process problems.

There is one setting on Microsoft SQL Server that affects the data being sent to the Performance Monitor. In the main configuration screen in the Enterprise Manager, shown in Figure 11.2, you will notice two radio buttons—On Demand Mode and Direct Response Mode. The mode you select can have a slight impact on performance and can affect the way the Performance Monitor displays data. If you leave the default (Direct Response Mode) selected, the information from Microsoft SQL Server to the Performance Monitor will be returned a bit faster. Using the alternative—the On Demand Mode—can result in a slight improvement in overall server performance. For more on how each mode is utilized, see Microsoft SQL Server Books Online.

The Performance Monitor uses the Probe user account to connect to the server and retrieve its information. Be careful not to gather information using too small a time slice; you could place an extra burden on the server and slow other processes down unnecessarily. Make sure the Probe user does not affect the way production users get their data.

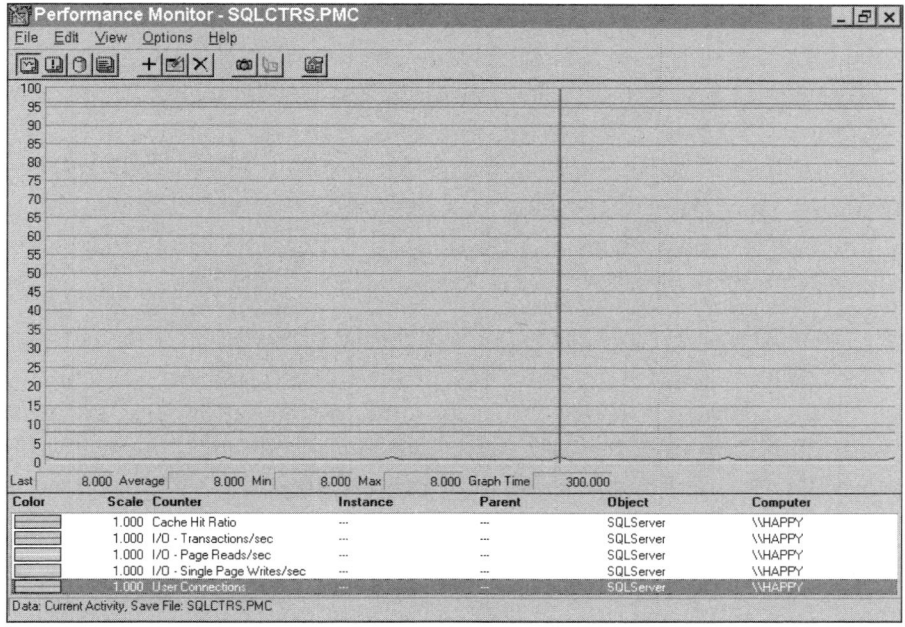

Chart view of the Performance Monitor.
Figure 11.1

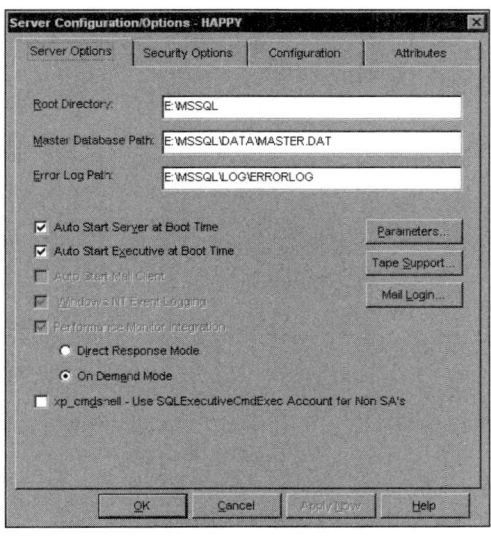

The Server Configuration/Options dialog box.
Figure 11.2

Performance Tuning And Optimization

The Performance Monitor actually looks at objects that exist in the operating system and applications on Windows NT. These objects number over 300 and have a great deal to tell us about how the server is running. You can pick and choose which objects to monitor and how often to capture data. This tool is not quite a "network sniffer"—more like a "machine sniffer." Table 11.1 lists some of the objects you should monitor periodically on your server and some of the expected values for a production system. You can save counters into files, which can be reopened later to save time and make checking performance faster and more efficient.

Although Table 11.1 is by no means a complete list of the objects you should monitor, it can be used as a starting point. Take some time to become familiar with how the Performance Monitor works. I recommend taking it slow, starting with a few counters and building up a few at a time. The Performance Monitor is a powerful product. It will take time for you to become good at using this tool, but it will be time

Object—Counter	Expected Values For A Production System
Processor—% Processor Time	When utilization is consistently over 90%, watch the load you are placing on the server. A maxed-out value (100%) is OK, but not for extended periods of time.
PhysicalDisk—Avg Disk Queue Length	This value should not be greater than 2. If multiple drives exist, divide this value by the number of physical disks to determine whether the transfer rate is higher than 2 on all drives.
SQLServer—Cache Hit Ratio	This value should be in the high 80s to mid-90s on a regular basis. Occasional processes may drop this value momentarily. If queries are running slow consistently and this value is low, you should consider adding more memory to the server.
SQLServer—User Connections	This displays the number of user connections currently attached to Microsoft SQL Server.
SQLServer Log—Log Space Used %	This can monitor the amount of space the transaction log for each database is using. Do not allow this to fill up!

Look up "SQL Server Object" in Microsoft SQL Server Books Online for more object definitions.

Table 11.1 Performance Monitor objects and their expected values.

well spent. See the Practical Guide of this chapter for more on the Windows NT Performance Monitor.

Windows NT

Although the importance of installing Microsoft SQL Server on a server by itself in production has been mentioned several times in this book, it bears mentioning in this chapter again. You should keep your server as dedicated as possible to the task of serving data. Do not use the server for file or print services, gateway services, or any other task that can slow you down. Do not put applications on the same server that runs SQL Server if those applications access the physical disks. You are asking for performance problems if you have another program writing to disk when SQL Server needs to read or write data.

Eliminate the extra services from your server. If you are not going to use the services that are enabled by default when Windows NT is installed, disable the ones that are not required to run SQL Server. Remember that the base install of any product will most likely fill only 75 percent of your needs, and you will get better results from your applications if you tune the server to better fit your needs. If your server is intended only to provide data to clients, the only required services are Server, Workstation, and MSSQLServer. In most environments, you should also leave the EventLog service running (for safety and troubleshooting), and also SQLExecutive (for scheduled tasks).

The last operating system issue you should be aware of—short of what has already been covered in earlier chapters—involves the behind-the-scenes processes associated with participating in a network environment. Load only the protocols that are required. A distributed-server environment gives you a set of servers that will be scalable and dependable if you keep them simple and segmented. Create role player-type servers as opposed to a single mission-critical machine that runs everything for your system.

Data Models

SQL Server supports many different data-modeling approaches and allows flexibility similar to that of desktop databases. If you apply desktop database methodology to Microsoft SQL Server, however, the price you will pay more often than not will be poor performance. Wide tables do not work well with SQL Server. Keep the rows and indexes as trimmed down as possible. The storage of indexes and data on your server and the amount of physical disk used are directly determined by how well thought out your data model is.

Do not let bad process logic lead to a poor data model. Store the data in the fashion that allows Microsoft SQL Server to access it the fastest and present it to the user in the form he or she expects. Convert the data into user-friendly form in your stored procedures and views instead of in the data model.

You can also improve performance by creating tables with only a few columns. This normalization can be done a number of ways. You can remove redundant data and put it into related tables that supply the row later through a join operation. The benefit of this is the increased number of data rows that can be stored per page in the database. The more rows per page, the better the performance. Along with fewer columns, consider fewer rows. If a table has a large number of rows, you might be able to increase performance by horizontally segmenting the data.

Data can be combined through UNION statements when needed and processed in smaller subsets for better throughput. One very useful technique is to migrate inactive records to other tables (a technique called "archiving"). Moving inactive records to history tables with the exact structure as the active table makes performing a union between the two data sets much easier while reducing the amount of data users must contend with for day-to-day operations.

Finally, keep an up-to-date backup of the schema at all times. No product guarantees that it will not introduce problems into a system once it is up and running. Be prepared.

Application Design

Application design is an area that affects the performance of systems at the user end. If the application is slow or hard to use, the whole system is slow or hard to use. Many programmers spend hours adding functionality to client applications that really belongs on the server. This methodology will not create a thin, fast client application.

All data-specific processing should be done on your data server. Keep all the logic regarding business rules and data validation on the server and off the client. The client application should be focused on presenting the data to the user and facilitating the modification of any data displayed. Keep the amount of network traffic down to a minimum, especially if the client application will be connecting through a modem. (Fewer packets mean more speed.)

When possible, load lookup data and static information locally on the client machines. Populating controls with lookup lists containing local data usually means better performance. Use as fast a method as possible for loading local data, and cache as much as possible during startup. Not all components available in Delphi, VB, or other development tools provide the fastest method. Shop around and stay current on advancements in third-party tools.

 Beware of memory leaks! Many third-party tools can be very appealing and some are even quite functional. Before placing add-ins into production, test them for memory leaks on your client machines.

Benchmark your application code often—both at the server level and the client level. Know how long the processes take individually. Troubleshooting a problem is very difficult if you do not know where the slow parts are located.

Establish A Baseline

I am often called upon to perform an analysis of Microsoft SQL Server installations where performance dropped off after months of running with few or no problems. One of the first questions I ask is: Are there any "baseline" measurements to which I can compare current process runs? More often than not, the answer is: No. If you have no idea what a normal load on your server is, how can you tell what an abnormal load is?

It is a good practice to run performance benchmarks after operating system installation to make sure the machine runs well without any other software installed. After running the benchmarks, install and configure Microsoft SQL Server based on the parameters discussed in Chapters 1 and 2. Then apply the TPC Benchmark Application to the server to get a feel for how well the box should run based on the current configuration. When the TPC test is finished, remove that code and begin system development.

When you create stored procedures, be sure to generate test scripts to ensure that data is manipulated exactly as required for client applications. Then use test scripts to generate baseline performance values for each process from strictly the server side of the application environment. This gives you documented execution times for your processes before client developers begin depending on them. If a problem arises that points toward SQL Server performance, you will have the numbers to support the server side of the process without having to rerun scripts.

Once the client and server pieces are joined, again benchmark the process to get a feel for how long each critical path process will take under no load. This allows you to determine if any problem found later is in the process logic or in the server load.

If the load on the server is to blame, you can then begin looking at load balancing or hardware configuration changes to get performance back into acceptable ranges.

 Who determines what speeds are acceptable? The developer, the DBA, the person who is writing the specification, or the user? The answer should always be the user. If the application runs poorly, the user is the one who suffers.

Keep It Simple

Check the easy-to-fix issues first. I always check the installation settings to be sure the memory and other server-level parameters are in line with the hardware configuration. Make sure you have not set too tight a window for Microsoft SQL Server with regard to physical memory on the server. Do not forget to start your production server with the "-x" option once you have configured and tested your processes. Remember that this startup option can improve performance, but it will also limit the amount of data maintained by Microsoft SQL Server regarding CPU and cache.

In calculating the amount of memory Microsoft SQL Server should use, keep in mind that logging on to the server console or firing off some utility can cause memory allocation on the server to change. Avoid moving Microsoft SQL Server into paged memory space. Leave a few megabytes of RAM available for checking things on the server without sending Microsoft SQL Server into a low-memory state.

Check the server for the simple things. Has someone logged on to the server and run an application from the server that is using available memory and slowing everyone down? Also, watch that ad hoc query tool! Users can bring a server to its knees with a few good queries at just the wrong time.

As DBA, you should know at all times what is running on your server. You are ultimately responsible for the performance and reliability of the server and the data. In most of the successful Microsoft SQL Server installations I have been involved with, developers are not allowed to write their own stored procedures. Index coverage and tuning issues are rarely the concern of the client developer and can be omitted from the data model. Always check the code running on your server before assuming it is complete and correct.

This might seem like a large burden for the DBA and a staff of programmers, but the results are well worth the effort. Faster performance and reliable code are the direct results of heavy DBA involvement in the installation and functioning of SQL Server.

SQL Server Trace Flags

When set, some trace flags can affect the performance of your server. Table 11.2 lists a few of them. Use trace flags on a server only after you have fully researched the use and meaning of the output generated by Microsoft SQL Server when these flags are used.

Trace flags are intended to "tweak" Microsoft SQL Server's functioning so that you can get an under-the-hood type of performance change. Some flags are used to allow Microsoft SQL Server to output additional results of processes over and above those that are normally returned. Read as much as you can in Microsoft SQL Server Books Online before attempting to use these trace flags or any others in your enterprise solutions.

SQL Trace

SQL Trace is basically an SQL "sniffer," included in version 6.5. With this utility, you can capture or filter commands sent to your server from client applications. Application names, login IDs, or host names can be filtered for output to the screen or to a log file for further review. This utility allows you to troubleshoot client/server applications with an increased level of confidence. You no longer have to copy and paste queries into the query tools to run them and monitor server activity.

Flag Number	Description Of Function
330	Allows for a more detailed output containing join information to be provided by the SHOW PLAN statement.
1081	Holds the index pages stored in the cache for one extra pass through the buffer. If a flush command is encountered on an index page with this flag set, the page is held in cache until the data is again referenced or a second flush command occurs.
3502	Prints messages to the log at the beginning and end of each checkpoint issued by Microsoft SQL Server.
3640	Stops the sending of DONE_IN_PROC messages to all client connections for each statement within a stored procedure. This action is very similar to issuing a SET NOCOUNT statement within your procedures, but at the server level.

Table 11.2 Trace flags and their functions.

You can define multiple filters and have more than one filter open at the same time. A really nice feature of SQL Trace is the ability to view the queries being passed to your server exactly the way the server does. You can copy the code right out of SQL Trace and run your own test scripts to further determine what is happening on the server. As with many tools supplied with Microsoft SQL Server, knowledge is power, and SQL Trace gives you the ability to know what is being run against your server. See the Practical Guide of this chapter for a step-by-step walk-through of creating a filter for use with the SQL Trace utility.

SQL Probe

SQL Probe is a third-party tool that can help you monitor many aspects of the performance and status of your Microsoft SQL Server machine and its databases. See Figure 11.3 for the SQL Probe main screen. This tool will run on Windows NT Workstation or Server without problem. I have tested it on Windows 95 and it appears to run OK; however, sources at Subquery Innovations (the SQL Probe software vendor) caution that they do not yet fully support the Windows 95 installation.

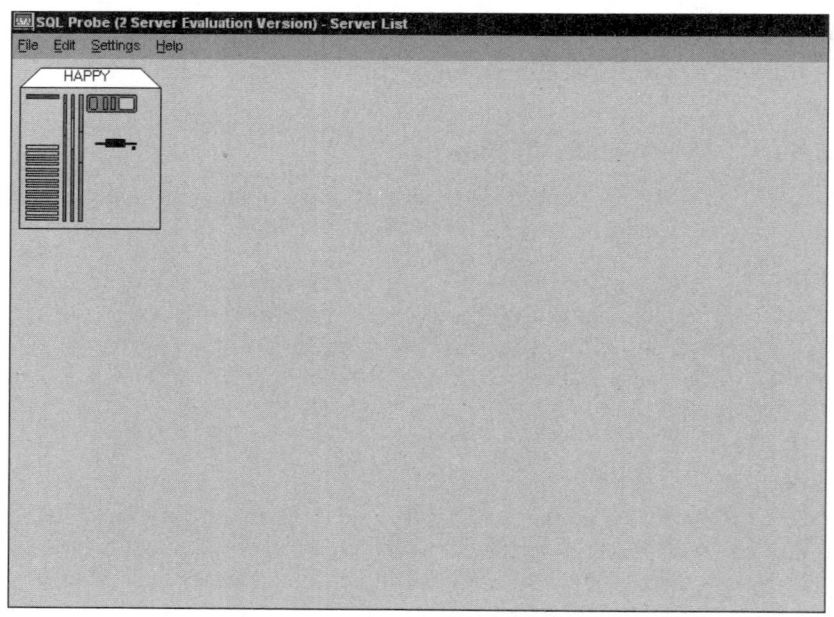

SQL Probe's main screen.
Figure 11.3

The main screen allows you to navigate easily between multiple servers for comparisons and checks that you may wish to perform. The demo copy included with this book will work on two servers for 30 days; after that, contact Subquery Innovations, Inc. (www.sqlprobe.com) for licensing and purchase questions.

Once you select a server on the main screen, a detail screen for the selected server appears, as shown in Figure 11.4. One of the nice features of this tool is that information can be refreshed automatically. All the important information regarding the health of the server is displayed in an easy-to-follow manner.

You can drill down even deeper into the server's health and current statistics by moving the mouse over the data being displayed and double-clicking when the magnifying glass appears. By double-clicking anywhere in the connection thread box at the top of the screen, you can display the processes currently being executed. See Figure 11.5 for the Processes display window. Although this window will update automatically, you can click the Refresh button (the one with chasing arrows) anytime to get current data from the server.

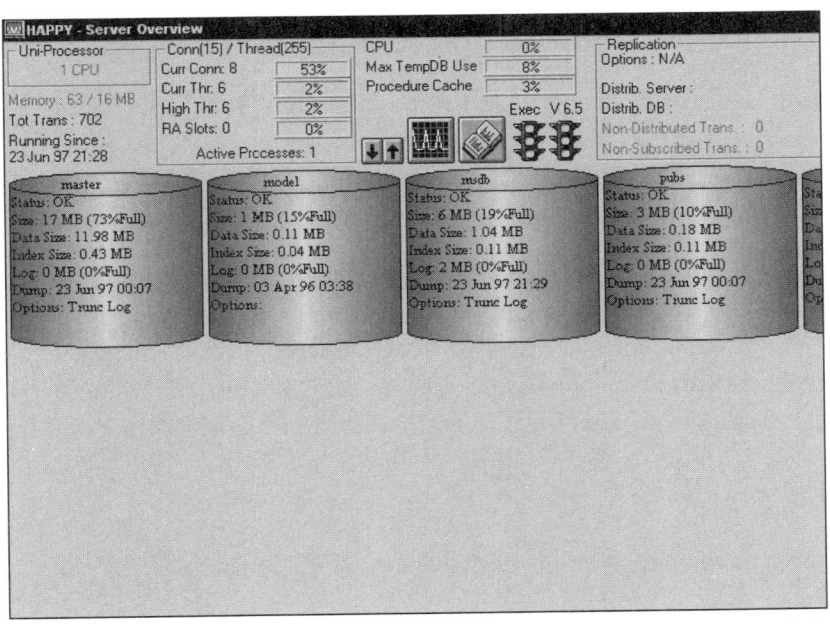

The Server Overview screen.
Figure 11.4

Performance Tuning And Optimization

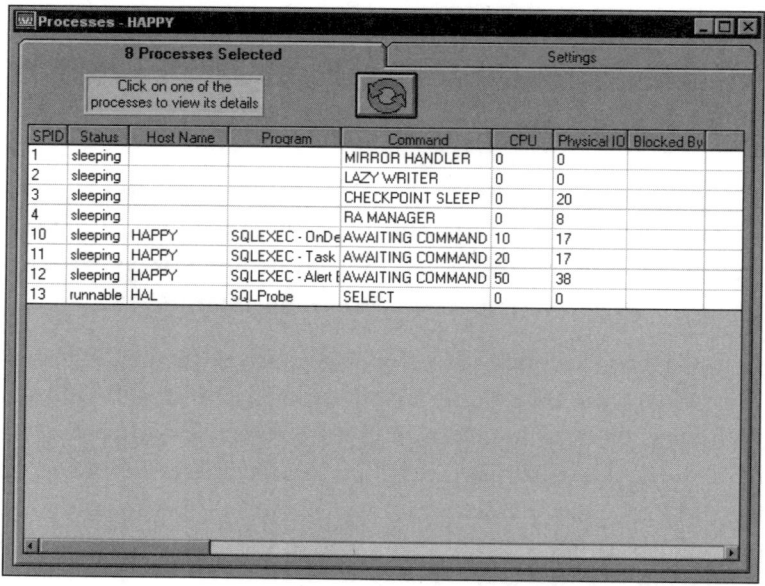

The Processes display window.
Figure 11.5

You can also use this tool to manage the health of the tables on your SQL server. If you click on the Pubs database graphic in the server detail window, the resulting window (the Pubs database detail window; see Figure 11.6) displays all the table-level statistics you would need to check in order to effectively manage your databases on Microsoft SQL Server.

You can drill down deeper still by selecting a table from the grid, or you can change the display order of the grid to suit your needs. Couple these features with the ability to monitor statistics and view the error log from SQL Server from a single interface and you have a great tool for managing and maintaining Microsoft SQL Server installations.

Summary

- Use trace flags to improve the performance of SQL Server.
- Monitor each process that runs on your SQL server.
- Create baseline benchmarks for comparison purposes.
- For reasons of speed, limit the number of columns in your tables.

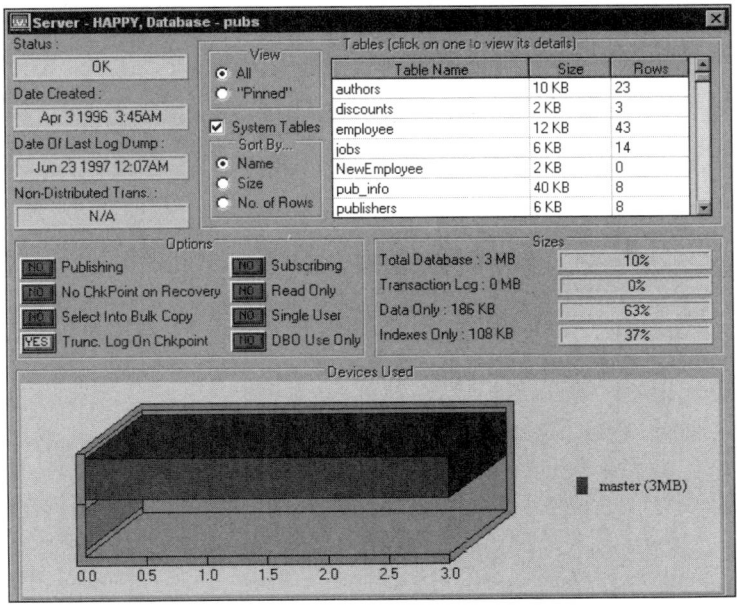

The Pubs database detail window.
Figure 11.6

- Monitor servers remotely so that you do not add overhead on the machine.
- Create thin clients.
- Manage data manipulation on the server.
- Consider the use of history tables to reduce the number of rows processed.

Practical Guide To Tuning And Optimization

In this section, you will walk through two important tasks on Microsoft SQL Server. One is the creation of a Performance Monitor script file with the counters discussed earlier in this chapter. The other is the creation of a filter in SQL Trace.

Using The Performance Monitor

As already mentioned, the Performance Monitor is valuable for troubleshooting many types of performance problems. This tool is flexible enough to monitor not only Microsoft SQL Server, but also other Windows NT machines on your network. This Practical Guide focuses on how it can be used to troubleshoot Microsoft SQL Server.

Opening The Performance Monitor

This operation is assumed to be carried out on a Windows NT 4.0 server. You can run this application remotely and in other versions of Windows NT without many changes in the steps described here. For clarity, illustrations are provided at key points in the process.

Make sure you are logged in to the server on which you are performing these steps. From the Start menu, select Programs|Administrative Tools|Performance Monitor. You should now see a blank Performance Monitor application window similar to that shown in Figure 11.7.

You can launch the Performance Monitor from the SQL Server menu group as well with a preloaded set of counters, but we'll walk through the process of creating your own chart from scratch. If you have not been able to launch the Performance Monitor successfully, verify that you have a correctly installed version of Windows NT and that the application exists in the Windows NT directory under the system32

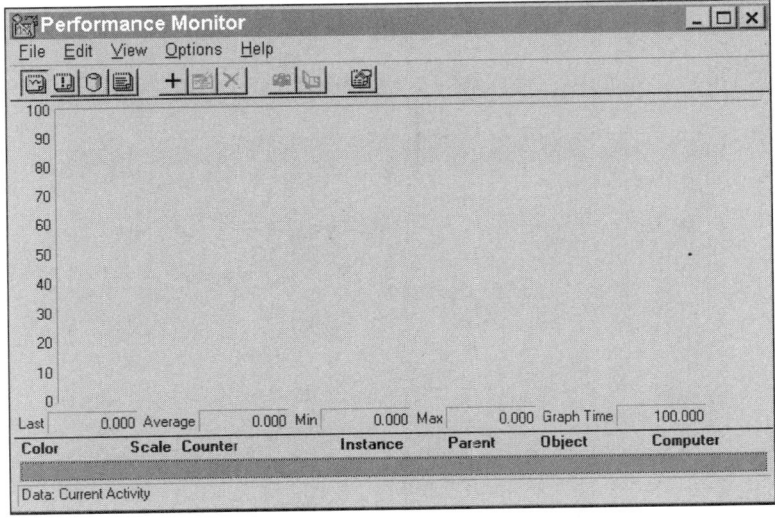

Blank Performance Monitor window.
Figure 11.7

subdirectory. The name of the application is "perfmon," and it should be appear in that directory.

 Many hours can be spent getting acquainted with the Performance Monitor and how it works. It is worth it, however. I find it surprising that Microsoft has chosen not to charge for this utility. The features are incredible and the interface is easy to master. The problem is that the interface is only the tip of the iceberg. Learning about the objects and their meanings and relationships is a whole career for some individuals.

Creating A New Chart

A chart graphically illustrates how well your server is performing by representing different object/counter values that compare related server functions. Creating a chart is fairly easy with the Performance Monitor. Following are the steps to create an example chart:

1. From the Edit menu, select Add To Chart.

2. The Add To Chart dialog box appears, as shown in Figure 11.8. Click the Add button to add the default object Processor and the counter % Processor Time to the chart.

3. From the Object drop-down box, select Physical Disk Object. The average disk queue length counter should be the default.

4. Click the Add button to place this object and counter on the chart.

5. Repeat Steps 3 and 4 for each of the counters listed in Table 11.1.

6. Select the Done button to close the dialog box.

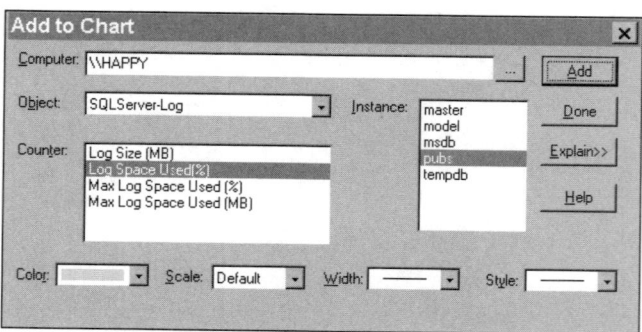

The Add To Chart dialog box.
Figure 11.8

346   Chapter 11: Practical Guide

You have now added the counters and objects to this chart and should see various lines of different colors being drawn across the screen. (If you want to learn more about the counters, you can click the Explain button in the Add To Chart dialog box for a text-based description of each object and counter.) A screen similar to Figure 11.9 should appear, but with different values. Relax and watch the data being gathered.

You should now run a query through the ISQL/W utility or some other means so that you can see the changes in chart data for yourself. I have run a simple SELECT statement of all columns from the Authors table in the Pubs database a few times back-to-back to illustrate activity. The resulting chart is displayed in Figure 11.10.

Although my processor activity only had small spikes, I can still see the change in load each time I run the SELECT statements. This is obviously not a real-world test; you should run your new stored procedures and queries through this process to see the impact each item has on the load of the machine.

Saving Charts To Files

To save this set of objects to a file, simply press the F12 key and select the name and directory for this PMC file. Once you have saved this chart, you can call it back up by opening the file from the Windows NT Explorer or through the File|Open command within the Performance Monitor itself.

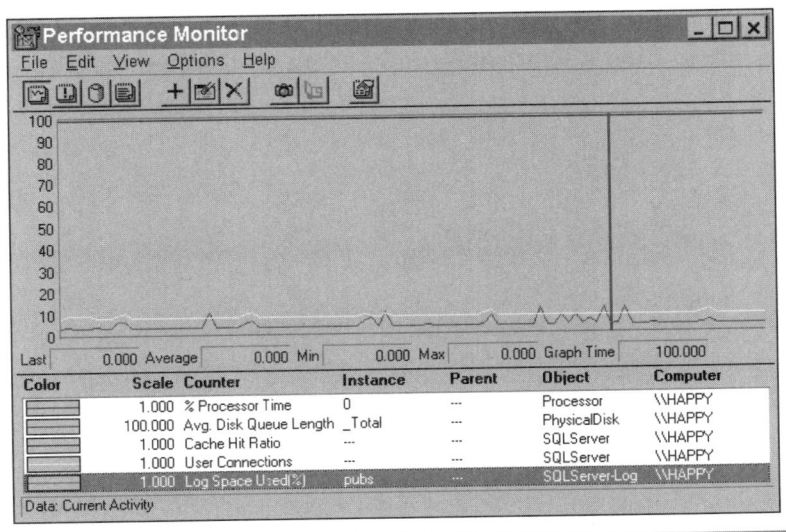

Performance Monitor with Table 11.1 counters loaded.
Figure 11.9

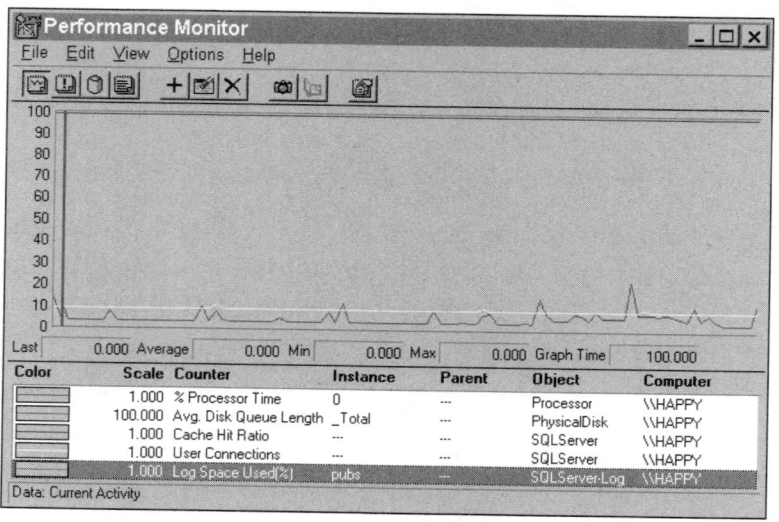

Chart showing Select statement activity on the server.
Figure 11.10

Create test files and give them real names after you are sure that they are going to be useful. Frequently, you will find that you experiment with different counters and settings only to find that you have gotten a bit off track. Save your settings to files periodically so that you can back up to a point where you still have the counters you intended and are getting data displayed in a form you can work with.

Organizing Charts

Group your charts by type of function that you wish to check. Disk I/O, Network, and SQL Server are just a few of the directories that I use to organize my Performance Monitor PMC files. I have a standard set of charts that I like to view each day to make sure certain values are still within a good range. In order to do this, I create an alias to the PMC files I want loaded at startup. When I come in and boot my machine, I start gathering data. I then can get a cup of coffee and check the logs on my server and see how well (or poorly) things are running with just a few steps.

Maintaining a good, proactive SQL Server environment takes more than what is outlined here. You must really understand the nuts and bolts of how SQL Server performs its tasks. Learn at least one object or counter per week for a while until you become familiar with what each object and counter means and how it reflects the performance of your server.

We have only scratched the surface of what the Performance Monitor can do. Spend some time with it—test it and attach it to other people's machines on the network. This tool can be used for performance monitoring of systems other than Windows NT and SQL Server. You should run this application from a remote machine, when possible, to limit the impact on data services in production.

Using SQL Trace

Another great tool included in version 6.5 is SQL Trace. As previously mentioned, this utility is an SQL "sniffer." With it, you can monitor, without interruption of service, the SQL calls made to Microsoft SQL Server. When you install SQL Server utilities on your machine, SQL Trace is added to the Program group. There are no other installation and configuration issues associated with this tool except for logging into the SQL Server and beginning the filtering process.

Overview Of SQL Trace

This tool is very useful for benchmarking and troubleshooting development problems on SQL Server. You can determine the order in which commands are sent and the performance times associated with those commands on a case-by-case basis. You can launch the SQL Enterprise Manager, ISQL/W, or the Windows NT Performance Monitor within SQL Trace.

In addition, the ability to define and save filters makes life as a DBA much easier. If you detect a problem user or someone who is having trouble with a program, you can create a trace file for that user and monitor the actions of the user without changing any code. You can watch execution sequences without interrupting the flow of business. This can be a powerful piece of the performance and tuning puzzle. If you use no other tool provided with SQL Server, use SQL Trace.

Running SQL Trace

Launching SQL Trace is accomplished through double-clicking on the icon in the Program Manager group for SQL Server or by selecting Start|Programs|Microsoft SQL Server 6.5|SQL Trace. Once you have launched SQL Trace, you are presented with a standard SQL login dialog box, where you provide a login ID and password to connect to SQL server. The first time you run this utility, there will be no filters defined and you will be prompted to create a filter. For the sake of this Practical Guide, you should select Yes. The New Filter dialog box appears, as shown in Figure 11.11.

You can now supply a name for the filter. Try to choose one that makes sense and is easily distinguishable from other filters. You can now choose to filter all login names, all applications, and all host machines. or to supply a more detailed list of filter criteria from the top of the dialog box.

The page frame at the bottom of the dialog box is where you specify the output you desire—whether it is to the screen, to a log file, or to both. You can even supply

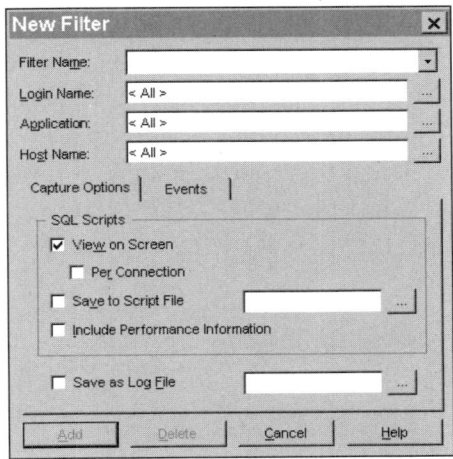

The New Filter dialog box.
Figure 11.11

specific events you wish to filter for, such as SELECT or UPDATE statements being passed to the server. Once you are happy with your filter, select the Add button to start the filter.

SQL Trace now displays your filtered information on the screen until you pause the filter or close the application. You can define many filters and run them individually or in sets depending on your needs. Figure 11.12 shows a sample filter created to supply all information to the screen.

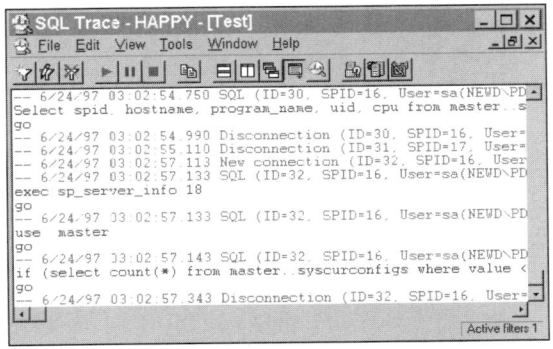

Running the test filter.
Figure 11.12

SQL Trace greatly simplifies the process of gathering the raw SQL commands being sent to your SQL Server. Although this utility, new to version 6.5, makes capturing the information easier, it still requires time and practice to analyze the results effectively. Practice is the only means of becoming proficient using SQL Trace. I recommend running SQL Trace on a periodic basis, even if your system is running well, to ensure you have a good picture of what is happening on your server. This practice of getting snapshots through SQL Trace will make troubleshooting easier in the long run.

And now for that obligatory reminder: *Back up the master database!*

Chapter 12

Newsgroups And The Internet

- Installing The Newsreader
- Configuring The Source News Server
- Subscribing To Newsgroups
- Preferences
- Newsgroup Etiquette

Administrator's Notes...

Chapter 12

Perhaps one of the most overlooked pieces of the troubleshooting puzzle is that incredible resource available to all of us, the Internet. You have access to more information and help than ever before through the Internet and the newsgroups that can be accessed for the cost of a dial-up connection. Throughout this book, I have referred to Microsoft SQL Server Books Online. Other resources are available to help fill in the blanks that Microsoft SQL Server Books Online might leave.

Newsgroups can be very useful tools for troubleshooting problems or finding out what's new with Microsoft SQL Server. Some very good DBAs are active in the newsgroups and are more than willing to help you with any problem.

Not all the users in the newsgroups are experts. No one is an expert on your system—except you. Do not take advice from anyone as the fix-all for your system and apply changes blindly to your machine without first testing to make sure things work the way you expect.

Another valuable resource available through the Internet is the Microsoft Knowledge Base. You can get good, current information right from the Microsoft SQL Server source anytime, day or night, through your Internet connection. You can also subscribe to the TechNet CD, which includes a smaller version of the Knowledge Base, without having a dial-up connection. I will cover these and other tools later in this chapter.

This chapter is not intended to change your view of any service, product, or vendor. Statements made here are my opinions and should be treated as suggestions. The companies mentioned have many fine qualities and are all good at what they do. In no way should anything in this chapter be taken to mean that I feel these companies do not provide quality services and products.

Accessing The Internet

Finding your way around the World Wide Web and newsgroups can sometimes be a frustrating task. I hope that, after reading this chapter, you will have a better understanding of the Internet and will be able to surf the Web with the best of them. The Internet is open 24 hours a day, 7 days a week, year round. It is growing at incredible rates. See Table 12.1 for some of the interesting facts about the Internet.

To become involved in newsgroups, you'll first need to get connected to the World Wide Web via an ISP (Internet service provider). Although the Microsoft Network (MSN), CompuServe, or America Online are easily available, I have found these services can be more trouble than they're worth. An ISP will charge you less overall, providing local service and, in many areas, unlimited usage for a flat monthly fee. Search around your local area, get prices, and compare the online time/cost benefits of several ISPs before making a choice.

Most ISPs offer hourly plans as well as flat-rate plans. If you plan to spend a lot of time online, you might want to look at a flat-rate plan—unlimited access for one

Users per day	Currently 30 million users per day; projections for the year 2000 estimate 250 million per day.
New users	Over 150,000 new users per day, or 1.74 new users per second.
Companies	In 1994, there were 1,000 companies or individuals on the Internet. As of April 1996, there were 316,217.
Revenue	In 1995, the Internet generated $75 million dollars in revenue. Projections begin at $1.65 billion for the year 2000.
Newsgroups	Most newsgroups, which are hosted by Internet service providers, see over 50,000 messages per day.

Table 12.1 Internet fast facts.

lump sum per month. However, very reasonable hourly plans are available as well. Choose the plan that best fits your needs.

Online services, such as America Online, MSN, and CompuServe, are available in most major cities throughout the world. By dialing a local phone number in your city, you can access the World Wide Web through these online services. They all work fairly well for the casual Internet user who only wants to browse and send and receive email.

Browsers

Before you do any surfing, you will need a browser to help you get around the Net. The most popular browser software packages available are Microsoft Internet Explorer and Netscape Communicator. Both browsers provide excellent user-friendly tools and icons; you should not have any trouble accessing Web pages with either one. If you do have problems, the Web site is probably not staying current and should be avoided anyway.

After deciding on an ISP and choosing a browser, get online and do a little searching until you feel comfortable with the browser. Each time you sign on, you will be sent to the browser's home page. From there, you can access any information on the World Wide Web.

Functions

All browsers have many areas of common functionality. This book is not intended to be an Internet how-to guide. I will give some of the basics to get you started; however, you will need to check the documentation for each product and follow your ISP's instructions when installing and setting up your connection and browser. I will use Microsoft Internet Explorer as an example. Figure 12.1 shows the blank window for Internet Explorer. The top toolbar helps you maneuver through different pages and Web sites.

Now let's go over the function of the buttons and controls you see in the Internet Explorer window:

- The *Back* button takes you back one page from the one you're currently viewing. You go back one step in the list of pages you have viewed—not back in the Web site itself.

- The *Forward* button does the exact opposite of the Back button. If you are moving forward by selecting URLs (links to other documents), you will not be able to select Forward.

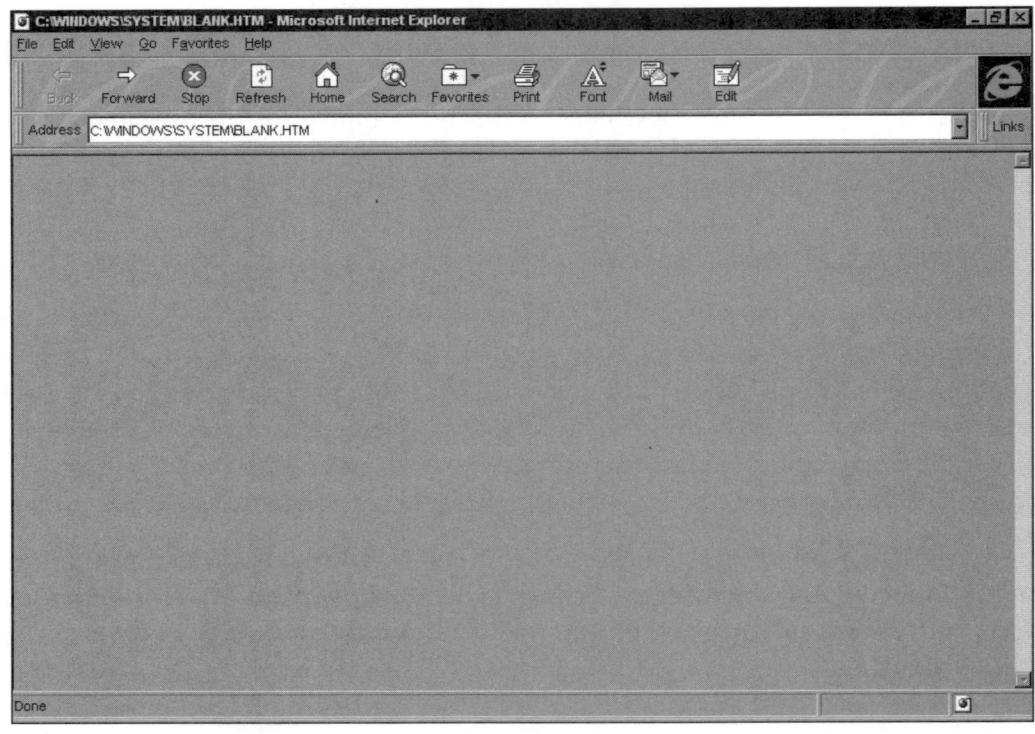

Microsoft's Internet Explorer.
Figure 12.1

- The *Stop* button is activated anytime you are changing pages or going to a new Web site. If you decide after changing pages that you want to stop the operation, simply click the Stop button, and all loading and transferring of information will cease. I often use this to halt a long-running page load.

- The *Refresh* button reloads the last Web page you successfully loaded. You can use the Refresh button if the Web page is loading slowly and you select Stop.

- When activated, the *Home* button sends you back to the browser's home page or to a page you have designated as your home page. You can change your home page through Options settings from the main menu.

- The *Search* button lets you search the Web for any topic you wish. Clicking on this button sends you to a search engine site, where you can choose different search engines or supply keywords to get a list of sites that contain those words. See the "Search Engines" section of this chapter for more on this subject.

- The *Favorite* button is particularly handy. It lets you keep track of addresses of Web sites that you like and allows you to organize them in any manner you wish. For example, you can create a folder for Web sites having to do with sports to keep all your sports information in one place.

> *Adding pages to your Favorites folder is simple. Anytime you are viewing a page you like, simply click the Favorite button and select Add To Favorites. You will be prompted to specify where to place the link. Then, in order to access that same Web page later, just click Favorites, open the folder where the site is located, and select that site. The browser then loads that Web page for you to view.*

- The *Print* button sends the current Web page to your selected printer.

- The *Font* button enlarges or shrinks the font of the Web page for better viewing. After clicking this button, you can choose from five different-size fonts. Some pages have very small print and may be more easily read by enlarging the text using this feature.

- When activated, the *Mail* button retrieves any email you have received. When you sign up with an ISP, be sure to ask if it has email capability and how to configure your software to send and receive mail. At this time, you should be given an email address.

- As shown in Figure 12.1, the *Address* field shows the Web address of the page you are currently on. You may also type an address into this field to go directly to a site. Also notice the drop-down list arrow at the end of the address window. You can click this arrow to receive a list of all the Web sites you have visited in the past. This is another shortcut to particular sites. However, to use this address field, you must know the exact Web site address or the IP (network) address.

This is by no means a complete description of the workings of Microsoft Internet Explorer, but it gives you the basics of how to move around and what the buttons do. Most browsers have the same functionality I have described here, so you can count on these features no matter which browser you choose. Many people never take the time to learn how to configure their browser for the tasks they want to perform. Browsers are getting more powerful with each release, so it is worth your while to familiarize yourself with your browser and to read the Help file for particulars on how it works. You will be glad you did.

Search Engines

Searching the Net can be as easy as typing a word and clicking the Search button. Many search engines are available on the Internet—Yahoo!, Excite, Infoseek, and WebCrawler, just to name a few. I use Infoseek and Yahoo! a lot, but I have no real preference as to which one to use for any given task. See Figure 12.2 for a screen capture of Yahoo!'s home page.

Most search engines are very user-friendly, with step-by-step guides to getting your request processed. Not all engines store the same information. If you do not get the results you expect from a query, try a different search engine. After a little research, you will be able to find out which search engines return the most Web-site matches for the topics you are interested in.

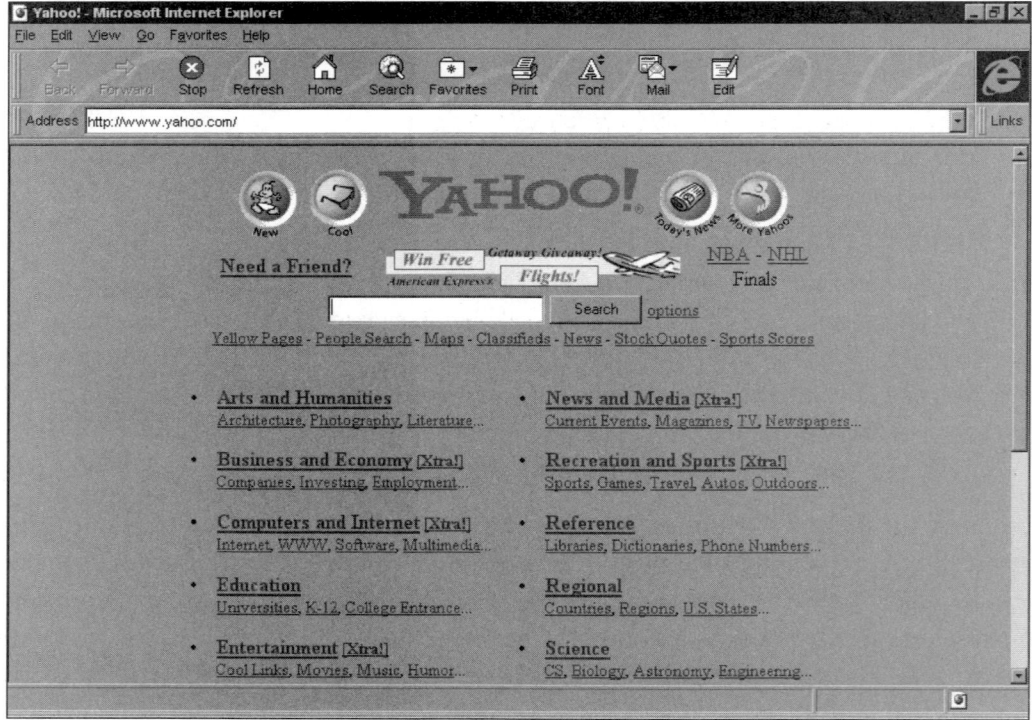

Yahoo!'s home page.
Figure 12.2

An important consideration when performing a search is the keyword(s) you use. For example, if you wanted to search for Web sites dealing with Microsoft SQL Server, simply type "SQL" in the search window and click the Search button.

Figure 12.3 shows the search results—314 matches—returned on the Yahoo! search engine for "SQL". Each time the search engine found either a word on a Web site's home page or an index match for "SQL," it returned that site's URL address and a brief snippet about the file it found. You can now click on any of the headings to access the Web site.

If the list of returned topics is too large, you can narrow the search by being more specific. If you ask for "SQL Server," or if you ask for "SQL" and "6.5," you will get fewer matches and have a shorter list to look through. [Some search engines will accept the use of plus (+) and/or the ampersand (&) to help restrict the search and return fewer matches.]

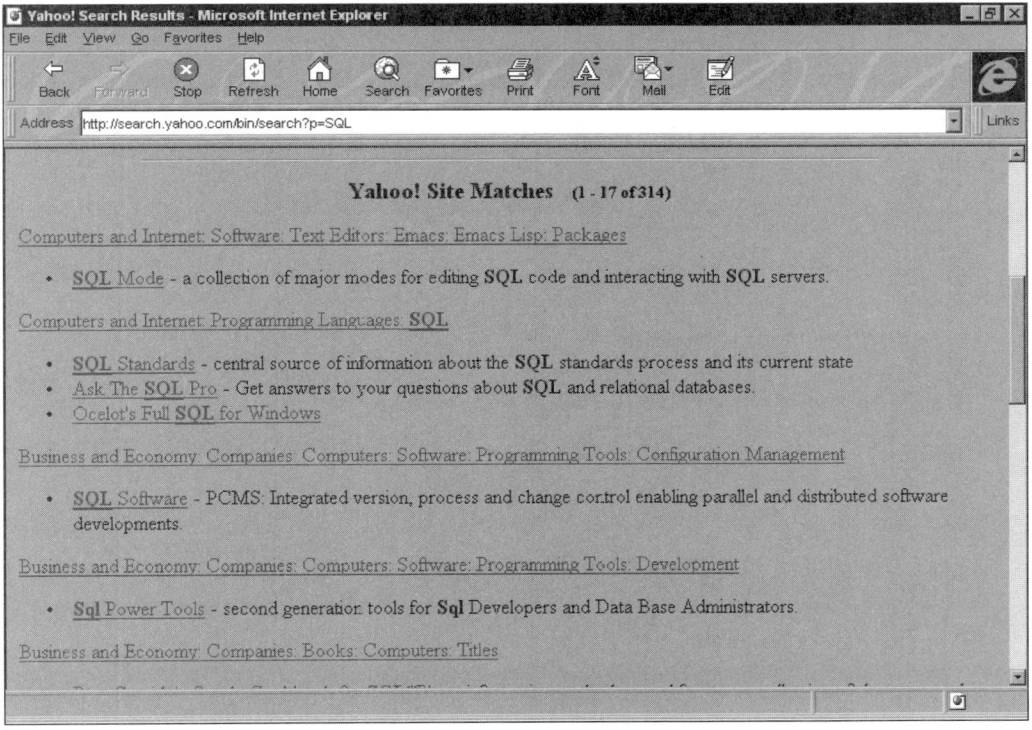

Yahoo! search results.
Figure 12.3

It's a good practice to start with a broad search and narrow the results down once you are sure that you have an idea of what will be returned from a search request. If you are too specific, you might not get any matches back for your query.

Knowledge Base

The Microsoft Knowledge Base, whether the Internet version or the one available on the TechNet CD, is an up-to-the-minute source for current problems and solutions other people are experiencing with all Microsoft products. The Knowledge Base also contains current fixes or service packs you can download to apply to your software. Locating the Knowledge Base on the Internet is simple: Just use a search engine or go to the Microsoft home page at http://www.microsoft.com. When you get to the Microsoft home page, click Support at the top of the page. Figure 12.4 shows the Knowledge Base home page.

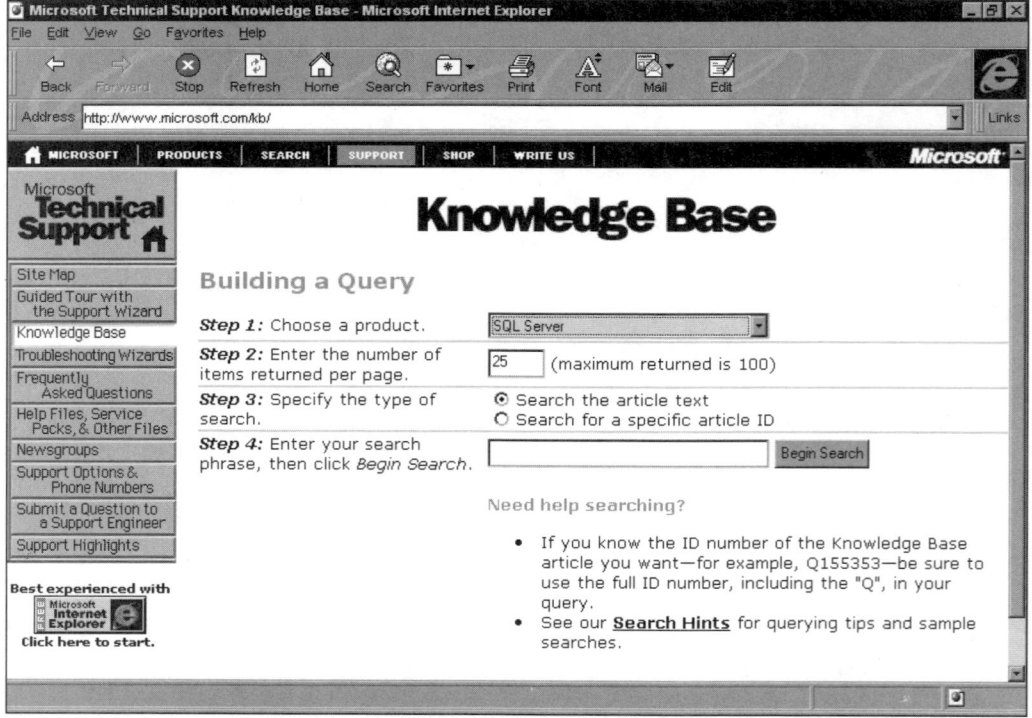

Microsoft Knowledge Base's home page.
Figure 12.4

Click on the list box arrow next to Choose A Product, and select a Microsoft product. Let's say that you want to search for information on Microsoft SQL Server. Simply choose SQL Server from the list and select Begin Search. You also can add additional requirements to the query, such as the number of rows returned and whether to search for your string in article text or just look for an article ID number. Figure 12.5 shows an example of the results returned from a Knowledge Base query for Microsoft SQL Server.

 If additional items are returned in excess of what will fit on a page, select the Show Next button to move further down the list.

You can supply key words to narrow the search in the Knowledge Base for the topic or problem you are interested in. Each search will return all articles available concerning your topic. Results are returned at a default of 25 per page or per your preference,

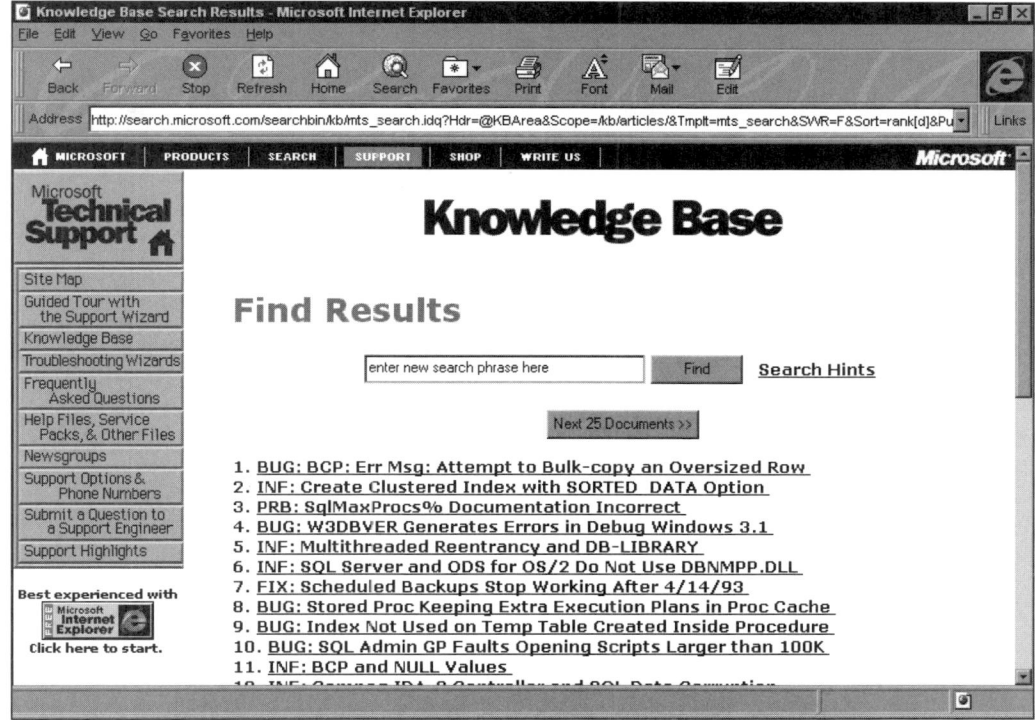

Knowledge Base search results.
Figure 12.5

which you would select from the Knowledge Base home page. Contained within each article are tips and information regarding error messages, bugs, and bug fixes.

Service Packs And Patches

You can obtain information relating to service packs, and—in some cases—you can link directly to a patch or service pack from the Knowledge Base Web site or off the TechNet CD-ROM. Once installed on your system, the service packs should fix the problems you are having, and they might prevent error messages in the future. Carefully read the installation instructions for the service pack or patch before applying them to your production machine. As a general rule, I check the newsgroups before applying a patch, to make sure people are not having trouble with the software I'm about to apply to my production machine.

TechNet CD-ROM

TechNet CD-ROMs are very useful Microsoft products. Each month, Microsoft gathers all of the articles from the Knowledge Base and any new information regarding Microsoft products and compiles them on CD-ROM for distribution. Developers and programmers will find these CD-ROMs to be a valuable tool in staying current with any Microsoft product. By subscribing to this CD-ROM-based service ($299 at this writing), you not only receive current information from the Knowledge Base, but you also have access to past articles and white papers. See Figure 12.6 for the TechNet home screen.

You search TechNet just as you do the Knowledge Base. Click on the Find icon (the pair of binoculars on the toolbar) and enter a keyword. TechNet comes with at least two CDs and may prompt you to insert the CD it needs to complete your task. You can also use the left pane of the search engine to browse through documents by product or by category.

Microsoft SQL Server Books Online

Microsoft SQL Server Books Online is such an important tool in developing a solid production server that I may mention it more than SQL Server itself. It is included in the SQL Server software package and is an optional installation on hard disk the first time you install Microsoft SQL Server. Books Online works exactly like the Microsoft TechNet CD-ROM. The main search screens look the same and provide much of the

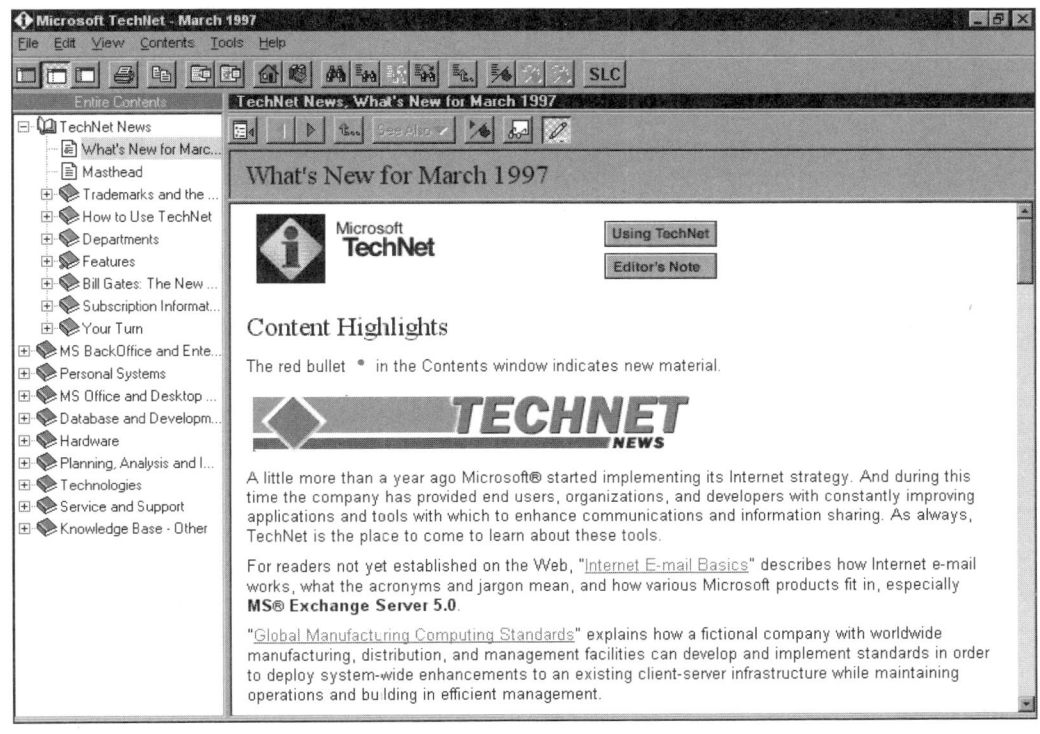

Microsoft TechNet home screen.
Figure 12.6

same search capabilities. Microsoft SQL Server Books Online is SQL Server-specific and carries about 15MB of data on Microsoft SQL Server and how it functions.

I install Microsoft SQL Server Books Online on developer machines only. Because Books Online is the "key to the kitchen," you might be asking for problems down the road if you put the books in the wrong hands.

Newsgroups

Newsgroups on the Internet are probably the second most useful reference tool at your disposal. A newsgroup is a group of people sending and receiving information in a single forum relating to a particular subject. You have access to thousands of newsgroups on the Internet, relating to subjects from A to Z. Let's look at what is available pertaining to Microsoft SQL Server in the newsgroups.

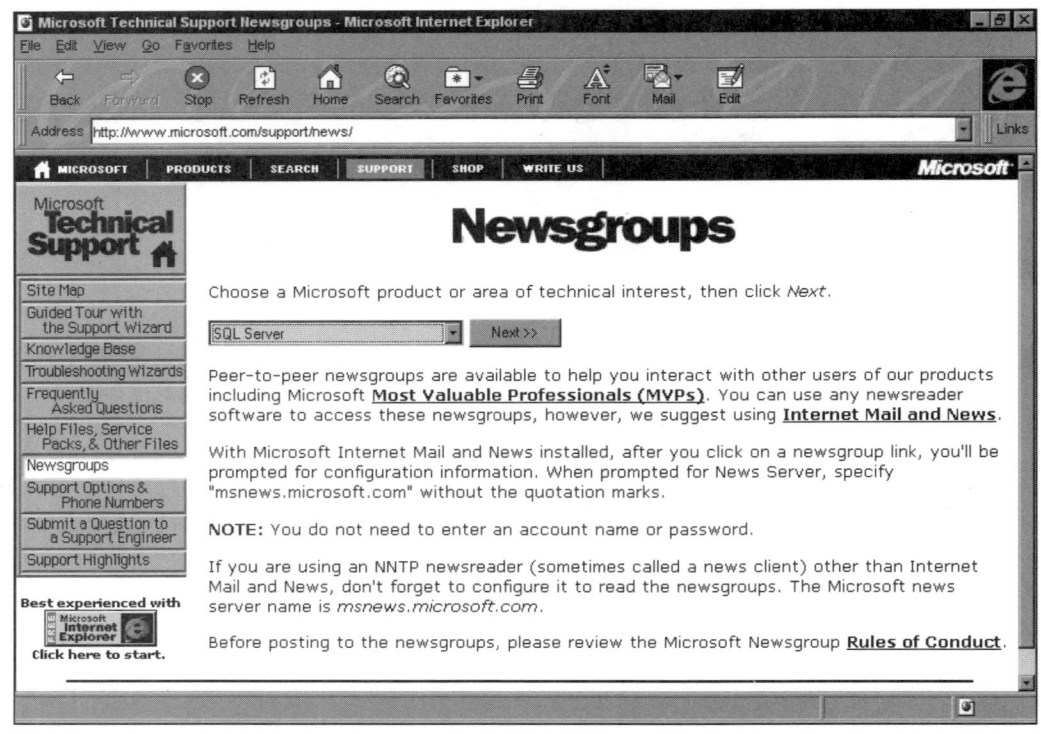

The Newsgroups home page.
Figure 12.7

On the Microsoft home page, select Newsgroups on the left pane. Figure 12.7 shows the Newsgroups home page with SQL Server selected as the area of interest.

Figure 12.8 shows the results returned after selecting SQL Server as a search topic and selecting Next. This page gives you more detailed instructions and the actual address of each newsgroup on the Microsoft news server.

Click on one of the topics listed to access that newsgroup. There is no fee for using the newsgroup. Microsoft personnel frequent these areas, so the information can be very useful. Once in the newsgroup, you can read and reply to messages and send out a request for information to the whole group. Be prepared; once you post a request, you might receive several email messages a day in reply. You should check the newsgroup periodically for answers to your postings, because the answers are not really addressed to you specifically, but rather to the group.

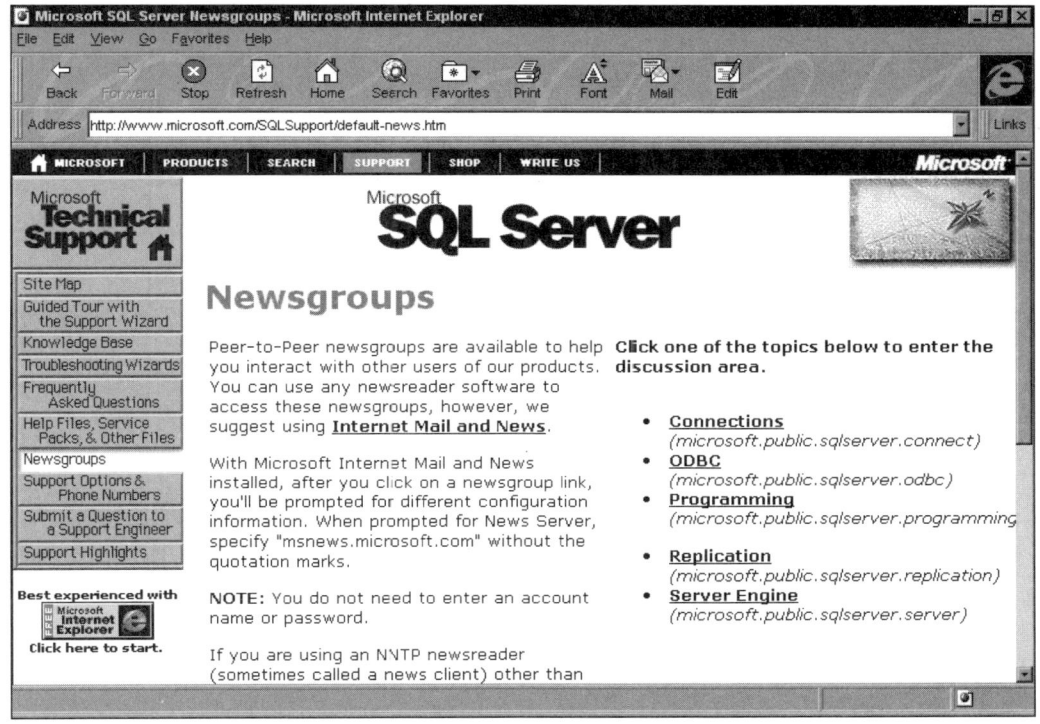

The Newsgroups selection page.
Figure 12.8

In addition to the newsreaders contained within most Web browsers, I highly recommend another newsreader software package. Contained on the CD-ROM accompanying this book is a newsreader called "Free Agent," a product from Forté Inc., located in San Diego. See Figure 12.9 for the Free Agent main screen. This tool is powerful yet easy to use, and with each release it is improving.

On the left of the Free Agent screen, you would see a list of the newsgroups you had subscribed to. By double-clicking on any one of these, you could access all of the messages posted for those groups. On the right of the screen would appear the subjects of messages that had been posted. Plus signs (+) would appear next to some of the messages, indicating that there were responses relating to any messages lower in the message tree. See the Practical Guide at the end of this chapter for a step-by-step walkthrough of how to use this screen. One helpful feature of Free Agent is its ability to keep track of certain messages and responses. When you click on the eyeglasses

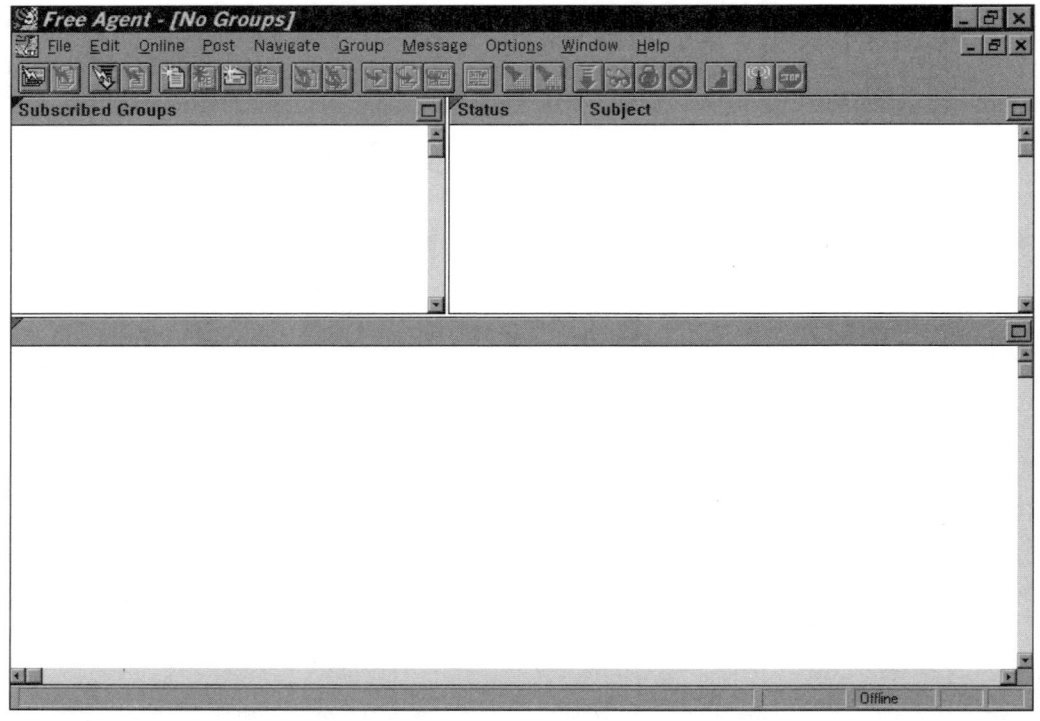

Forté's Free Agent newsreader main screen.
Figure 12.9

icon on the toolbar, Free Agent will monitor the highlighted message and all threads related to it. You can also lock messages into your list to keep them from being aged out before you have had a chance to read them. To read the body of a message, double-click on the header and Free Agent will retrieve the message and display it in the lower pane.

The entire layout in this product is tunable according to your preferences and may end up looking totally different than the example here. One of the nice things about Free Agent is that you can change the interface to suit your taste. This brief description does little justice to Free Agent. It is included on the CD-ROM, however, so you can experiment with it yourself. Be sure to consult the Help file.

Summary

- Research the alternatives before signing up with an ISP or Internet service.
- Choose a Web browser you are comfortable with.
- Use several search engines to get the maximum results.
- Use the Microsoft Knowledge Base and Microsoft SQL Server Books Online often.
- Frequent newsgroups to gain knowledge and to offer assistance regarding a wide range of products.
- Try the Free Agent newsreader.

Practical Guide To Free Agent Installation

In this section, you will walk through the step-by-step installation of the Free Agent software package.

Installing The Newsreader

You can install Forté's Free Agent newsreader two ways. We'll go through one of them here. Although Free Agent is included on the CD-ROM, we'll download a copy from the Internet to put into practice topics covered in this chapter. To access the Forté home page, simply type **www.forteinc.com** on the address line within your browser. Then click the Download Sites jump text to go to the download page for a copy of the software. Figure 12.10 shows Forté Inc.'s download page.

First, choose a site to download from. Any of the sites shown in blue text would be fine. Click on the site to start the file transfer process. (Your mouse pointer will change to a hand when you pass it over a URL.) Figure 12.11 shows the status window for the downloading file. Most Web browsers put the downloading file in a temporary directory within the browser. This default process prevents the file from getting mixed up with other important files. It's easy to locate the file once the downloading process is complete. The only other concern you might have is the possibility of catching viruses—but that's material for another book entirely.

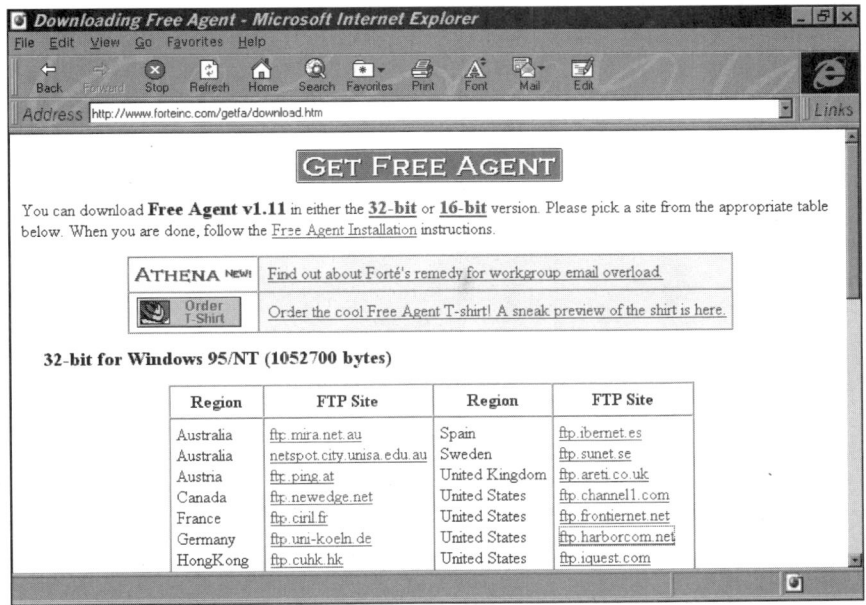

Forté Inc.'s download page.
Figure 12.10

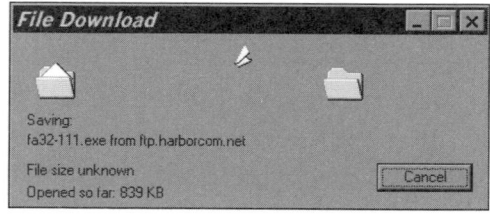

The File Download window.
Figure 12.11

Within the window in Figure 12.11, note that the file name is fa32-111.exe, and the site being downloaded from is ftp.harborcom.net. This information is not necessary to perform the download in Microsoft Internet Explorer, but it is useful if you use an FTP client to get the files. The download will take approximately 8 minutes, depending on your modem and processor speed.

After the download is complete, you can close the browser, disconnect from the Internet Service Provider, and prepare to install the Free Agent newsreader. If you are using Windows 95, find the file fa32-111.exe in the temporary folder using Windows Explorer. Double-click on the file within Windows Explorer to launch the install program. See Figure 12.12 for a screen capture of the install program startup screen.

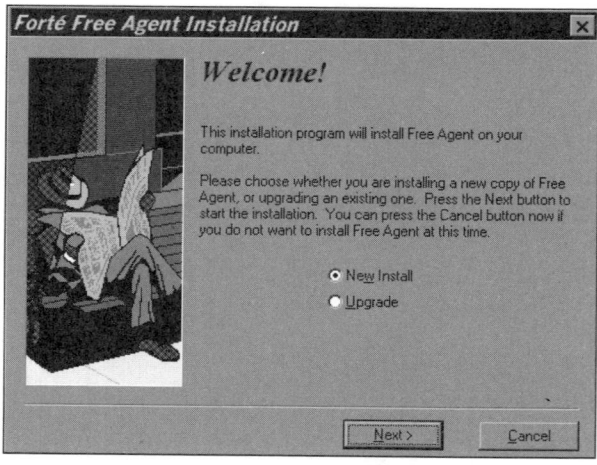

The Free Agent install program startup screen.
Figure 12.12

372   Chapter 12: Practical Guide

Because we are performing a new installation, click the New Install button. Then click Next. Now choose the folder or directory in which to place the Agent files. See Figure 12.13 for the folder or directory destination dialog box. Note the default is c:\program files\agent.

The next step is to decide whether to provide shortcuts for Free Agent. Selecting Yes installs a shortcut on your desktop so that you can start Free Agent without accessing the program groups in the Start menu. See Figure 12.14 for the shortcut selection screen.

The next step is to select the program group with which you want to associate Free Agent. You can select any of your existing program groups or use the default. If you wish, the install program creates a new program group named Forté Agent. It is your choice; place the program wherever you wish. See Figure 12.15 for the Start Menu selection screen.

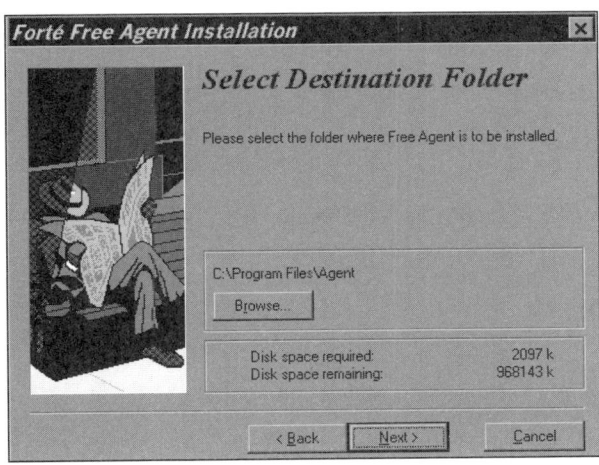

The Free Agent install destination dialog box.
Figure 12.13

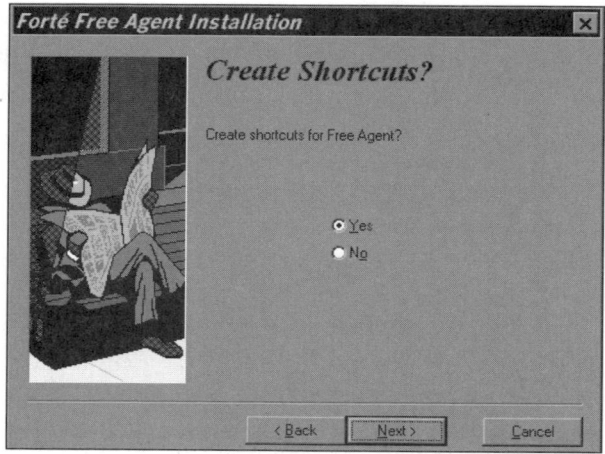

The Free Agent Create Shortcuts screen.
Figure 12.14

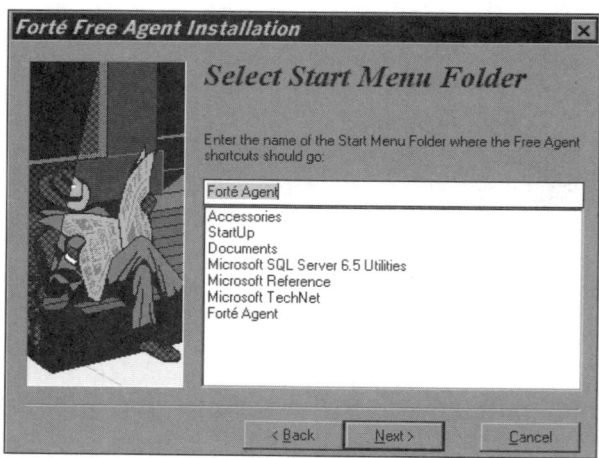

The Select Start Menu Folder screen.
Figure 12.15

The Free Agent install program is ready to install all files and folders needed to run the application. Click Start on the install screen to begin the install process (see Figure 12.16). This is the "keep-alive" screen intended to convince you to register and purchase the licensed copy of the product.

You are almost done installing Free Agent. After all of the files have been copied, a screen similar to the one in Figure 12.17 appears. If you get any other window, contact Forté's technical support through their Web site. Now choose from the options on the Installation Complete screen to run Free Agent now or later. For this example, let's run the program now. The next step is to configure the source news server so we can start checking out the news.

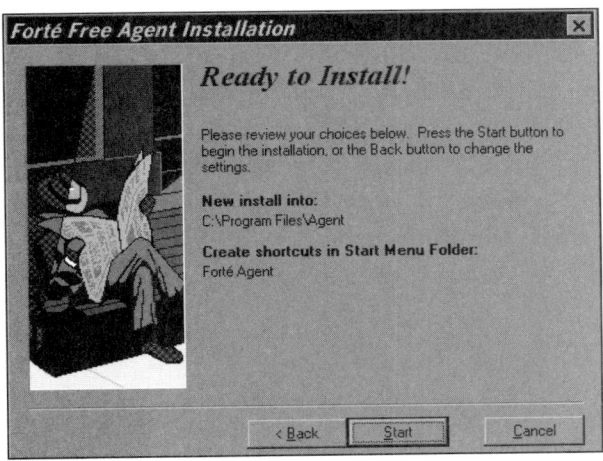

The Ready To Install screen.
Figure 12.16

The Installation Complete screen.
Figure 12.17

Configuring The Source News Server

The rest of the configuration is just as easy as the installation. Look at the figures carefully and pick up everything you can about the Free Agent newsreader and how it works. The Help sections within the program are a very good source of information should you become stranded or just have a general question.

The first time you run Free Agent after installation, you'll need to provide a little more information so that the reader can find a server and know who you are. See Figure 12.18 and use the data I have filled in as a guide. (Use your own email address and name, of course.)

You must input the name of the news server you wish to connect to. I have specified the msnews news server at Microsoft for this example in order to access all of the information available about Microsoft SQL Server. Type in the address for the news server exactly as shown in Figure 12.18. The next thing you need to do is get online and subscribe to some newsgroups. Select OK to start up the reader. As shown in Figure 12.19, Free Agent prompts you to go online to access all of the newsgroups. This process could take a few minutes if you are connected over a slow modem. If you haven't done so already, connect to your ISP and minimize your connection box. Select Yes, and Free Agent will go get all of the groups available on the server you have specified.

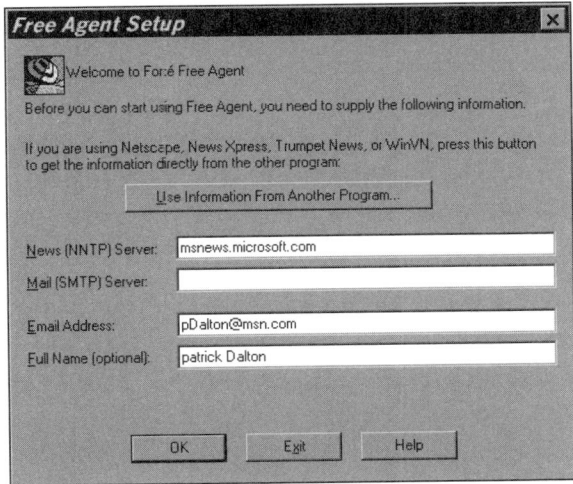

The Free Agent Setup screen.
Figure 12.18

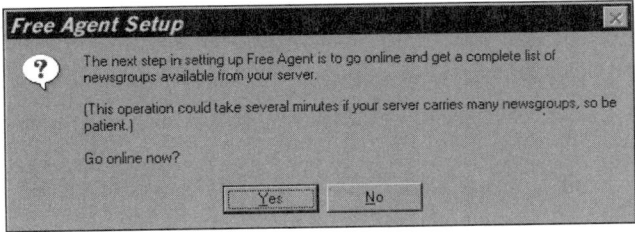

Go Online Now dialog box.
Figure 12.19

Free Agent Installation

Subscribing To Newsgroups

Now that you are online, you can subscribe to any newsgroups you wish, within the confines of the specified news server. This is the only major drawback to the Free Agent software—other full versions of newsreaders allow you to subscribe to multiple servers at one time. See Figure 12.9 earlier in this chapter for the blank screen you will see the first time you use Free Agent and want to load the available groups on the Microsoft news server.

Find the Online drop-down menu, select it, and choose Get New Groups. This is necessary only because you have not subscribed to any newsgroups yet. A list will appear in the left-hand pane; from this you can select which groups to read and monitor. In Figure 12.20, notice that microsoft.public.sqlserver.connect and microsoft.public.sqlserver.programming have been selected.

 Do not overload yourself. If you select too many groups, you won't be able to keep up with all the traffic. Take your time and build a set of groups that you can handle on a daily or every-other-day basis.

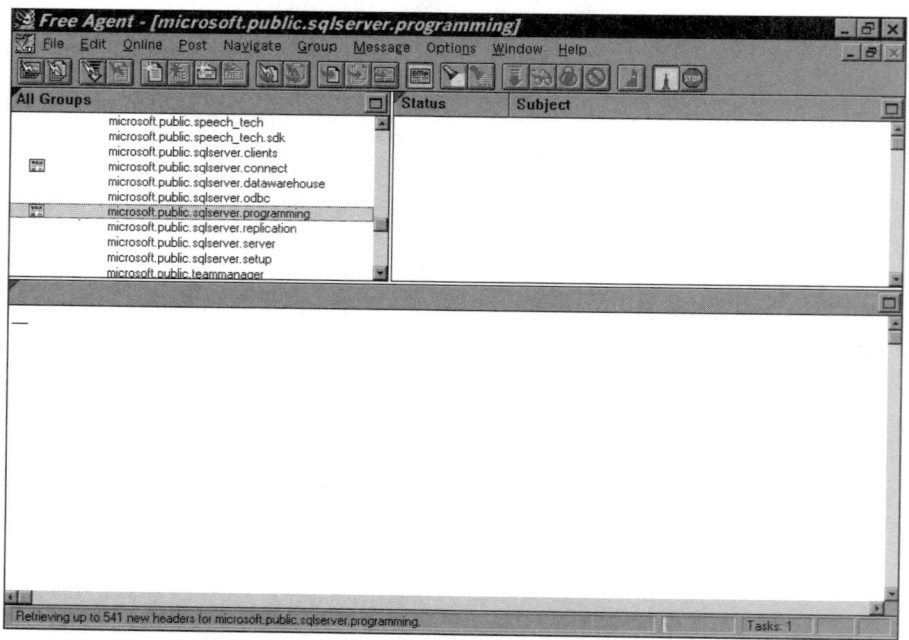

Selecting a newsgroup for subscription.
Figure 12.20

To subscribe to these groups quickly, highlight the group, right-click on the highlighted group, and select Subscribe from the drop-down menu. Once you have subscribed to a group or groups, you need to request which headers are available in those groups. To do this, you can use the menu or the toolbar at the top of the screen. Select the far-left button to get some headers.

Note that the bottom of the screen in Figure 12.20 indicates that the news server is returning 541 messages (your results, of course, will differ). You might think this is a lot, but I have seen over 3,000 messages returned for a single group in just a few days. If you don't go online every day and read, save, or discard the messages you don't want, they will add up—so be prepared.

See Figure 12.21 for a list of subjects that are available. The left frame shows the newsgroups you have subscribed to; the right frame shows the subject lists in those groups. When you choose a message to read, the message text will be displayed in the bottom frame. You can bring up the text by clicking on a message in the subject list.

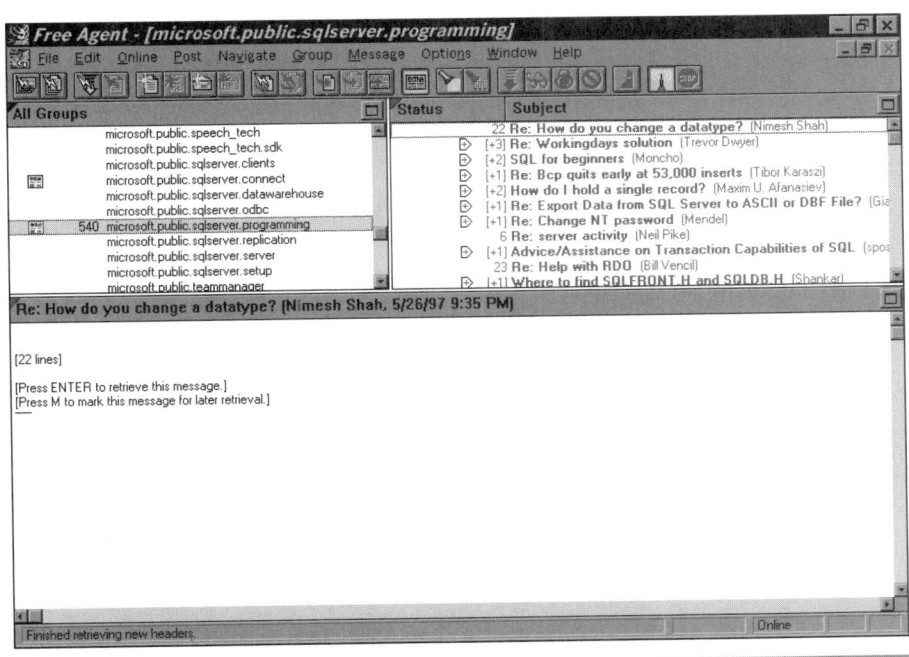

The Free Agent screen, showing lists of newsgroups and the subject list.
Figure 12.21

You can decide which messages to read by looking at subject lines. And when posting messages, be sure to use specific subject lines. Otherwise, people will skip over your message and look for something more interesting. As mentioned earlier in this chapter, a plus sign (+) will appear next to messages with replies, along with the number of responses. Figure 12.22 shows that there have been three replies to the highlighted message called "Workingdays solution." You can reply to a message by highlighting the message and clicking on the Post drop-down menu option. Select Follow Up Usenet Message, and fill in the email-like form.

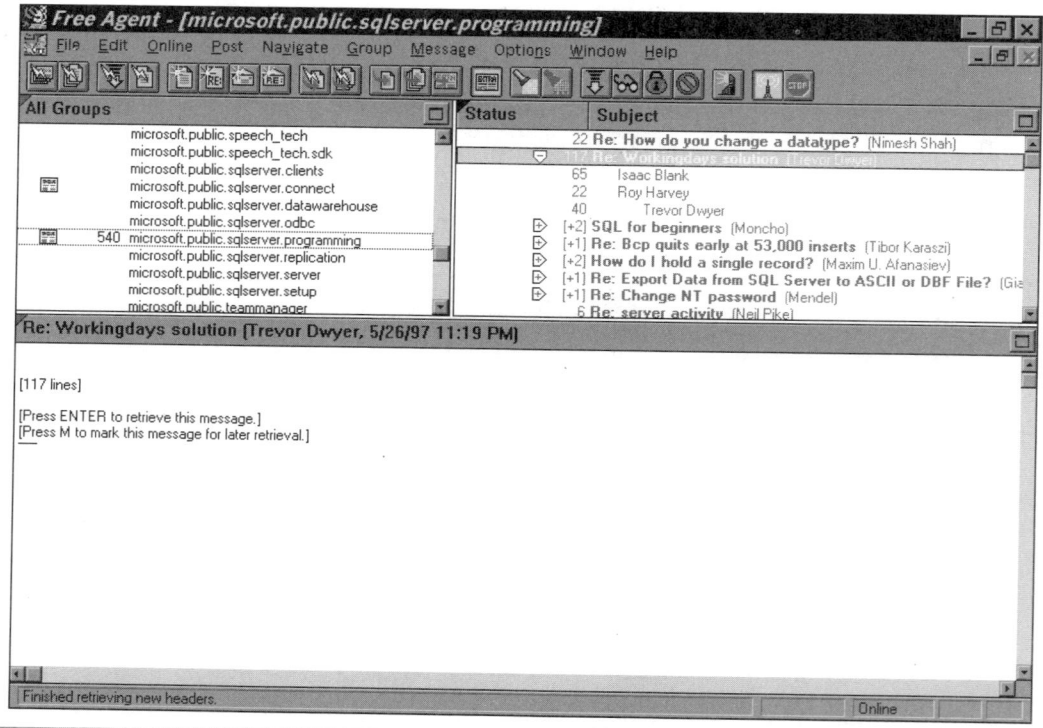

The Free Agent screen, showing an expanded Subjects pane.
Figure 12.22

Preferences

Setting preferences allows you to customize the newsreader to your satisfaction. You have many options if you know where to look for them. Start by selecting Options from the menu bar in the newsreader, then select General Preferences from the drop-down menu. Figure 12.23 shows the General Preferences dialog box and the options it presents. We'll touch briefly on each one. The preferences you will change the most after your initial setup will probably be User and System.

Under the *System* tab of the General Preferences dialog box, you can change news servers and email servers, should you decide to use this newsreader for email services. See Figure 12.24 for the *Fonts* tab. You can customize your reader with any combination of custom fonts as long as they are installed on your system. You can change the font of the entire browser or only of the messages.

Figure 12.25 shows the *User* tab. Here you can supply information to identify yourself to others in the newsgroups.

The *Dial-Up* tab can be useful in an office environment (see Figure 12.26). If your company allows you to browse the newsreader during working hours, the newsreader will prompt you to disconnect from your ISP when you close the reader. You can dial in, get your information, and read it offline when you have the time.

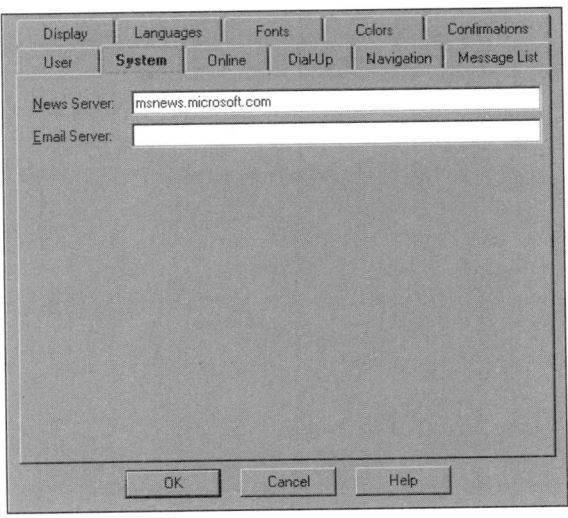

The General Preferences dialog box.
Figure 12.23

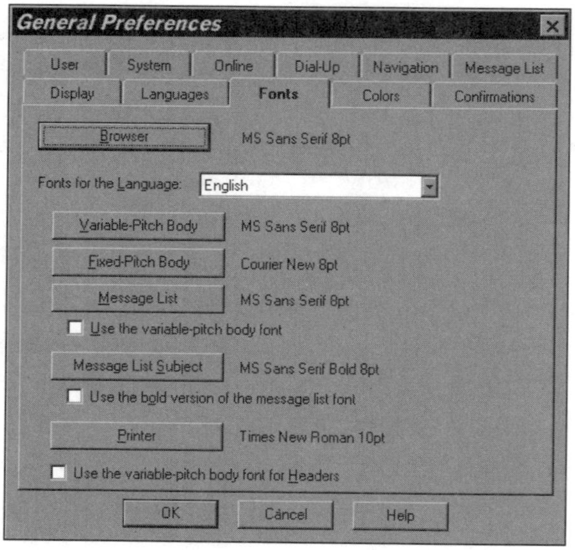

The Fonts tab.
Figure 12.24

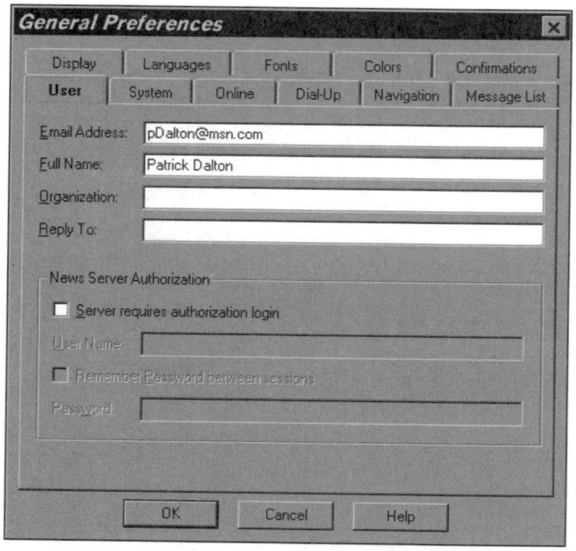

The User tab.
Figure 12.25

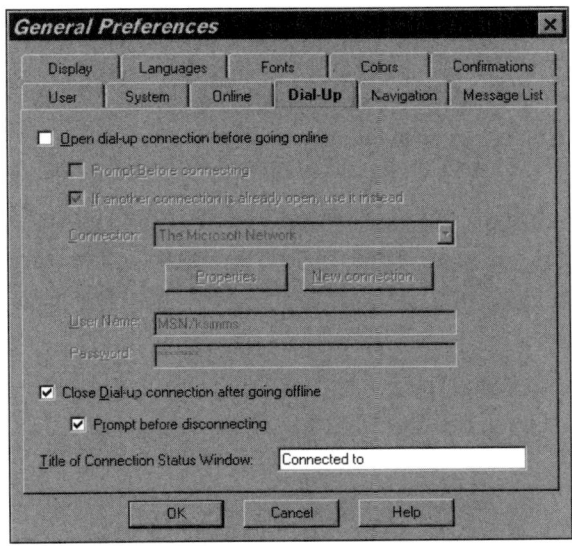

The Dial-Up tab.
Figure 12.26

The *Display* tab is shown in Figure 12.27. You can use this tab to customize the look of your reader. You can hide or display the toolbar and status bars, and set whether you want the email address displayed.

I advise against altering any of the settings on the *Confirmations* tab until you become more familiar with how your newsreader operates. Changes here can delete messages, mark messages as unread by mistake, or mark unread messages as read. See Figure 12.28 for the settings on the Confirmation tab.

The *Navigation* tab deals mainly with the reading and retrieval of messages. You can skip through messages one by one, or by group. You will develop your preferences for this over time. I suggest leaving the default settings until you are comfortable using Free Agent. See Figure 12.29 for an example of the Navigation tab.

The *Message List* tab allows you to control how messages are listed (See Figure 12.30). For instance, you can enable threads by subject or by message. If you wish, you can start a new thread when the subject changes on a watched thread. Or you can have Free Agent open the message window with just subject lines displayed or automatically show all messages and threads. If you like all your messages in a nice, neat row, you can change the followup indentation to 0, and all threads will be left-justified.

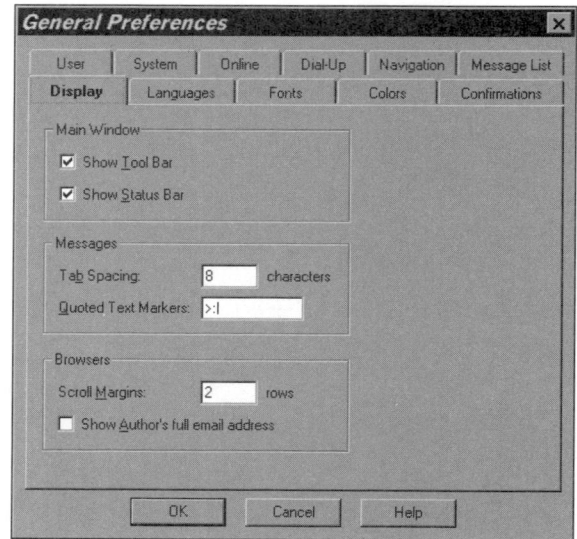

The Display tab.
Figure 12.27

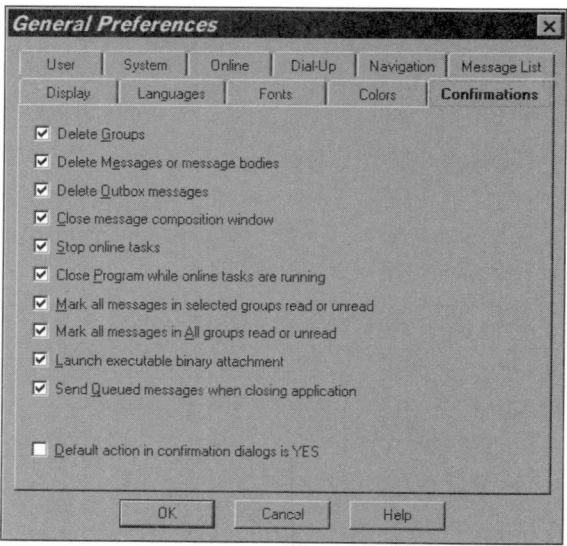

The Confirmations tab.
Figure 12.28

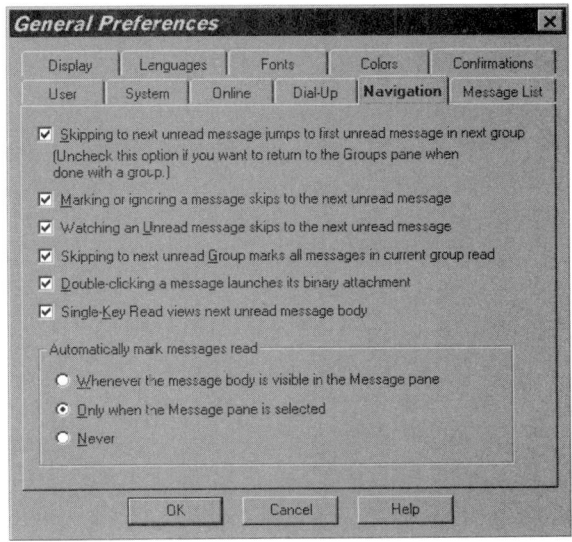

The Navigation tab.
Figure 12.29

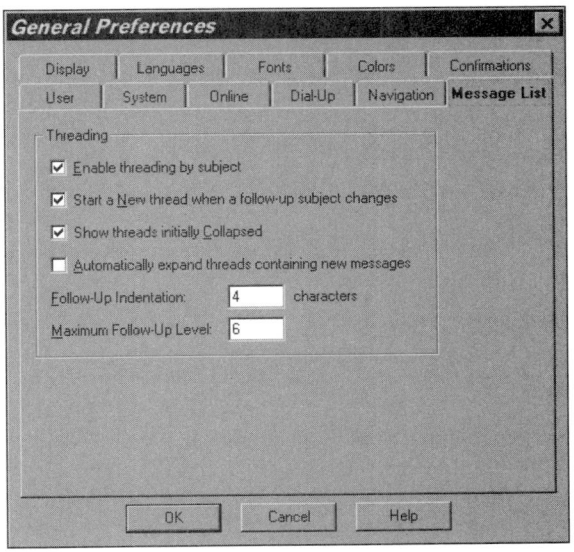

The Message List tab.
Figure 12.30

Two other tabs exist within the General Preferences dialog box: the *Colors* tab and the *Languages* tab. These are self-explanatory, however, so I won't go into them here.

There is one last feature in Free Agent that bears mention. Free Agent can automatically return all threads to all monitored messages. Because I am in the SQL Server forum frequently, I place a watch on a thread that interests me and monitor the traffic for that subject. This is a handy feature.

Newsgroup Etiquette

Many people think that newsgroups are just for hotshot programmers. That is just not true anymore. Many beginners and intermediate users are venturing into the newsgroups and posting questions. Computer professionals are coming to welcome novices, seeing this as an opportunity to foster a better understanding of the products they use. Unfriendly responses to "simple" questions are uncommon.

Newsgroup etiquette calls for participants to be patient and polite, and to pose their questions clearly. It is helpful to potential respondants to supply as much background as possible when posting a question. The more information, the better. If there are no responses in the first day or so, it is worthwhile to repost the message and see what happens. After all, nobody is being paid to spend time in the newsgroups answering all the questions that are posted.

When answering questions, keep the user in mind. He or she might not have the same level of understanding that you do. Spend an extra minute and be more specific than usual. Each day, thousands of people read newsgroup messages and take their content to heart. Therefore, be careful and check your facts as much as possible.

And now, once more, with feeling: *Back up the master database!*

Appendix A: Classes, Training, And Consultants

Classes For DBAs And Developers

I am often asked what classes I would recommend to someone who is new to Microsoft SQL Server. Because I have taken all the major courses and taught them all many times, my view may be just a bit biased (but well-informed!). Classes are integral to your professional growth. In today's business world, you must be technically proficient if you want to remain employed. Your professional development is your first responsibility.

Instructors And Trainers

The quality of a course comes from what the instructor brings to it. If your instructor has a lot to offer in addition to the manual used, then 9 times out of 10 that class will be a success.

Microsoft-certified classes are not exceptions to that rule, either. If the instructor has a substantial amount of real-world experience to add to the course content, then you will enjoy the class. Each instructor is unique and can deliver the same class in totally different ways. As a general rule, I prefer instructors who give as many examples as needed to clarify a point before moving on. I teach that way and believe students can learn a lot from using real-world examples as a reinforcement to learning.

Instructors who read directly from the manual without having anything to add are just not as effective. After all, you can read from the book yourself. I cannot see the value in spending hundreds of dollars for a class if all you get out of it is somebody reading to you for the class's duration.

Choosing Which Classes To Take

Microsoft offers certification classes in SQL Administration and SQL Database Design and Implementation that offer a solid foundation to the DBA or developer. In addition, the Windows NT Server class is valuable. Because Microsoft SQL Server runs in Windows NT and integrates very tightly with the operating system, knowing how NT Server works can be a big advantage.

You might also want to consider enrolling in the Performance Tuning class. The hands-on testing and analysis learned in this course are very helpful in troubleshooting performance problems.

Microsoft certification classes are offered at many training centers around the world. You can find out where these classes are offered by going to the Microsoft Web site and searching under "Training."

Although they provide a good foundation, none of these classes will make you an expert. It takes time and practice to get truly proficient at putting Microsoft SQL Server through its paces. Also, keep in mind that these courses do not cover the specific exam material used for certification. They cover most of what you will see, but not all. Microsoft certification exams test product knowledge in a very broad scope. You cannot get the background needed for success on these exams in a week or two of listening to someone talk about a product and what it does. It takes time, study, and a lot of hands-on experience.

Becoming a Microsoft Certified Solution Developer, for instance, required a great deal of my own time and money. I spent hours studying documentation and breaking things down to find out how they worked. The product knowledge gained by hands-on experimentation is much more valuable to the exam process than book knowledge or rote memorization.

The certification process that Microsoft, Novell, and others are using to test the proficiency of technicians is very valuable in today's job market. Most employers would hire a certified technician before hiring someone equally qualified with no certification. I am also a proponent of the training aids supplied by third-party manufacturers, such as Transcender. These tools help prepare you for the exams by pointing out thoroughly the whys and hows behind the questions. I use and recommend them in all my classes.

Training In General

Look for a training facility that is willing to work with you and provide you with a schedule that meets your needs. If the training center can meet your schedule, you should then research the prices of the courses. Certification classes are not cheap; expect to pay well over a thousand dollars for any of the courses recommended here. Most training facilities will give you discounts (if you ask for them) for group enrollment or for taking multiple classes and, if applicable, they will work with your account representative a little.

Also look for a facility that has current hardware and software; if you are taking a class using slow hardware, the course will drag on interminably. A comfortable classroom environment that is not crowded is a must for these technical courses. Most training facilities let you sit in on a class for an hour or so to get a feel for what is offered and how the class works. Ask for the chance to sit in, and see how other students feel about the experience they are getting.

Make sure the instructor for your class knows the product. Ask the hard questions to check whether the instructor is qualified. Find out how many times he or she has taught the course you want to take or even the number of courses he or she has delivered. If an instructor is new to training, you might prefer to choose a course taught by a more seasoned instructor. Of course, everyone must start somewhere, and novice teachers, while they might not have a lot of teaching experience, might still bring a lot of hands-on experience to the class. Be sure to ask about their background in the industry. Remember, it's easy to find instructors in today's training market, but it is very hard to find quality instructors.

Do not be afraid of contract instructors. Contract instructors can be a very good resource because they have probably taught the class many times. Instructors who travel widely delivering these classes are exposed to all sorts of questions week-in and week-out. Chances are they have already been asked any questions you might have and will have the answers.

Consultants

Although also a contract instructor, I am first and foremost a consultant and have been for many years. I have worked with many other consultants and numerous companies. With that in mind, a few guidelines to consider before selecting a consultant to help solve a problem in your company are listed on the next pages.

- Look for someone who takes pride in what he or she does. Some of the better consultants I have dealt with take workmanship and pride very seriously. This makes for better quality of work and superior product knowledge.

- Beware of discount consultants. More often than not, you get what you pay for. Thirty dollars an hour saved will not make up for the time wasted paying someone to learn "on the job." By the same token, expect more than your money's worth from the high-dollar consultant. Good consultants try to give a 110 percent effort in their contract and support roles so that each company feels it has made a good investment in their services. If you are paying premium prices for consultants, expect premium service in return.

- If you are deciding whether to solve a problem in-house or to hire a consultant, you should do some research and find out what the market pays for consulting in the technical area in which you require help. You might find that paying for a consultant is cheaper than performing certain tasks in-house. By the same token, understand that the tasks at hand might require a great deal of background and experience to solve, which would legitimately boost a consultant's fees.

- Be wary of consultants who want to get paid for determining the scope of a project. As a rule, when I do consulting work, I try to keep the planning time as productive as possible and keep that cost down. Make sure you agree with the consultant up front about what is billable time and what is not. A consultant should be able to determine within days if he or she can help and how long the work should take.

- Consultants usually request partial payment up front, as a safeguard against doing work "for free." This partial payment may amount to as much as half of the cost of a project. You should expect to make the final payment when the project is completed. That final payment is your protection against nondeliverable projects.

- Put everything in writing before entering into a working relationship with a consultant. A written contract can head off potential legal fees down the road. Supply a clear and concise specification of the work required of the consultant, including documentation and training. If he or she knows exactly what is expected, the consultant is more likely to meet your requirements. Many standard consulting contracts are available that can protect you from disreputable consultants. In addition, do not forget to include a nondisclosure agreement in the contract. You should take every precaution to ensure you are protected. If a consultant does not want to agree to any of these provisions, you should look for another consultant.

- Be flexible with your consultants with regard to their methods of implementing tasks. A consultant may have a different approach than you would, and it might save you time and money in the long run. Consulting work is rarely an exact science. Many hours can be spent solving what was initially considered a simple problem. Demand quality, yet be understanding and open to suggestions.

Appendix B: The Pubs Sample Database

The Pubs database is a collection of tables and data that is installed automatically when you install Microsoft SQL Server. See Figure B.1 for a graphic representation of the Pubs sample database. In this book, I have suggested that you remove this database from your production servers after installation, because it is not required. For development servers, however, I usually leave the Pubs database intact so that I have a common point of reference on each server. This point of reference can be used to test the functions involved in the client/server communication process.

I have used the Pubs database for the examples in this book so that all readers have a common data set to run the examples against. Destroying the data in this database will have no adverse effect on your server, so you can use it in a learning situation without fearing that you might destroy something important. You can rebuild the Pubs database with a script called "instpubs.sql," which can be found in the installation directory on your server.

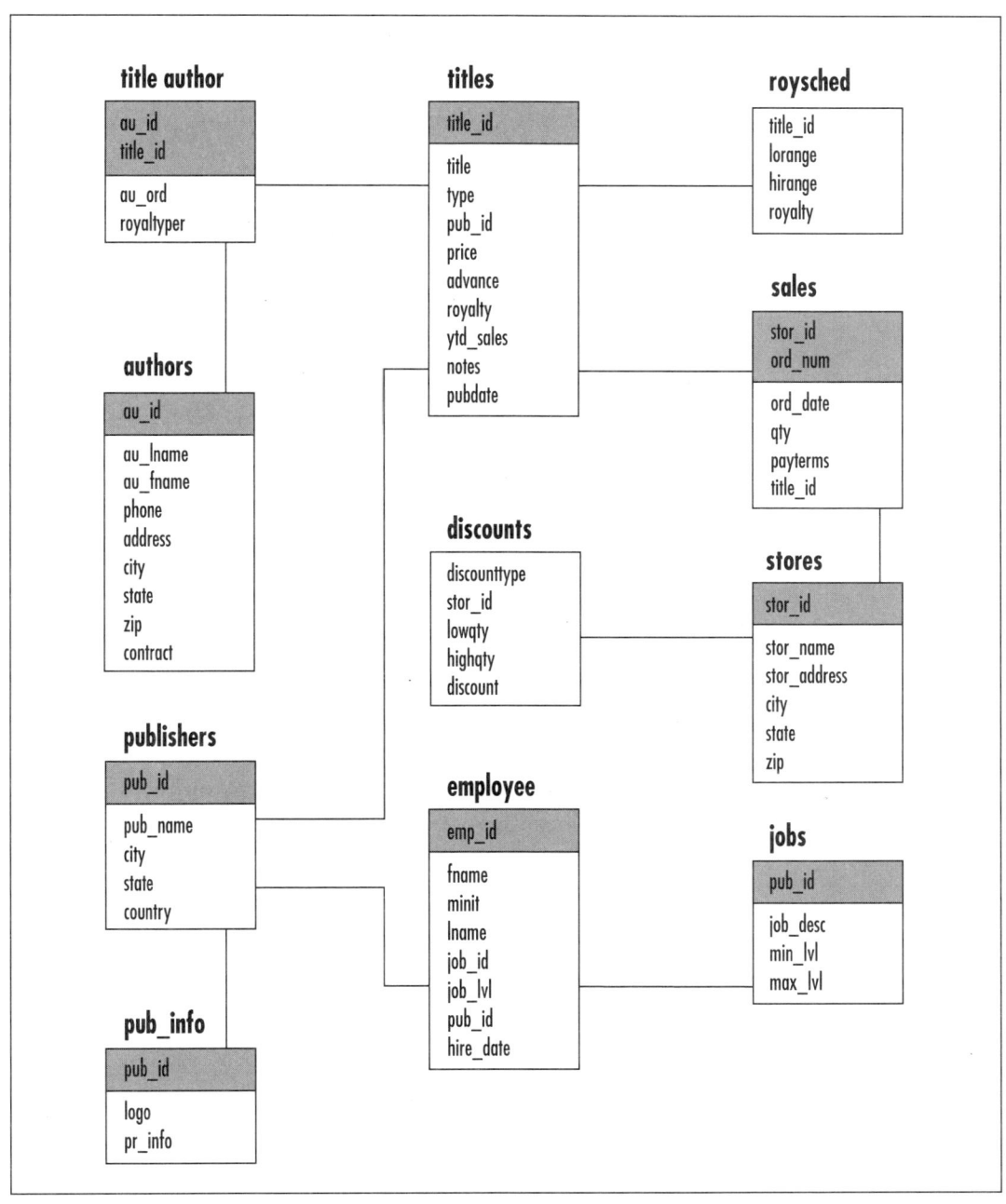

The Pubs sample database.
Figure B.1

Glossary

These definitions have been provided to help clarify some of the more common terms in the previous chapters. In addition, you can look up these and other terms in Microsoft SQL Server Books Online or the Microsoft Knowledge Base available through the Internet or on the Microsoft TechNet CD-ROM.

ad hoc query A query created for immediate execution. You can create an ad hoc query from scratch or by modifying an existing query that is saved in a text file.

algorithm A process or rule a machine uses for processing.

alias A database user name that is shared by several login IDs. An alias allows more than one person to be treated as the same user inside a database, giving all the designated users the same permissions. A common use for aliases is to allow several users to assume the role of database owner (DBO).

backup domain controller (BDC) In a Windows NT domain, a server that receives a copy of the domain's security database from the primary domain controller. A backup domain controller can be promoted to a primary domain controller.

bandwidth The difference between the highest and lowest frequencies in a given range. For example, a telephone line accommodates a bandwidth of 3000 hertz (Hz), the difference between the lowest (300Hz) and highest (3300Hz) frequencies it can carry. In computer networks, wider bandwidth gives faster data transfer and is shown in bits per second (bps).

batch   A set of SQL statements submitted together and executed as a group. A script is often a series of batches submitted one after the other.

BCP (bulk copy program)   A command-line utility that copies Microsoft SQL Server data to and from an operating-system file.

binary   A data type that holds as many as 255 bytes of fixed-length binary data. The binary data type can contain 0 bytes, but when specified, it must be a value from 1 through 255. Choose binary when you think the data entries in the column will be consistently close to the same size.

binding   Associating a default or rule with a column or data type. The sp_bindefault system stored procedure binds a default to a column or to a user-defined data type.

case-sensitive   Pertains to the ability to distinguish between upper- and lowercase letters. Some programs or class codes are case-sensitive—that is, they are specific to upper- or lowercase letters and must be input correctly.

central publisher   The database server between the publisher server and the subscription servers. The central publisher answers to the publisher server and distributes data to the subscription servers.

character set   A set of 256 letters, numbers, and symbols specific to a language. The selected character set when you first install SQL Server determines the types of characters that SQL Server recognizes in the databases. If, after installation, you need to change it, you must rebuild your databases and reload your data.

child record   A record that has a parent record. A child record can be a parent record that has been attached to another parent record.

computed values   The product of computations with data from numeric columns or on numeric constants in a SELECT list by using arithmetic operators. Arithmetic operators let you add, subtract, multiply, and divide numeric data.

constraint   A restriction placed upon the value that can be entered into a column or a row. Values can be equal to, greater than, or less than. A constraint limits the input.

cursor   Database objects with which applications manipulate data by rows instead of by sets. Using cursors, multiple operations can be performed row-by-row against a result set with or without returning to the original table. For example, a cursor can generate a list of all user-defined table names within a database. Cursors are extremely powerful when combined with stored procedures and the EXECUTE statement.

data replication   Distributing data automatically between one or more servers.

database   A collection of information, data tables, and other objects that are organized and presented to serve a specific purpose, such as facilitation of searching and sorting data.

DBMS (Database Management System)   An application that manages the data and structures that hold information.

deadlock   A situation that arises when two users, each having a lock on one piece of data, attempt to acquire a lock on the other's piece. Each user waits for the other to release his or her lock. SQL Server detects deadlocks and kills one user's process, returning error code 1205.

device   A file in which a database is stored. A database can be stored on several different devices. The two types of devices are *database devices,* which store databases, and *dump devices,* which store backups of a database.

distribution server   In replication, the server containing the distribution database. The distribution server receives all changes to published data, stores the changes in its distribution database, and when appropriate, transmits them to subscription servers. The distribution server can be the same computer that is acting as the publication server, or a different computer.

DMO (distributed management object)   An object exposed by Microsoft SQL Server that is used in the management of SQL Server and not data manipulation on SQL Server. Also can be used in creating your own Microsoft SQL Server management tools written in other object-oriented languages.

DTC (Distributed Transaction Coordinator)   An application that coordinates transactions across a network of Windows NT- and Windows 95-based systems. With DTC, SQL Server can update data that resides on two or more SQL Server systems.

FAT (file allocation table)   A method for managing disk storage. A FAT file system is used by an operating system to keep track of various segments of disk space.

fill factor   An option that specifies how full SQL Server should make each index page. The amount of empty space on an index page is important because when an index page fills up, the system must take time to split it to make room for new rows.

global variables   System-supplied, predeclared variables. Global variables are distinguished from local variables by two symbols (@@) preceding their names.

horizontal partitions   A subset of rows contained in a table. Horizontal partitions are the result of using a WHERE clause to filter only the rows you want.

IDC (Internet database connector)   A component provided by Microsoft as a communications component used by Internet Information Server (IIS) and Microsoft SQL Server to pass data requests back and forth between Web server and data server.

index   A set of pointers that are logically ordered by the values of a key. An index is a database object that provides access to data in the rows of a table, based on key values. Indexes provide quick access to data and can enforce uniqueness on the rows in a table. SQL Server supports clustered and nonclustered indexes. In a clustered index, data is stored in the same order as the index; in a nonclustered index, data is stored differently from the index.

integrated security   Security that allows SQL Server to use Windows NT authentication mechanisms to validate logins for all connections. Only trusted IPX/SPX or named pipes connections are allowed.

IPX/SPX   Network protocol primarily used by Novell networks.

ISP (Internet service provider)   A company you subscribe to for access to the Internet.

login ID   The unique name a user uses to log in to SQL Server. A login ID can have as many as 30 characters and must be unique for that server. The characters can be letters or numbers, but the first character must be a letter or the symbols # or _. With the integrated security available with Windows NT, you do not need to maintain a separate login ID for SQL Server.

master database   The database that controls all of the operations of SQL Server. It is automatically installed with SQL Server and keeps track of such things as user accounts. It also tracks other servers that the original server can interact with, the configurable environment variables, system error messages, the storage space allocated to each database, the tapes and disks available on the system, and the active locks.

mirroring   Continuous duplication of the information on one SQL Server device to another. Mirroring can provide continuous recovery in the event of a drive failure.

mixed security   Security mode that allows login requests to be validated using either integrated or standard security. Trusted connections (as used by integrated security) and nontrusted connections (as used by standard security) can be established.

model database   An SQL Server–supplied database that provides a template for new user databases. Each time a database is created, SQL Server makes a copy of the model database, sizes it to the requested size, and files the user database with the system tables and objects currently defined in the model database.

named pipes   A protocol that SQL Server and Open Data Service applications use to provide communication between clients and servers. Named pipes permit access to shared network resources.

NTFS (NT file system)   A disk storage method designed for use specifically with the Windows NT operating system. It supports long file names (but keeps shorter file names for compatibility with computers running the FAT file system). It supports object-oriented applications by treating all files as objects.

ODBC (open database connectivity)   A set of drivers provided by different manufacturers that allows client applications to connect to database servers without regard to native database language. These drivers interpret data requests and translate those requests into a format that the database understands.

Optimizer   The SQL Server component responsible for generating the optimum execution plan for a query.

parent record   The record that represents the "one" side of a one-to-many relationship.

password   A word or group of letters or numbers specific to a user. Passwords are used to access most systems and/or data within the systems.

primary domain controller (PDC)   In a Windows NT domain, a server that maintains the domain's security database and checks user logins. It also provides a copy of the domain's security database to backup domain controllers that share the user login load.

primary key   The column or combination of columns that uniquely identifies a table. It must always be non-null and will always have a unique index. A primary key is used for joins with foreign keys in other tables.

publisher server   In replication, a server that makes data available to distribution servers. A publisher server maintains publication databases, makes published data from those databases available for replication, and sends copies of all changes made to the published data to the distribution server.

Pubs database A sample database provided with Microsoft SQL Server. The Pubs database can be helpful when you are learning to use SQL Server. All Microsoft SQL Server documentation, as well as this book, utilize the Pubs sample database as the basis for examples.

pull subscription In replication, a subscription performed while administrative focus is set on the subscription server. Accessing information through the subscription server from the publication server is an example of a pull subscription.

push subscription In replication, a subscription performed while administrative focus is set on the publication server. The opposite of a pull subscription.

RAID (redundant array of inexpensive disks) Installation of several disk drives to a system. Some drives contain mirrored information so data is not lost. RAID disk drives can be replaced quickly in cases of disk failure. This technology is good for Web and database servers, so that no information is lost and the information is always available.

RAM (random access memory) Physical memory existing on a server or workstation.

RQBE (relational query by example) Applications that allow users to create ad hoc queries built graphically to run against a database server.

scheduled table refresh In replication, scheduled table refresh specifies that at scheduled intervals, all articles in the publication will be refreshed. Each time refresh occurs, all data will be applied to all destination tables.

schema change A description of a database the DBMS generated using the data definition language.

sort order The set of rules that decides how SQL Server collates and determines the order in which data is presented in response to SQL. You can change the order the data is presented by using ORDER BY and/or GROUP BY statements.

standard security Security mode that uses SQL Server's own login validation process for all connections. To log in to SQL Server, each user must provide a valid login ID and password.

stored procedures Transact-SQL statements stored under a name and processed as a unit. Stored procedures are stored within a database and can be executed with one request from an application. A stored procedure can also allow user-declared variables, conditional execution, and other powerful programming features.

Structured Query Language (SQL) A database query and programming language originally developed by IBM for mainframe computers. It is widely used for accessing data in database systems.

subquery A SELECT statement nested inside another SELECT, INSERT, UPDATE, or DELETE statement, or inside another subquery.

subscription server In replication, a subscription server maintains destination databases, which receive and maintain copies of published data. Also referred to as a *subscriber*.

synchronization In replication, the process that ensures the publication and destination tables contain the same schema and data. This process must occur before a subscription server can receive replicated transactions from an article or a publication.

syntax Order of characters in programming languages. A syntax error means something was typed incorrectly.

table A collection of rows that have associated columns.

TCP/IP (transfer control protocol/Internet protocol) A protocol for connecting to the Internet or other network hosts. The primary protocol for Unix networks.

Tempdb A database that provides a storage area for temporary tables and other temporary working storage needs. *All* temporary tables are stored in Tempdb.

Transact-SQL The standard language for communicating between applications and SQL Server. The Transact-SQL language is an enhancement to Structured Query Language (SQL) as implemented by Microsoft SQL Server.

transaction log A reserved area of the database in which all changes to the database are recorded. The transaction log is stored in the Syslogs system table and is used by SQL Server during automatic recovery.

trigger A special form of stored procedure that goes into effect when data within a table is modified. Triggers are often created to enforce integrity or consistency among logically related data in different tables.

vertical partitions A subset of columns contained in a base table. Vertical partitions are typically utilized through the column list in a SELECT statement.

Web browser A software program, such as Microsoft Internet Explorer, that retrieves a document from a Web server and interprets the HTML codes.

A Coriolis Group New Title
Bonus Chapter

http://www.coriolis.com.

The following chapter provides a preview of some of the topics you will find in *Visual Developer SQL Database Programming With Java*, now available in bookstores.

You can also order the book directly from the Coriolis Group by calling 1.800.410.0192.

Order ISBN 1-57610-176-2

SQL is currently the language of choice for handling relational databases, and Java is the most popular language for Web programming. *Visual Developer SQL Database Programming with Java* combines these two technologies, showing how they can create fast, efficient database applications for the World Wide Web and corporate intranets. This is a hands-on, practical book that includes specific guidance for using Java and SQL with popular databases, such as Microsoft Access.

Chapter 1	Introduction To Database Programming And Client-Server Systems
Chapter 2	Relational Data Basics
Chapter 3	Using Java To Access Databases
Chapter 4	SQL Queries
Chapter 5	The JDBC API
Chapter 6	Sorting And Grouping
Chapter 7	Joins And Unions
Chapter 8	Designing Databases
Chapter 9	SQL Data Definition Language
Chapter 10	SQL Data Manipulation Language
Chapter 11	Advanced SQL Queries
Chapter 12	Creating And Using Views
Chapter 13	Multiuser Considerations
Chapter 14	Database Security And Recovery

3
USING JAVA TO ACCESS DATABASES

In this chapter you'll begin your study of SQL database programming. To illustrate the principles of SQL programming, I'll present a Java application that uses an Access database to store data in a guest book of the sort that many people like to provide on their Web home pages. Of course, a real guest book would have to be implemented as an applet, rather than an application, so that it could be automatically downloaded and executed in the user's browser. Building the program as an application rather than an applet avoids some security-related complications, which I'll bring up in Chapter 14.

The emphasis in this chapter is on getting the application up and running and explaining its basic structure. This chapter also explains how the data types provided by SQL correspond to those provided by Access and Java. This information will help you choose the proper Java data types to correctly access values stored in any SQL database. You can then use the example program in this chapter as a pattern for building Java programs that similarly access your own databases.

The following two chapters will address the operation of the application in more detail. Chapter 4 deals with the SQL commands used by the application, and Chapter 5 more fully explains the JDBC API used in accessing the database.

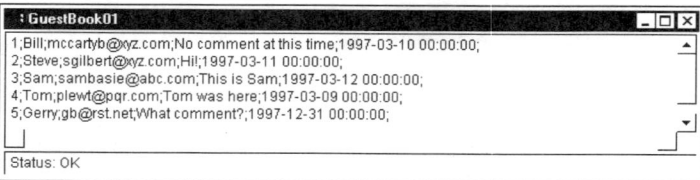

Figure 1
Running the GuestBook application.

The GuestBook Program

The user interface of the GuestBook application, shown in Figure 1, reports entries stored in the GuestBook database designed in Chapter 2. The application displays its output rather primitively; each row of the Visits table is shown as a line within a **TextArea** Abstract Windowing Toolkit (AWT) component. Fields within the row are separated by semicolons. The interface provides no Quit button; the user terminates the program by clicking on the Close icon on the application window's title bar. If this interface isn't exactly what you would enjoy using, never fear. I'll soon show you how to add a more suitable user interface that uses **TextField**s and **Button**s. The application as shown here is indeed clumsy to use, but it's easier to understand than a more attractive one.

Figure 2 shows the class hierarchy of the **GuestBook01** class. The application itself is shown beginning in Listing 1. It contains a single (public) class named **GuestBook01**, which extends the **Frame** class, as do most other graphical applications. The **GuestBook01** class defines an inner class, called **WindowHandler**, used to process the **windowClosing** message sent when the user wants to close the application window. **WindowHandler** extends the **WindowAdapter** class provided as part of the AWT 1.1 delegation event model. If you're not yet familiar with the delegation event model, you should pay careful attention to the way the application handles events, because the delegation event model is quite different from that used in AWT 1.0.

Just in case your Java is rusty, the explanations in this chapter will be a bit more thorough than those in subsequent chapters. If you find them wordy, just focus on the listings. Listing 1 shows the fields defined by the **GuestBook01** class, along with its **main( )** class. The application imports classes from three standard packages:

- **java.awt**—defines the graphical user interface.

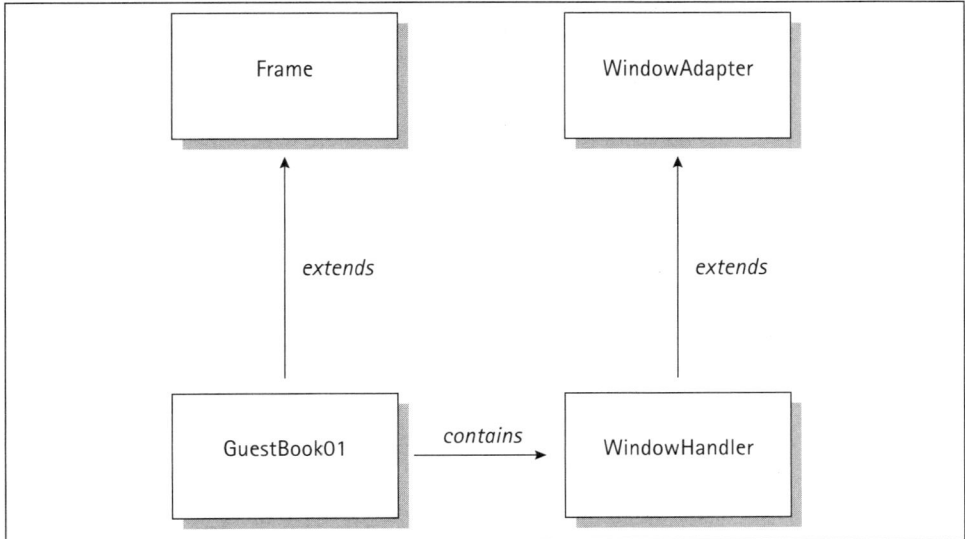

Figure 2
Class hierarchy of the **GuestBook01** class.

- **java.awt.event**—provides support for the AWT 1.1 delegation event model.
- **java.sql**—provides support for JDBC access of SQL databases.

The user interface consists of only two components:

- a **TextArea** named *theVisits*—displays the contents of the database.
- a **TextField** named *theStatus*—displays a message describing any error that occurs.

LISTING 1   THE GUESTBOOK APPLICATION.

```
import java.awt.*;
import java.awt.event.*;
import java.sql.*;

class GuestBook01 extends Frame
{

    TextArea    theVisits = new TextArea(6, 80);
    TextField   theStatus = new TextField("");

    Connection theConnection;
    Statement  theStatement;
    ResultSet  theResult;
    ResultSetMetaData theMetaData;
```

```
    String theDataSource;
    String theUser;
    String thePassword;

    public static void main(String args[])
    {
        new GuestBook01( ).init( );
    }
```

The class defines several fields used to support access to the database:

- **theConnection**—a **Connection** object used to represent an open connection to a database.

- **theStatement**—a **Statement** object used to represent a SQL command to be sent to the database for execution.

- **theResult**—a **ResultSet** object used to represent the results returned after execution of a SQL command.

- **theMetaData**—a **ResultSetMetaData** object that contains useful information about results returned after execution of a SQL command, such as the number of records in the result set.

- **theDataSource**—a **String** that contains the name of the database or data source being accessed, in the form of a special type of URL.

- **theUser** and **thePassword**—**Strings** used to gain access to a database that has security restrictions limiting access only to designated users, who must identify themselves and supply a proper password before a connection is established.

The **main( )** method of the class is starkly simple. It creates an anonymous instance of the class and invokes the **init( )** method on it. The arguments passed to **main( )** by the Java interpreter are not used.

Initializing The Application

Listing 2 shows the **init( )** method for GuestBook. The default layout manager of the application's frame is **BorderLayout**, so init( ) places the **TextArea** and **TextField** at the "Center" and "South" positions of the **Frame**, respectively. This way, the **TextArea** will expand to fill any available space, maximizing the room available for displaying database records. Both the **TextArea** and **TextField** are set to be noneditable, since the user doesn't need to type input into either one. An anonymous **WindowHandler** instance is set as a listener for window events, so that it can close the application when the user requests. The **pack( )** and **show( )** methods are invoked on the application frame (the default object) to cause it to resize itself according to the size of its components and display itself on the screen.

The **init( )** method then uses other methods to open a connection to the database, execute a SQL query (the results of which are formatted and displayed in the **TextArea**), and close the database connection. The next section will look at the way window messages are handled, followed by a detailed explanation of the database-related steps.

LISTING 2   INITIALIZING THE APPLICATION.

```
public void init( )
{
    setTitle("GuestBook01");
    add("Center", theVisits);
    add("South", theStatus);

    theVisits.setEditable(false);
    theStatus.setEditable(false);
    addWindowListener(new WindowHandler( ));

    pack( );
    show( );

    openConnection( );
    execSQLCommand("Select * from Visits;");
    closeConnection( );
}
```

Handling Window Events

The **init( )** method of the **GuestBook01** class defines an anonymous instance of its **WindowHandler** inner class as a listener for window messages. Details of the inner class are shown in Listing Clicking the Close icon of the application window generates a **windowClosing** event. When a **windowClosing** message is received, the **WindowHandler** hides the application frame and terminates the application. Rather than blindly invoking the corresponding methods, it checks to make sure the source of the event is truly a **Frame**, avoiding a possible **ClassCastException** if it turns out the object isn't a **Frame**.

LISTING 3 HANDLING WINDOW EVENTS.

```
class WindowHandler extends WindowAdapter
{
    public void windowClosing(WindowEvent event)
    {
        Object source= event.getSource( );
        if (source instanceof Frame)
        {
            ((Frame) source).setVisible(false);
            System.exit(0);
        }
    }
}
```

Opening A Database Connection

Listing 4 shows how the program opens its database connection. It first sets values for the fields **theDataSource, theUser,** and **thePassword.** The user ID and password should match those associated with the database that is the ODBC data source, as explained in the next section. If the database does not require a user ID or password, each can be specified as an empty string, as done here.

LISTING 4 OPENING A DATABASE CONNECTION.

```
public void openConnection( )
{
    theDataSource = "jdbc:odbc:GuestBook";
    theUser = "";
    thePassword = "";

    try
    {
        Class.forName ("sun.jdbc.odbc.JdbcOdbcDriver");
        theConnection =
          DriverManager.getConnection(theDataSource, theUser,
            thePassword);
        theStatus.setText("Status: OK");
    }
    catch (Exception e)
    {
        handleException(e);
    }
}
```

The string containing the data-source name is formatted as a special URL:

```
jdbc:<subprotocol>:<subname>
```

The protocol name, **jdbc**, is always present. The subprotocol and subname vary depending on the kind of data source used. The JDBC **DriverManager** uses the subprotocol to choose an appropriate driver for the data source. Common values for the subprotocol are "odbc" and "oracle". The subname contains additional information used by the driver. Often, this is a network name, such as that used for other Web services:

```
jdbc:<subprotocol>://<host.domain>:<port>/<databasename>
```

The documentation for your driver should specify the correct form of the subprotocol and subname. With ODBC, the host and port information is unnecessary, since the data source is already configured on the local host. The form used for an ODBC data source is:

```
jdbc:odbc:<data source name>
```

To open the database connection, you must instantiate the proper driver. Again, the documentation for your driver should specify how to do this. If you're using the JDBC-ODBC bridge, you can instantiate the JDBC-ODBC bridge driver by using the **forName( )** method of the class named *Class*:

```
Class.forName ("sun.jdbc.odbc.JdbcOdbcDriver");
```

You can then tell the **DriverManager** to open a connection to your data source by using:

```
theConnection =
    DriverManager.getConnection(theDataSource, theUser, thePassword);
```

The **getConnection( )** method returns a **Connection** object, which you should save, since it becomes your means of accessing the data source. Here, it is saved in the field named *theConnection*.

If an error occurs during the opening of the connection, a **SQLException** is thrown. By enclosing the statements that open the connection within a **try-catch** block, you can handle this contingency gracefully. The GuestBook application simply displays an appropriate message in its **TextField** by means of the **handleException( )** method, shown later.

Closing The Database Connection

When you're done accessing a data source, you should close the database connection, as shown in Listing 5, freeing any resources associated with the connection. Any open **ResultSet** or **Statement** objects you've created are closed automatically. Again, a **SQLException** may occur during the closing of a connection, so enclosing the operation in a **try-catch** block is advisable.

LISTING 5   CLOSING THE DATABASE CONNECTION.

```
public void closeConnection( )
{
    try
    {
        theConnection.close( );
    }
    catch (Exception e)
    {
        handleException(e);
    }
}
```

Executing A SQL Command

The **execSQLComand( )** method, shown in Listing 6, actually issues the SQL command, the most important task of the program. Fortunately, issuing a SQL command is easy with JDBC. In fact, your ability to work with a SQL database has much more to do with the depth of your SQL knowledge than the depth of your JDBC knowledge. JDBC itself is really quite simple to use. That's why this book focuses on SQL, rather than JDBC.

LISTING 6   EXECUTING A SQL COMMAND.

```
public void execSQLCommand(String command)
{
    try
    {
        theStatement = theConnection.createStatement();
        theResult = theStatement.executeQuery(command);
        theMetaData = theResult.getMetaData( );
        int columnCount = theMetaData.getColumnCount( );

        theVisits.setText("");

        while (theResult.next( ))
        {
```

```
            for (int i = 1; i <= columnCount; i++)
            {
                String colValue = theResult.getString(i);
                if (colValue == null) colValue = "";
                theVisits.append(colValue + ";");
            }
            theVisits.append("\n");
        }
    }
    catch (Exception e)
    {
        handleException(e);
    }
}
```

To perform the command, the program uses the **createStatement( )** method of the **Connection** object to create a **Statement** that can hold the query. Then it invokes the **executeQuery( )** method on the **Statement** object, passing a string containing the SQL query.

Chapter 4 will show how to construct some basic SQL queries. For now, just observe how the **init( )** method passes the query string—"Select * from Visits;"—as an argument. This simple query obtains all the rows of the Visits table and returns a **ResultSet** object. Like most other SQL queries, this one generates a relational table as its result. You can use **ResultSet** to access this result table.

Next the program invokes the **getMetaData( )** method on the **ResultSet** object. This returns a **ResultSetMetaData** value, which the program stores in a variable named *theMetaData*. Much useful data is available using **ResultSetMetaData** objects; here, the program uses the **getColumnCount( )** method to obtain the number of columns of the result table.

Finally, the program iterates through the result table, invoking the **next( )** method on **theResult** to obtain each row of the result table. This method eventually returns **false** when it runs out of rows.

Each row is processed using a **for** loop that iterates over the number of columns. The value of each row attribute is obtained using the **getString( )** method, which returns the value of a column as a **String**. As you'll see later in the chapter, there is a whole family of similar methods that return column values as other data types. The **getString( )** method is particularly useful, because almost any SQL value has a **String** representation of some sort. Therefore, the **getString( )** method can be appropriately called on a column of almost any type.

If a database column contains a SQL **null** value, perhaps resulting from an input field omitted by the user, the **getString( )** method returns **null**. The program tests the value returned by **getString( )**, transforming a **null** value to an empty string. Then the value is appended to the contents of the **TextArea**, **theVisits**. The entire operation is enclosed in a **try-catch** block so that a **SQLException** does not unexpectedly terminate the program.

Handling Errors And Exceptions

Listing 7 shows the **handleException( )** method, which the program uses to handle errors and exceptions. This method simply sets the status **TextField** to contain the error message related to the exception, which it obtains by using the **getMessage( )** method. It also prints a stack trace on **System.out**.

An interesting property of **SQLException**s is that they can be *chained*—that is, a **SQLException** can be linked to another **SQLException**. The **getNextException( )** method "walks" the exception chain, as shown here. The **handleException( )** method uses this technique to print each chained exception on **System.out**.

LISTING 7 HANDLING ERRORS AND EXCEPTIONS.

```
public void handleException(Exception e)
{
    theStatus.setText("Error: " + e.getMessage( ));
    e.printStackTrace( );
    if (e instanceof SQLException)
    {
        while ((e = ((SQLException) e).getNextException( )) != null)
        {
            System.out.println(e);
        }
    }
}
```

Setting Up The ODBC Data Source

To run the GuestBook application, you must first create an ODBC data source corresponding to the GuestBook Access database. You can use the database you created in Chapter 2 (if you're confident that you created it correctly), or you can copy the database file (GuestBook.mdb) from the CD-ROM directory that contains the source files for this chapter.

To use Access via ODBC, you must install the Access ODBC drivers. If you haven't done so, use the Access setup program to load them onto your system.

To configure the database as an ODBC data source, follow these steps:

1. From the Start menu, select Settings|Control Panel.
2. Click on ODBC-32, the 32-bit ODBC driver. (If this icon is not present, you need to install the Access ODBC drivers.)
3. Click Add and choose Microsoft Access Driver. (If this choice is not present, you need to install the Access ODBC drivers.)
4. Type in a data-source name, such as *Guest Book*, and a suitable description.
5. In the Database frame, click on the Select button.
6. Use the Select Database dialog to select the file that contains your database.
7. If your database is protected with a password, you can click the Advanced button and specify a user name and password.

Your ODBC data source is now configured and ready. This would be a good time for you to execute the GuestBook application and see how it works.

If you later find that you need to change a setting for this data source, follow these steps:

1. From the Start menu, select Settings|Control Panel.
2. Click on ODBC-32, the 32-bit ODBC driver.
3. Select the data source you wish to reconfigure, and click the Setup button.

An Improved GuestBook Program

Upon trying out the GuestBook program, you probably found its output awkward to read. In this section, I'll show how to improve the program's user interface. We'll continue making improvements through the next several chapters until we finally arrive at a program that makes full and effective use of the capabilities of Java and SQL.

Figure 3 shows the new version of the program, and Listing 8 shows its fields, along with its **main( )** method. The improved version does not make any significant changes to the **main( )** method. The main class is now named **GuestBook02**, to distinguish it from the original version. It implements the **ActionListener** interface, so it can receive and process event messages originating with the two buttons—Next and Quit—added to the user interface.

LISTING 8 THE FIELDS AND MAIN( ) METHOD.

```java
import java.awt.*;
import java.awt.event.*;
import java.sql.*;

class GuestBook02 extends Frame
implements ActionListener
{
    Panel      theDataPanel   = new Panel( );
    TextField  theName        = new TextField("", 32);
    TextField  theEMail       = new TextField("", 32);
    TextField  theComment     = new TextField("", 50);
    TextField  theTime        = new TextField("", 24);

    Panel      theBottomPanel = new Panel( );
    Button     theNextButton  = new Button("Next Record");
    TextField  theStatus      = new TextField("");
    Button     theQuitButton  = new Button("Quit");

    Connection theConnection;
    Statement  theStatement;
    ResultSet  theResult;

    String theDataSource;
    String theUser;
    String thePassword;

    public static void main(String args[])
    {
        new GuestBook02( ).init( );
    }
```

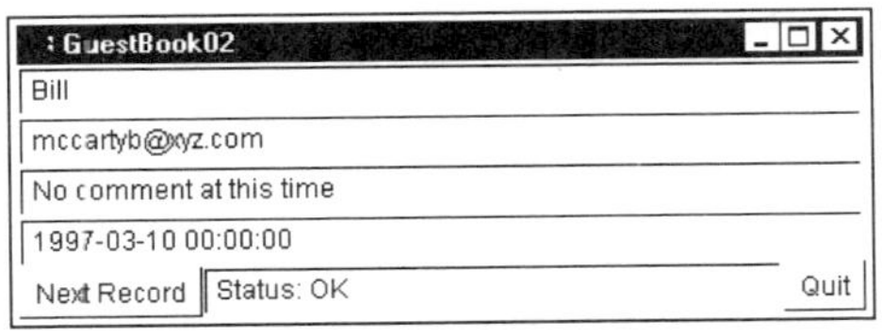

Figure 3
The improved GuestBook program.

Since the program now displays only a single record at a time, it provides a Next button to allow the user to scroll forward through the database. Note that it has no Previous button; moving backward through the database must await more sophisticated SQL programming techniques, which will be presented in Chapter 4. In addition to the Next button, the program now provides a Quit button, so the novice user can easily figure out how to stop the program.

The init( ) Method

The improved user interface constructed by the **init( )** method includes two **Panel**s. The center **Panel**, which expands to fill available space, contains **TextField**s for the visitor name, email address, comment, and time of visit. These are arranged into four rows—one **TextField** on each row—using **GridLayout**.

The bottom **Panel** is arranged using a **BorderLayout**. Its center component, the **TextField** that reports status, expands horizontally to fill available space. The Next and Quit buttons, to the **TextField**'s left and right, respectively, use only enough space to make their labels visible.

Each of the **TextField**s is set as noneditable, since they're used only for output. Each of the **Button**s has the **GuestBook02** object set as the listener for any **actionPerformed** events it generates; the **GuestBook02** object is also set as the listener for window events.

The remainder of the **init( )** method is little changed. Note, however, that the program no longer invokes the **Connection.close( )** method to close the database connection. In the new version of the program, the connection is closed only when the user decides to exit the program.

Listing 9 shows the revised **init( )** method. The **openConnection( )**, **closeConnection( )**, and **handleException( )** methods are left exactly as they were in the original version of the program, so they're not shown in the listing.

Listing 9 The init( ) method.

```
public void init( )
{
    setTitle("GuestBook02");
    add("Center", theDataPanel);
    add("South", theBottomPanel);

    theDataPanel.setLayout(new GridLayout(4, 1));
    theDataPanel.add(theName);
    theDataPanel.add(theEMail);
    theDataPanel.add(theComment);
    theDataPanel.add(theTime);

    theBottomPanel.setLayout(new BorderLayout( ));
    theBottomPanel.add("West", theNextButton);
    theBottomPanel.add("Center", theStatus);
    theBottomPanel.add("East", theQuitButton);

    theName.setEditable(false);
    theEMail.setEditable(false);
    theComment.setEditable(false);
    theTime.setEditable(false);
    theStatus.setEditable(false);

    theNextButton.addActionListener(this);
    theQuitButton.addActionListener(this);
    addWindowListener(new WindowHandler( ));

    pack( );
    show( );

    openConnection( );
    execSQLCommand("Select * from Visits;");
}
```

The execSQLCommand Method

The **execSQLCommand( )** method, shown in Listing 10, appears almost exactly as before. The only change is the addition of a call to a new method, **moveDataToForm( )**, which is invoked if the result set contains at least one row.

Listing 10 The execSQLCommand( ) method.

```java
public void execSQLCommand(String command)
{
    try
    {
        theStatement = theConnection.createStatement();
        theResult = theStatement.executeQuery(command);
        if (theResult.next( )) moveDataToForm( );
    }
    catch (Exception e)
    {
        handleException(e);
    }
}
```

The moveDataToForm( ) Method

The new method, **moveDataToForm**( ), shown in Listing 11, is responsible for getting the individual column values from the result set and setting the **TextFields'** contents appropriately. The method uses the **getString**( ) method of the **ResultSet** object to obtain a **String** representation of the specified column. A utility method, **noNull**( ), is used to avoid setting a **String** to a **null** value. The **noNull**( ) method is shown immediately below the **moveDataToForm**( ) method in Listing 11.

Listing 11 The moveDataToForm( ) and noNull( ) methods.

```java
public void moveDataToForm( )
{
    try
    {
        theName.setText   (noNull(theResult.getString(2)));
        theEMail.setText  (noNull(theResult.getString(3)));
        theComment.setText(noNull(theResult.getString(4)));
        theTime.setText   (noNull(theResult.getString(5)));
    }
    catch (Exception e)
    {
        handleException(e);
    }
}

public String noNull(String s)
{
    return (s != null) ? s : "";
}
```

Note that **moveDataToForm( )** does not include the first column, which contains the primary key of the Visits table. Including the field would have been simple, but the value of the primary key was considered to be of no importance to the user of this program; consequently, the field is not displayed.

The remaining columns are accessed sequentially. Drivers for some ODBC data sources require that columns be accessed only once, and in order. This is a good habit to form at the outset of your JDBC programming career.

The actionPerformed( ) Method

The **actionPerformed( )** method, shown in Listing 12, handles events generated when the user clicks either the Next or Quit button. The program establishes the **GuestBook02** object as the listener for all **actionPerformed** events. An alternative would be to create distinct objects to handle the events of each **Button**. This would avoid the need for **if-else** processing and would be quite helpful if the application had many **Button**s. With only two **Button**s, however, the simpler course is to handle events from each in a single object and method.

LISTING 12 THE ACTIONPERFORMED( ) METHOD.

```
public void actionPerformed(ActionEvent event)
{
    theStatus.setText("Status: OK");
    Object source = event.getSource( );
    if (source == theNextButton)
    {
        try
        {
            if (theResult.next( )) moveDataToForm( );
            else theStatus.setText("Status: No more records.");
        }
        catch (Exception e)
        {
            theStatus.setText("Error during next: "
              + e.getMessage( ));
        }
    }
    else if (source == theQuitButton)
    {
        destroy( );
    }
}
```

The **getSource( )** method distinguishes which button is the source of the event. If the user clicks the Next button, the routine attempts to obtain and display another row from the result set. A message is displayed if all records have been viewed.

Clicking the Quit button invokes a new method called **destroy( )**, described in the next section. This method has the task of closing down the application.

Notice that the **actionPerformed( )** method sets the status display to Status: OK at the outset of any requested operation. This eliminates "stale" messages caused by transient errors. If the error is "hard," it will recur and the **handleError( )** method will be invoked by the processing method to set the status display appropriately.

The destroy( ) Method

The **destroy( )** method, shown in Listing 13, closes down the application. It invokes the **closeConnection( )** method, which frees all JDBC resources and disconnects from the data source. It then hides the application frame and terminates the program.

LISTING 13   THE DESTROY( ) METHOD.

```
public void destroy( )
{
    closeConnection( );
    setVisible(false);
    System.exit(0);
}
```

The WindowHandler Inner Class

The **WindowHandler** inner class, shown in Listing 14, is little changed from the previous version. Instead of directly invoking the methods to close the data-source connection, it now simply calls the **destroy( )** method. This way, whether the user clicks the Close icon or the Quit button, the result is the same.

LISTING 14   THE WINDOWHANDLER.

```
class WindowHandler extends WindowAdapter
{
    public void windowClosing(WindowEvent event)
    {
        Object object = event.getSource( );
        if (object instanceof Frame) destroy( );
    }
}
```

Java And Access Data Types

Now you can use the pattern illustrated by the **GuestBook02** application to create your own SQL database applications, accessing ODBC sources, such as any Access databases you've created. You may want to work with data types other than **String** in your programs. Table 3.1 shows various Access data types, the corresponding Java data types, and the method used to obtain column values of each type. For example,

```
String theStringValue = getString(1);
```

could obtain the value of result set column 1 as a Java **String**. But

```
int theIntValue = getInt(1);
```

could obtain the value of the same column as an **int**. Chapter 5 will provide a more thorough treatment of Java data types, but Table 1 should be enough to get you started writing interesting and useful JDBC programs.

TABLE 1

DATA TYPES AND RESULTSET METHODS.

Java Type	Access Type	SQL Type	Method
String	Text	VARCHAR	getString( )
String	Memo	LONGVARCHAR	getASCIIStream( )
java.sql.Numeric	Number	NUMERIC	getNumeric( )
boolean	Yes/No	BIT	getBoolean( )
byte	Byte	TINYINT	getByte( )
short	Integer	SMALLINT	getShort( )
int	Long	INTEGER	getInt( )
long	Long	BIGINT	getLong( )
float	Single	REAL	getFloat( )
double	Double	DOUBLE	getDouble( )
byte[ ]	OLE object	VARBINARY, LONGVARBINARY	getBytes( ), getBinaryStream( )
java.sql.Date	Date/Time	DATE	getDate( )
java.sql.Time	Date/Time	TIME	getTime( )
java.sql.Timestamp	Date/Time	TIMESTAMP	getTimeStamp( )

Summary

The most important JDBC data types are **Connection**, which represents connections to data sources; **Statement**, which represents SQL commands; and **ResultSet**, which represents a relational table returned as the result of an executed SQL command. Another important data type is **ResultSetMetaData**, which provides information concerning a **ResultSet**, including the number of columns it contains.

JDBC data sources are referenced using a special form of URL. The author of the driver used to access the data source specifies the exact syntax.

A SQL command is executed by creating a **Statement** based on an open connection and invoking the **executeQuery( )** method on the **Statement**. The query will generally return a **ResultSet** object, which provides access to the relational table generated by the query. Rows of the table may be accessed sequentially by using the **next( )** method. You can access columns of each row with the **getString( )** method, or a similar method returning a different data type. The columns of each row should be accessed only once and in sequential order. Moving backward through the **ResultSet** requires special techniques.

When a SQL-related error occurs, a **SQLException** is thrown. These exceptions may be caught and handled as other exceptions. **SQLException**s can be chained together; the **getNextException( )** method can be used to walk the chain.

The ODBC driver manager, found in the Control Panel, can configure an ODBC data source. You must install the Access ODBC drivers before JDBC can access data in an Access database.

Index

A

Ad hoc query, 399
Add To Chart dialog box, 346
Aggregates, 157-160
Algorithm, 399
Aliases, 156-157, 399
ANSI-compliant SQL, 139-140
AppleTalk ADSP, 18
Application design, 336, 337
Application parameters
   DBCC PINTABLE, 78
   list-type tables, 79
   registry-type tables, 78-79
Archiving, 336
Articles, 107
AVG() function, 158

B

Backup
   master database, 11, 23
   strategy, 21
Backup domain controllers (BDCs), 10, 399
_BAK, 85
Bandwidth, 399
Banyan VINES, 18
Base-level server, 35-37
Batches, 172-175, 400
BCP (bulk copy program), 87-89, 251, 400
Benchmarks, 329-330
Binary, 400
Binary sort order, 7
Binding, 400
Books Online. *See* SQL Server Books Online.
Bottlenecks, 331-332
Browsers, 357-359

C

Calculated values, 161-163
Case-sensitive, 7, 400
CD-ROM, 22
Central publisher, 400
Central Publisher scenario, 113-114
Central Publisher With Remote Distribution scenario, 114-115
Central Subscriber scenario, 115-118
Character sets, 6-8, 55, 400
CHARINDEX() function, 160
Charts, 346-349

Check constraints, 287
Child record, 400
Choose Licensing dialog box, 51
Cleaning up, 17
CLOSE statement, 175-176
COL-LENGTH() function, 161
Comments, 141
Computed values, 400
@@CONNECTIONS, 199
Connectivity errors, 316-318
Constraints, 186, 285, 400
   Check, 287
   Default, 286-287
   Foreign Key, 286
   Primary Key, 285-286
Unique, 286
CONVERT() function, 158
Correlated subquery, 166
COUNT() function, 158
CPU, 8-9
@@CPU_BUSY, 199
CREATE TABLE statement, 288-289
Cursors, 175-178, 400
Custom stored procedures, 209-211

D

.DAT extension, 4
Data access, 90-91
Data distribution models, 103-104
Data integrity, 246-247
Data modeling, 71-72
Data models, 335, 336
Data replication, 401. *See also*
   Replication.
Database, 4-5, 401
Database/Object Transfer dialog box,
   84, 86

DATALENGTH() function, 161
DATEDIFF() function, 159
DATEPART() function, 159
DBArtisan, 70, 83, 180
DBArtisan Database Copy
   dialog box, 89
DBArtisan work area, 84
DBCC PINTABLE, 78
DBMS (Database Management
   System), 401
DDL, 212
Deadlock, 401
DEALLOCATE statement, 175-176
Debugging. *See* Errors.
DECLARE statement, 175-176
DECnet, 18
Default constraint, 286-287
Default gateway entry, 26
Defaults
   binding, 284
   changing, 284-285
   creating, 283-284
   dropping, 285
Defining a user, 91
DELETE statements, 172
DELETE triggers, 254-255
Deleted table, 252
Desktop, 60-62
Development environment, 69-70
Device, 3-4, 401
Dialog boxes
   Add To Chart, 346
   Books Online, 54
   Choose Licensing, 51
   Database/Object Transfer, 84, 86
   DBArtisan Database Copy, 89

Distribution Options, 129-130
Edit Publications, 131-132
Enter Name and Organization, 49-50
Free Agent Install Destination, 372-373
General Preferences, 381
Generate SQL Scripts, 82
Go Online NOW, 376-377
Install Replication Publishing, 127-128
Installation Options, 55
Manage Articles, 132-133
Manage Defaults, 284
Manage Publications, 131
Manage Rules, 282
Manage Subscriptions, 135
Manage Tables, 261-263, 297
Manage User-Defined Data Type, 288
MASTER Device Creation, 52-53
Multi Protocol Encryption, 57
New Filter, 350, 351
Novell Bindery Service Name, 57-58
Options, 49-50
Per Seat Licensing, 52
Query Options, 237-238
Register Server, 94
Replication Publishing, 129
Replication Subscribing, 134
Select Character Set, 55
Select Network Protocols, 55-56
Select Sort Order, 56
Server Configuration/Options, 333
SQL Executive Log On Account, 57
SQL Server Books Online, 54
Subscriptions Options, 135-136
TCP/IP Socket Number, 57-58
Transfer Scripting Options, 95-96
Verify Name and Organization, 49-50
Welcome, 49
Direct Response Mode, 332
Distribution Options dialog box, 129-130
Distribution server, 105, 110-111, 401
DMO (distributed management object), 61, 401
Domain controller, 10
Domains. *See* User-defined data types (UDTs).
DROP RULE statement, 282
DTC (Distributed Transaction Coordinator), 401
Dynamic link library (DDL), 212
Dynamic parameters, 72

E

Edit Publications dialog box, 131-132
Embarcadero Technologies, 70-71
Enter Name and Organization dialog box, 49-50
Enterprise Manager, 61, 82
Entries, 25-27
@@ERROR, 199, 253
Errors, 301-325
 connectivity, 316-318
 error 107, 307
 error 156, 307
 error 603, 310
 error 605, 320
 error 706, 311-312
 error 707, 311-312
 error 803, 321

error 806, 322
error 1105, 312-313
error 1108, 313
error 1205, 308
error 1511, 319
error 1608, 316
error 2506, 323
error 2610, 324
error 17809, 314
error 17824, 316
error 17825, 317
error 17832, 317
query/connection-based, 307-309
researching cause of, 303
service configuration, 310-315
service packs, 302-303
table and index, 320-325
transaction log, 319
EXECUTE (EXEC) statement, 195
Extents, 77
External stored procedures, 212

F

FASTFIRSTROW, 165
FAT (file allocation table), 401
FETCH statement, 176, 178
@@FETCH_STATUS, 199
File Copy in Progress status bar, 57-59
Fill factor, 76-77, 401
Filters, 340, 350-352
Foreign Key constraint, 286
Free Agent
  configuration, 376-377
  installation, 371-375
  main screen, 367-368

overview, 367-368
preferences, 381-386
subscribing to newsgroups, 378-380
threads to monitored messages, 386
FROM statement, 144
Functions, 157-160. *See also* System functions.

G

Gateway Services for NetWare, 10
General Preferences dialog box, 381
Generate SQL Scripts dialog box, 82
GETDATE() function, 159
Global variables, 198-200, 252-253, 401
Glossary, 399-405
Go Online Now dialog box, 376-377
GO statement, 175
GROUP BY clause, 151-153
Groups, 91

H

Hard drives, 9
Hardware Compatibility List (HCL), 25
Hats, 91
HAVING clauses, 152-153
High-end server, 39-40
History tables, 343
HOLDLOCK, 165
Horizontal partitions, 106-107, 228-229, 402

I

IDC (Internet database connector), 402
@@IDENTITY, 199, 253
Identity column, 170
@@IDLE, 199
Index, 332, 402
INDEX=, 165
INSERT/SELECT, 89, 184
INSERT statements, 168-170
INSERT triggers, 253
Inserted table, 252
Install Replication Publishing dialog box, 127-128
Installation
   default location for devices, 19
   hardware to use, 20-22
   mail client, 41-42, 47-48
   perinstallation checklist, 25-32
   post-installation issues, 63-65
   practical guide, 44-62
   production data servers, 35-40
   service rights, 47
   services, 19, 42
   setup program, 48-59
   SQL Executive account, 40-41, 45-46
   SQL Server service account, 41, 46-47
   third-party applications, 22
   user accounts, 40-41, 45-47
   where, 10-11
Installation Options dialog box (character set, sort orders), 55
Integrated security, 16, 402

Internet, 353-387
   accessing, 356-357
   browsers, 357-359
   Free Agent, 367-386. *See also* Free Agent.
   interesting facts, 356
   Microsoft Knowledge Base, 362-364
   newsgroups, 365-366, 387
   search engines, 360-362
   service packs/patches, 364
   Tech Net CD-ROM, 364
@@IO_BUSY, 199
IPX/SPX, 402
ISNULL() function, 161
ISP (Internet service provider), 356, 402
ISQL/W icon, 60

J

Join conditions, 153-156

K

Knowledge Base, 362-364

L

List-type tables, 79
Local variables, 198
Lock Escalation parameters, 75-76
   Lock Escalation Threshold Maximum, 76
   Lock Escalation Threshold Minimum, 76

Log On As A Service Right, 47
Log reader process, 120-121
Login ID, 402

M

Mail client
  installation, 47-48
  overview, 19
  set up, 28, 41-42
  testing, 64-65
Manage Articles dialog box, 132-133
Manage Defaults dialog box, 284
Manage Publications dialog box, 131
Manage Rules dialog box, 282
Manage Subscriptions dialog box, 135
Manage Tables dialog box, 261-263, 297
Manage User-Defined Data Type dialog box, 288
Mange Stored Procedures window, 205-206
MAPI, 19
Mapping, 91
Master database, 11-13, 402
Master device, 12
MASTER Device Creation dialog box, 52-53
MAX() function, 157
@@MAX_CONNECTIONS, 199
Max Worker Threads, 75
Medium-duty server, 37-39
Memory, 15-16, 29, 63-64
Memory leaks, 337
Microsoft Internet Explorer, 357-359
Microsoft Knowledge Base, 362-364
Microsoft SQL Server Books Online. *See* SQL Server Books Online.
Microsoft system requirements, 8-9
Microsoft TechNet, 364-365
MIN() function, 158
Mirroring, 402
Mixed security, 17, 402
Model database, 13, 403
Modular programming, 193
Monitors, 22
Msdb database, 14
Multi-Protocol, 18
Multi Protocol Encryption dialog box, 57
Multiple Publishers Of A Single Table scenario, 118-119

N

Named pipes, 18, 403
Naming conventions, 190-192
Nesting
  stored procedures, 204
  triggers, 250
@@NESTLEVEL, 199
Net-Libraries, 18-19
Network interface card, 22
Network traffic, 194-195
New Filter dialog box, 350, 351
Newsgroup etiquette, 387
Newsgroups, 365-366, 387
NOLOCK, 76, 164-165
Noncorrelated subquery, 166
Normalization, 226-228
Novell Bindery Service Name dialog box, 57-58
NTFS (NT file system), 403
NULLIF() function, 161
NWLink IPX/SPX, 18

O

Objects
  monitoring, 334
  scripting, 82-83
  transferring. *See* Transferring objects.
ODBC (open database connectivity), 60, 403
On Demand Mode, 332
OPEN statement, 175-176
Optimization. *See* Tuning and optimization.
Optimizer, 403
Optimizer hints, 164-165
Options dialog box, 49-50
ORDER BY clause, 149-150

P

PAGLOCK, 165
Parameters. *See* Application parameters, Server-level parameters.
Partitioned data, 228-229
Password, 403
Patches, 364
PATINDEX() function, 160
Per Seat Licensing dialog box, 52
Performance, 330-331. *See also* Tuning and optimization.
Performance Monitor, 332-334, 345-349
Permissions, 90, 99, 249
Point-and-click graphic interfaces, 83
Post-installation issues, 63-65
Practical Guide To Replication, 126-136
  creating publications/articles, 131-133
  installing distribution database, 127-128
  setting publication options, 129-130
  setting subscriptions options, 134
  subscribing to a publication, 135-136
Practical Guide To SQL, 179-186
  backing up data, 181
  cleaning up, 185
  converting/inserting old data, 184
  renaming objects to be modified, 182
  schema changes, 180
  scripting objects, 183
Practical Guide To Stored Procedures, 216-221
  calling procedures within procedures, 221
  parsing a string, 217
  reduced network traffic, 219-220
  redundant code, 218
Practical Guide To Triggers, 259-276
  check titleAuthor table, 270-271
  create trigger, 272-273
  define business rule, 264
  graphic representation of firing order, 266-267
  identify child records, 265
  remove foreign key constraints, 261-263
  testing, 274-276
  write test script, 268-269
Preinstallation checklist
  entries, 25-27
  installation issues, 30-32
  memory requirements, 29-30
  Windows NT section, 25-29

Primary domain controllers
    (PDCs), 10, 403
Primary key, 124, 403
Primary Key constraint, 285
PRINT statement, 178
Priority Boost, 75
Probe user, 332
Process display window, 341-342
@@PROCID, 199
Production data servers
    base level (SQL Server A), 35-37
    high end (SQL Server C), 39-40
    medium duty (SQL Server B), 37-39
Protocols, 18, 55-56
Publications, 108
Publisher server, 105, 109, 403
Publishing Subscriber scenario,
    114-116
Pubs database, 13, 141-143, 404
Pubs database detail window, 342-343
Pull subscription, 109, 404
Push subscription, 109, 404

Q

Query/connection-based errors,
    307-309
Query Optimizer, 164, 196
Query Options dialog box, 237-238
Query plan, 196-197

R

RA slots per thread, 74
RA worker threads, 74
RAID (redundant array of inexpensive
    disks), 20, 38-39, 404
RAM (random access memory), 9, 404

Rapid SQL, 83
Read-ahead optimization, 74
Readme file, 61
Recursion, 204-205
Register Server dialog box, 94
Registering servers, 94-96
Registry-type tables, 78-79
Remote stored procedures, 212-213
Renaming a table, 85-86
Replication, 101-136
    character set, 123
    communication failures, 122
    consistency, 104
    disk space, 123-124
    distribution server, 110-111
    granularity, 111-112
    limiting traffic, 111
    log reader process, 120-121
    major components, 120
    memory, 123
    ODBC, 112
    planning, 111
    practical guide, 126-136. *See also*
        Practical Guide To Replication.
    prerequisites, 122-125
    primary key, 124
    protocol, 123
    publisher server, 109
    replication distribution process, 121
    scenarios, 111-119
    server roles, 109-110
    SQL Executive service, 124
    subscriber server, 110
    synchronization process, 121
    terminology, 104
    trusts, 123
    user connections, 124
    what cannot be published, 112

working directory, 123
Replication Publishing dialog box, 129
Replication Subscribing dialog box, 134
Resource Timeout, 74
RETURN statement, 203
@@ROWCOUNT, 200, 253
RQBE (relational query by example), 404
RTRIM() function, 160
Rules, 279-280
  binding, 281-282
  changing, 282
  creating, 281
  dropping, 282-283

S

Scheduled table refresh, 404
Schema change, 404
Scratch pad, 13-14
Script, 79
Scripting objects, 82-83, 99
Search engines, 360-362
Security
  integrated, 16
  mixed, 17
  permissions, 90-91
  standard setting, 16
  views, 230
Select Character Set dialog box, 55
SELECT list, 144
Select Network Protocols dialog box, 55-56
Select Sort Order dialog box, 56
SELECT statements, 143-146
Server configuration errors, 310-315
Server Configuration/Options dialog box, 333
Server-level parameters
  dynamic vs. static, 72
  Lock Escalation parameters, 75-76
  Max Worker Threads, 75
  Priority Boost, 75
  RA slots per thread, 74
  RA worker threads, 74
  Resource Timeout, 74
  Sort Pages, 73
  Tempdb in RAM, 73
  User Connections, 73
Server Manager window, 94-95
Server Overview screen, 341
Server role questions, 28
Servers. *See* Production data servers.
Service packs, 302-303, 364
Service rights, 47
SET statement, 176
Setup keep-alive screen, 58-59
Setup program, 48-59
Setup scripts, 79-82
16-level rule, 204
Sort orders, 6-8, 55-56, 404
Sort Pages, 73
Sound cards, 22
SOUNDEX() function, 159
@@SPID, 200, 253
Spring cleaning, 17
SP_ADDEXTENDEDPROC, 207
SP_ADDLOGIN, 207
SP_ADDMESSAGE, 207
SP_ADDUSER, 207
SP_CHANGEDBOWNER, 207
SP_CHANGEDGROUP, 207
SP_COLUMNS, 207

SP_CONFIGURE, 207
SP_DATABASES, 208
SP_DBOPTION, 208
SP_DROPEXTENDEDPROC, 208
SP_HELP, 208
SP_HELPDB, 208
SP_HELPDEVICE, 208
SP_HELPPROTECT, 208
SP_HELPSQL, 208
SP_HELPSTARTUP, 208
SP_HELPTASK, 208
SP_LOCK, 208
SP_MONITOR, 208
SP_RECOMPILE, 208
SP_RENAME, 209
SP_SPACEUSED, 209
SP_STATISTICS, 209
SP_STORED_PROCEDURES, 209
SP_TABLES, 209
SP_WHO, 209
SQL Client Configuration utility, 61
SQL-DMO, 82
SQL Executive account, 40-41, 45-46
SQL Executive Log On Account dialog box, 57
SQL Instant Reference, 140
SQL Mail. *See* Mail client.
SQL Performance Monitor icon, 61
SQL Probe, 340-342
SQL script, 172
SQL Security Manager, 61
SQL Server A, 35-37
SQL Server B, 37-39
SQL Server Books Online, 364-365
   dialog box, 54
   icon, 61
SQL Server C, 39-40
SQL Server program group, 60-62

SQL Server service account, 41, 46-47
SQL Server Trace Flags, 339
SQL Server Web Assistant, 62
SQL Service Manager, 62
SQL Setup icon, 62
SQL statements
   CLOSE, 175-176
   CREATE TABLE, 288-289
   DEALLOCATE, 175-176
   DECLARE, 176
   DELETE, 172
   DROP RULE, 282
   EXECUTE (EXEC), 195
   FETCH, 176, 178
   FROM, 144
   GO, 175
   INSERT, 168-170
   INSERT/SELECT, 89, 184
   OPEN, 176
   PRINT, 178
   RETURN, 203
   SELECT, 143-146
   SET, 176
   TRUNCATE TABLE, 251
   UNION, 336
   UPDATE, 170-171
SQL Trace, 62, 339-340, 350-352
Standard security, 16, 404
Standards, 190
Startup stored procedures, 213-214
Statements. *See* SQL statements.
Static parameters, 72
Stored procedures, 170, 187-221, 404
   calls, 195-196, 221
   custom, 209-211
   encryption, 206
   external, 212
   getting data, 191-192

maintenance, 202-203
modifying data, 192-193
modular programming, 194
nesting, 204
network traffic, 194-195
NT server registry, 200-202
parameters, 198
practical guide, 216-221
pre-production tips, 214
query optimizer, 196
query plan, 196-197
recursion, 204-205
reduced client processing, 194
remote, 212-213
return codes, 203
rules, 203-204
startup, 213-214
system, 205-209
variables, 198-200
Structured Query Language (SQL), 139, 405. *See also* Practical Guide To SQL.
STUFF() function, 159
Subqueries, 165-167
Subquery, 405
Subscriber (subscription) server, 105, 110, 405
Subscriptions Options dialog box, 135-136
SUBSTRING() function, 146, 159
SUM() function, 157
Synchronization, 106, 121, 405
Syntax, 141, 405
System functions, 160-161.
 See also Functions.
System requirements, 8-9
System stored procedures, 205-209

T

Table, 405
Table and index errors, 320-325
TABLOCK, 165
TABLOCKX, 165
TCP/IP (transfer control protocol/ Internet protocol), 405
TCP/IP Socket Number dialog box, 57-58
TCP/IP Sockets, 18
TechNet CD-ROMs, 364
Tempdb, 13-14, 405
Tempdb in RAM, 73
The Free Agent Install Destination dialog box, 372-373
Third-party tools, 70-71
Timed tests, 330
Token lists, 217
TPC Benchmark Application, 337
Trace flags, 339
@@TRANCOUNT, 200
Transact-SQL, 405
Transaction log, 105, 405
Transaction log errors, 319
Transfer Manager, 84-85, 99
Transfer Scripting Options dialog box, 95-96
Transferring data
 BCP, 87-89
 DBArtisan, 89-90
 INSERT/SELECT, 89
 preliminary steps, 86
Transferring objects
 pitfalls, 99
 registering servers, 94-96
 renaming tables, 85-86

space problems, 95
Transfer Manager, 84-85, 99
transfer utility, 84, 97
warning messages, 98
Triggers, 243-276, 405
　business rules, 248-249
　creation, 247
　data integrity, 246-247
　DELETE, 254-255
　Deleted table, 252
　firing sequences, 247, 249
　global variables, 252-253
　INSERT, 170, 253
　Inserted table, 252
　limitations, 255-256
　logged/nonlogged operations, 250-251
　multiple-row considerations, 256-257
　nesting, 250
　performance, 257
　permissions, 249-250
　practical guide, 259-276. *See also* Practical Guide To Triggers.
　statements not allowed, 248
　syntax, 247-248
　UPDATE, 254
　virtual tables, 251-252
Troubleshooting. *See* Tuning and optimization.
Tuning and optimization, 327-352
　application design, 336-337
　baseline measurements, 337
　benchmarks, 329-330
　bottlenecks, 331-332
　data models, 335-336
　filters, 340, 350-352
　memory leaks, 337
　Performance Monitor, 332-334, 345-349
　performance, what is it, 330-331
　practical guide, 344-352
　server, 335, 338
　SQL Probe, 340-342
　SQL Trace, 339-340, 350-352
　tables, 335, 336
　trace flags, 339
Two-phase commit, 103-104

U

UNION statements, 336
Unions, 167
Unique constraint, 286
UPDATE statements, 170-171
UPDATE triggers, 254
UPDLOCK, 165
UPPER() function, 146, 160
User accounts, 40-41, 45-47
User Connections, 73
User-defined data types (UDTs)
　advantages, 290
　CREATE TABLE statement, 288-289
　defined, 287
　entity definition, 287-288
　maintenance/troubleshooting, 298
　placement of, in Model database, 298
　practical guide, 291-298
USER-ID() function, 161
USER-NAME() function, 161
Users, 91

V

Variables, 198-200
Verify Name and Organization dialog box, 49-50
Vertical partitions, 106, 108, 228, 405
Video memory, 22
Views, 186, 223-241
    computed values, 230
    creating, 226
    multiple tables, 229
    normalized data, 226-228
    partitioned data, 228-229
    performance, 231
    practical guide, 234-241
    restrictions, 232
    security, 230
    underlying objects, 231
    updates, 230-231
Virtual tables, 251-252

W

Web browser, 405
Welcome dialog box, 49
WHERE clause, 147-149
Windows NT Registry, 200-202
Windows NT4 Administrator's Black Book, 25
WINS Server IP address entry, 26
WITH ENCRYPTION option, 206

X

XP_REGDELETEVALUE, 201
XP_REGREAD, 201
XP_REGWRITE, 201
xp_sendmail, 42

Y

Yahoo!, 360-361

Administrator's Notes...

Administrator's Notes...

Administrator's Notes...